Handbook for
Child Protection Practice

We dedicate this book to:
All the professionals dedicated to enhancing
children's safety, health, and well-being
and

by Howard:
To my wife, Diana, for being my best friend, and to my
children, Nikki and Andy, for all the joys of being a dad

by Diane:
To my husband, Joseph Gene Wechsler, for being my partner,
consultant, computer guru, and friend, and to my son,
Jacob Hae Wechsler (age 9), for helping remind me to
"slow down and take time out"

Handbook for
Child Protection Practice

Edited by
Howard Dubowitz • Diane DePanfilis

Sage Publications, Inc.
International Educational and Professional Publisher
Thousand Oaks ■ London ■ New Delhi

For information:

Sage Publications, Inc.
2455 Teller Road
Thousand Oaks, California 91320
E-mail: order@sagepub.com

Sage Publications Ltd.
6 Bonhill Street
London EC2A 4PU
United Kingdom

Sage Publications India Pvt. Ltd.
M-32 Market
Greater Kailash I
New Delhi 110 048 India

Printed in the United States of America

Library of Congress Cataloging-in-Publication Data

Main entry under title:

Handbook for child protection practice / edited by Howard Dubowitz and Diane DePanfilis.
    p.   cm.
Includes bibliographical references and index.
  ISBN 0-7619-1370-X (cloth: alk. paper)
  ISBN 0-7619-1371-8 (pbk.: alk. paper)
  1. Child abuse—United States—Prevention—Handbooks, manuals, etc.
2. Child welfare—United States—Handbooks, manuals, etc. 3. Social work with children—United States—Handbooks, manuals, etc. 4. Family social work—United States—Handbooks, manuals, etc. I. Dubowitz, Howard. II. DePanfilis, Diane.
  HV6626.52.H36 2000
  362.76'0973—dc21   99-005958

00 01 02 03 04 10 10 9 8 7 6 5 4 3 2 1

Acquiring Editor:	C. Terry Hendrix
Editorial Assistant:	Anna Howland
Production Editor:	Diana E. Axelsen
Editorial Assistant:	Nevair Kabakian
Typesetter/Designer:	Janelle LeMaster
Indexer:	Jeanne Busemeyer
Cover Designer:	Candice Harman

Contents

PART I: REPORTING AND SCREENING

PART II: ENGAGEMENT

PART III: INTERVIEWING

PART IV: INITIAL ASSESSMENT
Section A: General

Section B: Neglect

Section C: Physical Abuse

Section D: Sexual Abuse

PART V: FAMILY ASSESSMENT
Section A: Emphasis on the Child

Section B: Emphasis on Parents and Caregivers

Section C: Emphasis on Families

PART VI: SERVICE PLANNING

PART VII: INTERVENTION
Section A: Emphasis on the Child

Section B: Emphasis on the Parent or Caregiver

Section C: Emphasis on the Family

PART VIII: EVALUATION AND CLOSURE

PART IX: LEGAL AND ETHICAL ISSUES

PART X: CHILD PROTECTION PRACTICE: SPECIAL ISSUES FOR THE PRACTITIONER

Preface

Working in the field of child abuse and neglect presents many challenges. On an emotional level, seeing children hurt and families struggling is painful. The resources needed to substantially help families are frequently in short supply. Also, even when we have good resources, changing the complex circumstances contributing to children's maltreatment is an immense challenge. It is the nature of this field that it spans several disciplines, including social work, mental health, medicine, public health, nursing, law enforcement, law, and education. Many professionals in each of these disciplines, however, have not been adequately prepared for their work with abused and neglected children and their families. In addition, professionals working in this field need to know a good deal about the related disciplines—pediatricians need to be knowledgeable of the law, and social workers need to know about medicine—thus presenting another challenge. In this context, important decisions must be made: We say to families, "Your child has been abused or neglected," "You need help," "Your child is not safe in your care and we need to place him or her elsewhere," and "Your child cannot return to your care."

We hope that this book will provide valuable and practical guidance to professionals confronting these challenges. We recognized that it is often not easy in the course of busy days to fully examine and learn about the many complex issues that present in practice. This book is a compromise. With the help of leading experts in many areas, we have prioritized the most important information on a wide array of clinical issues and tried to present it in a way that should be easy to access and be useful. We have the busy practitioner in mind, and we have strived to succinctly convey key information. For those seeking additional information, many chapters recommend key books, chapters, and articles as well as other excellent resources.

How did we determine the contents of this book? We first drafted a long list of topics we thought were important. We sent this list to approximately 30 professionals in our field of child abuse and neglect (Appendix 1), and we asked them to rate the importance of each topic and to recommend topics we had omitted. Their input helped us develop the final contents. It was impossible to cover everything identified; some tough choices had to be made. Inevitably, there will be some disagreement about what is included and what is not. Nevertheless, this book represents a reasonable consensus among a fair number of professionals in the field. We also welcome your feedback. Please let us know your ideas.

Projects such as this book involve many people, and there are many we wish to thank. First, we are grateful to Terry Hendrix at Sage for his enthusiastic support. He did not need much convincing and quickly agreed that this book should meet an important need. Also, Kassie Gavrilis and Diana Axelsen at Sage have been a pleasure to work with. The contributing authors have done a terrific job. It is surprisingly difficult to distill a great amount of information into a few pages, and we are very appreciative of their fine work. We thank the many professionals who carefully considered this project and provided excellent guidance. On a daily basis, our work in this field is sustained by working with wonderful colleagues at the University of Maryland, many professionals across the disciplines in Baltimore and Maryland, and members of the American Professional Society for the Abuse of Children. Jan Miller provided invaluable clerical support.

Despite the many challenges, working in this important field is deeply satisfying and a real joy. We have learned much from editing this book. We hope that others will benefit as we have. Most important, by constantly striving to improve our practice, the children and families we serve will benefit.

Part I

REPORTING AND SCREENING

1

How Do I Decide Whether to Accept a Report for a Child Protective Services Investigation?

■ *Susan Wells*

Accepting a report for a child protective services (CPS) investigation is a legal decision. The appropriateness of this decision depends on the ability of the worker to elicit critical and accurate information and apply law and policy to the information gathered.

1. Review law and policy and determine how it is applied in practice.

   • Refer to state law as it is outlined in your agency manual.

   The law will define what is considered child abuse and neglect under your state statutes. These definitions are your ultimate source of guidance. For example, some statutes specify whether educational neglect is an appropriate problem for agency response; others may specifically include all cases of infants who test positive on drug toxicology screens.

   • Go to procedures in the agency manuals.

   Policies and procedures will include state and local guidelines. They may include additional information on defining terms, guidelines on what questions to ask the reporter, and how to respond to specific types of reports. One common example of differential response among states and localities is the response to anonymous reports. This is also true of self-reports.

- Clarify the meaning of written materials.

    Determine through group discussions (that include your supervisor or agency administrator or both) how these guidelines are implemented in your office. Wherever possible, be sure that clarifications are in writing so that all in the agency have the same understanding of the situation.

    When you are a new worker or have recently transferred to an office, verify any suggestions you are given by others with your supervisor. There are often geographic variations in worker decision making, even about what reports to investigate or who will receive services.

    Sometimes, customs develop with workers or in teams that may not reflect the agency guidelines. This is rarely a matter of staff refusing guidance from the agency. It is often a result of many years of practice in the same office, helping one another respond to difficult situations, and improvisation over time. These adaptations to circumstances, however, may in some cases lead workers away from carrying out their legislatively mandated job. Therefore, it is very important that you understand the actions required by your agency. For example, people who report that they are worried about hurting their child are systematically referred out in some places because "they know they need help and are likely to get it." In many or most agencies, this blanket practice would be contrary to law and policy.

- Nothing in this chapter (or book) should override state or local law and policy.

2. Obtain immediately, as specifically as possible, all the information suggested by agency guidelines and the intake or screening form.
    - Get specific descriptions of who did what to whom, the context in which the event(s) occurred, and the result for the child(ren) involved.

- Remember to ask the reporter to describe the actual acts, or lack of action, that occurred. Also remember that the description of the context is as important as the alleged maltreatment.
- Who was there, where were they, what were they doing, why were they doing it, and what leads the reporter to think the maltreatment occurred (i.e., what did they see or hear)? Who else can provide information, what is their relationship to the child and family, and how can they be contacted?

3. Referral for CPS investigation or to other community agencies.
   - If the child appears to be at risk of harm due to circumstances other than direct parental (or relative or caregiver, depending on law) neglect or abuse, are there other agencies that can intervene quickly enough to guard the safety of the child? In cases of domestic violence with a child in the home, the police are most often the most appropriate first responders. The child protective agency may also be required if the child is also at risk of harm.
   - Problems that may be more appropriately served by other agencies include parental substance abuse, parental or child mental health, health or developmental disability problems, lack of resources to meet basic needs due to poverty, lack of information about appropriate parenting, lack of sufficient support systems in crisis, lack of day care, the child's constant truancy, or severe learning problems that do not endanger the child.
   - CPS must determine to what extent the parental or familial circumstances could result in imminent danger, whether a simple referral to the appropriate agency will ensure service delivery, whether the connection between appropriate services and the family is so tenuous that the child may not receive the needed intervention, thereby requiring protective intervention, or whether the initial report that may focus on the need for other services is masking other more serious dangers (refer to information gathering).

- The decision is heavily based on having accurate and sufficient information, the ability of the worker to assess and use the information given to develop an accurate picture of the situation, and the clarity with which law and policy can be applied. Screening tools can be very helpful, but it is not possible to rely totally on any formula because a formula can never fully account for human idiosyncrasies and the incredible variation in circumstances that confront screening workers every day. An actuarial formula provides probabilities of future occurrences. The worker and supervisor use those probabilities as part of their decision making.

■ Further Reading

Morton, T. D., & Holder, W. (Eds.). (1998). *Decision making in children's protective services; Advancing the state of the art.* Atlanta, GA: Child Welfare Institute.

Wells, S. J., Fluke, J. D., & Brown, C. H. (1995). The decision to investigate: CPS practice in twelve local agencies. *Children and Youth Services Review, 17*(4), 523-546.

2

What Criteria Are Most Critical to Determine the Urgency of Child Protective Services Response?

■ *Susan Wells*

Determining the urgency of response to a report is the first step in safety assessment. The worker will be able to determine the speed and degree of intervention with carefully obtained, specific knowledge of the child and his or her circumstances. The criteria that inform the worker concern the incident, the child, the person(s) responsible for the alleged abuse or neglect, the family, and the family's situation. Many states have their own criteria for response times based on the nature of the report.

The following factors are generally used to distinguish among emergencies requiring instant response, those requiring responses within 24 hours, and reports that require child protective services (CPS) response but do not involve fear of immediate, continuing danger of serious harm. CPS should respond immediately when the child is unprotected and

- injury is severe or the alleged maltreatment could have easily caused severe injury—for example, shooting a gun or throwing a knife at a child, throwing or pushing a child down stairs, not providing enough food to eat day after

day, and locking toddlers out of the house without supervision;

- the child is especially vulnerable to the caregiver's behavior due to age, illness, disability, or proximity to the
alleged perpetrator or the child is a danger to himself or
herself or others (e.g., other children in the home);
- the caregiver's behavior with, or ability to take care of,
the child is known to have caused harm or endangered
the child or others, or the caregiver's behavior is unpredictable and could potentially result in serious harm or
both;
- there is no one who can intervene to protect the child,
either by removing the alleged perpetrator or keeping the
child safe; this includes the degree of certainty the CPS
worker has about whether the potential protector is able
to and will act on the child's behalf in the time that is
required and whether the child will be kept safe long
enough for CPS to arrive; and
- the family may flee with, or abandon, the child.

The issue is not that all these must occur together but rather that,
when examined as a whole, there is a clear opportunity for the
child to be seriously harmed if there is not immediate intervention. For example, the child may not have been harmed and the
caregiver may not have yet endangered the child, but the caregiver is known to have been violent in the past and is highly
agitated and is threatening the child. The worker's effective
performance rests on his or her ability to obtain all the details
needed to understand the situation and the skill to combine them
into a constellation of facts that provides a meaningful picture of
the child's situation.

Possible immediate responders include the police (alone or
with the CPS worker); someone else who is already with or near
the child—for example, a relative who can and will provide
immediate protection; and CPS alone. Information that indicates
the child is in current danger requires the first or second re-
sponder. In these cases, it is often advisable to send the police or
to ask them to accompany you for the first contact.

At the second level of response, a 10-year-old child's face
might be bruised from a hand slap, but there are no prior reports
or history of violence in the family, and it is certain that the family

is not unstable or highly crisis ridden. This is a serious injury (on the face or head) with potential for serious harm (e.g., concussion, continued battering of the child's head, or both). All other factors, however, indicate that injury has not occurred before, caregivers have not been reported before, and that before this report there has been no other problem with their child-rearing behaviors. Response within 24 hours (depending on law and agency policy on timeliness of response) is indicated, but it is not an emergency that requires urgent response within 1 hour.

The most important questions to ask, after all the pertinent information has been obtained, are the following: What is happening to the child now, what could happen if CPS is not there, and how likely is this to occur based on the information known to date? The most difficult problem for the worker in determining priorities is to not succumb to the overgeneralizations that inevitably result after handling many cases. There is a difference between using experience to inform a response and believing that certain types of reports are never (or always) high risk.

As a caution, lack of information on the questions listed previously should not discourage response. Instead, depending on what type of information is missing (e.g., what happened to the child and whether there was beating or continued beating after the witness saw the parent beating the child), lack of information may be an indicator of the need for immediate action.

■ *Further Reading*

DePanfilis, D., & Salus, M. (1992). *Child Protective Services: A guide for caseworkers* (U.S. Government Printing Office No. 1992-625-670/60577). Washington, DC: National Center on Child Abuse and Neglect.

Holder, W., & Corey, M. (1995). *Child Protective Services risk management: A decision making handbook.* Charlotte, NC: ACTION for Child Protection.

3

What Is Child Neglect?

■ *Howard Dubowitz*

hild neglect is usually defined as omissions in care resulting in significant harm or the risk of significant harm to
children. In most states, child welfare laws specify that
the parent(s) or caregivers are responsible for the omission in
care, thereby not becoming involved with lapses in care by others.
Similarly, neglect laws may exclude circumstances in which children's needs are not met primarily due to poverty.

Legal definitions do not specify what qualifies as "significant
harm" or as "significant risk of harm." Rather, this is left to local
child welfare agencies and professionals to interpret; not surprisingly, there is great variation in how these terms are defined. In
general, the child welfare system frequently screens out cases
without actual harm, unless the circumstances are extremely
worrisome (e.g., when young children are left home alone); this
is a serious problem because the harmful effects of neglect may
only be apparent later.

It is necessary for professionals to know their state law and
agency regulations regarding neglect. For the different professionals working with children, however, a general approach to
defining neglect will be suggested, including how this can be
applied in practice. If our main reason for defining child neglect

is to ensure that children receive adequate care and protection, neglect can be seen as occurring when children's basic needs are not adequately met, for any reason. From the child's perspective, a basic need is not met, and this is a crucial bottom line. The reasons why this need is not being met are important for guiding appropriate interventions but not for deciding whether or not a situation meets a definition of neglect. Generally, there are multiple causes, including parental behavior, that contribute to neglect. In many circumstances of neglect, community interventions are the appropriate first approach. In accordance with state laws, child protection services (CPS) are likely to become involved only when parents or caregivers are deemed responsible.

What are children's basic needs? Adequate food, clothing, a home, health care, education, supervision, protection from environmental hazards, nurturance, affection, support, and love may be considered basic needs; currently, none of these in the United States are luxuries. The following are more detailed definitions of these forms of neglect, clarifying the threshold of adequate or inadequate care:

Nutritional neglect occurs when children repeatedly experience hunger for hours or a large part of the day, and no food is available. This form of neglect may manifest as poor growth or failure to thrive, usually diagnosed by a pediatric health care provider. It is important to ensure that the poor growth is not due to a medical problem. Occasionally, children may have specific nutritional deficits when they are placed on unusual diets (e.g., vitamin B_{12} deficiency with a macrobiotic diet). Another form of nutritional neglect occurs when children are grossly obese, and recommendations for intervening are not followed. There are clear short-term and long-term complications from obesity, and, although rare, children can die from obesity.

Clothing neglect occurs when children lack clothing so that they are dangerously exposed to the elements—for example, not having shoes or warm clothes for winter. Clothes that are much too big or too small may be uncomfortable and provoke teasing, as may dirty clothes. When children believe they "need" a particular article of clothing and enormous peer pressure may apply, however, these circumstances should not be considered neglect. It is not a basic need to have designer jeans.

Homelessness can be considered another form of neglect, considering the importance of having a safe and secure place to live. Living on the street and even in a shelter surely qualifies as neglect in terms of a child's basic need not being met. More difficult is the "near homeless" situation in which families may temporarily have to move in with friends or family and sometimes need to make frequent moves.

Neglected health care refers to situations in which children do not receive adequate health care, resulting in actual or potential harm. This may involve a lack of primary preventive care, failure or delay in getting care for a sick child, or when recommendations for care are not followed. This form of neglect includes regular medical care, dental care, and mental health care. For example, a depressed, suicidal child who does not receive professional care is probably being neglected.

Educational neglect occurs when a child is not enrolled in school or when there is significant absenteeism without reasonable cause. The increasingly widespread use of home schooling, however, probably needs to be viewed as adequately meeting children's educational needs. For children attending school, the failure of the school system to evaluate and address significant learning problems is another form of neglect.

Inadequate supervision occurs when children are left alone in a manner and for a period of time that is not appropriate for their developmental level. For an infant, 1 minute unattended in a bath tub can be fatal. For a toddler, brief lapses in supervision in a dangerous area, such as near a swimming pool, can be lethal. Many states have laws or regulations stating at what age children can be left with older children of a certain age. Even in these cases, it is important to consider the specific circumstances, such as the kind of neighborhood, the maturity of the children, and the availability of help from neighbors or someone by phone.

Protection from environmental hazards includes dangers in and out of the home. Young children need to have the home safety-proofed, with poisonous substances and small objects on which they could choke placed out of their reach. Stairs need to be guarded with gates. Smoking can be a hazard, particularly for children with asthma or lung disease. Smoke alarms are important. If there is a gun in the home, it should be securely stored, out of the reach of children, and not loaded. Outside the home, children need to wear seat belts or sit in car seats, and those riding bikes need to wear helmets. These are a few examples of preventing noninflicted injuries (previously called accidents).

Inadequate nurturance, love, affection, and support may be the most serious form of neglect, although it is difficult to quantify and assess. Often it co-occurs with other forms of neglect that are easier to identify. Every child needs to know that at least one adult is there for him or her, feels positively toward him or her, and is able to provide affection and support. Parents who are depressed or addicted to drugs may have great difficulty meeting these crucial emotional needs of children.

It remains challenging to decide at what point one would define the inadequacy of care as neglect. For example, one would not report the occasional failure to wear a bike helmet to CPS.

The category of "mild" neglect comprises many cases that may justify a community intervention (e.g., a pediatrician advising on bike helmets), but not warrant a CPS report. In the category of "moderate" neglect, less intrusive efforts have failed or moderate harm is involved (e.g., persistent poor growth), and CPS probably needs to be involved, often with other community supports. Finally, the category of "serious" neglect involves severe or long-term harm (e.g., a child with severe asthma who repeatedly does not receive necessary medications despite the efforts of a home visitor and has multiple admissions to an intensive care unit [ICU]); CPS and perhaps legal involvement are needed. It is clear, however, that the child welfare system is usually focused on cases in which parental responsibility is a major contributor to the neglect.

The following are important issues regarding how neglect is viewed:

1. How do I determine potential harm? Information on the specific child may help (e.g., if this child does not receive her asthma medications, she could return to the ICU). Sometimes, common sense serves to make the determination (e.g., feeling hungry often is not good). Research data can

also be useful (e.g., the risks of secondhand smoke, not wearing a seat belt, and not going to school).

2. Should I be concerned with long-term harm? Yes; it can be severe, even though the child currently appears to be well.

3. Should I be concerned with emotional harm? Yes; it can be devastating, often more so than the physical harm.

4. Should I be concerned with occasional incidents of neglect? Yes, although patterns of repeated neglect are especially worrisome. Also, "occasional" neglect may not be so infrequent; rather, it may be a part of a chronic pattern of neglect.

5. What about neglect that is mostly due to poverty? This calls for interventions other than CPS, including advocacy to tackle this serious problem.

6. What about different cultural practices that may be considered neglect? Respect for and understanding of different cultures is critical, avoiding ethnocentric views (i.e., "my way is the right way"). Neglect should be considered only if it is clear that the practice or lack of care is causing or risks significant harm and that beneficial alternatives exist. This avoids a dangerous approach that accepts any practice of another culture regardless of its effect on children simply because a parent states "that's how we do things." Cultural differences, however, need to be addressed with great sensitivity and humility, and frequently a reasonable compromise can be reached.

A child-focused definition of neglect requires a response to many conditions that harm children, not all of which warrant CPS involvement. Professionals need to carefully evaluate the nature of the neglect, what is causing it, and what kind of intervention is most appropriate.

4

What Is Physical Abuse?

■ *Howard Dubowitz*

hysical abuse is usually defined as an inflicted act that results in a significant physical injury or the risk of such injury. In most states, the child welfare system is concerned with acts by parents or caregivers; physical assault by others is typically addressed by law enforcement or informally (e.g., fights among siblings).

■ At What Point Is Hitting Children in the Course of "Discipline" Abuse?

This is a crucial question because corporal punishment, including hitting children with various objects, is still widely accepted and used in the United States. Although many child advocates oppose all hitting of children and several researchers have found a harmful psychological effect of corporal punishment, most hitting does not meet the threshold for defining abuse in the current child welfare system. Instead, abuse is often defined as occurring when there is an injury beyond the temporary redness (e.g., a bruise, broken bone, cut, burn, and bleeding around the brain).

In addition to hitting, other acts, such as grabbing, shoving, and using a weapon, can lead to abusive injuries.

Professionals may recommend alternative disciplinary approaches (e.g., time-out), but they usually do not consider "minor" hitting as abuse. Infants are an exception; their dependence and vulnerability evoke more concern, and any hitting may be construed as abuse. Shaking can also be dangerous for infants and should be considered a form of abuse. Also, where the child is hit is important. The hands, backs of legs, and the bottom are typical sites for corporal punishment; hitting the face or head is more likely to be considered abuse.

■ What About Potential Injury?

Clearly, physical abuse may risk serious injury (e.g., when a heavy object is thrown at a child), but due to good luck or poor aim the child might escape unscathed. Such incidents should be viewed as physical abuse, although as a practical matter they seldom come to professional attention, unless an injury occurs or the incident is witnessed. Potential injury raises the possibility of emotional harm. It is clear that children may suffer emotional effects long after the bruises have faded or the fractures healed. Also, as mentioned previously, research suggests that even minor hitting is harmful (e.g., increased aggression and depression). Although I believe we should foster the use of preferable alternatives to hitting while discouraging all corporal punishment, defining "minor" hitting as abuse is currently unlikely to be an effective strategy. The widespread belief in corporal punishment and in parental rights could aggravate "the backlash" against child welfare.

■ How Should Different Cultural Practices That Physically Hurt Children Be Considered?

There are many examples of cultural practices that physically hurt children, including circumcision (male and female), moxabustion (an Asian folkloric remedy that can burn the skin), and *cao gio* (a folkloric approach in which the body is rubbed vigorously with a hard object such as a coin, causing bruising in an effort to treat the illness). In all such instances, the motivation is helping the child by following a hallowed tradition. The same argument, however, may be made by proponents of corporal punishment. Different cultural practices are generally respected and not defined as physical abuse. If the injury or harm is significant and if clearly preferable alternatives exist, however, professionals should sensitively encourage alternative approaches (e.g., medicine for the fever). The threshold for intervening should be high. Intervening may jeopardize a family's important ties to their minority community; addressing the concern with community leaders may be valuable. As with corporal punishment, defining these different cultural practices as abuse is unlikely to be constructive. These issues illustrate the challenges that must be dealt with when abuse is defined as deviation from community standards but there are practices that may harm children that are accepted by a community.

In summary, physical abuse is defined as inflicted acts causing physical injury to children. Potential injury is a concern but is seldom addressed by the child welfare system. All hitting of children should be discouraged but should not be termed abuse. Similarly, different cultural practices that clearly harm children should be discouraged and preferable approaches suggested. Most of these practices should not be labeled abuse. Of note, female genital mutilation has recently been made illegal. See Chapter 20, this volume, for more information on handling cross-cultural issues.

5

What Is Sexual Abuse?

■ *Lucy Berliner*

C*hild sexual abuse* is a general term used to refer to nonconsensual sexual acts, sexually motivated behaviors involving children, or sexual exploitation of children. These activities are associated with a variety of emotional and behavioral sequelae; being sexually abused increases the risk of psychiatric conditions and functional impairment. Although not all children develop problems as a result of these experiences, many do.

■ *Laws and Legal Definitions*

Criminal statutes at the state and federal levels define sexual behavior that is illegal. Each state has laws, variously named, that prohibit certain sexual conduct and define the elements of the criminal behavior that must be proven to convict the accused. These laws apply to adolescents and children as well as adults. States set an age at which children are presumed capable of forming the intent to commit a crime and can be prosecuted, usually between 10 and 14 years of age, and an age below which children cannot be prosecuted, regardless of conduct. In certain circumstances, the courts may determine that a child who is younger than the age at which competence is presumed did engage in criminal conduct and authorize prosecution. Although rare, this means that a prepubertal child could be charged with a sexual offense if force is used or there is an age differential. Laws also establish an age of consent at which adolescents are permitted to make their own decisions about sexual relationships. Incest is illegal regardless of age; states determine the degree of relatedness.

Child protection statutes in every state explicitly include sexual abuse as a form of child abuse that warrants state intervention. States vary in the degree to which they specify the exact behaviors or activities that constitute sexual abuse, however. Some child abuse statutes refer to the criminal laws of the state, whereas others define what constitutes sexual abuse more broadly. These laws may encompass behaviors that are inappropriate or suggest risk but do not rise to the level of sexually explicit acts or criminal conduct.

■ *Nonconsensual Behavior*

Lack of consent makes sexual activity abusive. Sexual activity can be nonconsensual in the following ways:

1. Force or coercion is used, regardless of the ages of the persons involved.
2. Consent is not possible (e.g., incapacitation by virtue of drugs, alcohol, or disability).
3. The target is a child. Children are presumed unable to give informed consent to sexual relationships with adults or when there are significant disparities in age, size, or development. In some cases, children perceive themselves to be consenting to the sexual activity, but developmental limitations on their capacity to objectively evaluate relationships or to understand the consequences call such judgments into question.

■ *Sexually Motivated Behavior*

Sexually motivated behavior consists of intentional acts that produce sexual arousal or gratification:

1. Explicit sexual acts: Sexual motivation is presumed for sexual penetration (vaginal, oral, anal, digital, and with an object), sexual touching (intentional contact with genitals, buttocks, or breasts), and sexual kissing. It is also presumed when adolescents or adults instruct children to engage in such behaviors with each other.
2. Indecent exposure, voyeurism, and frottage (i.e., rubbing against a person): Sexual motivation is inferred when sexual arousal is present or the context of the behavior is public and does not have a plausible nonsexual explanation.

■ *Sexual Exploitation*

This term refers to sexual behaviors or situations in which the motivation may or may not be sexual, but there is a clear sexual component. For example, in some cases the motivation is financial:

1. Taking pictures or videos of children engaging in sexual activities or in sexually explicit poses
2. Making children available to others for sexual purposes

■ *Problems in Determining Whether Behavior Is Sexual Abuse*

Some behaviors that are assumed to be sexually motivated in extrafamilial situations may be normative in intrafamilial situations. For example, parental nudity, looking at a child who is undressing or unclothed, joint bathing, and kissing on the mouth may be innocuous and acceptable in many families, but sometimes they are sexually motivated. Such behaviors frequently accompany intrafamilial sexual crimes, but by themselves they are not sufficient to conclude abuse.

Several factors may be used to assess whether behavior is sexually motivated. Specific evidence of deviant motivation may be found (e.g., holes drilled into bedroom walls). Behavior that is secretive or is accompanied by warnings not to tell raises strong suspicion. Repeated "accidental" touching or "inspections" of sexual body parts, especially in pubertal children, is suggestive of sexual motivation, as is "sex education" accompanied by touching. Also, there may be overt indication of sexual arousal when the person is nude or engaging in physical contact with the child. Explicit sexual remarks or observations may signal that a sexual component is present (e.g., lascivious comments about the child's physical developmental or intrusive inquiry into the child's sexual thoughts, feelings, or behavior).

■ *Developmentally Inappropriate But Not Sexually Motivated Behavior*

Parental nudity, joint bathing or showering, extensive bodily touching, or having children sleep in the parental bed are quite normal with younger children but may become uncomfortable for older children. For example, with the onset of puberty or sexual awareness, kissing on the mouth may make some older children uncomfortable or confused. In other cases, parents may expose children to sexually explicit activity or materials without any sexual intent. This may be the result of poverty and overcrowding, the level of parental supervision, or values about sexuality. There is no clear line for when these activities become abusive, if ever, when sexual motivation is not present.

■ *Sexual Activity Between Children*

It is sexual abuse when adolescents engage in sexual contact by use of force or with younger children. Sexual contact between adolescent siblings, even when consensual, is ordinarily considered a form of sexual abuse. Sexually aggressive or persistent sexual contact by prepubertal children, except in the rare cases in which criminal intent is present, is best considered a sexual behavior problem. This does not mean that the child who is the recipient of the behavior has not been victimized, but this conceptualization does not require that the aggressing child be labeled an offender. Such behavior in children may signal that they have been sexually abused, but it may also result from exposure to sexually explicit activity or a high level of family stress. Sexual intercourse between prepubescent children, regardless of consent, is developmentally inappropriate. Sexual curiosity and touching between similar age children up to early adolescence is common; as long as the activity does not involve coercion, is not a preoccupation, and is private, it can be considered normal.

■ *Family and Cultural Variations*

Family relating style or cultural traditions will strongly influence the nature of physical expression of affection, privacy accorded children, and openness about sexuality. In situations in which the behavior does not involve coercion or sexual motivation, it is important to assess the context and family values before making a determination. Some practices may be acceptable in a country of origin but violate legal or child protection standards in the United States, whereas others may simply reflect variations in family practices. Consultation with culturally competent experts may help in uncertain situations.

6

What Is Psychological Maltreatment?

■ *Marla R. Brassard and Stuart Hart*

■ *Definition of Psychological Maltreatment*

Psychological maltreatment usually accompanies other types of abuse and neglect, and research suggests that this is what makes them so harmful. Therefore, professionals should always check for the presence of psychological maltreatment when they are evaluating possible sexual abuse, physical abuse, or neglect.

Psychological maltreatment is "a repeated pattern of caregiver behavior or extreme incident(s) that convey to children that they are worthless, flawed, unloved, unwanted, endangered, or only of value in meeting another's needs" (American Professional Society on the Abuse of Children, 1995, p. 2; Brassard, Hart, & Hardy, 1991). Psychological maltreatment includes both abusive acts against a child (e.g., verbal attacks by a caregiver) and failure to act—neglectful behavior, when appropriate action is required for a child's healthy development (e.g., when a child is shown no affection). It can occur as part of an extreme one-time incident (e.g., a parent frustrated about continual bed-wetting forces a 6-year-old to wear diapers in the neighborhood) but is usually chronic. Many states and child welfare professionals use terms such as "mental injury" and "emotional abuse and neglect" to mean the same things. We prefer the term *psychological maltreat-*

ment because we think it best represents the breadth of types of abuse, neglect, and injury that the child experiences.

■ *Forms of Psychological Maltreatment*

Table 6.1 identifies six forms of psychological maltreatment. The first five forms have been identified through research, clinical experience, and a consensus of expert opinion. The sixth form includes types of neglect embedded in or derived from the other forms and traditionally of concern to society. Children may experience one or more of these forms either singly or together with other forms of abuse and neglect. Many professionals find those forms helpful in understanding their cases. States use different terms for these types of behavior, however; therefore, professionals should apply the forms described in Table 6.1 according to their state law. For example, terrorizing and spurning might be classified as emotional abuse, denying emotional responsiveness and isolating might be classified as neglect, and some forms of corrupting and exploiting would be abuse (e.g., telling a child to shoplift if he or she wants spending money), whereas others (e.g., permitting a teenager to use illegal drugs at home) may be classified as emotional neglect.

■ *Identification of Psychological Maltreatment*

Where should the line be drawn as to what is psychological maltreatment and what is inadequate or poor parenting? All caregivers, at some point in time, may behave in a way that is psychologically hurtful to their children. This is not necessarily psychological maltreatment. Psychological maltreatment usually occurs when hurtful behavior (e.g., ignoring a child's bids for attention and affection) becomes a consistent caregiving style. Some isolated behaviors are so psychologically hurtful, however, that even one incident would be psychological maltreatment (e.g., blaming a parent's suicide attempt on a child's behavior). To determine if the hurtful caregiver behavior that one observes is psychological maltreatment, several factors must be considered. The level of severity of the caregiver behavior is a guiding

Table 6.1   Psychological Maltreatment Forms

*Six Major Types of Psychological Maltreatment Described
and Further Clarified by Identification of Subcategories*

A repeated pattern or extreme incident(s) of the conditions described in this table constitute psychological maltreatment. Such conditions convey the message that the child is worthless, flawed, unloved, endangered, or only valuable in meeting someone else's needs.

Spurning (hostile rejecting and degrading) includes verbal and nonverbal caregiver acts that reject and degrade a child. Spurning includes the following:

Belittling, degrading, and other nonphysical forms of overly hostile or rejecting treatment

Shaming or ridiculing the child for showing normal emotions, such as affection, grief, or sorrow

Consistently singling out one child to criticize and punish, to perform most of the household chores, or to receive fewer rewards

Public humiliation

Terrorizing includes caregiver behavior that threatens or is likely to physically hurt, kill, abandon, or place the child or child's loved ones or objects in recognizably dangerous situations. Terrorizing includes the following:

Placing a child in unpredictable or chaotic circumstances

Placing a child in recognizably dangerous situations

Setting rigid or unrealistic expectations with the threat of loss, harm, or danger if they are not met

Threatening or perpetrating violence against the child or the child's loved ones or objects

Exploiting/corrupting includes caregiver acts that encourage the child to develop inappropriate behaviors (self-destructive, antisocial, criminal, deviant, or other maladaptive behaviors). Exploiting/corrupting includes the following:

Modeling, permitting, or encouraging antisocial behavior (e.g., prostitution, performance in pornographic media, initiation of criminal activities, substance abuse, and violence to or corruption of others)

Modeling, permitting, or encouraging developmentally inappropriate behavior (e.g., parentification, infantalization, and living the parent's unfulfilled dreams)

Encouraging or coercing abandonment of developmentally appropriate autonomy through extreme overinvolvement, intrusiveness, and/or dominance (e.g., allowing little or no opportunity or support for child's views, feelings, and wishes and micromanaging child's life)

Restricting or interfering with cognitive development

Denying emotional responsiveness (ignoring) includes caregiver acts that ignore the child's attempts and needs to interact (failing to express affection, caring, and love for the child) and show no emotion in interactions with the child. Denying emotional responsiveness includes the following:

Being detached and uninvolved through either incapacity or lack of motivation

Interacting only when absolutely necessary

Failing to express affection, caring, and love for the child

(continued)

Table 6.1   Continued

Isolating includes caregiver acts that consistently deny the child opportunities to meet needs for interacting or communicating with peers or adults inside or outside the home. Isolating includes the following:	*Mental health, medical, and educational neglect* includes unwarranted caregiver acts that ignore, refuse to allow, or fail to provide the necessary treatment for the mental health, medical, and educational problems or needs for the child. Mental health, medical, and educational neglect includes the following:
Confining the child or placing unreasonable limitations on the child's freedom of movement within his or her environment	Ignoring the need for treatment for serious emotional and behavioral problems or needs of the child; failing to provide or refusing to allow such treatment
Placing unreasonable limitations or restrictions on social interactions with peers or adults in the community	Ignoring the need for treatment for serious physical health problems or needs of the child; failing to provide or refusing to allow such treatment
	Ignoring the need for treatment for services for serious educational problems or needs of the child; failing to provide or refusing to allow such treatment

SOURCE: Office for the Study of the Psychological Rights of the Child, Indiana University-Purdue University at Indianapolis, 902 West New York Street, Indianapolis, IN 46202-5155.

standard used by most states. All parents criticize children's behavior, but psychologically abusive parents offer more frequent criticism of the child (e.g., repeatedly saying "You never do anything right") or more extreme criticism ("You are so stupid I wish you had never been born"). Many caregivers occasionally ask children to take on inappropriate responsibilities, but psychologically neglectful parents do this routinely (e.g., a 7-year-old is her mother's confidant and makes many of the family decisions). Professionals should be aware, however, that research shows that apparently mild forms or levels of psychological maltreatment (e.g., frequent critical remarks) can be as damaging to children as more severe forms.

Some states also require evidence that a child has been emotionally or mentally harmed by the caregiver (e.g., that a child has developed an anxiety disorder because of terrorizing). Assessment of psychological maltreatment is discussed in Chapter 45, this volume.

The family's circumstances must also be considered when assessing psychological maltreatment. Families living in violent neighborhoods severely restrict their children's movement in the community and their choice of friends, as a matter of survival. Some families who have recently immigrated require children to take on what would be considered adult responsibilities in our culture; for example, an 11-year-old girl may be expected to manage a household and four younger siblings after school while the parents work very long hours to support the family. Careful consideration by professionals of the cultural demands and realities faced by children and families in their environment may prevent both the misidentification of parents as maltreating and the acceptance of potentially damaging cultural practices.

■ *Further Reading*

American Professional Society on the Abuse of Children. (1995). *Practice guidelines on the psychosocial evaluation of suspected psychological maltreatment in children and adolescents.* Chicago: Author.

Brassard, M. R., Hart, S., & Hardy, D. B. (1991). Psychological and emotional abuse of children. In R. T. Ammerman & M. Hersen (Eds.), *Case studies in family violence* (pp. 255-270). New York: Plenum.

Part II

ENGAGEMENT

7

How Do I Connect With Children at Different Developmental Levels?

■ *Brenda Jones Harden*

Engaging children requires a special set of strategies built on a knowledge of child development, a high comfort level with children, and good interpersonal skills. The interpersonal skills that facilitate engagement with adults and children include (a) empathic responding (sharing in what the person is feeling and experiencing), (b) unconditional positive regard (accepting the person in a nonjudgmental way), (c) genuineness (displaying who you are in an honest manner), (d) active listening (showing with your words and body that you are attuned to what the person is saying), and (e) the capacity to help solve a problem or manage a crisis.

The practitioner who works with children should have as a foundation the previously mentioned interpersonal skills but should also be aware of the unique characteristics of the child-adult interaction process. Children have very little power and often do not believe that they are engaged in voluntary equitable interpersonal relationships with adults. Moreover, children in the child welfare system often view adults suspiciously because of their experiences of adults as abusive or neglectful and as having the power to disrupt their families. In addition, children do not have the cognitive or coping skills that allow them to understand or manage fully their life circumstances. Children also have different temperaments, which make them more or less amenable to social interaction. Finally, because children are continuously developing, the strategies used to engage them change as a function of their age and developmental level.

The following general engagement strategies are useful in work with children:

- Getting on the same level as children (e.g., sitting on the floor or in a child-sized chair)
- Using modes of communication with which children may be more comfortable (e.g., play, stories, poems, rap music, and art activities)
- Nurturing children in a case-appropriate way (e.g., feeding them, using touch judiciously, providing a small present, responding to their needs immediately, and attending to their thoughts, interests, and wishes)
- Following the child's lead (e.g., determining how directive to be, how to manage behavior, and how deeply to address feelings by what messages the child gives about these issues)
- Being trustworthy (i.e., being true to your word, keeping appointments, following up on issues you agreed to, not making empty promises, and ensuring that what the child tells you will remain confidential if possible)
- Providing a safe haven for the child (i.e., letting the child know with your words and behaviors that he or she is not only physically safe with you but also psychologically safe—that you will not hurt him or her and that you will respond to his or her needs)

Engagement strategies vary with the different developmental levels through which children proceed. It is important to note that chronological age does not always coincide with children's developmental level. Many children encountered by child welfare practitioners may be developmentally delayed. Thus, it is important to determine at which developmental level children are through an informal interview with caregivers about general developmental milestones. The following are some engagement strategies specific to developmental levels:

Infants and toddlers: The developmental predilection of infants and toddlers to attach to a few primary caregivers suggests that practitioners should not attempt to engage them. This is particularly true for children between 6 and 24 months of age, when they may evidence varying levels of separation and stranger anxiety. Attempts to work with these children should ideally be conducted in the context of the child's current home environment in the presence of the child's current caregiver. Young children need to see that their caregivers (no matter who they are) approve of their relationship with another adult. These children should have to develop relationships only with another permanent caregiver, however, and not a caseworker or other practitioner. Observational strategies, rather than engagement per se, should be employed to determine how the case should progress.

Preschoolers: Preschool children have made considerable cognitive, social, and emotional advancements that allow them to interact capably with strange adults. Because play is the preschooler's most salient medium of communication and learning, these children should be engaged through play. Adults who get on the floor and use the children's toys (or who have their own stash of toys) to create a joint play experience often expedite the engagement process. Similarly, joint storytelling and art activities invite the preschool child to interact more fully with the strange adult. Accepting how these children view the world (e.g., fantasizing about their ideal biological parents) is also important. Assuring the children that you will try to make sure they are safe (e.g., throwing the monsters out the window and keeping the bad guys away) is also an effective engagement strategy.

School-aged children: Children during this developmental period are invested in self-identity, peer relationships, and task accomplishment. Adults engage school-age children by expressing interest and belief in these children's abilities and accomplishments. In addition, exposing them to different experiences and ideas that are related to their interests facilitates engagement (e.g., providing a child with a magazine that has pictures of the cars he or she has talked about). Because these children are sometimes reluctant to express their feelings verbally, engaging in activities that draw on their cognitive capacities may be a better way to address emotional issues (e.g., drawing faces of different feelings, completing sentences about the child's experiences and feelings, and jointly creating a book about a child with a similar experience). The best format to use for first interviews with these children is often a game or other activity that is enjoyable to the children.

Adolescents: Because adolescents have the cognitive capacity to understand the world in general, the best approach is to be honest and straightforward. Their complex thinking and verbal skills allow them to discuss their situations candidly. Their inability to construct their futures, however, requires that the practitioner balance respect for their ideas with structure and a strong message that they will be supported through the transition to adulthood. The engagement process is also facilitated by the practitioner's willingness to become a student of (not an expert in) the adolescents' world, including the pop culture they follow, their perceptions of their environment, and their experiences. Maintaining confidentiality is crucial with adolescents. In addition, using an age-specific peer group approach may be helpful.

In conclusion, engaging children is a process that requires good interpersonal skills and an understanding of the unique characteristics of children. Practitioners should give children a strong message through their words and actions that they are trustworthy and sensitive to children's needs. Engagement strategies should be selected that capitalize on the capacities and preferences of children at different developmental levels.

■ *Further Reading*

Fahlberg, V. (1991). *A child's journey through placement.* Indianapolis, IN: Perspectives Press.

Gumaer, J. (1984). *Counseling and therapy for children.* New York: Free Press.

Zigler, E., & Finn-Stevenson, M. (1993). *Children in a changing world: Development and social issues.* Pacific Grove, CA: Brooks/Cole.

8

How Do I Develop a Helping Alliance With the Family?

■ *Diane DePanfilis*

M any families at risk for child maltreatment may have a history of difficulty in forming and sustaining mutually supportive interpersonal relationships. Furthermore, they may not have had positive experiences with formal systems. One of the essential challenges for practitioners is to form positive connections and partnerships with families so that families will have an opportunity to handle the difficult challenges in their lives. Experience has demonstrated that successful intervention and treatment depend heavily on the quality of one's relationship with the client or family. Whether one's role is to interview family members as part of the initial assessment or to target outcomes for risk reduction, the quality of one's work is directly dependent on one's ability to develop a working relationship with family members. This chapter outlines skills that are effective in building the helping alliance.

■ *Communicating Concern for All Family Members*

Simply stated, this involves sincerely caring about what happens to the client and communicating that you care to all family members. This can be particularly difficult in the field of child protection. For example, when confronted with an angry, hostile outburst from a client, it is important to be aware of your own feelings toward the person. To the extent that you can, you must communicate concern for the person while not condoning the person's behavior.

■ *Clarifying Expectations and Purposes*

One of the best ways to develop a helping alliance with your clients is to clearly explain the helping process and your role to work together toward solutions. Many of the difficulties labeled a "resistance" or "lack of cooperation" can be attributed to a lack of clarity or unrealistic expectations by your client about what you will or will not do. Each helping relationship has a unique, individual purpose. Depending on your role with the agency, this purpose may be short term if you conduct initial assessments, or it could be longer term if you provide continuing services. Although the purpose of your relationship with your clients may be clear to you, it may not be clear to your clients. Thus, part of your responsibility is to work with your clients to come to agreement about the purpose of your relationship with them.

■ *Clarifying Your Authority and Power*

There are two aspects of authority in child protection practice helping relationships. The first is usually referred to as the institutional aspect in that it is derived from your position and function within your agency. The second aspect is psychological in that clients give workers the power to influence or persuade because they accept them as sources of information and advice— as experts in their field. This is an especially crucial element for child protective services workers. Mistakes can be made by abdicating one's authority (e.g., "My supervisor made me do it"). Abuses of power and authority can also jeopardize your relationship with your clients (e.g., "If you don't do this, I will see to it that your kids are taken away"). Particularly with families that require the use of court intervention, it may be necessary for you to repeatedly explain what authority and power you carry, the limits of your authority and power, and how you use it.

■ Clarifying Commitment and Obligation

In the helping relationship, both client and worker must be bound by commitments and obligations if the purposes of intervention are to be achieved. A commitment to the conditions and purposes of the relationship allows the client to feel safe and reduces the testing behavior that usually marks the beginning of a relationship. Once a commitment to the relationship has been established, and the limits of time, place, and purpose have been accepted, each participant is able to depend on the predictability of the other's behavior, attitudes, and involvement. With some families, this may mean mutually agreeing on what you and the family will work on together, who will do what and when, and for how long you and the family will work together. For other clients, arriving at agreement on commitments and obligations may be an evolving process. This may be something that you work on together over time as your client increasingly trusts you.

■ Communicating Acceptance and Expectation

This element emphasizes the importance of individualization, acceptance, client self-determination, and a nonjudgmental attitude. One of the most effective ways to communicate acceptance is to try to understand the position and feelings of each client as a unique human being with distinctive feelings, thoughts, and experiences. As this concept relates to child protection practice, it means that one does not talk about the "sexual abuse case" and make certain assumptions about what individual family members will be like based on certain characteristics or facts. Each new "case" is actually a family made up of individual members, all of whom are individual human beings. Each of them, and the family as a whole, should be looked to for help in understanding their problems and life circumstances from their individual and collective points of view. Acceptance does not mean that we will always agree with our clients. It also does not mean that we forego our own values to support a client's values, particularly if they interfere with the protection of the child. Acceptance means that we "understand," not that we accept the factors that create risk or concern.

■ *Communicating Empathy*

Practitioners and researchers agree that empathy is a necessary quality of the helping relationship. The process of entering into the feelings and experiences of another—knowing what the other feels and experiences—should begin before we even meet families for the first time. This "tuning in" that we do before we first talk with the child, mother, father, or other caregiver opens the door to understanding more completely the actual experience of the child and family. This process is especially important when working cross culturally (see Chapter 9, this volume). It is important that beginning workers distinguish between the capacity to feel an emotion deeply and the need to remain professionally separate from their client's situation. In their effort to be empathic with children in particular, some new workers lose their objectivity and "overidentify" with the children's perspective. This position makes it difficult for them to be empathic to other family members, which leads to counterproductive outcomes for the family as a whole.

■ *Communicating Genuineness and Congruence*

In some ways, communicating genuineness and congruence combines many of the other concepts already discussed. To do this, we must seek (a) an honest knowledge of ourselves—of who and what we really are; (b) a clear knowledge of agency procedures and policies and of the professional role both in their meaning to the worker and in their meaning to the clients; and (c) an internalization of the first two aspects and our concern for the other, acceptance of clients, and commitment to their welfare and to the authority aspects of the workers' role and position so that these qualities are so much a part of us that we no longer need to be consciously aware of them and can turn our full attention to clients and their situation. The congruence aspect of this dimension means that what we say is really consistent with our attitudes and beliefs. This subtle dimension means that our clients should more likely trust that we "mean what we say."

■ *Further Reading*

Compton, B. R., & Galaway, B. (1999). *Social work processes* (6th ed.). Pacific Grove, CA: Brooks/Cole.

Hepworth, D. H., Rooney, R. H., & Larsen, J. (1997). *Direct social work practice*. Pacific Grove, CA: Brooks/Cole.

9

What Principles and Approaches Can I Use to Engage Clients Across Cultures?

■ *Veronica D. Abney*

Currently, there is much talk in the human service field about the need to find ways to engage clients from a multitude of different cultures. Although there are those who debate the necessity of having a multicultural approach, the need seems very clear. It occurs because of the increasing diversity in the United States, inadequate service delivery to people of color, and fewer numbers of professionals of color in the field than clients of color.

There are three essential principles that must operate in the background when we work cross culturally. First, we need to believe that diversity is a good thing and understand that having different ideals, customs, attitudes, practices, and beliefs does not, in and of itself, constitute deviance or pathology. If we approach culturally different clients from this perspective, we will more likely communicate respect. Second, it must be understood and accepted that we all have biases and prejudices. If we are not aware of our own prejudices, we will not be challenged by new experience, nor will we understand intense emotional reactions to clients caused by such biases and prejudices. Finally, it is necessary to be aware that the role of helper provides power, and that a professional may also have power because of ethnicity or gender or both. This power impacts the client-helper interaction and may work against efforts to empower the client.

With these principles well established, I present the following concrete approaches:

1. Gain basic knowledge of culture by reading and talking with colleagues, recognizing that it is impossible to learn everything about every culture in a multicultural society. Basic knowledge includes information on family values, strengths of the culture, religious and spiritual views, language and communication styles, views of wellness, behavioral and emotional expressiveness, views on sex roles and sexuality, child-rearing beliefs and patterns, the level of assimilation and acculturation, racial and ethnic identity, and time perspective. Remember that there is heterogeneity within cultures, and that this information should provide only an initial framework for understanding a client's culture. Even when this information is not available, be aware that these are the areas in which one can expect variations and differences attributable to culture as opposed to pathology. Clients are a good source of information regarding their particular culture; in the field of child maltreatment, however, professionals must be careful to guard against the possibility of cultural camouflage by perpetrators. One still needs enough information and resources to delineate what is culturally deviant.

2. When making introductions, it is important to introduce yourself by your professional title. For those from many cultures, this builds their confidence in you. The client should be addressed formally and then asked how he or she would like to be addressed. This connotes respect.

3. Explain your role and how you can help. Different cultures have different ways of helping and may not know what you can do to help.

4. Explore the client's understanding of the problem. The client may have a different view due to particular cultural values. It is essential to keep both perspectives in mind when addressing the problem to establish and maintain an alliance with the client.

5. Communicate that you are listening and are interested in what the client has to say by making direct eye contact, brief utterances, and nonverbal communication. When the client has finished talking, summarize what you have heard.
6. Identify and acknowledge client strengths. This helps the client to see that, despite the problem at hand, areas of competence are recognized.
7. Be open to exploring the client's feelings about working with someone outside his or her own culture.

It is important to realize that these are only basic guidelines for engaging clients across cultures. Professionals should seek out training opportunities to more fully understand their feelings and beliefs about diversity and multiculturalism and to explore the impact of their own cultural experience on their interactions with clients.

■ *Further Reading*

Abney, V. D., & Gunn, K. (1993). Culture: A rationale for cultural competency. *APSAC Advisor,* 6(3), 19-22.

Sue, D. W., & Sue, D. (1990). *Counseling the culturally different: Theory and practice.* New York: John Wiley.

10

How Can I Use Authority Effectively and Engage Family Members?

■ *Ronald H. Rooney*

Effective use of authority reduces opposition and assists in engaging families. Several factors make this a difficult proposition. First, there may not be agreement between the practitioner and the family about the nature of effective intervention. From the child protective services (CPS) worker's perspective, effectiveness may be related to the availability of services and the manner in which services are offered. From the perspective of family members served by CPS, effectiveness is influenced by their perceptions of the value of services and the extent that they believe that their perspective is heard and included in the assessment and service plan. A second factor is related to recent changes in the nature of the CPS response. Although in some agencies services include an assessment and actual service provision, in other agencies the emphasis may be on only an assessment of danger focused on protecting children at imminent risk. Using authority effectively and engaging the family will be much easier within some of these frameworks than in others. A third factor relates to the worker's perception about the family. Views of parents range from being hostile adversaries unconcerned with their children's needs to being active, positive participants who wish their children to be safe and healthy. If workers perceive family members as uncooperative, it is much less likely that they will be engaged as partners (see Chapter 8, this volume). An additional factor in the current context is the overrepresentation of low-income children of color in the child welfare system at large, and particularly in out-of-home care. Workers may not be adequately prepared to successfully engage families across culture (see Chapter 9, this volume). As a consequence of these adversarial circumstances, child welfare recipients have reported feeling "invaded" by child welfare investigators. A final factor is the fact that although CPS workers initiate contact with legally delegated authority to conduct assessments and offer services, they may lack their client's respect and therefore do not have the psychological authority to influence the change process (see Chapter 8, this volume). The following recommendations are made based on these circumstances:

1. Contact with families in an assessment role should be carried out in a courteous, respectful fashion, assessing strengths and assets as well as problematic circumstances.

2. CPS workers should quickly elicit the parent's view of concerns and wishes for assistance, conveying understanding of the parent's viewpoint, including reservations about CPS involvement. Child welfare service recipients who feel threatened by a situation are apt to defend themselves verbally or physically. They may deny harm, blame others, or challenge authority. Rather than consider such responses as pathological, as indicators of refusal to take responsibility for one's actions, or as personally directed at the CPS worker, it is more useful to consider these responses as normal reactions when valued freedoms are threatened. Hence, to state that "most people don't like someone coming into their home to talk about child safety" can convey empathy and help establish rapport.

3. CPS workers should be matter-of-fact, explanatory, and nondefensive in explaining the legal authority that permits them to conduct an assessment of child safety. It is important not to get into a debate about this authority but, rather, to state what it is and what legal recourse the client might have to challenge it. Such an explanation need not be adversarial and should explain how it is the job of CPS to assist parents and the community in ensuring safety for children. Legally delegated authority also entails nonnegotiable require-

ments. It is important to be specific about nonnegotiable legal requirements such as provisions of court orders. In addition, service recipients must be informed of their rights, free choices, and options available to them.

4. Opposition to contact can be reduced by clarifying available choices, even when they are constrained; by emphasizing freedoms still available; and by avoiding labeling. For example, CPS recipients may be able to select from a list of providers of parenting classes or chemical-dependency assessors.

5. To earn the respect needed to psychologically influence parents, in addition to the power of legally delegated authority, the CPS worker should be a good listener who strives to understand the potential client's viewpoint. In addition, making and keeping commitments to CPS recipients enhances the CPS worker's credibility.

6. The CPS worker should explore and include, where possible, parental wishes for the health and safety of their children in service agreements to enhance their co-ownership of the plan.

■ Further Reading

Courtney, M. E., Barth, R. P., Berrick, J. D., Brooks, D., Needell, B., & Park, L. (1996). Race and child welfare services: Past research and future directions. *Child Welfare, 75,* 99-137.

Diorio, W. (1992). Parenting perceptions of the authority of public caseworkers. *Families in Society, 73,* 222-235.

Rooney, R. H. (1992). *Strategies for work with involuntary clients.* New York: Columbia University Press.

11

How Do I Manage Difficult Encounters With the Family?

■ *Ronald Zuskin*

W hen you enter into a relationship with someone who has not invited you to do so, you are likely to be facing a difficult encounter. Ronald Rooney (1992) termed the normal reactions of people to unwanted intrusions by professionals *reactance* instead of *resistance*. If you have not been freely sought as a helper, try to normalize the reactance responses that can appear as resistance, denial, and hostility. Do not personalize these reactions. In fact, the most difficult encounter you may have is with the apparently compliant person. Although compliant people may seem welcoming and willing, they may be less likely to engage with us and move toward change.

One of the most difficult encounters, particularly during the initial contact, is with the person or family with a history of violence. During these encounters, or at critical points in your work with people with a history of violence, their emotions and behaviors may escalate. Escalation begins when the typical reactance responses become filled with mounting anxiety. Pacing, sweating, stammering, shakiness, and breaks in eye contact signal mounting anxiety. Anxiety can build to agitated defensiveness. Belligerence, yelling, intimidation, pressured speech, or staring indicate mounting escalation that, if continued, will lead to acting out. Verbal threats, rapid movements, standing or movement toward you, and actual assaultive behavior signify the peak of escalation—and danger. Acting out is usually followed by tension reduction. Crying, blushing, avoidance, fear, and even remorse typify deescalation.

It is important to deal effectively with normal reactance responses to address client concerns without inviting people to escalate. To deal with normal resistance, denial, and hostility:

- Expect it as normal.
- Emphasize specific, not global, changes.
- Avoid labeling.
- Attribute difficulties and problems to situations and not individuals.
- Clarify areas of choice from areas of limited, or no, choice.
- Establish small feasible steps.
- Build in early success and recognize or reward efforts and progress.

The following are statements you might say:

- "It must be difficult to have to talk with me about this."
- "Many people I talk with are frightened at first that I have come to take their children away, but I want to let you know that I am here to make sure they are safe and to work with you to make sure that you will be able to stay together."
- "Some people have found that talking with a group of other people in similar circumstances is helpful, and others find that working with one person is better for them. What do you think would work best for you?"
- "I guess you would rather see me disappear, but since that can't happen right now, would it be better for you if we met again on Wednesday morning or Friday afternoon?"

Dealing with the escalating, potentially violent person requires responses that are tuned in to the stage of agitation or escalation. Recognize escalation early, and act in ways that diminish the likelihood of acting out. When there are signs of mounting anxiety:

- Be supportive and understanding.
- Use active listening.
- Assess the person's ability to accurately judge your comments.
- Facilitate and do not limit expression of emotion.
- Clarify your role and expectations.
- Use distance consciously and do not get too close.

The following are statements you might say:

- "It might help to let me know how you are feeling."
- "It's like you don't know where to turn and you're getting so frustrated."
- "Golly, what you heard isn't what I meant to say. Let me try that one more time."
- "I do need to understand what's been happening at home and I need you to take a few minutes to let me know."

When you see agitated defensiveness:

- Provide structure and focus.
- Set reasonable and enforceable limits.
- Practice self-control without defensiveness or threats.
- Sit and encourage the person to remain seated.

The following are statements you might say:

- "I get confused if we talk about too many things at once. Which topic would you like us to stick to?"
- "Shouting won't help either of us. If things don't calm down we will have to stop our meeting and try again later."
- "Golly, I don't know you well enough to know whether or not I should be frightened when you stand up like that. Can you sit down while we try to figure that out?"

When you see acting out:

- Follow through on limits.
- Indicate the realistic consequences of the behavior.
- Use furniture as a protective barrier.
- Terminate the meeting.

The following are statements you might say:

- "If you need a break, we can take a few minutes."
- "What you are doing is frightening me, and I wonder if we can just take a few steps back and think about what is happening?"
- "I don't want anything to happen that will just make things worse for you, or for me. Let's stop for now."

When you see tension reduction:

- Reinstitute active listening and reconnect.
- Acknowledge that the person has regained control.
- Restate the mutual goal.

The following are statements you might say:

- "I can hear in what you are saying that you regret going off like that."
- "You know that we both want what is best for your family, even if we see it differently sometimes. And neither of us wants anything bad to happen to you."
- "I certainly don't want to stir the pot again, but I was wondering how your buttons got pushed. I couldn't tell exactly what it was, whether it was something I did, or something else. What do you think?"

Your self is your only tool for handling difficult encounters. You may be uncomfortable with a person's normal reactance but still actually be quite safe. It is important to differentiate when you are uncomfortable from when you are unsafe (see Chapter 119, this volume). Use the signs of mounting anxiety and agitated defensiveness to determine whether you are actually at risk.

Recognize mounting anxiety and use it to stop agitation and escalation before they start. Do not be afraid to be afraid, and do not pretend that your professional role requires you to either take command or stick it out no matter what. Stay within your limitations. Discretion is the better part of valor. It is better to put things on hold than to pick up the pieces of a shattered difficult encounter. Be strategic, but, above all, be safe.

■ *Further Reading*

Irwin, D. (1996/1997). Safety training for human services professionals. *Protecting Children, 12/13,* 8-11.

Rooney, R. H. (1992). *Strategies for work with involuntary clients.* New York: Columbia University Press.

12

How Do I Respond to Feelings (Mine and My Client's)?

■ *David Corwin*

The focus of this chapter is emotional reactions, yours and your client's, and how awareness of these feelings can make your child protection work more effective and less stressful. When the possibility of child abuse is raised, powerful emotional reactions often occur. It is common for suspected abusers to express anger, for the parents who learn their child may have been abused to feel horror and grief, and for the children to feel frightened, embarrassed, and ashamed. Child victims and their families may also experience anxiety, confusion, depression, and sadness. As a child protection professional, you are exposed to all these intense feelings. You experience them through the lens of your own personal history, education, training, and previous professional experience. Your work conditions, which may include limited resources, a high workload, a modest salary, and inadequate work space, can make it even more difficult for you to be empathetic and respectful while remaining clear and focused in your effort to ensure that children are safe and adequately cared for.

■ *Acknowledging Feelings*

Learning how to enhance your work through awareness of emotional reactions begins with simply paying attention to emotional reactions and considering the possible thoughts, beliefs, and concerns associated with them. One of the most empathic things that you can do for a person is to acknowledge that person's feelings. By addressing a client's feelings, you can open up important thoughts, beliefs, and concerns for discussion. Doing this can also decrease the intensity of the client's emotional reactions and enable you to provide information to address the client's speculations and fears.

Attending to our own emotional reactions is equally important. Strong emotions can be contagious. Anger is especially infectious. By remaining aware of feelings, you can decide when to address them with words or with actions. If you determine that a client's rage is beginning to kindle your own anger or fear, you may want to defuse the situation by taking a break or offering the enraged person something to eat, even if it is only crackers or candy. Food is a universal peace offering. Empathizing with angry clients may also help diffuse their anger.

Acknowledging one's own feelings can also be appropriate and healthy, especially with colleagues and friends. Colleagues, supervisors, and family members can help us deal with our most challenging feelings and can often provide different perspectives on difficult situations.

One of the challenges of child protection work is to avoid expressing negative feelings toward people who we think have abused children. Remembering that many persons who abuse children were also abused during their childhood lessens this temptation. It is possible to empathize with the pain in a person's life that may have contributed to their committing child abuse without condoning abusive behavior.

■ *A Balanced Perspective*

It is important to keep in mind when dealing with clients' intense feelings that we usually have very little to do with what is really driving their emotions. Childhood experiences, unspoken thoughts, and other things beyond our control often have major roles in triggering strong emotional reactions. Although it is useful to acknowledge another's feelings, it is also important to remember how peripheral we are to most of the people we encounter. We should not take personally most of the intense emotional reactions associated with child protection work. As a professional working in an emotionally charged area, it is important not to become emotionally overinvolved and unnecessarily vulnerable.

Part III

INTERVIEWING

13

How Do I Interview Young Children About Suspected Sexual Abuse?

■ *Kee MacFarlane*

Because child sexual abuse almost always occurs in secrecy and rarely has witnesses or accompanying medical findings, cases often are based on the words of children. This is particularly problematic for very young victims because they are not forthcoming, their language is limited, and their credibility is frequently in question. Therefore, investigatory interviews are critical elements in these cases not only to determine the need for protection but also because the way that interviews are conducted can influence the legal viability and the outcome of court cases. Currently, interviewers are under more scrutiny than in the past because their actions are often the target of defense cases. There are many things to keep in mind before undertaking the exacting task of interviewing this population.

■ *Things to Remember Before You Begin*

---

1. Young child interviews take time. When there is insufficient time or interviewers become impatient, they may put too much pressure on themselves or a child and either push too hard for answers or give up too easily. Young children get anxious, distracted, and fade quickly; therefore, they may

need several breaks, or more than one interview with the same person may be necessary.

2. Remember that not all children you interview have been sexually abused, regardless of how credible a report or reporter may sound. Conversely, an improbable sounding report from a seemingly unreliable source may be true. Research indicates that many child victims show no initial symptoms. Do not prejudge information, assume nothing, and be open to all possibilities.

3. When victims disclose abuse, they usually do so reluctantly, often following initial denial. They may disclose in bits and pieces, saving whatever they consider the "worst" for last. Some young victims, however, may blurt out disclosures, especially when they do not fear consequences.

4. Most sexual abuse is accompanied by some kind of threat or admonishment not to tell. It is frequently the belief that the threat will come true that keeps very young children quiet. Uncovering the threat (i.e., "What would happen if you told me the secret?") and allaying the fear may be key.

5. Watch what you say or imply about a suspected abuser. Not only may it unduly influence a child's report and be prejudicial to a case, but it may inhibit disclosure due to a child's positive feelings for and attachment to an abuser.

6. Despite their initial comfort level, young children who have been sexually abused may be afraid not only to tell but also of what you will think of or do to them (including molest them). If they become scared or need a break from you, let them know that they can go, and bring them back later.

7. Having disclosed sexual abuse, some children fear (or observe) the consequences and immediately (or later) retract the disclosure. Recantations, like disclosures, are not automatically true or false. It is important to carefully evaluate for both motive and believability.

8. Those who work with very young children usually do so within a play therapy framework. Although this makes sense developmentally, it can compromise a forensic interview because it is viewed as encouraging fantasy, confounding information, and producing findings that are subject to multiple interpretations. An interviewer's role is different from that of a therapist. Although a sensitive interview can have a therapeutic effect, it is not the place to encourage

children to communicate metaphorically or project feelings, even when doing so might benefit them personally. This is not to say that some of the tools and techniques of play therapy are not useful in helping children describe events, but they should be used to impart or clarify information and be carefully controlled.

■ General Principles of
Interviewing Young Children

The primary goals of interviewing include (a) increasing accuracy and reliability of information, (b) decreasing potential suggestibility, and (c) minimizing trauma. Very young children are somewhat more compliant, suggestible, and easily confused than older children. In addition to various abuse-related factors, accuracy is influenced by a child's age, understanding of events, repeated verbal recall, interviewer style and position of authority, and demand for details, as well as by the structure and nature of questions. Interviewers can do the following to help increase accuracy:

1. Diminish aspects of power and authority over the child. Position yourself at eye level with the child. Reduce formality, and speak simply and slowly. Reiterate that you do not know what happened. This helps diminish omnipotence or the idea that you are trying to confirm what you already know. Similarly, do not use the authority of others (i.e. "Your mom wants you to tell me what daddy did").

2. Use the funnel approach (i.e., begin with open-ended questions and later ask increasingly specific questions as necessary). *Leading* questions (those with an answer embedded in the question) are at the bottom of the funnel and should be avoided with young children. Young children, however, especially victims, rarely provide narrative answers or details in response to open-ended questions. Specific information is often only obtained from specific questions. The funnel approach is often necessary to demonstrate or justify the need for more directive questions—that is, those that direct children to particular issues or subject areas (e.g., touching) and not to particular answers. It is important to alternate specific questions with open-ended questions such

as "Tell me more about that" or "What else do you remember?"

3. Adjust requested details to fit developmental levels. The paradox associated with the need to ask specific questions is that accuracy decreases when extensive detail is required. Children younger than 6 years of age rarely have the cognitive skills to provide common forensic details, such as time frames, intent, and number of times. The problem is that they do not know this information and may provide answers that reduce their credibility, even though they may have detailed memories of an event. Know their cognitive limits. It is better to have fewer forensic details than much information that threatens the integrity of a case.

4. Talk less, listen more, and follow the child's cue. Do not be quick to fill in empty spaces in conversation. Young children need time to think and formulate answers. Apply reflective listening. When asking directive questions, avoid introducing abuse information that might be incorporated by a child.

5. Know the case history. Although repeated recall of memories tends to improve later recall, there is research indicating that repeated suggestive questioning could distort recall. You cannot change the past, but you should be familiar with the amount and nature of previous questioning, including, if possible, circumstances and accounts of exactly what was said.

6. Do not repeat yes-no questions. Although it is sometimes necessary or useful to repeat questions, young children may change answers to a yes-no question because they think they answered wrong the first time. If you repeat a question, rephrase it and keep it as open-ended as possible.

7. Do not bribe (with things or promises), threaten, or cajole. You are not there to "prove" that abuse occurred. The harder you try, the more you may reduce both the reliability and credibility of what you get and the possibility of a narrative disclosure later. Abused children need to trust you and the process. Nonabused children should not be or appear to be coerced.

8. Beware of selective reinforcement. Adults are used to reinforcing young children when they do well and comforting them when they are upset. Depending on their use, however, these responses can impart interviewer bias and potentially

influence a child. Reinforcement should be applied to general behaviors (answering questions, following instructions, etc.), not to specific answers. Comfort should be low key. It is better (for the child and the case) to underreact than overreact.

There is debate regarding the wisdom of using anatomical dolls or other communication aids in forensic interviews (despite the fact that the research does *not* support concerns that they will increase suggestibility). Nonetheless, some young children will be unable to provide much information on a strictly verbal basis, but they may be able to show you what happened with simple drawings (such as "gingerbread man" outlines) or other visual aids. There are many ways in which young kids tell us something is wrong; we should remain open to hearing them.

■ *Approach and Methods:*
 Structure of the Interview

There is no accepted, standardized "recipe" for forensic interviews, especially those involving young children. Interviewers need the flexibility to follow a young child's lead as long as it is within the structure of their own agencies' protocols or guidelines. It is helpful, however, to view an interview within the framework of the following stages:

> *Introductory and assessment phase:* The first goal with young children is to enable them to feel comfortable enough to talk freely to you. This phase should focus on encouraging narrative dialogue from children by limiting questions that elicit single-word answers. Rapport building may include explaining who you are, asking what children were told (or think) about why they are there, and finding out who populates a child's world, but it does not include direct questions about abuse unless introduced by the child. Simple objects can help with rapport and aid in assessing general levels of development and whether relational concepts (such as prepositions) are understood. Some interviewers determine names for body parts and conduct assessments of legal competency. Others test the extent to which a child is suggestible by misstating simple facts or asking innocuous,

misleading questions. "Questioning rules" should be explained during this phase and repeated later if needed.

Information-gathering phase: This phase may begin abruptly, based on a child's cue. If not, proceed in stages using the funnel approach. The use of "wh" questions (who, what, where, when; why is more problematic) is a good guideline. The following are possible starting points:

- *Problems focus:* Discuss why kids come to see you. For example, you might ask whether they have any problems, if something has happened to them, or if there are things or people who bother them and that they wish they could change.

- *Feelings focus:* Discuss things or people that make them feel happy, angry, upset, loved, scared, and so on.

- *Circumstances, location, and events focus:* Discuss location, surroundings, or events associated with the allegation or potential abuse situations; probe for narrative; and ask about positive and negative aspects.

- *Individuals and relationships focus:* Discuss positive and negative aspects of significant adults and older children, especially those with access and/or who are suspected of abuse.

- *Secrets, touching, and private parts focus:* Discussion should focus on both good and bad secrets and/or touch.

- *Direct abuse inquiry focus:* If the previous discussions are avoidant, unconvincing, or contradict nonverbal cues, it may be time to narrow the funnel with direct questions about possible acts of abuse or suspected abusers. It is less suggestive to keep the two separate, but it is often necessary to inquire about both. Remember that asking a question is not the same as suggesting an answer.

Closure phase: Some young children may be anxious to leave, and little time may be needed for closure; others may need reassurance and a chance to process the aftermath of disclosure:

- Invite children to ask you questions and ask if there is anything you "forgot" to ask them.

- Thank the child for staying and talking with you and not for the content of what was said.
- Provide the option of talking again with you or another adult (identify who) if children remember something later.
- Ask what they want or think should happen next. Reassurance should focus on safety, truth, and the limits of your role. Do not make promises you cannot keep.

■ *Questioning Rules for Young Children*

The following are statements that can be used for interviewing young children:

1. "There are no right or wrong answers; only the things that you know. I'm not there in your life, so I don't know the answers to my questions. I need you to tell me what you know."
2. "The truth is the best answer; no pretending or making things up. Only what's real."
3. "No guessing. 'I don't know' is a good answer if you really don't know something."
4. "If a question doesn't make sense or you get confused, say 'I don't understand' or 'huh?' "
5. "If you used to know something that you can't remember anymore, just say, 'I forgot.' "
6. "If you know the real answer but you don't want to tell me something, just say you don't want to talk about it. That's OK."
7. "If I get something wrong or I don't understand what you mean, I want you to tell me. I won't get mad. Sometimes I might get confused and need your help."

■ *Final Thoughts*

The average age of children being referred for assessment of sexual abuse has decreased dramatically in the past 20 years. Whether this reflects a change in abusive behavior or in awareness and reporting is unknown, but the result for interviewers is the same. There is a need for more knowledge of child development, more experience relating to young children, and more versatility in communication. Even so, forensic interviewing has become a specialized field that is usually best left to specialists once clear indications of possible sexual abuse are established.

Increased legal involvement and research in this area have demonstrated the need for caution when interviewing very young children. But they also have resulted in so many guidelines that it is difficult to remember them all, and in so many cautions that some interviewers are afraid to ask anything directly. It is important for interviewers to read the literature and receive all the training and ongoing supervision available. But it is also important to remain flexible and tuned in to the child. Interviewing guidelines have been developed, in part, to withstand the scrutiny and standards of proof of our criminal courts—a place that few sexual abuse cases involving young children ever reach. Fear of that arena or concerns about its proscribed boundaries should not dictate intervention to the extent that they prevent other avenues of protection for young victims who remain unidentified as a consequence. You cannot do more than be well prepared and do your best. We ask abused children to stand up and speak out despite their fear of the potential consequences. We must ask no less of ourselves.

■ *Further Reading*

Faller, K. C. (1996). *Evaluating children suspected of having been sexually abused.* Thousand Oaks, CA: Sage.

Kuehnle, K. (1996). *Assessing allegations of child sexual abuse.* Sarasota, FL: Professional Resource Press.

MacFarlane, K., & Waterman, J., et al. (1986). *Sexual abuse of young children.* New York: Guilford.

Saywitz, K., & Goodman, G. (1996). Interviewing children in and out of the courtroom. In J. Briere, L. Berliner, J. Bulkley, C. Jenny, & T. Reid (Eds.), *The APSAC handbook on child maltreatment* (pp. 297-318). Thousand Oaks, CA: Sage.

Steinmetz, M. (1997). *Interviewing for child sexual abuse: Strategies for balancing the forensic and therapeutic factors.* Notre Dame, IN: Jalice.

14

How Do I Interview Older Children and Adolescents About Sexual Abuse?

■ *Lucy Berliner*

■ *Purpose of the Investigative Interview*

The primary purpose of interviewing children about possible sexual abuse is to obtain accurate and complete information about whether abuse occurred. The interview is especially important because it is usually the most significant source of information in sexual abuse cases. Decisions about interventions will often be made on the basis of children's statements because definitive medical evidence or witnesses are available in very few situations, and admissions by the accused are uncommon.

The forensic or investigative interview is designed to gather factual information and not to be therapeutic for the child. Therefore, the interviewer must maintain an objective, neutral stance. It is possible, and desirable, to be supportive and warm and at the same time not try to help the child with any of his or her emotional problems. Even if this seems like what the child needs, doing so during this interview may compromise an investigation and eventually result in a child being worse off.

■ Goals of Investigative Interviews

There are two central considerations in interviewing children or adolescents. One is creating an environment in which children who have actually been abused are willing to tell what happened despite their fears. The second is ensuring that children do not have their memories distorted and are not in any way pressured to describe abuse that did not happen. Because a few children may intentionally lie about abuse, it is also essential that interviewers not be too credulous or be reluctant to challenge improbable accounts.

■ Preinterview Considerations

It is very important to start with a completely open mind, regardless of the information contained in the initial report to child protection authorities. A confirmatory bias or seeking to confirm a preexisting belief can cause the interviewer to misconstrue responses, follow only certain leads, reinforce answers that conform to expectations, and fail to rule out alternative explanations. This error is frequently inadvert on the part of the interviewer; therefore, it is crucial to make a point of having no preconceived ideas. It also has been shown to help children provide more accurate information when the interviewer explicitly tells the child that he or she does not know what happened and is only interested in hearing the truth.

There are some specific considerations that are developmentally based and others that relate to the nature of sexual abuse in older children and teenagers. These children may be self-conscious, very concerned about how others view them, or in a stage in which they are asserting independence from adults. Adolescents in particular can sometimes be flippant or uncooperative. In addition, it is more likely that abused older children and adolescents will have self-blame or guilt about actions taken or not taken that may have contributed to the abuse. They may be reluctant to tell the whole story.

The interviewer should make no promises about what will happen and should explain that there is no confidentiality. The interviewer should inform children if they are being audiotaped or videotaped, explain why notes are being taken, or both. A good way to handle this is for the interviewer to say that it is to ensure that he or she or others know exactly what the child says so there is no confusion or misunderstanding.

■ *Obtaining Accurate and Complete*
  Information in Investigative Interviews

The first component of an interview is to establish rapport. This is the process of making the child comfortable with the situation so that he or she will be willing to talk openly. Making a developmentally appropriate connection with the child facilitates the remainder of the interview. Children generally respond best to adults who are relaxed, natural, and respectful; they are put off by adults who try too hard, seem fake, or are excessively formal.

Asking the child to talk about him- or herself before beginning the substantive part of the interview is a good way to begin. This shows the child that the interviewer is genuinely interested in him or her and provides an opportunity for the child to warm up. It also provides the interviewer with a basis for gauging the child's cognitive and communication abilities. In addition, research has shown that asking the child about family, school, and a recent event in a completely open-ended fashion serves as practice for providing longer, freely recalled narratives during questioning about possible abuse. The more the child can tell about what happened from his or her own memory, the less chance there is of distortion or error.

Another critical component of the initial stages of the interview is establishing ground rules. Children need to know what is expected because a forensic interview is unlike other conversations with adults. Interviewers should tell children that they want to know only the truth about what did or did not happen. Research has shown that it helps to inform children that there is no right or wrong answer, that they should say they "don't know" when they really do not, and that they should ask for clarification if they do not understand a question or a word.

The substantive part of the interview should always begin with an open-ended question, such as "Can you tell me why you are here?" and "I understand something may have happened to you?"

The interviewer should continue to use open-ended prompts as long as the child can give information. Facilitative prompts are comments such as "Can you tell me more about that?" and "Is there anything else you can remember?" In cases in which a child has confirmed that something happened, a strategy that can be effective in eliciting more information is "context reinstatement." This involves asking the child to picture him- or herself in the situation and then to describe everything, no matter how trivial or seemingly unimportant, from the beginning to the end.

■ Reducing Errors in Investigative Interviews

Leading questions should be avoided because they include interviewer-introduced information that may be incorporated into children's accounts. Asking specific questions, however, is invariably necessary at some point for clarification purposes. Once a child gives information in response to direct questions, the interviewer should immediately return to the open-ended prompts. This is the hardest part about conducting interviews with children. Research has repeatedly shown that even when interviewers are trained in the importance of open-ended questioning, they almost always resort to specific questioning very quickly and rarely return to open-ended prompts. A good way to keep track of this is to constantly monitor who is doing most of the talking. Pauses and silence, even when the interviewer feels slightly uncomfortable, are excellent strategies. A good interview is one that consists of more child verbalizations than adult questioning.

A problem that children may encounter is that they become confused about the source of information. They may not be sure that what they are remembering or saying is something they have thought about or heard in a previous conversation but did not actually happen. Because parents or others will almost always have talked to children before the investigative interview, children may need help in source monitoring. Research has shown that it helps to ask children specifically if what they are reporting really happened.

Of course, there are times when children are extremely reluctant or even refuse to talk. Encouraging the child is appropriate, and a slight amount of pressure can be necessary. It is never acceptable, however, no matter how urgent it may seem, to insist, bribe, or threaten a child. Children's denials of abuse should not be disconfirmed except in extraordinary circumstances (e.g., the child has a sexually transmitted disease or there are sexually explicit photographs). Even in these circumstances, great care should be taken because the child clearly has reasons why he or she does not want to tell what happened. The extent to which an interviewer pursues the topic with a child who is not responding or is denying depends on the level of evidence for abuse suspicion that exists.

■ Completing Investigative Interviews

Once the interviewer has secured all the information that the child can supply about possible abuse, there may be other topics that should be addressed. For example, in the case in which a child has reported sexual abuse, it is important to ask what concerns or fears the child may have about the consequences of telling. The child should always be given an opportunity to ask questions, and the interviewer should give honest answers. The child should be thanked for the effort he or she has made during the interview and told of the likely next steps that will occur.

■ Further Reading

Poole, D. A., & Lamb, M. E. (1998). *Investigative interviews of children.* Washington, DC: American Psychological Association.

Reed, L. D. (1996). Findings from research on children's suggestibility and implications for conducting child interviews. *Child Maltreatment, 1,* 105-119.

Wood, J. M., McClure, K. A., & Birch, R. A. (1996). Suggestions for improving interviews in child protection agencies. *Child Maltreatment, 1,* 223-230.

Yuille, J. C., Hunter, R., Joffe, R., & Zaparnuik, J. (1993). Interviewing children in sexual abuse cases. In G. S. Goodman & B. L. Bottoms (Eds.), *Child victims, child witnesses* (pp. 95-115). New York: Guilford.

15

What Tools Are Appropriate to Facilitate Interviews With Children?

■ *Barbara W. Boat and Mark D. Everson*

Caveats Concerning Tools

- Any tool is dependent on the skill of the user.
- No tool is a substitute for thorough knowledge of child development and forensic interviewing approaches.
- No behavior with any tool or prop by itself is conclusive that abuse has occurred.

Tools Most Commonly Used

Anatomical dolls: Use dolls with genitalia and breasts proportional to body size and appropriate to gender and age of doll and with clothing easily removable and appropriate to doll's age and gender.

Anatomical drawings: One can use ready-made anatomical outlines or draw a simple outline and have child describe or add sexual features.

Appropriate Uses of Dolls and Drawings

Be able to state clearly the function(s) that the tools are serving in your evaluation.

Anatomical Doll Uses

Icebreaker: Dolls can serve as a conversation starter, cueing the child that the interviewer wants to talk about body parts, possibly enhancing the child's comfort level.

Anatomical model: This is one of the most common uses of the dolls. The child's labels for body parts and functions can be assessed (e.g., "What do you call this?" and "What is it for?"). It also serves as a body map on which the child can indicate where touching occurred.

Demonstration aid: This is the most commonly used function of the dolls. It enables a child to demonstrate behaviors that he or she has described to confirm an interviewer's understanding and reduce miscommunication. Some children with limited verbal skills may use the dolls to show rather than tell what happened.

Memory stimulus and screening tool: Exposure to dolls may trigger a child's recall of specific events of a sexual nature or the child may demonstrate a specific sexual act while interacting freely with the dolls. Any sexualized acts or comments should be followed up with appropriate questions.

Anatomical Drawing Uses

Icebreaker: An outline drawing of a child or adult body can be used to focus the child's attention on sexual parts of the body.

Anatomical model: The interviewer asks about location, names, and functions of body parts. This also serves as a body map on which the child can indicate touching. Anatomical dolls are not superior to anatomical drawings for this purpose.

■ Common Questions and Concerns

Can nonanatomical dolls be used instead of anatomical dolls? Yes. Research suggests that children do not disclose differentially depending on the type of doll used. Nonanatomical dolls are used to show where and how the child was touched. Lacking sexual features, nonanatomical dolls are less useful as anatomical models and as a memory stimulus.

What about using puppets? Puppets have not been researched as an interview tool. Puppets may be useful during rapport building, but dolls and drawings may be better choices for actual disclosure work.

What are the most concerning practices (inappropriate uses) when using anatomical dolls?

- Introducing the dolls too soon: If the child is giving an adequate verbal account, the dolls may not be necessary.
- Drawing definitive conclusions about the likelihood of abuse based solely on interpretation of a child's behavior with the dolls: There is no known behavior with the dolls that is a definitive marker of sexual abuse.
- The child is encouraged to view the dolls as toys by using words such as play and pretend instead of telling the child that the dolls are used to help talk about and show things that really happened.

Are some children too young to be able to benefit from using anatomical dolls or anatomical drawings? This depends on the function served. Using dolls or drawings as interview props to focus attention and serve as a body map may be necessary when interviewing young children about genital and anal touching. Be cautious when using dolls as demonstration aids with very young children because they may not be able to use dolls to represent themselves in behavioral reenactment, and the dolls can be distracting.

What behaviors with the dolls are concerning and warrant follow-up?

- Explicit positioning of dolls suggesting that the child has detailed knowledge of the mechanics of sexual acts, especially oral and anal sex
- Sexual behavior accompanied by anxiety, fear, behavioral regression, or anger and aggression

What behaviors with the dolls are relatively common among nonabused young children?

- Undressing the dolls
- Touching breasts and genital areas on dolls

What are the current controversies concerning anatomical dolls?

- Do the dolls add important information? There is no definitive answer regarding the cost-benefit ratio of using dolls in forensic interview settings. Interviewers must continually update their knowledge in this area.
- Research to date includes several studies that have little or no relevance to actual forensic practice. Use of the dolls has been confounded with other props and leading questions, distinct uses of the dolls have not been tested, and recall events have not included touching that is conspicuous and noteworthy to the child.
- Although research indicates that the dolls are not too suggestive and overly stimulating to be useful in sexual abuse investigations, this controversy continues. Specifically, mere exposure to the dolls does not appear to induce nonabused, sexually naive children to have sexual fantasies and engage in sex play that is likely to be misinterpreted as evidence of sexual abuse.

■ *Documentation of the Interview*
When Anatomically Detailed Dolls
or Drawings Are Used

Ideally, an interview in which props are used will be videotaped. This is especially important when the dolls are used as demonstration aids. One advantage of the anatomical drawings is that the drawing is memorialized on paper. At the very least, the interviewer's questions, the child's responses, and spontaneous comments by the child should be recorded verbatim. The child's interactions with the dolls should be described in detail. Audiotape recording may be helpful.

■ *Further Reading*

American Professional Society on the Abuse of Children. (1995). *Practice guidelines: Use of anatomical dolls in child sexual abuse assessment.* Chicago: Author.

Boat, B. W., & Everson, M. D. (1988). Interviewing young children with anatomical dolls. *Child Welfare, 68*(4), 337-352.

Everson, M. D., & Boat, B. W. (1997). Anatomical dolls in child sexual abuse assessments: A call for forensically relevant research. *Applied Cognitive Psychology, 11,* 55-74.

Steward, M. S., & Steward, D. S. (with Farquhar, L., Myers, J. E. B., Reinhart, M., Welker, J., Joye, N., Driskill, J., & Morgan, J.). (1996). Interviewing young children about body touch and handling. *Monographs of the Society for Research in Child Development, 61*(4/5, Serial No. 248).

16

How Do I Interview a Child About Alleged Physical Abuse?

■ *David J. Kolko*

■ *Setting the Stage for an Abuse History Interview*

There does not seem to be a standard set of questions or method for conducting interviews with children who may have been physically abused. Beyond differences in the types of questions used to elicit this history, there are differences in children's understanding of the meaning of various terms, willingness to disclose such information, and recollection of details from one or more incidents. Establishing certain interview conditions, however, may enhance the consistency and utility of the child's reports, such as conducting the interview in a private and quiet setting. These conditions may promote rapport building, which is a vital initial interview objective.

■ *General Considerations*

Certain circumstances may minimize child compliance and participation, which may be as important to understand as the child's actual experiences. Patience and sensitivity to the child's situation should be exercised to determine when and how a successful interview can be conducted. This should include giving the child an opportunity to ask questions and making an effort to reduce any anxiety associated with the interview. Furthermore, the child's interview responses should be integrated with other information and observations to provide a comprehensive account of the abusive incident and its context (Kaufman, Jones, Stieglitz, Vitulano, & Mannarino, 1994). Finally, general guidelines for interviewing child victims should be understood and heeded to ensure that the interview is attentive to the explicit purpose of the interview, relevant legal and ethical standards, and the best interests of the child.

■ Interview Purpose and Limits of Confidentiality

It is also important to consider at the outset the manner in which an interview is conducted and certain prerequisites to enhancing the child's overall comfort and compliance with the interview. For example, children often benefit from being told the purpose of the interview (e.g., to understand what happened), the types of questions they will be asked (e.g., what parents said and did at that time), and the potential consequences or impact of key answers (e.g., "protect you and your brother" and "be able to help your family best"). Whenever possible, the abuse history interview should be contrasted with other types of interviews, such as a clinical treatment interview. Efforts to reassure the child realistically may also enhance accurate recall, but the child should be clearly told the limits of confidentiality. Of course, a clear determination of any possible abuse is more likely if multiple informants (e.g., siblings) are available and clear interview questions are used.

■ Normalizing Discipline and Punishment

Because physical abuse may occur in the context of routine parent-child conflicts, initial questions may be asked in a nonjudgmental manner that examine caregiver use of disciplinary strategies and types of punishment. Asking open-ended questions initially may elicit a more complete response for further discussion. Children can be provided with brief segues that normalize the use of punishment and encourage discussion of the details surrounding relevant incidents, such as "Children can get punished (disciplined) for doing different things; how often do you get punished, and in what ways?" This inquiry may be less threatening than probes into the alleged abusive incident. Specific questions about discipline with the child or other children may be helpful in highlighting caregiver practices. Examples include the following:

- "How often do you get punished—for example, sent to your room, had privileges removed, and got lectured?"
- "How often does this involve any physical force or discipline, such as spanking, slapping, or grabbing?"
- "What kind of physical discipline or punishment is used with you?"
- "What is the most extreme or serious kind of physical discipline or punishment that is used with you?"
- "How worried are you that someone living with you could lose control with you—that is, where you could get hurt?"

■ Details of Abusive Experiences

After the child has an understanding of the reason for referral, open-ended questions can be asked for details about the offender and the relationship to the child, the incident(s) that took place, the nature and timing of the act(s), the setting in which the act(s) occurred, the child's injuries, the level of pain, other consequences such as medical treatment and personal impact, and potential antecedents or triggers that describe the circumstances in which the incident(s) unfolded.

As found in structured interviews of specific problems (e.g., posttraumatic stress disorder), children can be asked to identify events or situations they have experienced or witnessed that were upsetting, scary, or frightening. For some children, this general question may elicit abusive incidents. For others, specific questions may be needed, such as "Have you ever been injured or hurt by someone older than you?" If necessary, the interviewer can refer to the referral incident to encourage discussion ("the incident that led to your family coming to see me; the one that led to the report"). Follow-up questions include the following:

- "Please tell me what happened?"
- "How did it start?"
- "Where did it take place?"
- "What happened afterwards?"

This general line of questioning allows the interviewer to determine if the child reported the "abuse incident" without prompting, acknowledged that the incident did happen, even with prompting, or described the incident as upsetting or scary.

For children who acknowledge such an incident, the following specific questions may be administered:

- "Were you physically hurt?"
- "Was there an injury?"
- "How were you hurt?" or "What did he or she do or use?"

Sometimes, it is possible to document the severity of the act and its consequences (e.g., pushing or shaking; spanking; hitting, punching, hitting with object, and threatening with a weapon; and beating or burning with serious injury; Barnett, Manly, & Cicchetti, 1993; Chaffin, Wherry, Newlin, Crutchfield, & Dykman, 1997). It is also helpful to know when these incidents may have started and ended (month and year).

Other questions address the context for the abusive interaction. Children's perspectives may help to identify the adult's motive (e.g., "Why do you think this happened? What was the reason?"). Several common circumstances may be reported (e.g., child misbehavior, adult parenting problems, adult conflict, accidents). Open-ended questions can also be asked about what happened after the incident ("What did he or she say or do afterwards?") to document any acceptance of personal responsibility or blame for the incident (e.g., saying "Sorry") or attempts to discourage reporting of the incident ("Did he or she ask you to keep it a secret?"). Finally, the cooperative child may be able to provide details about prior incidents or experiences ("Were you involved in something like this before? About how many times?").

■ *Concerns Regarding
Child Safety and Protection*

Child participation in interviews documenting abuse may yield key information highlighting that child's high risk for reabuse or violence. Certainly, safety plans must be developed in accord with the child's risk level. Furthermore, the child should be well informed about any initial plans and efforts to protect the child and, possibly, other family members. Highest priority should be given to the protection of children who are least able to protect themselves or least likely to be protected by caregivers. In some cases, an initial safety plan that articulates concerns about the child's general welfare may be needed before the interview is concluded.

■ *Further Reading*

Barnett, D., Manly, J. T., & Cicchetti, D. (1993). Defining child mal-treatment: The interface between policy and research. In D. Cicchetti & S. L. Toth (Eds.), *Child abuse, child development, and social policy* (pp. 7-74). Norwood, NJ: Ablex.

Chaffin, M., Wherry, J. N., Newlin, C., Crutchfield, A., & Dykman, R. (1997). The Abuse Dimensions Inventory: Initial data on a research measure of abuse severity. *Journal of Interpersonal Violence, 12,* 569-589.

Kaufman, J., Jones, B., Stieglitz, E., Vitulano, L., & Mannarino, A. P. (1994). The use of multiple informants to assess children's maltreat-ment experiences. *Journal of Family Violence, 9,* 227-247.

17

How Do I Interview Non-Maltreating Parents and Caregivers?

■ *Denise Pintello*

The primary focus of the non-maltreating parent or caregiver interview is to ascertain what the parent or caregiver knows about the alleged maltreatment, collect essential information to determine the level of risk to the children, and assess the parent's or caregiver's capacity to protect the child. In this chapter, I describe the interview process and use the term *parent* to refer to the non-maltreating parent or caregiver.

This initial interview and the manner in which the caseworker interacts with the parent will forever influence the remainder of the case. It is imperative to keep in mind the involuntary nature of the child protective services interview. The maltreatment referral, followed by the caseworker's physical presence, has initiated a crisis response. Every resource available to the parent is centered on coping with the crisis of his or her child's maltreatment disclosure.

■ *Parameters Surrounding the Interview*

Location and Setting

On receipt of the intake referral, the caseworker will attempt to determine when and where the face-to-face interview with the parent will take place within the agency-mandated time period. Depending on the circumstances surrounding the case, a decision with the supervisor must be made to determine whether it is in the child's best interest for the caseworker to (a) initiate an unannounced face-to-face visit to interview the parent or (b) contact the parent (i.e., by telephone) to schedule the interview at the agency, at the parent's home, or at another location.

Interview Sequence

Whenever possible, it is optimal for the parent interview to be conducted immediately after interviewing the maltreated child, siblings, any additional children residing in the home, or other children who have had access to the alleged perpetrator. This sequence maximizes the quality and precision of the information and may result in reducing denial, minimization, and resistance from the parent.

Building in Adequate Time for the Interview

Although it can be difficult for caseworkers investigating numerous emergency referrals, it is important to schedule enough time to comfortably complete the interview. This will allow time for parents to disclose sensitive information about childhood histories, marital or relationship difficulties, and special concerns about their children.

■ *Essential Information to Collect*

It is recommended that the caseworker collect information in the following sequence (examples of probing statements are included in parentheses):

1. Determine what the parent knows about the alleged mal-treatment ("Before my visit, have there been any events or situations that seem to be of concern to you?").

2. Explore the parent's feelings, perceptions, and expectations about the maltreated child, siblings, and other children in the home.

3. Assess parenting practices, child-rearing approaches, and discipline methods ("Describe for me how you handle your children when they bring home a good grade. Tell me how you handle your children when they do something you don't want them to do.").

4. Inquire about the parent's prior history, including child maltreatment, domestic violence, substance abuse, employ-ment, educational history, and physical and mental health experiences.

5. Investigate the intensity of the relationship between the alleged perpetrator and the non-maltreating parent, the role of the parent in the family, and the relationship of the parent to the children.

6. Evaluate the parents' perception of what they believe hap-pened concerning the maltreatment and who they believe is responsible ("Share with me your perspective. . . . Are you willing to consider the possibility that your child may have been maltreated?").

7. Collect information about the parent's capacity to protect the children ("Knowing what you know now, tell me your greatest concerns for your child . . . for your family.").

8. Explore sources of social, emotional, and financial support that can reduce crisis ("How might your friends or family be able to help? Let's explore how I can help.").

■ *Interview Strategies*

Gaining parental cooperation may be difficult. The following strategies can enhance the caseworker-parent working relation-ship while also maximizing the meaningful content of the infor-mation to be collected:

- *Use of descriptive questions:* During the early phase of the interview, ask the parent for help in gathering generic, descriptive information that is not emotionally threatening. In this early stage, encourage parents to ask questions, which may diminish their anxiety.

- *Universalize:* Inform parents that other families have experienced similar problems. It can be helpful to use this as an opportunity to teach them about what has worked well for other families ("Other parents have told me what they found helpful was . . .").

- *Typical-day interview:* When a parent appears anxious or upset, the typical-day interview is a productive strategy. This approach reduces the immediacy of the crisis for the parent while simultaneously exploring how the family functions ("Let's talk about what a typical day is like in your home. Who wakes up first in the morning? What happens next?").

- *Prediction:* When it is clear that the child has been maltreated and the parent initially believes the child, it is crucial for caseworkers to inform the parent that ambivalence about the believability of the child can be anticipated or predicted at a later point in time. Ambivalence may occur after hearing the alleged perpetrator's denial or during financial hardship after the disclosure. Use of prediction can inform parents that many factors, over time, can influence the level of parental support for the child. This strategy may also reduce the likelihood of future recantation from the maltreated child.

- *Mutual cooperation:* Successful anticipation of stressful reactions from parents may lead to enhancing mutual cooperation between both parties. Inviting the parent to talk about what the maltreatment may mean to his or her family in the future and offering to join with the parent can lead to a productive partnership ("Are you willing to work with me as we prepare together to find out the truth about what has happened to your child?").

- *Control the pace of the interview:* The caseworker must maintain control of the meeting. When a parent appears upset or angry, it is the caseworker's role to de-escalate the situation. Neutralizing responses such as "I'm sorry that this is so difficult" may reduce the tension and allow the parent to continue the interview. Speaking in a calm voice, slowing the pace, and using silence if the parent becomes distressed ("I think this is a good time to stop and take a few moments") are additional approaches to diffuse a tense exchange.

■ *Summary*

Various strategies have been presented in this chapter to enhance the initial interview with the non-maltreating parent or caregiver. It is important to approach the interview not only as a method to collect required information but also as an opportunity to help turn a poignant family crisis into a powerful transformation that can strengthen the well-being of the children and family.

■ *Further Reading*

DePanfilis, D., & Salus, M. (1992). *Child protective services: A guide for caseworkers* (Government Printing Office No. 1992-625-670/ 60577). Washington, DC: National Center on Child Abuse and Neglect.

Gil, E. (1994). *Family play therapy.* New York: Guilford.

18

How Do I Interview
the Alleged Perpetrator?

■ *Donna Pence*

Workers must gather factual information from caregivers and others who may have abused a child physically or sexually. At times, the worker will have reason to believe the child was abused but have to assess who, among several caregivers, may have committed the abuse. We must recognize that sometimes we interview persons who have not done anything improper, whereas others may deliberately try to deceive us. Throughout this process, we are trying to gain information and build a relationship.

The worker must allow every possible perpetrator the opportunity to present his or her information concerning the situation. The interview with the alleged perpetrator requires as much forethought as that of the interview with the child. There is no one best way to gain accurate information from someone who may be deliberately trying to mislead the worker or to minimize what has happened. Each individual will have different motivations and gains from the behavior. When interviewing an alleged perpetrator of serious physical abuse or sexual abuse, it is generally wise to coordinate the interview with law enforcement, allow law enforcement to take the lead, or both because they often have more training in this type of interviewing.

The role of the interviewer is to elicit as much accurate, complete information as possible to make informed decisions concerning the validity of the allegation, the safety of the child, and the appropriate action to be taken. One needs to understand what, if anything, happened; who is responsible; who will be protective; and what other risk factors are present (e.g., history of alcohol and drug abuse, domestic violence, mental illness, or antisocial behavior).

The interviewer strives to create an atmosphere that will encourage communication between the alleged perpetrator and the interviewer. The interview should be conducted in a private location with as few interviewers as possible. The location should be selected, when feasible, to ensure the safety of the worker.[1]

The interviewer should have a good grasp of the case facts, including an understanding of any medical findings and any statements from other witnesses that would help fix the time frame of any abuse. An understanding of the facts is vital to developing critical questions and evaluating proffered alibis and explanations.

The interviewer should convey openness, adaptability, and flexibility. The interviewer should project him- or herself as a seeker of the truth. The interviewer should observe the alleged perpetrator's behaviors throughout the process and listen carefully during the questioning period.

■ Stages of the Interview

An effective interview has several stages. In some ways, these mirror the stages of a proper child interview. The stages are as follows:

1. Introduction: This should explain who you are, your agency name and mission, and why you are there and should establish your credentials (e.g., you frequently talk with people about things that have happened with children or in families) and that you are requesting truthfulness and accuracy.

2. Rapport building: Identify commonalities between you and the interviewee; you want this individual to be as comfortable with you as possible.

3. History and biographical information: You should explore general topics, such as recent employment history, relationship and marital history, current household composition, cultural and religious beliefs pertinent to the allegations, childhood history (general abuse or neglect history), social services history, and criminal history (investigations, arrests, and convictions).

4. Screening of general adult functioning: During the history phase, you are also gaining an understanding of the interviewee's comprehension of the process and questions (i.e., receptive and expressive communication ability), general educational level, linguistic comprehension, the presence of mental health issues (current or historical: Are they currently using any psychotropic medication?), and current alcohol and drug use (including the level of sobriety at the time of the interview). The interviewer also needs to gain an understanding of the normal eye contact and body language (appropriate for cultural background) when talking about general subjects.

5. Introducing the topic of concern: Explain your understanding of the allegation in very general terms (e.g., "I understand Billy got hurt recently").

6. Questions concerning the act(s) under investigation: Ask them to explain the events as they understand them and when they first became aware of the allegation. Begin by moving from general questions about specific topics to abuse- or event-focused questions. Note affect, body language, and eye contact and any change in response to specific areas of inquiry. Critically listen, noting consistencies and inconsistencies with what is already known of the events (from medical reports, other interviews, and the child's statement).

Allow the interviewee to discuss one incident or time period from beginning to end without interruptions. Evaluate the story for completeness. Follow up by asking specific questions to check the consistency of the account and to gain additional details (e.g., what happened, who said what, what happened then, what time was this, and how did the child react?).

Ask the alleged perpetrator to start the narrative at a point in the middle and retell it in reverse (e.g., "So you said she was crying after she fell, tell me what happened just before you heard the cry?"). Using a technique called cognitive interviewing, you may want to ask the person to change perspective and describe the event as if he or she were someone else observing the event from another vantage point (e.g., "What would someone standing at the bedroom door have seen?").

Explore how the interviewee describes the child. Encourage him or her to talk about the child's physical appearance, development state, and behavior (e.g., how does the child act when asked or told to do something he or she does not want to, is there any drug or alcohol abuse, and what is the child's capacity for truthfulness). Ask who the child confides in and who are the child's best friends.

Special issues for sexual abuse: What is the alleged perpetrator's role in caring for the child, does his or her responsibilities place him or her alone with the child (e.g., bathing the child, putting the child to bed, and helping dress the child) or, when appropriate, has the alleged perpetrator ever accidentally touched the child's genital area? If yes, in what circumstances, how many times, and for how long? Explore the caregiver's views of the child and, if appropriate, his or her perceptions of the child's sexuality. Remain neutral: Do not react to statements or admissions. Explore the caregiver's sexual interest in children (e.g., how old is the youngest person that he or she has ever had sexual contact with? How old was the caregiver? Does he or she sometimes think of kids in a sexual way?). Avoid judgmental terms such as rape, molestation, and abuse.

Special issues for physical abuse: Explore the alleged perpetrator's views of the child. Does he or she report provocative behaviors on the part of the child that make him or her angry (e.g., "What type of things does Billy do that make you angry?")? Who else cares for the child? Search for the opportunity to confirm facts that can be related to medical findings (e.g., the doctor says the child would immediately loose consciousness after the blow, and the caregiver says the child was alert and fine when put to bed after the fall).

Explore rationalizations for alleged behaviors (e.g., spouse no longer interested in sex and child deliberately tries to provoke anger by wetting pants).

Ask questions that appear to accept the suspect's rationalization. These types of questions allow you to identify interview themes that will have the greatest likelihood of resonating with the interviewee. They also allow him or her to hear acceptable reasons for behaviors under question. If the alleged perpetrator believes you understand the pressures that he or she is under, this person will be more likely to confide the truth to you.

Explore reasons why any individual could commit such an act (e.g., many people lose their tempers when children will not stop crying).

Explore reasons why individuals try not to commit the act alleged (it would injure the child, it is illegal, it is morally wrong, the spouse would divorce, religion prohibits the act, etc.).

If the individual still denies the allegation and the child has named this individual as the perpetrator, inquire as to why the child is doing so.

Explore external issues surrounding the abuse event(s):

- Venue: Where did the act tale place? How did they come to be there together?
- Witnesses: Where were other adults? If not present, why were they absent?
- Witnesses: Where were other children? If not present, why were they absent?
- If the interviewee is not related to the child, why was he or she with the child? Where were the parents?

At some point during the interview, it may become necessary to challenge something the alleged perpetrator has said. Because the alleged perpetrator may feel threatened, he or she may verbally attack the interviewer to redirect the issue or gain control of the process. The person conducting the interview needs to be comfortable in the role of interviewer, realizing the meeting may move from pleasant to confrontational. Even when confronting the suspect, the interviewer should do so with firmness and retain a respectful tone.

At the point the interviewer decides to end the interview or the suspect declines to continue, the interviewer should attempt to leave on a positive note. Thanking the individual for his or her time, requesting to be contacted if the individual has additionally information, and providing a business card are appropriate ways of terminating the meeting.

If the interview was not audiotaped or videotaped, a detailed report should be written as soon as possible. Complete documentation of the entire interview is needed to make a reasonable assessment of the truthfulness of the individual's statement.

■ Note

1. If the interview is conducted in a "custodial" situation in which the alleged perpetrator is not free to leave, the interview should proceed after ensuring that the individual has been advised by law enforcement of his or her constitutional rights per Miranda.

19

What Kinds of Questions in My Initial Assessment Interviews Will Generate Solutions and Enhance Safety?

■ *Insoo Kim Berg*

Contrary to the sensational stories portrayed in the mass media, the majority of protective services cases are not about brutal physical or sexual abuses or children who are killed by their caregivers. The most difficult and persistent, and thus most frustrating, cases are those that make you feel uneasy and not sure what to do. These are the multiple investigation cases, the serious neglect cases, and those that fall between the cracks of what the rule says and what your common sense tells you. The majority of your work is not clear-cut, does not involve prolonged investigation, and may involve only a single visit. This chapter addresses how to make the most of these single visits and how to ensure the safety of the children when things fall between the cracks. The questions discussed in the following sections are fully elaborated by Berg (1994), Berg and Kelly (1999), and DeJong and Berg (1997).

■ *Seeking Exception Questions*

All problems have exceptions. Contrary to what terms such as *abusive parent* convey, most children are not maltreated 24 hours a day, 7 days a week. A helpful key to successful assessment and prevention is to find these exceptions and encourage the parent to repeat these successful strategies, however inadequate or meager they may seem. Making exceptions into rules is the easiest, simplest way to build parents' self-confidence and prevent additional abuse.

Exceptions are those times that the parent could have lashed out or neglected the child but somehow managed to restrain, control, or successfully negotiate more appropriate ways of handling the situation. The questions presented here will help you to learn that the parent has skills, and they will help the parent to feel better about him- or herself and about the child. They will recognize, perhaps for the first time, that they have small but significant successes that they can repeat on their own. Remember that until you elicit these small successes, parents frequently do not know that they are successful. This recognition enhances self-confidence and self-esteem, which in turn is played out with their children. The questions are as follows:

- "Tell me about the time, in recent days, when you could have hit [screamed at, called him names, etc.] Tommy but somehow managed to handle it differently?"
- "Can you explain how you did that? That must have been very difficult. How did you know it would work with him? What else did you do?"
- "Like all parents, I am sure there are days or times, when you just feel like walking out on your child[ren] or just saying to yourself, 'Oh, to hell with it, I don't care what happens' and just sleep through the day [or scream and holler at your child or smack him on the head]. I wonder what you find yourself doing instead that seems to help, even a little bit?"
- "How do you suppose Tommy [your best friend, your mother, and other supportive person] would say how you do it when life is so tough nowadays?"

Allow much time for the parent to ponder because he or she may not have thought about these questions before and might think that they are trick questions. After the parent provides answers to these questions, follow up with questions such as "Wow, how did you know that these would work with your child?" "You must know your child very well," and "You really think about what is good for your child, don't you?" This kind of admiring commiseration helps parents take a fresh look and see themselves as loving, caring, and gentle persons rather than as inadequate, incompetent parents who are often viewed with suspicion.

■ *Scaling Questions*

Scaling questions are a self-assessment tool that both you and your clients can use to gauge safety and plan for the future. For example, when you are not confident about the parent's ability to repeat his or her successful behaviors or have concerns about the level of safety, you can use the following questions to ask yourself and the parent to rank the safety issues on a scale from 1 to 10:

- "I am going to ask you a different kind of question this time. On a scale from 1 to 10, where 10 indicates that you are as confident as any parent can be about the safety of your child and 1 stands for the opposite, that is, you are very shaky about how safe you feel about your child's safety, where would you say you are between 1 and 10 right now?"
- "Suppose I was to ask your best friend: Where would he or she say you are on a scale from 1 to 10?"
- "Wow, I wonder how you managed to go up to 5 when your life is so tough?"
- "On the same scale, what would it take for your number to go up one point higher?"

Asking yourself and the parent the previous questions will help both of you to assess the safety needs and what can be done realistically so that you will know what steps to take to increase the margin of safety. Scaling questions are very versatile. You can ask the parent to scale his or her confidence, hopefulness, and willingness to increase the safety for the child. My experience with using this type of question is that parents usually become very thoughtful about their own situation, and many of them become much more accurate about their own assessment and, at times, become painfully honest about themselves. These two types of questions will build cooperative working relationships with your clients.

■ *Further Reading*

Berg, I. K. (1994). *Family based services: Solution-focused approach.* New York: Norton.

Berg, I. K., & Kelly, S. (1999). *Building solutions in child protective services.* New York: Norton.

DeJong, P., & Berg, I. K. (1997). *Interviewing for solutions.* Pacific Grove, CA: Brooks/Cole.

Part IV

INITIAL ASSESSMENT

Section A: General

20

How Do I Differentiate Culturally Based Parenting Practices From Child Maltreatment?

■ *Sherri Y. Terao, Joaquin Borrego, Jr., and Anthony J. Urquiza*

Because of the rapid growth in population of people from different ethnic and cultural backgrounds in the United States, clinicians are often faced with the daunting challenge of providing responsive services that are culturally sensitive (i.e., a sensitive and respectful response with knowledge about the culture and values of a particular group). A difficult issue is the clinician's ability to accurately distinguish between child maltreatment and culturally based parenting practices (i.e., practices acceptable or normative to one's cultural group). This chapter provides a pragmatic decision-making model to help differentiate between appropriate and inappropriate parenting practices.

Scenario 1

Mr. and Mrs. Nguyen, recent Vietnamese immigrants, were referred by the local school district after the school nurse discovered that Lan Nguyen, a 7-year-old student, had bruises on her back. They were referred to the local medical center.

A medical examination revealed that the parents were performing coining (rubbing the edge of a coin on the back), which is a traditional healing remedy in Southeast Asia. What is the most appropriate response?

Scenario 2

Mr. and Mrs. Diaz, Guatemalan immigrants who have resided in the United States for the past 15 years, were reported to child protective services by their next-door neighbor for publicly disciplining their 6-year-old daughter with a flyswatter to the buttocks. A medical examination did not reveal any physical evidence. What is the most appropriate response?

■ Reporting Versus Response

Before examining the issue of culturally based parenting practices, it is important to distinguish between reporting child maltreatment and providing a clinical response. In the first instance, all children, regardless of sex, race, ethnicity, or religious beliefs, should have the opportunity to be raised in an environment free of physical, sexual, and emotional abuse and neglect. Furthermore, although state statutes governing child abuse reporting vary, it is the ethical and legal responsibility of all clinicians to report all instances of suspected child maltreatment. We know of no parenting practice that would supersede a clinician's legal and ethical obligation to ensure the safety of a child. Therefore, it is essential that all clinicians respond by reporting suspected child endangerment, regardless of the ethnic or cultural background of the family.

■ Current or Future Risk of Harm

Issues of cultural diversity, however, may play a very important role in how clinicians respond to families of different cultural backgrounds. Although the clinician's obligation is clear (typically to report suspected child maltreatment), parents have broad discretion in the manner in which they interact with and discipline (i.e., parent) their children. Irrespective of culturally based parenting practices, it is important to assess whether the child is at risk for current and future harm (sexual and physical harm or neglect or both). Although a parenting practice may be considered normative (e.g., Scenario 1), if there is a clear risk of harm to the child, it must be reported to the appropriate authorities. In contrast, if there is no clear risk of harm, this should not be considered maltreatment. The decision to report parents to authorities is more difficult when clinicians must deal with cases such as that presented in Scenario 2. This "gray area" involves issues such as questionable parenting practices that are not clearly harmful to the child. It may be preferable to seek a compromise solution, respectfully raising concern and suggesting preferable alternatives but not involving child protective services.

■ *Acculturation and Treatment*

In addition, acculturation should be taken into consideration when determining a probable course of action. People with a low level of acculturation should be offered psychoeducational services (e.g., teaching or informing parents about acceptable parenting practices and alternative methods of discipline). Due to their limited knowledge of American parenting practices, this approach provides less acculturated parents with alternative and effective methods of discipline that are acceptable and lawful. People who are well acculturated (who understand that it is against the law to harm their child) should be provided a therapeutic response (i.e., psychotherapy)—for example, a parent-child treatment program that focuses on improving the quality of the relationship and addresses the parent personality or behavioral characteristics that placed the child at jeopardy.

In conclusion, multidisciplinary caseworkers need to be cognizant of the multitude of parenting practices across cultures. Regardless of what parenting practices are acceptable to particular cultures, it is imperative to assess for current or future risk of harm to the child. In sum, we offer a six-step decision making model to guide clinicians' judgment in differentiating child maltreatment from cultural parenting practices.

■ *A Six-Step Model*

The following is a six-step decision-making model for accurately distinguishing child maltreatment from culturally based discipline strategies:

1. Is the child at risk for physical, sexual, or emotional harm or neglect or both, or is there actual harm?

2. If "yes," it is the clinician's legal (given the state statute governing child abuse reporting) and ethical responsibility to report suspected maltreatment or harm. It is important to note that no type of cultural parenting practice should supersede the clinician's obligation to report child maltreatment. The cultural background of the family, however, may be essential in determining the most appropriate intervention strategy.

3. If the child is not at risk for physical, sexual, or emotional harm or neglect or both, assess the family's level of acculturation (e.g., language use, duration of time in the United States, ethnicity of friends, and involvement in religious and cultural traditions).

4. An assessment of the family's level of acculturation will determine whether a psychoeducational or therapeutic response is most appropriate.

5. If clients have minimal knowledge of acceptable U.S. laws and acceptable child-rearing practices, a psychoeducational approach is recommended. Parent persistence in harmful parenting practices after completion of a psychoeducational intervention may warrant assessment for a therapeutic intervention.

6. If clients have an acceptable knowledge level of U.S. laws and practices, a therapeutic approach is recommended.

■ *Further Reading*

Abney, V. D. (1996). Cultural competency in the field of child maltreatment. In J. Briere, L. Berliner, J. A. Buckley, C. Jenny, & T. Reid (Eds.), *The APSAC handbook on child maltreatment* (pp. 449-462). Thousand Oaks, CA: Sage.

Derezotes, D. S., & Snowden, L. R. (1990). Cultural factors in the intervention of child maltreatment. *Child and Adolescent Social Work Journal, 7*(2).

Korbin, J. E. (1994). Sociocultural factors in child maltreatment. In G. B. Melton & F. D. Barr (Eds.), *Protecting children from abuse and neglect* (pp. 451-459). New York: Guilford.

21

How Should Child Protective Services and Law Enforcement Coordinate the Initial Assessment and Investigation?

■ *Charles Wilson and Donna Pence*

hild abuse and neglect is a crime in all 50 states and territories. Therefore, the responsibility to protect children from child maltreatment is shared by the child protection system (including the civil court systems) and the criminal justice system (including law enforcement, prosecutors, and the criminal courts). Generally, by law or practice or both, law enforcement agencies' interest is reserved for child homicides, sexual abuse, serious physical abuse, and other more egregious incidents of child maltreatment for which public expectations of accountability are aroused.

Child protection and law enforcement approach child maltreatment issues with significantly different missions and philosophies. Child protection is focused on reducing the risk to the child of future maltreatment and on trying to maintain and strengthen as much of the child's family as possible. Law enforcement is focused on holding those who break the law accountable for their actions—in effect, punishment. These two apparently contradictory roles may collide when serious child abuse is reported. In many communities, this potential conflict is managed only through avoidance. The child protection and law enforcement professionals conduct their duties separately and in a parallel fashion. Such parallel investigations serve no one. Parallel investigations require children and other witnesses to undergo multiple recountings of painful memories because the interveners are not willing to talk to one another. The parallel investigations often create conflict between investigating agencies as the investigators encounter different, and sometimes contradictory, information at various points in the process. Uncoordinated efforts also result in the action of one system adversely impacting on those of another (such as when a premature, unilateral interview of a potential sex offender leads to the destruction of physical evidence, such as pornography), with resultant conflict and ill feelings.

To reduce the secondary trauma of the investigative process and to improve the effectiveness of all agencies involved, a coordinated or team approach such as a child advocacy center is needed. Such collaboration requires planning and hard work, but it can pay off in improved services for the child and family, less trauma for the child, more accurate information on which all can act, mutual support for the investigators, and more efficient use of scarce resources.

■ *Establishing Systems Protocols and Operational Agreements*

The first step in formal coordination is the establishment of working agreements or protocols. This step is usually initiated by management of the agencies involved (child protective services [CPS], local law enforcement, prosecutors, or sometimes outside advocates). One of the biggest perceived challenges is agency information confidentiality and record keeping. Agencies must resolve questions of

- who has access to what information,
- how information obtained from another investigative agency is preserved in the record, and
- how the differing discovery processes in juvenile or family court and those in criminal court will be managed.

The community agencies must determine the structure of collaboration, including the roles that representatives from each agency will play in the process, from taking initial information to investigation and evidence collection and case decisions about child protection and prosecution. Coordinated investigations are best managed through cooperation and trust, which are facilitated by regular meetings or case reviews in which all parties share critical case information. A decision as to which agency will lead such meetings should be made at the inception. Joint and cross-training also reduce the risk of misunderstandings regarding pertinent policies and procedures and enhance investigative skills. Conflict in such collaboration is normal and can, in fact, be healthy as long as the agencies have a strategy for solving problems and resolving conflict.

■ *Establishing Joint and Team Investigative Protocol*

The actual protocol should, at a minimum, include the following:

- *Receiving reports:* Who will the public contact when they suspect child abuse? What information do all investigative agencies need from the reporter at the time of referral?
- *Notification of other parties:* Once the report is received, the agencies need to agree on the nature and timing of notification. What type of cases require immediate notification of the other agencies (i.e., in what circumstances does CPS call law enforcement as the intake worker is being notified)? In general, immediate notification of law enforcement is indicated in child death cases, serious abuse cases in which there is immediate danger to the child or other children, cases in which fresh physical evidence may be present (pornography, computer records of sexual acts, weapons, objects used as sexual devices, bloody clothing or furnishings, etc.), or when access to the child or flight by the abuser is in question.
- *Creating a common investigative protocol:* Agencies need to agree on the usual course of the investigative process.

This includes the steps CPS and law enforcement will take to determine what, if anything, happened to the child and in what order these steps (e.g., interviewing the child, other witnesses, nonoffending parents, and suspects; assessment of medical evidence, crime scene evidence, and psychological information; and collection of other evidence) will be performed. Such protocols serve as a framework for the investigation and lay out expectations of all involved, but they can easily be modified by the participants as needed based on the unique aspects of individual cases.

- *Team decision making:* Agencies need to determine how decision making concerning child safety and protection will be made.

These systems responses must be augmented by the efforts of individual protective service workers. Individuals must reach out to their colleagues in law enforcement and prosecution and build social relationships, personal familiarity, and trust, share professional information from the literature and training, and help the relationship move from one between agencies to one of trust between individuals.

■ *Further Reading*

Best practices manual: A guidebook to establishing a child advocacy center program. (1994). Washington, DC: Network of Children's Advocacy Centers.

Cage, R., & Pence, D. (1997). *Criminal investigation of child sexual abuse.* Washington, DC: U.S. Department of Justice, Office of Juvenile Justice and Delinquency Prevention, Office of Justice Programs.

Martin, S., & Besharov, D. (1991). *Police and child abuse: New policies for expanded responsibilities.* Washington, DC: U.S. Department of Justice, National Institute of Justice, Office of Justice Programs.

Pence, D., & Wilson, C. (1994). *The team investigation of child sexual abuse: The uneasy alliance.* Thousand Oaks, CA: Sage.

World Wide Web resources: National Children's Advocacy Center. www.ncac-hsv.org; National Children's Alliance, www. nncac.org.

22

How Do I Screen a Caregiver's Use and Abuse of and Dependence on Alcohol and Other Drugs and Their Effects on Parenting?

■ *Ronald Rogers and Chandler Scott McMillin*

Harmful involvement with alcohol and drugs is a factor in as many as 80% of situations involving child maltreatment or neglect. In such cases, child protection depends on the professional's ability to recognize, assess, and intervene with an often resistant caregiver.

■ *Obstacles to Identification*

Screening for substance-related problems is hampered by the omnipresent denial associated with addiction. By definition, the addict or alcoholic is unable to accurately self-assess either the extent of his or her impairment or the severity of its impact on others, including the child.

To complicate matters, the caregiver is often keenly aware of the possible legal or social sanctions that may accompany an admission of drug or alcohol problems. This may motivate outright attempts to deceive or mislead the professional, resulting in a situation in which the caregiver is, in the words of one physician, "lying first to self, second to family, and third to me." The screening process may also be complicated by

- Substance-induced impaired thinking and organic brain effects
- "Blackouts" or other memory loss
- Panic or extreme anxiety associated with drug withdrawal
- Psychological defenses such as rationalizing, externalizing, and minimizing drug use and associated problems
- Misconceptions about the nature and symptoms of addiction
- Codependency and enabling by family and friends

Given these obstacles, it is apparent that specialized training is necessary to prepare for effective assessment and intervention in child maltreatment cases.

■ *Abuse Versus Dependence*
_____

Substance *abuse* disorders generally reflect alcohol or drug consumption that creates significant problems in one or more major areas of functioning. Symptoms may include job, family, legal, and relationship problems. Substance *dependence,* however, refers to a pattern of chronic, usually progressive dysfunction characterized by

- The presence of withdrawal symptoms of varying intensity and type
- Loss of control over the amount used, time or place where use occurs, or duration of episode
- Continued use despite adverse life consequences

Obviously, abuse and dependence can and do coexist in the same individual. Symptoms vary with drug of preference. Cocaine users, for example, may experience more financial and psychological disruption than alcoholics, who in turn are prone to a variety of medical and health complications not found among marijuana users.

■ *Screening and Assessment*

No specific, widely accepted screening tool exists to meet the unique challenge of assessing drug or alcohol use among caregivers in a situation involving child maltreatment. More generic instruments used by addiction treatment clinicians include the following:

- The Michigan Alcoholism Screening Test (MAST) and its counterpart for drug use: Although the MAST may take more time to administer, its validity and effectiveness are worth the time. A MAST and MAST KEY are provided in Appendix 2.
- The Addiction Severity Index, a detailed assessment of drug- and alcohol-related life problems, is often used as an aid to case management.
- Screening for drugs in urine specimens: This may be helpful, but it may be misleading if the test results are negative due to episodic use.

■ *Conducting the Interview*

The following are important to assess:

1. Is there a family history of alcoholism or drug abuse? Addiction clearly runs in families. Even someone in deep denial is often willing to discuss a parent's or grandparent's history of alcohol and drug problems. In doing so, the caregiver reveals an important risk factor in his or her own situation.
2. Are there alcohol- and drug-related social consequences? These may include problems that are caused by intoxication, withdrawal, drug-seeking behavior, or all three. These problems may not have provided enough motivation for the addict to seek help.
3. Is there an identified withdrawal syndrome? This may include insomnia, sweats, nausea, tremors, seizures, vomiting, and extreme anxiety. Often, the addict blames these symp-

toms on external stressors. Extreme emotionality is to be expected in the alcohol- or drug-addicted client.

Despite the obstacles to uncovering drug or alcohol problems in a caregiver, many clinicians have developed, with practice, a remarkably accurate "ear" for the telltale signs of abuse and dependence—a skill that can mean the difference between child protection and child endangerment.

■ *Further Reading*

Rogers, R. L., & McMillin, C. S. (1992). *Freeing someone you love from alcohol and other drugs.* New York: The Body Press/Perigee.

U.S. Department of Health and Human Services, National Institutes of Health, National Institute of Alcohol Abuse and Alcoholism. (1993). *Alcohol and health: Eighth special report to Congress.* Washington, DC: Author.

23

How Do I Screen Caregivers If I Suspect That They May Be Dangerous to Themselves or Their Children?

■ *David Corwin*

Concerns about dangerousness of caregivers to themselves or their children are common in child protection work. Caretakers who are depressed, hopeless, or enraged or threatening may pose increased risks to themselves and others. To further screen caregivers' dangerousness, a worker must gather information about their past and current behavior, thoughts, and plans. From these facts and observations, the worker can apply common sense, knowledge of risk factors, standardized risk assessment methods, and consultation with peers and supervisors to determine whether the caregivers present a serious enough risk to themselves or their child to require emergency intervention.

■ Suicidality

When screening for suicidality, worker must directly ask about suicidal thoughts and plans. If suicidal plans are present, emergency assessment by a mental health professional is needed. Until the assessment for suicidality is completed, appropriate precautions include having family members prevent access to guns and having someone stay with the suicidal person at all times. Hanging and jumping from high places are also highly lethal suicide methods used most often by males. Overdosing is a frequent method of female suicide attempters. Ultimately, if a person is determined to commit suicide, it is very difficult to stop him or her. Intent to commit suicide warrants emergency evaluation for psychiatric hospitalization.

When assessing the suicidality of a caregiver, it is important to explore the caregiver's thoughts and plans about the children in his or her care. Suicidal caregivers sometimes think that killing their children before committing suicide will rescue the children from circumstances they view as intolerable.

In addition to talking with the caregiver, who may or may not reveal dangerous past behavior, thoughts, or plans, it is important to interview others who have interacted closely with the caregiver, including children, spouses, neighbors, close friends, and relatives. Talking to other informants allows the worker to estimate the reliability of information obtained directly from the caregiver. Different sources usually offer slightly differing perspectives, but major discrepancies suggest that someone is mistaken or lying. Thoughts and plans are difficult to assess without a cooperative and truthful informant, but caregivers who choose to understate the seriousness of their thoughts and plans to a child protection worker may have shared their real thoughts and feeling with others close to them.

Signs of impending suicide include a lack of future plans or hopes, disposing of prized possessions, writing a will, making alternative care arrangements for children, and attempts to secure the means for committing suicide (e.g., buying a gun or rope). Past suicide attempts, or relatives and loved ones who have committed suicide, increase the individual's risk of suicide. Other factors that increase the risk of suicide include being adolescent, a young adult, or older than age 45; alcohol dependence; persistent rage or history of violence; male gender; unwillingness to accept help; depression; prior psychiatric hospitalization; recent loss or separation; loss of physical health; unemployment; and single, widowed, or divorced marital status.

Although some advise contracting with suicidal persons to deter them from attempting to kill themselves, it is unclear how much confidence should be placed in antisuicide contracts. Suicidal persons develop "tunnel vision" in which suicide seems to them the only reasonable way to proceed. When a person is prepared to give up everything, including life, a promise to a stranger may offer little protection.

■ *Screening Questions for Risk of Suicide*

The following questions, which focus on some of the strongest risk factors identified by research on suicide, are drawn primarily from the Columbia Teen Screen, which has demonstrated usefulness in screening high school students for risk of suicide:

- Have you been losing your temper, been in a bad mood, or have little things been making you upset?
- Have you been feeling unhappy or sad?
- Have you thought about suicide?
- If yes, do you have a plan? If yes, what is it?
- Have you ever tried to commit suicide?
- Has any close friend or relative of yours ever committed suicide?
- Have you been having a problem with drugs or alcohol?

If an individual has suicidal thoughts and a plan for how to kill him- or herself, the more developed and lethal the plan, the greater the risk of suicide.

■ *Danger to Children and Others*

Estimating dangerousness is a challenging but necessary task for child protection workers. It is very important to remember that past behavior is the best predictor of future behavior. Past incidents of assault on spouses, children, and pets are important risk factors for future assaultiveness. Some child protection agencies use standard risk assessment forms, but the ultimate judgment of dangerousness relies on careful consideration of the facts and observations in a particular case compared to what is known about predicting dangerousness.

The following factors increase the potential for violence: age in the late teens or early 20s; male gender; low socioeconomic status; low intelligence; limited education; unemployment; residential instability; impulsivity; low frustration tolerance; frequent and open threats; access to weapons; chronic anger, hostility, or resentment; enjoyment of inflicting pain; lack of compassion; self-view as victim; childhood victimization or deprivation; early loss of a parent; witnessed domestic violence as a child; reckless driving; isolation; chronic alcohol abuse; history of psychiatric hospitalization; history of arrests or antisocial behavior; and hallucinations, delusions, depression, mania, and paranoia. The more a caregiver presents these factors and, most important, if the caregiver has a known history of violent or aggressive behaviors toward people, the more dangerous he or she is to others and to his or her children.

■ Further Reading

Kaplan, H. I. (1995). Psychiatric emergencies. In H. I. Kaplan, & B. J. Sadock (Eds.), *Comprehensive textbook of psychiatry/VI* (6th ed.) (pp. 1739-1763). Baltimore, MD: Williams & Wilkins.

Shaffer, D., Wilcox, H., Lucas, C., Hicks, R., Busner, C., & Parides, M. (1966, October). *The development of a screening instrument for teens at risk for suicide.* Poster presented at the 1996 meeting of the Academy of Child and Adolescent Psychiatry, New York.

24

How Do I Decide Whether to Substantiate a Report?

■ *Brett Drake*

In this chapter, I discuss what it means to substantiate a case and how to best make this decision. The reader must keep in mind that these comments are general and intended for a national audience. There is no substitute for a thorough knowledge of statutes and substantiation guidelines that relate specifically to one's state.

■ What Is Substantiation?

Substantiation is basically a statement by the worker that "I have enough evidence to believe that child maltreatment has occurred." To make effective decisions, one needs to understand what constitutes maltreatment and "good enough" evidence. What constitutes child maltreatment in one state may not constitute child maltreatment in another state. Similarly, some state policies dictate the substantiation of cases based on having adequate "credible evidence," whereas other states substantiate at more restrictive levels such as a "preponderance of the evidence." The substantiation decision depends on the answers to two questions: "Is the harm to the child severe enough to constitute child maltreatment?" and "Is there sufficient evidence to support this being a case of child maltreatment?" For the case to be substantiated, both questions must be answered "yes." Substantiation decisions must also reflect other state laws or agency guidelines. For example, under Missouri law, drug-exposed infants are not generally considered to be victims of child maltreatment, whereas in other states this is not the case. Although many states use a simple substantiated-unsubstantiated dichotomy, some states use a three-tier system of substantiated, indicated, and unsubstantiated. The middle classification usually means that the worker has some belief or evidence that maltreatment has occurred but not enough to substantiate the case.

■ What Is Not Substantiation?

Substantiation is not a risk assessment or an evaluation of what services the client will need in the future. Risk assessments are attempts to predict the likelihood that the child will be maltreated in the future. Substantiation is a statement about what the worker believes happened in the past. In fact, a report may be unsubstantiated based on available evidence about what has already occurred, but there may be substantial future risk to the child. Similarly, in substantiated cases, the child is sometimes no longer at risk, such as in instances in which the perpetrator no longer has access to the child.

■ Evaluating Harm

Sometimes, harm is so severe that it is easily evaluated, as in the case of serious physical trauma or neglect. In these cases, evaluation is straightforward. Often, however, the severity of harm is ambiguous. When is a bruise inflicted during corporal punishment severe enough to warrant classification as child maltreatment? This depends on the seriousness of the bruise, the location on the body, the age of the child, the situation in which the punishment occurred, the laws of the state, the guidelines of the child protective agency, and many other factors.

In addition to the issues of severity and circumstance, another complicating factor is that sometimes workers are forced to deal with potential rather than actual harm. For example, an infant who was permitted to repeatedly crawl into a busy street would be evaluated by most workers as a victim of serious neglect even though the harm was only potential. Such potential harm can be far more serious than the actual harm found in other cases.

Skill in evaluating complicated cases is developed only with experience and with a thorough knowledge of one's agency's procedures, both formal and informal. Most agencies recognize this and provide extensive on-the-job training. Supervisors and experienced workers are generally able to provide useful guidance.

■ *Evaluating Evidence*

As with harm, evaluating evidence can be straightforward or tricky. The worker must evaluate all available information regarding its reliability and the degree to which it contributes to the overall picture. Often, there is simply not sufficient evidence available to determine if a particular injury or other form of harm could be attributed to maltreatment. This is especially likely when dealing with preverbal or young children. Sometimes, however, if enough evidence is gathered, a clear picture will emerge. For example, consider a report alleging that a 14-month-old child has two black eyes. The parents report that the child had fallen forward and hit the bridge of his nose on a coffee table, and that the bruises formed soon after. They also report that their family doctor told them not to worry about the bruising because a sharp blow to the bridge of the nose could easily cause such bilateral bruising. What evidence is available? The child was clearly learning to walk, and the coffee table did have a sharp edge and was the correct height for the child to hit his nose on it. Furthermore, close examination of the child revealed a slight lateral bruise or abrasion across the bridge of the child's nose that was so small that even the parents did not notice it. This mark was perfectly straight, consistent with hitting a hard, level edge. In this case, despite the age of the child and the seriousness of the injury, the evidence forms a clear and internally consistent picture that does not indicate the possibility of child maltreatment.

■ *Some Ways Your Assessment Can Help Your Substantiation Decision*

Prior planning in the assessment process can help you to obtain better information. It is best to interview people before they can compare their stories or alter evidence. It is also important to be as prepared as possible before you interview the victim so that you can ask more detailed and specific questions. It is helpful to interview the reporting party first both to learn more and to evaluate reliability. It is also important to interview the victim in a neutral setting if possible (see Chapters 13 and 14, this volume). It is important to evaluate the reliability of all information received and to place more importance on statements or physical evidence in which you have greater confidence. It is helpful to ask yourself, "Of all this information, what am I more or less sure of?"

■ *Where to Go for Help*

The inability to make a substantiation decision is usually due to the worker having inadequate information. Therefore, if you are in a quandary, the first question you should ask is "Where can I get more information?" Potential sources include other witnesses to the event and other people who know the child, family, or alleged perpetrator well. As you analyze the information that you have collected, it may be helpful to talk through what you know with your supervisor or a senior colleague or professionals representing other disciplines, such as medicine or law enforcement. If your agency supports multidisciplinary teams, these can be both a great source of information and a good means of working through the decision-making process. To maximize your consultation with others, you should briefly outline the main points of the case and then ask specific questions. Sometimes, the simple act of recalling the specifics of the case and formulating your questions can be all the help you need.

■ *Further Reading*

Drake, B. (1996). Unraveling unsubstantiated. *Child Maltreatment,* *1*(3), 261-271.

Giovannoni, J. (1989). Substantiated and unsubstantiated reports of child maltreatment. *Children and Youth Services Review, 11,* 299-318.

U.S. Department of Health and Human Services. (1998). *Child maltreatment 1996: Reports from the states to the National Child Abuse and Neglect Data System.* Washington, DC: Government Printing Office.

Part IV

INITIAL
ASSESSMENT

Section B: Neglect

25

How Do I Determine
If a Child Is Neglected?

■ *Diane DePanfilis*

Chapter 3 outlined the various ways in which omissions in care to meet a child's basic needs may result in significant harm or a risk of significant harm. Although the actual determination of whether a child should be considered neglected must be made based on definitions in specific state laws, this chapter outlines methods for analyzing information to determine whether basic needs are unmet at a level that may be termed neglect. Other chapters in this book outline methods for interviewing children and other family members, making observations about the home, and using medical reports and other documents to determine whether a child has been maltreated. Particularly with neglect, it is important that the assessment be broad and consider the ecological context in which the child exists—the family, the home, the neighborhood, and the broader community.

■ *Analysis of Information
and Decision Making*

The decision about whether certain conditions or circumstances should be considered neglect is made based on the answers to two questions: (a) Do the conditions or circumstances indicate that a child's basic needs are unmet? and (b) What harm or threat of harm may have resulted?

Unmet Basic Needs

This section provides examples of ways in which a child's basic needs may be unmet. Because other chapters in this book focus on psychological maltreatment (including emotional neglect), the examples provided here emphasize the ways in which a child's physical and educational needs may be unmet. In some cases, additional discussion is provided in other chapters. For other examples, suggestions are offered to further assess the degree to which the condition has reached a threshold that might be labeled neglect due to harm or a threat of harm to the child. The examples are as follows:

- Inadequate or delayed health care: failure to provide a child with needed care for physical injury, acute illnesses, physical disabilities, or chronic condition or impairment
  - □ Generally, this does not include routine health care, which is optimal to a child's health but does not lead to immediate negative consequences (see Chapter 26, this volume).

- Inadequate nutrition: failure to provide a child with regular and ample meals that meet basic nutritional requirements or when a caregiver fails to provide the necessary rehabilitative diet to a child with particular types of physical health problems (see Chapter 27, this volume)
- Poor personal hygiene: failure to attend to cleanliness of the child's hair, skin, teeth, and clothes
  - □ This often prompts a report, but it is difficult to determine the difference between marginal hygiene and neglect. The chronicity, extent, and nature of the condition need to be considered as well as the consequences to the child. For example, if poor personal hygiene results in the child being shunned by peers, this can lead to isolation in school, which in turn can lead to difficulties in academic performance. Frequently, this type of neglect occurs in combination with other types.

- Inadequate clothing: chronic inappropriate clothing for the weather or conditions
  - ☐ If a child does not have adequate clothes for the weather and must stand outside in below-freezing temperatures to wait for the bus, the potential consequences can be severe. The nature and extent of the condition need to be considered in context with the potential consequences.

- Unsafe household conditions: the presence of obvious hazardous physical conditions in the home
  - ☐ This condition can affect children differently, depending on age and developmental status. For example, needles or other drug paraphernalia could be deadly for a toddler who is unsupervised. Although unhealthy for an older child, the potential consequences would be less concerning. Particular areas of concern include the presence of toxic or poisonous materials; improperly vented heating devices, broken windows, knives, or weapons; high-rise apartments with open or broken windows; lead paint; and the presence of matches, lighters, or a gas stove with potential for fire. The potential consequences of these conditions are multiplied if children are left without adequate supervision.

- Unsanitary household conditions: the presence of obvious hazardous unsanitary conditions in the home
  - ☐ Areas of concern include rotting food, human or animal feces, lack of running or clean water, and rodents or insect infestations that present higher potential of harm to young children, particularly if unsupervised.

- Unstable living conditions: changes of residence due to eviction or lack of planning at least three times within a 6-month period or homelessness due to the lack of available affordable housing or the caregiver's inability to manage finances
  - ☐ Although being homeless should not be considered neglect, instability can have serious consequences to children. Generally, these conditions are considered neglect when the instability is the result of mismanagement of financial resources or when spending rent resources on drugs or alcohol results in frequent evictions.

- Shuttling: child repeatedly left at a household due to apparent unwillingness to maintain custody or chronically and repeatedly leaving a child with others for days or weeks at a time
  - □ In these situations, children are often not enrolled in school and are not able to develop sustaining connections to others who may be able to protect them.

- Inadequate supervision: child left unsupervised or inadequately supervised for extended periods of time or allowed to remain away from home overnight without the caregiver knowing the child's whereabouts (see Chapter 28, this volume)

- Inappropriate substitute caregiver: failure to arrange for safe substitute child care (e.g., when the caregiver leaves the child with an inappropriate caregiver) (see Chapter 28, this volume)

- Abandonment: desertion of a child without arranging for reasonable care and supervision in situations in which children are not claimed within 2 days and when children are left by caregivers who give no (or false) information about their whereabouts
  - □ Frequently, this behavior becomes chronic before a report is made.

- Expulsion: blatant refusals of custody without adequate arrangements for care by others or refusal to accept custody of a returned runaway
  - □ Community resources should be exhausted to provide assistance to families to avoid placement when possible.

- Chronic truancy: habitual truancy (a minimum of 20 days within a school year) without a legitimate reason
  - □ Another example is the situation in which children who are supposed to be home schooled are obviously not being provided an education at home.

- Failure to enroll or other truancy: a child (age 6) is not enrolled in school or a pattern of keeping a school-age child home for nonlegitimate reasons (e.g., to work and to care for siblings) an average of at least 3 days a month

- Unmet special education needs: child fails to receive recommended remedial educational services or treatment for his or her diagnosed learning disorder or other special educational needs of the child
  - ☐ Special needs that are unmet can lead to long-term consequences for children. An educational specialist is usually needed to document this condition as neglect.

Significant Harm or Threat of Significant Harm

Because of the various ways in which a child's basic needs may be unmet, it is impossible to identify the ways in which children are harmed as a result of their experiences with the previously discussed conditions. Both short-term and long-term consequences result from neglect. Both need to be considered because sometimes neglectful conditions are not detected until the pattern is chronic and someone notices the harm. The effects of harm are as follows:

- Physical effects: Certain types of neglect (e.g., nutrition and health care) will result in obvious physical effects that are best assessed by a pediatrician. Physical injury or death may result from lack of supervision (e.g., falling out of upstairs windows and injuries from fires or other household hazards; see Chapters 26, 27, and 28, this volume).
- Social and behavioral effects: Neglected children are sometimes characterized by passive, nonassertive, or withdrawn behaviors. For example, a child who is chronically dirty and therefore shunned by her peers may withdraw from social activities. Alternatively, a chronically hungry child may be observed begging for or stealing food. A child who is afraid to go home to an empty house after school may get into trouble so that he or she will have to stay after school.
- Cognitive, academic, and language effects: Neglected children may have lower IQ and language abilities, do poorly on standardized tests, and receive lower grades in school than children who are not maltreated.

■ *Summary*

Determining whether a child is neglected requires the collection of adequate information to assess the degree to which omissions in care have resulted in significant harm or a significant risk of harm. Unlike other forms of maltreatment, this determination may not be possible by assessing one incident; rather, it is often understood by examining patterns of care over time. Therefore, assessments must consider the nature of the current care in addition to the history of care. In general, younger children are more vulnerable to certain types of omissions because these may result in significant harm, even after short periods of time.

The analysis of information should focus on understanding how the child's basic needs are met and identifying situations that may indicate specific omissions in care that have resulted in harm or a risk of harm. Community and cultural standards should be considered when determining whether conditions or circumstances harm children. It must be acknowledged, however, that sometimes community practices, such as leaving young children home alone, may still be harmful to children and considered neglectful even though they may be common practices. With certain types of neglect, specialists are needed to document that the harm is likely related to a specific omission in care. When concern suggests a threat of harm, this becomes even more complicated; therefore, when possible, community resources should be employed to help families address needs before specific negative consequences are observed.

■ *Further Reading*

Magura, S., & Moses, B. S. (1986). *Outcome measures for child welfare services*. Washington, DC: Child Welfare League of America.

U.S. Department of Health and Human Services, National Center on Child Abuse and Neglect. (1996). *Study findings: Study of national incidence and prevalence of child abuse and neglect* (NIS-3). Washington, DC: Author.

26

How Do I Determine If It Is Medical Neglect?

■ *Howard Dubowitz*

There are a few useful principles that help determine whether the circumstances should be considered neglect (see Chapter 3, this volume). Neglect is usually a concern if the lack of care results in actual harm or the risk of significant harm, but specific state definitions need to be considered. Many lapses in health care do not meet this definition. Recommendations may be made for medical care, and although it is best to follow these recommendations, it is possible that no harm is likely if the recommendations are not followed. An example is a follow-up appointment for a child who had an ear infection but now appears to be fine. Such situations should not be considered neglect.

The following are important questions to answer. In most instances, it is necessary to work closely with health care professionals to assess possible medical neglect.

Does the child's condition reflect inadequate health care? The answer is sometimes straightforward, such as when an infant is severely dehydrated and there is a delay in seeking care that aggravates the baby's condition. This question is often difficult to answer, however. A child may have terrible asthma and still have frequent problems, despite doing everything in the medical plan. It is also possible that the medical plan is inadequate, but this would be the physician's responsibility—a different form of medical neglect. One needs to know about the child's health problem and condition, what care was recommended, and what care was received before attributing the problem to inadequate care. Another complicating factor is that often it is not known how much care is "enough." For example, few people take every dose of a course of antibiotics; at times, receiving 80% of the medicine is adequate. Therefore, each case needs to be considered individually to judge whether the partial care is adequate.

How does one know the risk of significant harm? To answer this question, knowledge of the specific child's condition is valuable. For example, it may be clear from past experience that if a child does not receive his or her seizure medicine, a seizure could result. Knowledge of some conditions can also help answer this question. Research has determined, for example, that children with high lead levels are prone to complications; if the problem is left untreated, it is neglect.

How does one assess the different levels of severity of harm? Situations vary enormously. Some are life threatening, whereas others are relatively minor. The specific circumstances and risks need to be weighed in each case to assess the level of severity and determine the appropriate intervention. Less serious situations may be best handled by the health care system and other community agencies, and child protective services should be involved only if the efforts of these agencies do not succeed.

How does one assess single or rare lapses in care? There is a natural inclination to recognize "human fallibility" and accept single lapses in care. It may seem reasonable, for example, that the parent did not appreciate the level of lethargy of the child. It may not be reasonable, however, when a child has been vomiting and in pain for days before medical care is sought. From a child's standpoint, even a single lapse in care could have fatal results. In practice, it is understandable that repeated or chronic lapses in care will be viewed much more seriously.

How does one assess care that may not benefit the child? Medical treatment may be recommended when it is not clear that the child will benefit or the side effects of treatment raise questions regarding the net benefit. An example is experimental treatment for some cancers. Neglect occurs only when it is clear that a child is being denied a significant benefit by not receiving an available treatment.

What if reasons other than parental omissions are responsible for the child being medically neglected? This is often true. An adolescent may refuse to take a medicine. There may be domestic violence contributing to a chaotic home. There may be a lack of health insurance. Physicians may not communicate the plan carefully. These are a few examples of possible contributors to medical neglect. The child, parents, family, and medical system as well as the health problem, the treatment, and the doctor-family relationship and communication need to be assessed to understand why a child's need for medical care is neglected to intervene appropriately.

Parental beliefs about health care based on their religion or culture may result in children not receiving necessary medical attention, sometimes leading to serious harm or death. Most states have "religious exemptions" laws excluding different religious healing practices from being viewed as neglect. The American Academy of Pediatrics, however, has advocated that every child should have access to necessary medical care, and this should be the priority regardless of the parents' religious beliefs. From a child's perspective, the lack of medical care, for any reason, that results in significant harm should be considered medical neglect. When this is due to different religious or cultural beliefs, it is best that the situation be handled with the utmost sensitivity and an attempt to forge a reasonable compromise should be made. Chapter 20, this volume, discusses this difficult dilemma.

■ *Further Reading*

Dubowitz, H. (1999). Neglect of children's health care. In H. Dubowitz (Ed.), *Neglected children: Research, practice and policy.* Thousand Oaks, CA: Sage.

27

How Do I Determine Whether a Child's Nutritional Needs Are Being Met?

■ *Howard Dubowitz*

P arents may feel frustrated that their child is "a picky eater." The concern of inadequate nutrition, however, usually occurs when a health care provider notes that a child's growth pattern is poor, making the diagnosis of "failure to thrive." Using growth charts based on many children, one can follow growth trends for girls and boys. Failure to thrive (FTT) is diagnosed when a child's weight or height decreases below the 5th percentile or across two major percentile lines (e.g., from the 80th to the 40th) or when a child's weight/height (how much the child weighs considering his or her height) decreases below the 10th percentile. Chronic undernutrition may result in short children (height per age lower than the 5th percentile), whereas their weight may appear satisfactory. Physicians have often considered FTT as *organic* when there is a serious medical condition, *nonorganic* when there is no medical condition and the cause is considered to be "psychosocial," or *mixed* when there are both medical and psychosocial problems.

Poor growth, however, does not always reflect poor nutrition. Some medical conditions, such as cyanotic heart disease, can limit growth. Some children are normally small, particularly if they have small parents. Their growth increases with a normal trend, but they remain small. Some children may have had problems while they were fetuses (e.g., infection and exposure to alcohol) and may similarly remain small. Premature infants who are otherwise healthy need to be plotted on special growth charts to account for their true age, and they usually "catch up" by age 3. Young children may not grow well if they do not receive nurturance and warmth, even though they receive enough food. Some small children have none of these factors—their diet appears adequate, and there are no apparent psychosocial problems; thus, it is unclear why their growth is poor. If there are no other problems (e.g., with development), such children are probably "small but normal." These possibilities all need to be considered before concluding that a growth pattern represents inadequate food.

■ How to Assess the Adequacy of the Diet

History

A child may describe frequently being hungry without there being food in the home. Family members, a teacher, and others may support the child's view. Parents may acknowledge the problem of running out of food. Pediatricians can assess whether there are gross deficiencies, such as when children receive excessive fruit juice. Nutritionists may ask a parent about everything the child ate in the past 24 hours to estimate more precisely the adequacy of the diet. Also, children can experience considerable hunger without it affecting their growth.

Observation

A child may be observed by health care professionals, teachers, or others to be obviously hungry, looking for or asking for food. The effect on behavior may be more subtle, such as when a hungry child has difficulty concentrating in school. The physical examination usually reveals little information in cases of mild undernutrition. Certainly, growth may be affected; growth is the most used characteristic. A child may appear pale (anemic). Other physical signs are present if the problem is more severe, including (paradoxically) a large belly, an enlarged liver, and coarse hair.

Deficiencies in specific nutrients (e.g., vitamin D) lead to specific diseases (e.g., rickets) with characteristic findings. Nutritionists may perform more refined measurements of skin folds and the arm circumference to assess nutritional status.

Laboratory Tests

These tests are often done to rule out the possibility of medical problems accounting for poor growth. Tests also sometimes confirm undernutrition, such as when a lack of iron causes anemia or blood protein or zinc levels are low. Very rarely, children who are short lack growth or other hormones.

■ Summary

In summary, caseworkers can obtain useful information from children, family members, and teachers regarding hunger, availability of food, diet, and behavior. Talking to the child's primary health care provider should be valuable, and in more serious cases a nutritionist's evaluation is recommended. Ideally, an interdisciplinary team that is expert in growth and failure to thrive should help assess and manage moderate or severe growth problems. If a child's nutritional needs are not met for any reason, this is a form of neglect. An appropriate response should be tailored to the specific reasons for the inadequate nutrition.

28

What Is Inadequate Supervision?

■ *Diane DePanfilis*

When can a child be left alone? When is lack of supervision neglect? In what circumstances should child protective services intervene? It is known that many children experience inadequate supervision because caregivers are overburdened or overwhelmed, have alcohol or drug problems, are poor and live in poor housing, have conflict with other caregivers, lack adequate child care resources when they are at work, are unable to manage parent-child conflict problems, or all these. It is also known that children who experience inadequate supervision are likely to have psychosocial adjustment problems, such as problems with peer relations and behavior. Intervention will be most successful if we identify and respond to problems early.

■ *Types of Supervision Problems*

1. Child left unattended: A child is left alone unsupervised.
2. Child left in the care of an unsuitable substitute caregiver: The person responsible is unable to provide adequate care (e.g., the child is left in care of young sibling, a known child

abuser, and someone with alcohol or drug addiction problems).

3. Child left in the care of a suitable caregiver but without proper planning or consent: The caregiver leaves the child but does not return when scheduled or has a history of leaving the child without providing essentials for care (e.g., diapers).

4. Caregiver inadequately supervising child: The caregiver is with the child but is unable or unwilling to supervise (e.g., the caregiver is under the influence of alcohol or drugs, is depressed, sleeps during the day, or has inadequate parenting knowledge or skill).

5. Child permitted, encouraged, or not restrained from engaging in harmful activity: The child is locked out of the house or permitted to stay out all night, uses alcohol or drugs, is chronically delinquent, is involved in prostitution, or demonstrates aggressive behavior.

■ Factors to Consider When Determining Whether Inadequate Supervision Is Neglect

Unfortunately, there is no formula to help one to decide when a child can safely be unsupervised. As practitioners that care about children, it is important that we consider a range of possible intervention responses to help caregivers meet the supervision needs of their children. The factors that guide assessment of the nature of supervision are the following:

1. Age of child: A consensus on a standard age by which children can be left unattended has not be achieved. Most professionals agree that children who are under the age of 8 and left alone are definitely neglected, and that children older than age 12 are able to spend 1 or 2 hours alone each day. The following factors need to be considered, particularly when children are between the ages of 8 and 12.

2. Child's personal resources: The child's physical condition and mental abilities, coping capacity, maturity, competence, knowledge about how to respond in an emergency, feelings about being alone, and so on need to be assessed.

3. Degree and format of indirect adult supervision: Is there an adult nearby who is available to the child or in frequent contact with the child by telephone, and has the child been prepared about how to deal with an emergency or threat?
4. Duration and frequency: Is this something that occurs for short periods of time, or is the child left alone all day, every day (e.g., during the summer)? Are the unattended periods during the day or during the night?
5. Nature of the child's residential environment: There is a need to assess the degree of safety in the environment—for example, the level of crime, urban versus rural, access to a telephone, other children in the household, safety of the home, the presence of gangs or groups that encourage delinquent activity, vulnerability in the neighborhood to sexual exploitation or abuse, physical injury, and exposure to substance abuse.

■ Conclusions

Many families need to make arrangements for their children that are not optimal. The number of latchkey children is increasing, not decreasing. The previously discussed factors should be considered in helping families make safe arrangements for their children.

■ Further Reading

Defining child abuse: At what level should we intervene? (1993, Spring). *Virginia Child Protection Newsletter, 39,* 1-7, 10-11, 14-16.
Jones, M. A. (1987). *Parental lack of supervision: Nature and consequence of a major child neglect problem.* Washington, DC: Child Welfare League of America.

29

How Do I Assess Neglect Among At-Risk Adolescents?

■ *Margarete Parrish*

For caseworkers, clinicians, and researchers in the field of child maltreatment, neglect poses some of the thorniest of assessment decisions. The assessment of neglect among adolescents may be further compounded by social norms and by normal adolescent behavior, such as risk taking, defiance, sexual acting out, and rebellion. Typically, neglect is defined with regard to adult or parental omissions in relation to a child's needs. Perhaps neglect is best considered along a continuum and contextually. Many needs are subject to considerable variation. Questions of "ideal" versus "adequate" are not absolutes, particularly regarding adolescents. Specific types of neglect are the same as those for younger children: medical, educational, emotional, and supervisory. Regardless of adolescent status, the basic needs of childhood remain the same (see Table 29.1).

The developmentally normal tasks of adolescence entail developing responsibilities for decision making and increasing autonomy and self-reliance. Their simultaneous needs for supervision, nurturance, and affection continue. Balancing autonomy and supervision can be difficult. Rebellious or apathetic behaviors may create considerable tension between normal needs, parental response, and the clinical assessment of neglect. Crucial aspects of assessment include the following:

■ 137

Table 29.1   Needs of Childhood and Examples of Neglect

Needs	Examples of Neglect
Physical and mental health care	Delay in seeking medical or psychiatric help, failure to sign required surgical consent forms
Education	Knowingly tolerating or colluding with truancy
Emotional well-being	Disregard for self-injurious behavior
Adequate nutrition	Disregard for dietary balance and well-being
Affection, nurturance, support, and stimulation	Failure to visit hospitalized child or teen
Hygiene, housing, and sanitation	Refusal to provide or maintain housing or safety
Protection from hazards in the home and environment	Exposure to hazards (e.g., toxic fumes and illicit drug usage in the home)
Stable and secure home	Refusal to accept custodial responsibilities
Supervision	Abandonment, disregard for well-being

Family education: Are the adolescent's parents adequately informed regarding their teen's developmental, educational, medical, and social needs? Do they clearly understand the implications of their teen's behavior? Are their responses based on misunderstanding, frustration, ignorance, or anger? If so, are they responsive to corrective suggestions? How do the adolescent and the family perceive responsibilities in general? For example, does the teen blame the parent for having "transmitted" his or her diabetes? Is the adolescent functioning at or below an age-appropriate level? Do the parents have unrealistic expectations of an adolescent's adherence to a medical treatment? For example, it may be unrealistic to expect the teen to be responsible for ensuring that prescriptions are kept up-to-date and refilled. Neglect may take the form of parental under-responsibility and, in some cases, overinvolvement at the expense of an adolescent becoming self-sufficient.

Communication: Are the adolescent and his or her family members capable of reasonable and productive communication? Do they have a positive framework for solving differences or problems together? For example, if an adolescent is not taking his or her medicine as prescribed, is a parent able to discuss this in a constructive manner, or is it ignored? Does it become an argument or crisis without being corrected? In such cases, what are the possibilities of establishing improved communication in the interests of a healthier outcome?

High-risk behaviors: What are the rules, roles, and behavioral norms in the family? Does the family abide by consistent rules and consequences of behavior? For example, is a parent aware of an adolescent's choice of friends and sexual partner(s) or of school attendance?

With the increasing autonomy that characterizes adolescence, conflicts often occur regarding parental culpability to supervise and exert control over defiant or self-destructive adolescent behavior. For example, is a parent aware of an adolescent's skipping school to pursue a high-risk sexual relationship? What do the parents know? How do they perceive the problem? What have they tried to do? Is the parental response constructive or counterproductive? Are they responsive to suggestions or alternative problem-solving approaches?

■ Conclusion

Questions of neglect typically include issues of deficient adult attention. The medical and socioeconomic consequences associated with adolescent drug use, exposure to sexually transmitted diseases, and risks of violence have escalated during the past decade. Adolescents and their parents are thus facing increasingly dire consequences of poor judgment as well as actual neglect. Therefore, it is crucial for professionals to take an assertive role in the assessment of and response to neglect as it relates to at-risk adolescents.

Part IV

INITIAL
ASSESSMENT

Section C:
Physical Abuse

30

How Do I Determine Whether a Child Has Been Physically Abused?

■ *Howard Dubowitz*

Chapter 4 on defining physical abuse set the stage for answering this chapter title's question. The key question is "Could this injury have occurred in a nonabusive manner?" There should always be a careful effort to obtain a history from a child and separately from the parent(s) and possible witnesses of what led to the injury. The challenge is to then consider whether the explanation given plausibly explains the physical findings. Different explanations for an injury, sometimes by the same person, suggest that the true history is not being revealed. The following are additional "red flags" in the history suggestive of abuse:

- *History does not reasonably fit with the injury:* Some fractures, for example, require considerable force so that a history of a baby rolling over would be very unlikely to explain the baby's broken femur (thigh bone). It is valuable to know about the child's developmental capabilities to assess the plausibility of some explanations (e.g., an infant climbing out of the crib with the sides up).

- *No history offered:* Perhaps due to denial, perhaps because the person genuinely does not know what happened, or perhaps in an effort to hide abuse, it is common to not receive any history for an injury ("I don't know how this happened"). This requires interviewing all primary caregivers about what might have happened ("Did the baby fall?" and "Did anyone drop the baby?") to explore both abusive and noninflicted trauma.

- *Disclosure of abuse:* If possible, it is critical to interview the child separately (see chapter 16, this volume). Sometimes, other family members, including siblings, disclose what they have witnessed, and occasionally perpetrators acknowledge their acts.

- *Delay in seeking medical care:* Denial about the seriousness of the child's condition, a wish to conceal the abuse, or a hope that the injury will heal without medical care may lead to a delay in seeking medical care. It is also true, however, that with many health problems one's first assessment may be that it is minor. Only when the problem persists or worsens is the need for medical attention clear.

■ Nature of the Injury

For some injuries, the characteristics are quite specific for abuse. For example, an infant with blood around the brain (subdural hematoma), retinal hemorrhages (bleeding in the back of the eyes), and fractures of the long bones strongly indicates shaken baby (or impact) syndrome; there really are no acceptable alternative explanations for this case. Bruises shaped by the implement that caused them or in places that seldom get injured accidentally (e.g., under the neck) may clearly indicate that they were inflicted. Burns with a pattern that can only have resulted from a child being forcibly held in hot water are another example. Nevertheless, the injury alone is often not conclusive, and there is a need to combine the history with the physical findings and pertinent psychosocial information.

■ *Psychosocial Information*

Risk factors for abuse, such as substance abuse, mental health problems, poverty, recent unemployment, domestic violence, and social isolation, provide a context for understanding what may have happened to a child. Although they are rarely conclusive in determining whether abuse occurred, knowledge of the risk factors can contribute to an assessment of what happened. In addition, together with assessing strengths and resources, knowing the risk factors helps guide appropriate interventions.

31

What Medical Evaluation Is Needed When Physical Abuse Is Suspected?

■ *Howard Dubowitz*

The following are needed when physical abuse is suspected:

History of the current incident: The crux of the medical diagnosis of physical abuse is to determine whether the injury is reasonably explained by a mechanism other than inflicted trauma. This means interviewing the child (separately if possible), the parents, and others who may have witnessed the incident. Before discussing the details of the alleged abuse, it is useful to develop a basic understanding of the family, caregiving arrangements, family relationships (e.g., how people get along), views of the child, and approaches to discipline. Regarding the suspected abuse, what happened, who was present, the precipitating events, when and where it occurred, who the child told, and that person's response should be determined. The parents' acceptance of the child's account, level of support, concern about the child's condition, and motivation to protect the child are all important to assess.

Past medical history: The family and the primary care provider should be asked about past health problems, injuries, ingestions, hospital admissions, and visits to emergency departments. This may reveal a worrisome pattern of repeated injuries that could reflect inadequate supervision, abuse, or Munchausen syndrome by proxy (parents simulate or cause injury or illness and repeatedly seek medical care for "the problem"). Talking to the primary health care provider is recommended to obtain the history and to discuss impressions of the family, both positive and negative. Understanding the family situation helps determine whether abuse occurred and is key for guiding appropriate interventions.

Family history: Health problems in the family, such as multiple fractures or easy bruising, may help determine a diagnosis other than abuse. Again, psychosocial problems, such as domestic violence and substance abuse, are areas to probe.

Physical examination: A thorough head-to-toe examination should be done on all children suspected of having been abused. There may be hidden signs of trauma (e.g., bruises in unlikely places) or clues to conditions other than abuse (e.g., blue color to the white part of the eye in children with the genetic bone disease, osteogenesis imperfecta). The child's growth pattern should be checked; poor growth may reflect failure to thrive and possible child neglect. If the child's condition permits, a developmental assessment is often valuable (e.g., Denver Developmental Screening Test). Some of this information can also be obtained from parents. Knowing a child's capabilities helps assess the plausibility of the explanation for the injury (e.g., was the baby able to roll over and off the bed?).

Consultation: Subspecialists can offer valuable assistance in many instances. If there is access to a pediatrician expert in the area of child maltreatment, consultation can help determine the likelihood of abuse. Ophthalmologists are generally consulted to examine the eyes of babies who may have been violently shaken. Depending on the specific problem, consultation with the relevant subspecialist should be considered.

Laboratory tests and special investigations: These studies need to be tailored to the child's age and the specific problem. Children younger than 3 years of age who are thought to have sustained serious trauma should have a complete skeletal survey to check for possible fractures. If the skeletal survey is normal but there remains the clinical suspicion of a recent or subtle fracture, a bone scan is needed. Concern about substantial head trauma warrants a head computed tomography (CT) scan, and head magnetic resonance imaging is generally advisable to detect subtle findings that may be missed on CT and to help determine the timing of an injury. Ultrasound is a useful screen for head trauma in infants. A history of "easy bruising" warrants screening for bleeding problems (prothrombin time, partial thromboplastic time, platelets, and bleeding time) and a careful family history; note that children with bleeding problems can also be abused. In a few children with clinical features (e.g., multiple fractures) of the genetic bone disease osteogenesis imperfecta (OI), a culture of a skin biopsy can help confirm the diagnosis. Usually, the distinction between OI and abuse can be made by the clinical appearance.

In summary, suspected physical abuse requires a comprehensive evaluation (i.e., history, examination, special tests, and consultation) and careful consideration of alternate explanations for the child's injury.

32

How Do I Interpret Medical Tests for Physical Abuse?

■ *John M. Leventhal*

The purposes of ordering medical tests in the evaluation of suspected physical abuse are to determine

1. The cause of the child's injury or problem: Is the injury due to an abusive or unintentional (accidental) event, or is there a medical explanation for the child's problem?
2. The location and severity of the injury and whether other parts of the body are involved: This information can help the clinicians decide on the appropriate therapy, such as casting of a fracture or drainage of a subdural hematoma (bleeding around the brain), and on the child's prognosis.
3. The age of the injuries, which can help in deciding whether abuse has occurred.

The following types of tests can be helpful in the evaluation:
- X rays (or tests of diagnostic imaging because some of the tests do not actually use X rays)
- Ophthalmologic examination
- Blood tests
- Special tests (e.g., skin biopsy)

■ *X Rays*

X rays or diagnostic imaging can be used to evaluate the bones, the head, and the abdomen and chest.

Bones

An X ray of an injured area of the body can provide information about the presence of a fractured bone, the type of fracture (e.g., transverse [through the shaft of the bone] and spiral [spiraling around the shaft]), the location of the fracture on the bone, the age of the fracture, and whether the bones appear normal or have an underlying problem, such as osteogenesis imperfecta (or brittle bone disease), that makes them more susceptible to break. Certain types of fractures are particularly worrisome for abuse, including the following:

- Fractures in children who are not walking (although such children can be injured from falls from beds, down stairs, from parent's arms, etc.)
- Rib fractures, especially rib fractures that occur posteriorly (or adjacent to the spine)
- Corner fractures near the growth plate of bones, such as the tibia (large bone in lower leg) and femur (thigh bone)

The X ray can provide information that allows an estimate of the age of the fracture: acute or recent, 10 to 14 days old, or at least several weeks old. An acute or recent fracture shows the fracture line and, if seen shortly after the event, may show swelling surrounding the fracture. The first sign of healing that can be seen on an X ray is the formation of callus or new bone, and this occurs approximately 10 to 14 days after a bone is broken. As the healing becomes more pronounced (evidenced by more extensive callus formation), the injury is estimated to be several weeks old.

A skeletal survey includes X rays of all the bones in the body. This can be a particularly helpful test to determine whether the child has other fractures (either acute or healing) that are not suspected from the clinical examination. This test is ordered if the child has a fracture or another injury, such as a subdural hematoma, that is possibly due to abuse. The test usually is not ordered in children older than 36 months of age because of the very low yield. In younger children, depending on the original injury, the skeletal survey is positive in 5% to 35% of cases. Such a finding is particularly important because it indicates that there are other unexplained injuries in addition to the original worrisome injury.

At some medical centers, another test that can be used to detect fractures is a bone scan. In this test, a radioactive substance is injected intravenously into the bloodstream and then localizes at fractures sites. This test often is used to search for new rib fractures, which can be difficult to detect by X ray until callus formation occurs 10 to 14 days after the injury.

Head

X rays can determine whether a bone of the skull is fractured or whether there is soft tissue swelling on the outside of the skull. X rays, however, cannot show the brain and therefore are less helpful than other tests, including computed tomography (CT) and magnetic resonance imaging (MRI).

CT can provide information about the brain, the skull bones, and tissue swelling outside the skull. A CT provides images of the head in thin slices so that details of the anatomy can be examined. A CT is necessary to detect injuries of the brain, such as subdural hematomas (bleeding around the brain), intracerebral hematomas (bleeding in the brain tissue), or swelling of the brain tissue. A CT also can be useful in estimating the age of the injury. Because CT scanners are widely available, the CT is the test of choice in evaluating children with suspected head injuries.

A MRI is the best test to detect small areas of bleeding in or around the brain and to follow the progression or resolution of an injury of the brain. Thus, a MRI can be helpful in determining the child's prognosis related to the brain injuries. In conjunction with the CT, the MRI can be helpful in estimating the age of the injury. Like the CT, the MRI provides images of the head in thin slices. Young children often need to be sedated or given anesthesia so that they will not move during the scan.

Abdomen and Chest

CT or MRI scans can provide detailed information about internal injuries, such as lacerations of the liver or spleen.

■ Ophthalmologic Examination

An eye exam by an ophthalmologist is requested when a young child has an injury of the head that might be due to shaken baby syndrome. The ophthalmologist dilates the pupils and examines the retina (back of the eye) for signs of retinal hemorrhages (bleeding). Such hemorrhages occur very infrequently in accidental head injuries but very commonly in infants with shaken baby syndrome. This examination of the eyes is also commonly requested as part of an evaluation of an infant whose major injury does not affect the head but there is concern about possible abuse.

■ Blood Tests

Hemoglobin

Almost every child admitted to the hospital takes a hemoglobin test to determine whether the child is anemic. In children with internal bleeding (e.g., in the head, abdomen, and thigh), the hemoglobin often is low. If it is dangerously low, a child may require a transfusion.

Clotting Tests

Blood tests (including platelet count, prothrombin time, partial thromboplastic time, and bleeding time) can be helpful in determining whether the child's blood clots normally or whether the child has a medical condition that predisposes the child to easy bleeding and bruising. For example, children with very low platelet counts often have areas of bleeding into the skin that may look like multiple bruises from physical abuse.

In some children with serious brain injuries, the fresh tissue damage in the brain can result in abnormal clotting studies. When these studies are repeated later in the course of the child's recovery, they are normal, indicating that the clotting abnormality was the result and not the cause of the head injury.

■ *Special Tests*

Many special tests and consultations with pediatric specialists can be obtained when evaluating a child with an injury suspicious for child abuse. For example, a genetic consultation from an expert in the areas of genetics, diseases of metabolism, and congenital abnormalities can sometimes be helpful in determining whether the child's growth failure is due to an underlying problem or a failure to provide the child with adequate calories. A test that should be discussed is a skin biopsy.

Skin Biopsy

Osteogenesis imperfecta (OI; brittle bones) is a very rare disease in which bones are more susceptible than normal bones to break from minor trauma. Although this disease can usually be detected by examination of the child and a review of the X rays, mild forms of the disease may occasionally be confused with child abuse. To confirm the diagnosis of OI or to distinguish between abuse and OI, it is helpful to obtain a skin biopsy from the child. This biopsy is sent to a special laboratory in which the fibroblast cells in the skin are grown and then tested to determine if the disease is present. In 85% of individuals with clinical signs of the disease, the test is positive for OI.

■ *Further Reading*

Feldman, K. W. (1997). Evaluation of physical abuse. In M. E. Helfer, R. S. Kempe, & R. D. Krugman (Eds.), *The battered child* (5th ed., pp. 175-220). Chicago: University of Chicago Press.

Smith, W. L. (1997). Imaging in child abuse. In M. E. Helfer, R. S. Kempe, & R. D. Krugman (Eds.), *The battered child* (5th ed., pp. 221-247). Chicago: University of Chicago Press.

33

What Conditions May Be Mistaken for Physical Abuse?

■ *Charles F. Johnson*

■ *What Types of Conditions May Be Mistaken for Abuse?*

A child with a variety of conditions may appear to have been injured. Determining the type of injury is generally easier than determining if the injury was self-inflicted, inflicted intentionally, or noninflicted. Types of injuries include burning with heat and caustics, impacting, puncturing, cutting, tattooing, pinching, freezing, suction, and ligating or binding. Children may be accidentally or intentionally injured by a variety of means. Because the body surface of skin is most accessible to the child, caretakers, and the environment, it is important to recognize birthmarks, self-inflicted trauma, and common inflicted and noninflicted injuries and to understand how the skin reacts to trauma.

■ *Bruises and Other Color Marks*

Bruises are the most common manifestations of injury seen by hospital-based pediatricians who report abuse, and the hand is the most "available" instrument used to explore the environment and mete out discipline and anger. Individuals who care for children must be familiar with how bruises form, their color changes, typical marks from the open hand and fist, and those body surfaces most likely to be injured by intent and accident.

Bruise colors include black, blue, red, purple, green, yellow, and brown. Birthmarks or paint and stains of these colors may be mistaken for injury. Mongolian spots are slate blue birthmarks that are most commonly found on the back and buttocks of dark-skinned infants, but they may appear on any part of the body. Capillary hemangiomas, or "stork bites," are red birthmarks that appear on the base of the nose and nape of the neck. Both types of birthmarks fade by 6 years of age and may have been noted on birth records. They are easily differentiated from bruises that fade by 14 to 21 days and undergo color changes as they resolve. Pigmented nevi, another form of birthmark, can range from deep black and blue to light brown (café au lait) in color. They do not resolve in time. Dark-skinned children may show patches of vitiligo or loss of skin pigment, which may resemble depigmented scars from burns or other trauma. Dark-skinned children may also have scars with increased pigment.

■ Impact and Skin Color Change

A mild impact to the skin will cause blood vessels to enlarge, resulting in erythema or redness that fades in hours. More severe impact results in rupture of blood vessels. Small ruptures cause petechiae (or dot-like bruises), and large ruptures cause bruises over a wider area. A variety of infectious diseases may cause erythema or petechiae. Their location and association with systemic symptoms including fever should decrease the possibility of a misdiagnosis of intentional injury. As blood vessels dilate, fluid leaks out, causing edema or swelling. A hive, which results from erythema and edema, can be blanched by putting pressure on the skin. Children, peers, or caretakers can apply various pigments to a child's skin. Applied colors generally are easily removed. Dyes such as henna may persist for weeks. Puncturing the skin with pigment (tattooing) is an unusual form of inflicted injury and results in deep and permanent color changes.

■ *Burns*

Heated skin will turn red (erythema or first-degree burn) and then blister or vesiculate (second-degree burn). In third-degree burns, caused by higher temperature and longer exposure, the skin may be charred from flames or white and senseless from scalds. The burn source may be from a heated object, which will leave an imprint, or hot liquid or caustic that may flow or splash. Lime and garlic juice may erode the skin, resulting in what appears to be a burn. Severe diaper dermatitis from monilia (yeast) may involve the entire diaper area with bright red skin in a pattern that suggests an immersion burn. At the edge of the red area, red papules or satellites are seen and represent new colonies of yeast. Immersion burns have a straight or slightly wavy border and spare skin creases that are protected when the child flexes various body parts.

■ *Allergy, Infection, and Poor Hygiene*

Any redness from allergy, infection, or poor hygiene in the anal or genital region may be mistaken for redness from sexual abuse. Lichen sclerosis, an unusual skin disease that causes redness and fragile skin in the genital area, should not be mistaken for genital trauma. Falls rarely tear the hymen. A torn hymen is diagnostic of penetration. The most common infectious disease resulting in vesicles (fluid-containing bumps) is chicken pox. In bacterial infections that cause vesicles, the skin is tender, and the fluid is thicker and generally yellow. The size of craters from healing chicken pox vary and are generally 3 or 4 mm in diameter. If the lesions are scratched, they become larger. Impetigo, a common skin infection, begins as a papule (skin bump) that progresses to a pustule (bump with yellow or white pus). When the pustule ruptures, the red pit left in the skin may resemble the round red pit that results when a blister from a cigarette burn ruptures. Generally, impetigo occurs in clusters, and the primary lesion, a small pustule, is generally present. Scratching the lesions thickens the skin and spreads the infection. Insect bites, which are found on exposed skin surfaces, begin as small, red macules (flat skin mark) that may progress to papules or vesicles. Children may dig at the bites with their fingers, causing deeper excoriation and infection. Tinea corporus, or ringworm of the skin, begins as a red papule and expands in an irregular raised circle with scales. As the center of the lesion clears, the borders may resemble the arch of a human bite mark.

The green and yellow color pattern of resolving bruises is not seen in other skin diseases. A caregiver may claim that a child bruises easily. This observation is generally for a fair-skinned child, who shows bruises more readily than a dark-skinned child. Laboratory tests can rule out bleeding problems. In rare bleeding disorders such as hemophilia, the blood vessel must be traumatized for bleeding to occur. Children with hemophilia are at increased risk for abuse, as are children with other chronic diseases who stress their parent's emotional and financial resources. Parents may claim that a baby with multiple fractures easily breaks his or her bones. Osteogenesis imperfecta, in which bones are fragile, exists in mild to severe forms. A normal family history for fractures, review of bones fractured, normal bone mineralization, and otherwise normal physical examination should rule out this very rare condition. A skin biopsy can establish the diagnosis with 85% certainty.

■ Unusual Marks

Children may puncture or lacerate themselves intentionally or unintentionally. Retarded or emotionally disturbed children may self-mutilate. Deep scratching may create lines that may be mistaken for lacerations from cords. The marks from an intentional scratch are linear but narrower than expected from an adult hand, and they are found only on areas of the body that the child can reach. A child may apply suction marks. The oval-shaped bruises appear on parts of the body the child can reach with his or her mouth. Sucker ("love") bites may be applied by perpetrators in Munchausen syndrome by proxy and during sexual abuse. The marks are larger than those from a child's mouth. Intentional smothering with a soft object, which can cause brain damage or death, results in autopsy findings that cannot be distinguished from those of sudden infant death syndrome. Occasionally, adult hand marks are found on the face of a child who was smothered. Strangling about the neck causes petechiae of the face; straining during coughing or vomiting may cause a similar pattern of petechiae.

■ *How to Examine the Skin*

When examining the skin, all lesions should be carefully mapped on a drawing of the body. The pattern, shape, size, and location are helpful in determining the cause. When questions exist about the cause of an injury, medical consultation should be sought. The pattern of marks and surfaces injured may suggest intentional injury. Leading body surfaces, such as the brow, shins, elbows, and forearms, are more likely to be injured in accidents. The protected genitalia and anus are rarely injured unintentionally. Attention needs to be paid to the structures underlying the skin. Blows to the skin may result in trauma to deeper structures, such as muscles, bones, and other organs. The curved pattern of tear-shaped knuckle marks on the abdomen may overlie a ruptured liver, spleen, or bowel.

■ *The History May Help Make the Diagnosis*

Reporting accidental, congenital, or self-inflicted injury as child abuse will have adverse consequences to the child and family. In contrast, the failure to recognize and report child abuse will have adverse affects on the child and the professional. The history of how the injury occurred must be evaluated to determine if it is in keeping with the child's developmental level and the injury. One should report suspected child abuse to appropriate agencies when an injury is not congruent with the history or the child's development. Injuries that are commonly or easily preventable should be reported as "safety neglect." Children who are older than 3 years of age have sufficient language ability and should be asked about the cause of the injury.

■ *Further Reading*

Johnson, C. F. (1990). Inflicted injury vs. accidental injury: The diagnosis of inflicted injury. *Pediatric Clinics of North America, 37,* 791.

Oates, R. K. (1984). Overturning the diagnosis of child abuse. *Archives of Diseases of Childhood, 9,* 665-667.

Schwartz, A. J., & Ricci, L. R. (1996). How accurately can bruises be aged in abused children? Literature review and synthesis. *Pediatrics, 97,* 254-257.

Vorenberg, E. (1992, June). Diagnosing child abuse: The cost of getting it wrong. *Archives of Dermatology, 128,* 844-845.

Wardinsky, T. D., Vizcarrondo, F. E., & Cruz, B. K. (1995). The mistaken diagnosis of child abuse: A three-year usual medical center analysis and literature review. *Military Medicine, 160,* 15-20.

34

What Are the Telltale Differences Between Abusive and Noninflicted Injuries?

■ *Charles F. Johnson*

The skin (see Chapter 33, this volume) and other organs have limited responses to trauma. A history must be obtained for every injury sustained by a child. Parents who injure their children, however, rarely give an accurate or truthful history. They may avoid bringing children with minor injuries to medical attention or delay seeking attention for more severe injuries, hoping that they may heal. Children with new injuries must be thoroughly examined to search for old injuries. Deep skin injuries heal with a scar that mimics the shape of the offending instrument. Fractures may heal so completely that they cannot be detected. If healing fractures or injury scars are found, in addition to acute injuries, this suggests "child abuse syndrome" or inflicted injuries that have occurred on more than one occasion. The mark from an object wielded by a perpetrator may not be different from a mark that results when the child runs into or falls onto the object. In the latter case, the force of impact by the child will depend on the child's weight, speed, and distance traveled to the object as well as the character of the surface struck. Similarly, marks from instruments wielded by a perpetrator will also depend on the characteristics of the surface and the force used for hitting the child. If the injury has the shape of a hand, paddle, cord, spoon, shoe, or pan, it is unlikely that the child ran into or fell onto the object. Impact marks from falling on toys will mirror the shape of the toy edge contacting the skin.

■ *Child Development and Recognizing Child Abuse*

One must be familiar with child development to determine if the history of an injury is credible. Perpetrators may blame the child or a sibling for causing an injury. They may state that the child rolled off the bed, crawled or ran into an object, fell down stairs, or turned on hot water or turned off cold water. If the child's development, or tested capability (some children are advanced, whereas others are delayed), is not compatible with the history, inflicted injury must be suspected.

■ *Vulnerable Body Parts*

The leading edges of the body, such as the shins, forearms, and brow, are most likely to be injured in falls. Children who are running generally fall forward. The buttocks and thighs, back, ears, upper arms, and genitalia are areas most likely to be injured by caregivers.

The pattern of a burn also indicates its origin. Stocking, glove, and diaper area burns that spare areas of the body that are protected by flexion are likely due to immersion. This burn pattern and a lack of splash marks are diagnostic of an immersion burn.

Highly suspect injuries for child abuse include metaphyseal, rib, scapula, and sternum fractures and spiral fractures of the legs or arms in preambulating children. Falls rarely cause geometric, patterned, paired, or symmetrical burns or bruises. A blow to the nose or forehead (which leaves a mark) can cause the soft tissue around both eyes to bruise (black eyes). A basal skull fracture can cause bruises about the eyes or behind the ears.

A caregiver may claim that a child became unconscious after a fall from a bed, table, or chair. If the child's head struck an object during the fall, one would expect to see the mark of the object on the skin. A young child with no external signs of injury who is reported to have been well and then suddenly becomes unconscious and requires resuscitation is likely to have been shaken. Examination in the hospital will reveal subdural (the dura is a covering over the brain) bleeding, often between the two halves of the brain (interfalcine), and retinal (eye) hemorrhages. A fall from 3 feet onto a lightly carpeted floor, as determined by several studies, does not result in death or serious central nervous system injury, such as unconsciousness, apnea (a period without breathing), and seizures. Rarely, such a fall may cause a simple skull, clavicle, or humerus fracture. A fall to cement requires less distance for a fracture to occur.

■ Changing Stories

After caregivers have obtained legal consultation, the original story may change or be denied. A careful record of each history is necessary to document this behavior. Neglect must be considered in all poisonings, especially those with mind-altering drugs. Caregivers on medication may intentionally give children their medications to change the children's behavior. Such drugs may impair judgment, coordination, and balance. Cases in which children are not in proper and required restraints and are involved in auto accidents should be reported for safety neglect.

■ Summary

One must approach each injury of a child with an open but suspicious mind about possible causes. A detailed history, with a time line and verification of all data from other sources, should be carefully recorded on specific forms that ensure that all information is collected and all necessary laboratory work ordered. The size, shape, age, color, and cause of each injury should be charted along with details of the child's developmental capabilities.

■ *Further Reading*

Brewster, A. L., Nelson, J. P., Hymel, K. P., Colby, D. R., Lucas, D. R., McCanne, T. R., & Milner, J. S. (1998). Victim, perpetrator, family, and incident characteristics of 32 infant maltreatment deaths in the United States Air Force. *CAN, 22*, 91-101.

Chadwick, D. L., Chin, S., Salerno, C., et al. (1991). Deaths from falls in children: How far is fatal? *Journal of Trauma, 31*, 1353.

Johnson, C. F., & Showers, J. C. (1985). Injury variables in child abuse. *CAN, 9*, 207.

Ludwig, S., & Kornberg, A. E. (1992). *Child abuse: A medical reference.* New York: Churchill Livingstone.

Nimityongskul, P., & Anderson, L. (1987). The likelihood of injuries when children fall out of bed. *Journal of Pediatrics and Orthopedics, 7*, 184.

35

What Is Shaken Baby Syndrome?

■ *John M. Leventhal*

S haken baby syndrome (SBS) refers to a constellation of symptoms and signs that occur after an infant, usually less than 1 year of age, has been violently shaken. Such an infant often has bleeding around the brain, bleeding in the back of the eyes, and other signs of abuse, such as bruises and fractures.

■ *Presenting Symptoms and Signs*

Infants with SBS may be brought to the physician because of irritability, decreased appetite, vomiting, or sleepiness. In more severe cases, the child may be unresponsive and have seizures or difficulty breathing. Important clues on the physical examination include irritability, lethargy or coma, a bulging anterior fontanelle (soft spot on the head), an enlarged head circumference, seizures, decreased frequency of breathing or even apnea (periods of not breathing), and bruises. Because parents do not provide information about the shaking when the child is first brought for care, other diagnoses, such as gastroenteritis and meningitis, are sometimes considered, and the diagnosis of SBS can be delayed. When the parents do provide a history of trauma, it is often of a minor fall, such as a fall from the couch; the injuries from this type of fall are not consistent with the kinds of injuries suffered in SBS.

■ Making the Diagnosis

Because infants with SBS often are very sick (and may even die), clinicians will first stabilize the child by giving medications to control seizures and ensuring that the child is breathing at a normal rate; this sometimes requires inserting a breathing tube and placing the child on a ventilator (breathing machine). The following diagnostic tests can be helpful:

Computed tomography (CT) and magnetic resonance imaging (MRI): The diagnosis of SBS is usually made by CT when subdural or subarachnoid hemorrhages (bleeding around the brain) are noted. Additional findings include evidence of fractures of the bones of the skull, bleeding in the brain, shearing injuries of the brain, and brain swelling. Findings on the CT and MRI can help estimate the age of the injury and determine whether there was a single episode or more than one episode of bleeding. The MRI is also helpful in detecting smaller areas of bleeding in the brain and in following the progression or resolution of the abnormalities.

Ophthalmologic evaluation: In approximately 75% of children with SBS, there is evidence of retinal hemorrhages (bleeding in the back of the eye). These hemorrhages usually resolve within several weeks and usually do not affect the child's ability to see.

Skeletal survey: The most frequently noted fractures in children with SBS are rib fractures. These fractures are usually located posteriorly next to the spine or laterally. At the time of the diagnosis of SBS, the rib fractures often have callus formation, indicating that these fractures are healing and at least 10 to 14 days old. Healing fractures of the ribs and an acute subdural hematoma indicate that the child has been abused on at least two different occasions. There may also be evidence of fractures of other bones.

■ How SBS Occurs

The injuries of a child with SBS are due to violent shaking of the infant; in many cases, the child's head is also struck on a hard surface, such as a mattress or a crib railing. The abuser is often a male caretaker, such as the father, stepfather, or mother's boyfriend, but can also be the mother or baby-sitter. The injuries occur when the adult becomes frustrated with the infant's behaviors, such as crying or spitting, grabs the infant under the arms, loses control, and vigorously shakes the baby. During the shaking, the infant's head snaps back and forth causing shearing strains that result in bleeding around the brain and injuries in the brain. Some experts believe that shaking alone is not enough to cause the bleeding and the injuries in the head; these experts believe that the damage occurs due to the rotational forces when the infant's head strikes a firm surface. Skull fractures occur when the infant's head strikes a hard object. The rib fractures occur from the squeezing of the rib cage. Normal care of children, including playful tossing of an infant in the air, does not cause SBS.

■ Prognosis

SBS is the major cause of death due to abuse in young children. Of the children who survive, many have moderate or severe neurological symptoms, including seizures, mental retardation, learning disabilities, motor abnormalities, and visual impairments.

■ Further Reading

Duhaime, A. C., Christian, C. W., Rorke, L. B., & Zimmerman, R. A. (1998). Nonaccidental head injury in children—The "shaken-baby syndrome." *New England Journal of Medicine, 338,* 1822-1829.

Feldman, K. W. (1997). Evaluation of physical abuse. In M. E. Helfer, R. S. Kempe, & R. D. Krugman (Eds.), *The battered child* (5th ed., pp. 175-220). Chicago: University of Chicago Press.

Reece, R. M., & Kirschner, R. H. (1998, Summer). *Shaken baby syndrome/shaken impact syndrome* (pp. 4-5). Ogden, UT: National Information, Support, and Referral Service on Shaken Baby Syndrome. (Child Abuse Prevention Center of Utah, 2955 Harrison Blvd., Suite 102, Ogden, UT 84403; phone: 888-273-0071; website: *www.capcenter.org*)

36

How Do I Assess Possible Histories of Physical Abuse Among Assaultive Adolescents?

■ *Margarete Parrish*

Adolescents are a remarkably heterogeneous and unpredictable population. Not all abused adolescents become aggressive or assaultive, nor have all assaultive or aggressive adolescents been abused. Thoughtful, comprehensive assessments are necessary to serve the needs of assaultive adolescents and to diminish the likelihood of a subsequent assaultive adulthood or abusive parenthood.

By definition, assaultive incidents are more than outbursts of unmanaged temper and impulsivity, and they represent a variety of problem behaviors and circumstances. Ironically, despite clear indications that adolescent court involvement, ungovernable behavior, delinquency, and substance abuse are often associated with child abuse histories, such adolescents are more likely to be routed through the juvenile justice system than the child protection system.

The role of social work in the assessment of assaultive adolescents is crucial to address the context in which violence occurs. A comprehensive assessment necessarily requires multiple historians and considerable finesse. Ideally, teachers, siblings, parents, and neighbors will contribute. Whether the nature of the assault is physical or sexual, the use of violence must be considered in terms of physical, cognitive, social, and moral development along with the environment and possible psychopathology.

■ *Cognitive*

Is the adolescent intellectually capable of understanding the nature of his or her behavior and its consequences? In cases of mental retardation or borderline intellectual functioning, such factors necessarily guide treatment decisions. Adolescents with histories of abuse (including prenatal drug exposure and childhood head injuries) frequently do not achieve their academic potential and may be misperceived. Intellectual testing may be necessary to establish cognitive limitations.

■ *Development*

Is the adolescent functioning at or below an age-appropriate level for problem solving? Problems with self-management, impulse control, social skills, and anger management are frequently noted among children with abuse histories. Does the behavior reflect prolonged parent-child separations, social isolation, or early deprivation that may impede secure attachment? Does the assaultive behavior reflect a long-standing history of antisocial behavior or a recent development? An early onset of antisocial behavior generally indicates a worse prognosis, especially among adolescent males.

■ *Environment*

Has the adolescent been exposed to violence (against himself or herself or within the family) to such an extent that violence is perceived as an acceptable means of expressing frustration or resolving problems? Relevant histories include exposure to multiple types of violence and exposure to parental substance abuse or criminality. Who are their role models? What behavioral norms do they admire? Ideally, multiple sources of information apply to such an assessment, including family members, neighbors, medical records, and academic and community resources.

Open-ended questions such as "What happens in your home when there is disagreement?" and "What do you consider the most difficult situation you've ever experienced, and who or what helped you to cope?" may elicit adolescent perspectives on family and environmental norms. Questions of exposure to neighborhood violence and media depictions of violence are also pertinent. Parents', siblings', and peers' views on the adolescent's history of responding to threats or difficulties are typically informative.

In cases of juvenile sexual assaults, adolescents should also be assessed for prior sexual trauma. Sexual assault offenders of all ages are substantially more likely to have physical or sexual abuse histories.

■ Psychological

Does the adolescent manifest symptoms of psychopathology? If so, does this influence his or her culpability for the assaultive behavior? The diagnoses most frequently involved include conduct disorders, reactive attachment disorders, depression, intermittent explosive disorder, posttraumatic stress disorder, substance abuse (especially of cocaine and steroids), and psychotic disorders including schizophrenia.

In any case involving assaultive adolescent behavior, a comprehensive mental health assessment is indicated to establish the presence of suicidal, homicidal, or psychotic features. Such factors necessarily need consideration in terms of how an adolescent may be expected to respond to various stressors and in terms of treatment planning.

■ Conclusion

Because assaultive adolescent behavior frequently reflects severe problems with early origins, the sooner such children are recognized and helped, the better the outcome. By adolescence, these children typically are a very troubled and troubling population with tremendous needs. Effective intervention necessarily begins with a thorough, thoughtful, and accurate assessment.

■ *Further Reading*

Chafin, M., Bonner, B., Worley, K., & Lawson, L. (1996). Treating abused adolescents. In J. Briere, L. Berliner, J. Bulkley, C. Jenny, & T. Reid (Eds.), *The APSAC handbook on child maltreatment* (pp. 119-139). Thousand Oaks, CA: Sage.

Raine, A. (1993). Familial influences. In *The psychopathology of crime* (pp. 243-266). San Diego, CA: Academic Press.

Wolfe, D. (1997). Children exposed to marital violence. In O. Barnett, C. Miller-Perrin, & R. Perrin (Eds.), *Family violence across the lifespan* (pp. 133-157). Thousand Oaks, CA: Sage.

Part IV

INITIAL
ASSESSMENT

Section D:
Sexual Abuse

37

How Do I Determine If a Child Has Been Sexually Abused?

■ *Joyce A. Adams*

A suspicion of child sexual abuse usually arises in one of the following ways, and the approach to investigation may be slightly different in each case:

1. A child has made a statement that he or she has experienced some type of sexual contact with an adult or another child.

2. A parent or another caregiver has either observed certain behaviors that raise the suspicion of abuse or has noticed physical findings, such as redness of the genital or anal area, complaints of pain, or blood or discharge on the child's underclothes.

3. A health care provider has discovered evidence of an infection that may have been sexually transmitted or has found something that he or she thinks is abnormal on the examination.

4. A child in therapy for other reasons has made a statement that may indicate that he or she has been abused, has made drawings that raise suspicion, or has indicated in doll play that something may have happened.

5. A child has had contact with someone who is suspected of sexually abusing another child in the home or in another child care setting.

6. A child was found or accused of perpetrating sexual abuse on another child.

■ *What You Need to Ask to Help Determine Whether or Not Abuse Has Occurred*

The following questions should be asked when attempting to determine whether abuse has occurred:

1. Who is reporting that the child has said something? Beware of separated or divorced parents who are accusing one another or angry grandparents who want custody.

2. Who is reporting suspicious physical findings? If the report is from a health care provider who notices signs of possible infection or injury, is this person experienced in examining young children's genitalia? Medical providers who do not routinely examine the genitalia of young children may not be aware that there are many normal findings for the appearance of the genitalia and anus. Has the medical provider checked his or her impressions with someone else in the community who is an expert in evaluating possible sexual abuse? Is the provider aware of conditions that may be mistaken for abuse? (see Table 37.1).

3. What exactly did the child say? Beware of young children using terms that are too sophisticated for their level of development. A 3-year-old, for example, would be unlikely to describe sexual touching as "My dad has been sexually molesting me" but rather would probably say something such as "Dad hurts my pee-pee." Can the child give details as to place, time, and what may have been said by the alleged abuser? (Refer to the section on interviewing.)

4. When did the child make a statement, start showing behaviors, or develop the symptoms that are causing concern? What else was occurring in the child's life at the time? Had someone been repeatedly asking the child if he or she had been abused? Was it a spontaneous remark? Was the child being treated for any type of medical condition that might

cause genital or anal irritation? Has the child been exposed to X-rated movies or videos or witness to adult sexual activity that led to sexualized acting out behavior?

5. Where does the child say that the alleged molestation took place? Does it make sense that molestation could have occurred in that setting? Is it possible that the child is describing genital touching that was not of a sexual nature, such as cleansing or application of medication?

■ Putting All the Information Together

A spontaneous, clear, detailed, and consistent statement from a child that describes sexual abuse in terms appropriate to that child's developmental level is the best evidence that abuse has occurred. If information on specific behavior changes and examination and laboratory findings are also available, it is helpful to use a system to integrate all the information.

Too much emphasis has been placed on the medical examination findings of children who describe being sexually molested. Most kinds of touching leave no signs. Genital touching, genital rubbing, oral genital contact, rubbing of the anal area, or even having objects inserted into the anus usually cause no injury, and a perfectly normal examination is to be expected. Nonspecific findings, such as redness of the genital or anal area or discharge from the vagina, can also be caused by many other conditions besides sexual abuse and should not be overinterpreted. If the suspicion of abuse is based solely on a medical provider's examination findings, it is highly recommended that a second opinion be sought by a specialist in child sexual abuse medical evaluation as soon as possible.

A two-part system for classifying genital findings and determining the overall likelihood of sexual abuse has been published (Adams, 1997). An abbreviated form of this classification system is shown in Table 37.1.

Table 37.1   Two-Part System for Classifying Genital Findings and Determining the Overall Likelihood of Sexual Abuse

---

Part 1: Interpretation of genital and anal findings

Class I: Normal

Tags, bumps, or mounds on the edge of the hymen

Thickening of the hymen due to estrogen

Clefts or notches in the upper half of the hymen when the child is examined supine (on her back)

Pale area in the midline of the posterior fourchette below the hymen

Class II: Nonspecific or normal variants—findings that may be the result of sexual abuse, depending on the timing of the examination with respect to the abuse, but that may also be due to other causes or may be variants of normal

Redness of the genital or anal tissues

Vaginal discharge (may or may not be due to a sexually transmitted infection—must await testing)

Labial adhesions (sticking together of the labia majora or outer lips)

Genital warts (condyloma) in the vaginal or anal area in a child younger than 2 years of age (may have been acquired from the mother at birth)

Anal skin tags or smooth areas in the midline around the anus

Dark pigmentation around the anus or a purple coloration caused by venous congestion

Flattening or irregular appearance of the anal skin folds

Class III: Concerning for abuse—findings that have been noted in children with documented abuse, and may be suspicious for abuse, but for which insufficient data exists to indicate that abuse is the only cause

Very large hymenal opening as determined by measurements taken from colposcopic photographs or slides and compared to the normal sizes that have been published

Dilation of the anus of 2.0 cm or more, documented on photographs or slides (highly recommended), with measurements taken from the photos and with no stool seen in the rectal vault

Notches or clefts (sharp indentations) in the lower rim of the hymen, with the child supine (on her back)

Genital warts (condyloma) in children older than age 2 years, proven by biopsy (highly recommended)

Bruising or abrasions of the genital or anal tissues with no clear history of accident

Class IV: Suggestive of abuse or penetration— findings that can reasonably be explained only by postulating that abuse or penetrating injury has occurred

Scars of the posterior fourchette or anal area

Fresh laceration of the posterior fourchette not involving the hymen

Class V: Clear evidence of blunt force or penetrating trauma—findings that have no explanation other than trauma to the hymen or perianal tissues

Fresh laceration of the hymen or bruising of the hymen

Fresh laceration of the perianal tissues beyond the external anal sphincter

Areas where the hymen has been torn through all the way to the base so that there is no tissue remaining between the vagina and the vestibular wall

Part 2: Likelihood of sexual abuse based on the psychosocial and medical information

Class I: No evidence of abuse

    Normal exam, no history, no behavioral changes, no witnessed abuse

    Nonspecific findings with another known or likely explanation and no history of abuse or behavior changes

    Child considered at risk for sexual abuse but gives no history and has only nonspecific behavior changes

    Physical findings of injury consistent with history of accidental injury, which is clear and believable

Class II: Possible abuse

    Class I or II findings in combination with significant behavior changes, especially sexualized behaviors, but child unable to give a history of abuse

    Condyloma acuminata or herpes type I anogenital lesions in a prepubertal child in the absence of a history of abuse and with an otherwise normal examination

    Statement by child not sufficiently detailed, given the child's developmental level, or not consistent

    Class III findings with no disclosure of abuse or behavior changes

Class III: Probable abuse

    Child gives a clear, consistent and detailed description of being molested, with or without physical findings

    Class IV findings in a child, with or without a history of abuse and with no history of accidental penetrating injury

    Positive culture (not rapid antigen test) for chlamydia trachomatis (child older than 2 years), positive culture for herpes type II, positive test for trichomonas

Class IV: Definite evidence of abuse or sexual contact

    Class V physical findings with no history of accident

    Finding sperm or seminal fluid in or on a child's body

    Pregnancy (from nonconsensual intercourse)

    Positive cultures for gonorrhea or positive test for syphilis or HIV, for which sexual transmission is the only possible way the child could have contracted the infection

    Witnessed abuse or cases in which photographs or videotapes show child being abused

    Confession by the alleged perpetrator to the acts described by the child

■ *Further Reading*

Adams, J. A. (1997). Sexual abuse and adolescents. *Pediatric Annals, 26,* 229-304.

American Professional Society on the Abuse of Children. (1998). *Practice guidelines: Descriptive terminology in child sexual abuse medical evaluations.* Chicago: Author.

Botash, A. (1997). Examination for sexual abuse in prepubertal children: An update. *Pediatric Annals, 26,* 312-320.

Heger, A., & Emans, J. (1992). *Evaluation of the sexually abused child. A medical textbook and photographic atlas.* Oxford, UK: Oxford University Press. (Second edition in press)

38

What Developmental Factors Should Be Considered in Interpreting a Child's Disclosure of Sexual Abuse?

■ *Nancy Davis*

When investigating an allegation of sexual abuse, it is important to recognize that younger children are limited in their ability to describe and effectively verbalize the conduct at issue. Although factors other than age (intelligence, disabilities, and social and language skills) may affect a child's ability to recall and describe, generally children within a particular age range will possess similar abilities and limitations. Being alert to developmental status assists in understanding and evaluating the child's account. In evaluating reports from children of all ages, it is important to consider if the language used to describe the conduct is consistent with the child's age and social skills. The following general guidelines may be helpful:

> *Ages infant to 4 years:* Generally in this age range, an investigator must rely on medical evidence, information provided by caregivers, and any reported symptoms of trauma because children in the first 4 years of life make simple verbal allegations. Sleep problems, nightmares, and acting out a sexual act are common symptoms. Children 4 years old and younger rarely are

qualified in court because at this developmental stage they are unable to verbalize their understanding of the difference between a lie and the truth, which is a requirement for being allowed to testify. Memories of trauma are recalled in single incidents, like a snapshot rather than a videotape. Young children are much more likely to respond to an abuser's attempts to convince them that sexual abuse is a game or normal. Although able to identify a familiar person, if an abuser is not a regular part of a young child's life, he or she rarely can describe or identify the abuser in person or by photo. Before age 4, children generally cannot use anatomically correct dolls to demonstrate what happened to them; instead, they show what happened by using their own bodies.

Ages 5 to 7: Because of improved language and memory skills, children of this age are usually able to describe sexual abuse; because they lack sexual knowledge and adult vocabulary, however, their descriptions are often simplistic. Children younger than 8 years of age usually remember traumatic events as a single incident and may illustrate the event by drawing without being directly aware of doing so (such as in school). Although possessing a memory as good as that of an adult, children do not have memory cues to help them retrieve their memory. Interviewers who use questions that facilitate memory retrieval obtain more detailed information (e.g., "Did anything happen to your head? Your eyes? Your nose? Your mouth? Did anything happen in the living room? The bedroom? The bathroom?").[1] In this age range, sexual abuse often causes sleep difficulties, nightmares, and sexual acting out in play or interactions with other children.

Ages 8 to 11: Referrals in this age range are primarily by females, perhaps because of a reluctance of males to reveal sexual abuse. Sexually abused females in this age range may begin puberty prematurely. Memory and language have improved; therefore, allegations of sexual abuse may be clear and specific. Older children may blame themselves for being sexually abused. By age 8, children are gaining the skills to access sexual material on cable television or the Internet that may result in sexualized behavior.

Ages 12 to 16: Males at this age are even more reluctant to reveal male-to-male abuse. Females may be embarrassed or resist disclosure because they believe themselves mature enough to be sexually active. Young adolescent girls may not understand that seduction by a much older male is abuse. Language skills and memory are excellent; therefore, allegations can be clear and specific. A pattern of having sex with multiple partners may have begun as a result of being sexually abused. For abused teens, depression, withdrawal, and suicide attempts are frequent.

Learning disabled, developmentally delayed, and retarded children: A child with a disability is especially at risk of being sexually abused because his or her body is more mature than his or her emotional or social functioning, which makes the child easier to manipulate. Before questioning a disabled child, having his or her teacher explain the child's disability and functioning level can be helpful.

■ Note

1. Because a variety of questions are asked that can elicit a "yes" or "no" response, this is not likely to suggest a particular response and, therefore, not an inappropriate leading question.

■ Further Reading

Downs, W. R. (1993). Developmental considerations for the effects of childhood sexual abuse. *Journal of Interpersonal Violence, 8*(3), 331-345.

Putnam, F. W. (1996, March 26). *Developmental pathways in sexually abused girls; Psychological and biological data from the longitudinal study.* Research presented at the Psychological Trauma conference, Boston, MA.

39

How Do I Interpret Sexualized Behavior in Children?

■ *Esther Deblinger*

It has been well documented that sexually abused children exhibit significantly higher rates of age-inappropriate and abusive sexual behaviors compared to nonabused children in the general population. Furthermore, although sexually abused children share many of the same psychological problems exhibited by other emotionally troubled children, problematic sexual behavior seems to distinguish sexually abused children from psychiatrically disturbed children who have not been sexually abused. Thus, when children engage in age-inappropriate or abusive sexual behaviors or both, a possible history of child sexual abuse should be considered.

It is important to recognize, however, that many sexual behaviors exhibited by children are neither age inappropriate or abusive. In fact, sexual behaviors of various forms are exhibited by children of all ages.

■ *What Kinds of Sexual Behaviors May Be Considered Normative in Young Children?*

Recent research has documented that many sexualized behaviors, including walking around in underwear, scratching one's crotch,

■ 183

touching one's own sex parts at home, walking around nude, and undressing in front of others, are commonly exhibited by young nonabused children. Some common sexual behaviors also may involve more than one child, as in the case of "playing doctor" or "I'll show you mine, you show me yours." These types of normative sexual behaviors reflect children's natural naïveté concerning social inhibitions and their curiosity about their bodies. Thus, these behaviors generally are not suggestive of abuse. Note, however, that as children grow older and gain a greater understanding of societal norms concerning sexuality, the public display of many sexual behaviors naturally diminishes.

■ *What Kinds of Sexual Behaviors May Be Considered Age Inappropriate or Abusive When Exhibited by Children?*

When a child exhibits sexual behavior or knowledge or both that seems to be beyond that typical for children of his or her age group, additional exploration is warranted. Age-inappropriate sexual behaviors may best be described as imitations of adult-like sexual behaviors, including oral genital contact, inserting objects in the vagina or anus, imitating intercourse, and asking to engage in sex acts. In addition, there is cause for concern when children engage one another in adult-like sexual interactions, particularly when there are significant differences in the children's ages, either child uses any type of coercion or force, or both.

■ *How Can Sexual Behaviors in Children Be Assessed Most Effectively?*

Age-inappropriate sexual behaviors may sometimes be observed directly by child protection workers. If this occurs, it may be useful to question the child at that time in as calm and as nonjudgmental a manner as possible about where they learned the sexual behaviors. Direct observation of these behaviors by professionals, however, may be rare because sexually inappropriate behaviors in children are low base-rate behaviors. Thus, in assessing sexualized behaviors in children, child protection workers generally need to rely on information elicited from parents or other caregivers or both. Children may also be questioned about such behaviors, although they may be reluctant to acknowledge problem behaviors. Also note that there are several standardized instruments that are available to assess sexualized behaviors in children, including the Child Sexual Behavior Inventory (a parent report measure) and the Trauma Symptom Checklist for Children (a child self-report measure) (Briere, 1989; Freidrich, 1993; Freidrich et al., 1992; Horton, 1996). Scores on these measures may help to determine whether the quality and frequency of the sexualized behaviors are within the normal range for children in an identified age group.

■ *What Are Other Reasons Children May Exhibit Age-Inappropriate or Abusive Sexual Behaviors?*

When children exhibit age-inappropriate or abusive sexual behaviors, the possibility that they have been sexually abused should be carefully investigated. In the context of a comprehensive investigation, child sexual abuse, exposure to other forms of violence, and other alternative explanations for sexual behavior problems should be considered. Alternative explanations include but are not limited to the following:

1. Lack of understanding of societal norms (e.g. sexually impulsive behavior exhibited by a mentally retarded adolescent who has limited understanding of social inhibitions)
2. Sexual curiosity, exploration, or both beyond what may be considered normative among age mates who have no known history of abuse
3. Exposure to adult sexual activity, viewing of explicit sexual behavior on television or in movies, or viewing of pornography

It is possible for this type of exposure to occur accidentally when a child is inadvertently exposed to the sexual activity of parents, an older sibling, teenage baby-sitters, and so on. Such exposure may also occur as a result of parental negligence or extremely relaxed moral standards. Note, however, that exposure to explicit sexual materials may also occur when sex offenders deliberately expose children to such materials as part of the grooming process.

Finally, there generally tends to be greater cause for concern when children's sexual behavior problems have been observed in different settings, by different caregivers, and seem to be unresponsive to limit setting. Ultimately, whether a child's age-inappropriate sexualized behaviors are reflective of an abuse history will be determined by a comprehensive investigation that includes forensic interviews, medical examination, and the collection of collateral information.

■ *What Kind of Treatment Should Be Recommended for Children Who Exhibit Age-Inappropriate Sexual Behavior?*

For psychiatric and child protection purposes, it is important to determine the etiology of age-inappropriate sexual behaviors exhibited by children. Regardless of the etiology, however, children exhibiting sexual behavior problems should receive specialized treatment for such behaviors. This is important because such behaviors generally do not disappear on their own, and they may increase a child's risk of being sexually victimized or engaging in sexual offenses in the future or both. Furthermore, preliminary research evidence suggests that age-inappropriate sexual behaviors may be most effectively treated when nonoffending parents are involved in treatment and when they obtain some training in behavior management. Thus, children exhibiting such difficulties with or without an identified history of child sexual abuse should be referred to counselors with specialized expertise in this area.

■ *Further Reading*

Briere, J. (1989). *The Trauma Symptom Checklist for Children (TSS-C)*. Los Angeles: University of Southern California.

Freidrich, W. N. (1993). Sexual victimization and sexual behavior in children: A review of recent literature. *Child Abuse and Neglect, 17,* 59-66.

Freidrich, W. N., Grambsch, P., Damon, L., Hewitt, S., Koverola, C., Lang, R., Wolfe, V., & Broughton, D. (1992). Child sexual behavior inventory: Normative and clinical comparisons. *Psychological Assessment, 4*(3), 303-311.

Horton, C. (1996). Children who molest other children: The school psychologist's response to the sexually aggressive child. *School Psychology Review, 25*(4), 540-557.

40

The Medical Evaluation for Possible Child Sexual Abuse:

When Is It Needed, Who Should Do It, How Should One Prepare for It, and What Will Be Done?

■ *Robert A. Shapiro*

The following are the objectives of the medical evaluation:

- Medical treatment: to assess for and treat sexually transmitted infections, injuries, and pregnancy
- Forensic evaluation: to collect forensic evidence, such as semen or saliva, and to document trauma
- Psychological reassurance: to reassure the child that her or his body is healthy and that he or she is physically well

A medical examination is required when

- The abuse involved the child's genitalia or anus
- The child has symptoms of vaginal or rectal pain, itching, burning, bleeding, or discharge
- The child or parent has concerns that can best be answered by a physician or nurse
- The child would be reassured by an examination
- The extent or type of abuse is unclear and may be clarified by an examination

Many experts recommend that all children believed to have been sexually abused should have a medical evaluation.

The following are indications for an emergent (immediate) or urgent (same-day) evaluation:

- The child should be seen as soon as possible if the abuse occurred within the past 72 hours and included sexual activities that may have left forensic material on the victim's clothing or body. Forensic material includes semen, saliva, blood, skin or hair of the perpetrator, and fibers or material from the crime scene. Examples of sexual activity that may leave forensic evidence include ejaculation, contact with the perpetrator's genitalia, licking, bleeding, biting, scratching, or other similar acts within the prior 72 hours. The likelihood of recovering forensic material decreases with passing time. The child should not bathe or change clothing prior to the examination.
- The child is in pain, bleeding, or has other serious physical symptoms.
- The child is suicidal or threatening to harm himself or herself.
- The child was assaulted or abused within the past 72 hours by a perpetrator with HIV or hepatitis.

The following are indications for an evaluation within a few days:

- The child has less serious symptoms, such as discharge, pain with urination, and itching.
- The child or family is unwilling to wait because of anxiety, stress, or other reasons.
- The child could be pregnant as a result of the abuse.

An evaluation within a few weeks is indicated in all other circumstances.

■ *Seek a Medical Examiner Who Has*
Been Trained in Sexual Abuse Evaluations

In most situations, an examiner who has specific training in sexual abuse will provide a more complete and accurate evaluation compared to an examiner without such training. Clinics or other practices that specialize in child abuse evaluations are preferable to emergency departments or general practitioners. Urgent evaluations for forensic evidence collection or serious symptoms may require the use of an emergency department.

■ *Prepare the Child for the*
Medical Evaluation

Explain the evaluation process to the child and reassure him or her that the evaluation should not be painful. The evaluation for most children will include a medical history, a short general physical examination, and an external inspection of the genitalia and anus. It is highly unusual for a preadolescent child to require an internal vaginal or rectal examination. Explain to the nonoffending caregiver that the examination is different and less invasive than an adult pelvic examination. This preparation should reduce the child's and caregiver's anxiety and will contribute to a more comfortable and informative examination.

■ *Provide the Examiner With*
  Helpful Information

To avoid unnecessary and potentially harmful and repetitive questioning of the child, a detailed history should be provided to the examiner prior to the evaluation.

■ *Questions That May Be Asked*
  During the Medical Evaluation

The child, the parent, or both will be asked questions about the child's current health, past medical history, medications, recent behavior changes and any current complaints or symptoms, information about possible earlier trauma or abuse involving the anogenital area, other problems in this area, and possible sexual activity. Questions about the alleged abuse may also be asked if a forensic interview of the child has not been performed or if the examiner was not given the history of the alleged abuse. In some cases, the examiner may need to ask the child specific questions about the abuse when the information is needed to determine the need for medical testing and treatment.

■ *A Description of the Medical Evaluation*

Each examiner will have an individualized approach that may include the following:

- Dialogue with the child and caregiver to "break the ice"
- Specific questions about the child's medical history and the alleged abuse
- A brief general physical examination
- External inspection of the genitalia and anus while the child is lying on his or her back
- External inspection of the genitalia while the child is kneeling, head down and rump up (girls only)

- Vaginal speculum and digital exam (adolescent girls only)
- Photographs or video recordings of the examination
- Collection of specimens for testing
- Concluding discussion with the child and the caregiver about the findings

■ *Tests That May Be Obtained*
  During the Medical Evaluation

Depending on the history and examination findings, tests for sexually transmitted infections and pregnancy may be obtained. These tests are discussed in detail in Chapter 41, this volume.

■ *Further Reading*

Emans, S. J. (1992). Physical examination of the child and adolescent. In A. Heger & S. Jean Emans (Eds.), *Evaluation of the sexually abused child: A medical textbook and photographic atlas.* New York: Oxford University Press.

Giardino, A. P. (1992). Physical examination and laboratory specimens. In A. P. Giardino (Ed.), *A practical guide to the evaluation of sexual abuse in the prepubertal child.* Newbury Park, CA: Sage.

41

How Do I Interpret Laboratory Test Results for Sexually Transmitted Diseases?

■ *Robert A. Shapiro*

Definition: Infectious diseases that are transmitted through sexual contact are referred to as sexually transmitted diseases (STDs).

Prevalence of STDs in sexually abused children: Abuse victims are more likely to have an STD if they were abused by multiple perpetrators, abused multiple times, live in a community with a high prevalence of STDs, or were abused by a perpetrator who had high-risk behaviors. High-risk behaviors include intravenous drug use, crack use, prostitution, or multiple sexual partners. In addition, sexually active adolescents have the highest rates of STDs of all age groups. Relatively few abused children have an STD, however (usually less than 5%).

Sexual transmission and nonsexual transmission: Some STDs are caused by microorganisms that live exclusively in, or near, the genitalia or rectum of an infected person. These STDs are almost always transmitted through sexual contact. Other microorganisms, in addition to living in or near the genitalia or rectum, also live in nonsexual areas of the body. Infections by these microorganisms can be transmitted by sexual or nonsexual contact. Appendix 3, Table A3.1 summarizes the likelihood of sexual transmission of specific STDs.

Certain STDs are transmitted to children in the perinatal period, during or before birth. A physician can differentiate most perinatal infections from infections due to sexual abuse. Some infections, such as those from chlamydia or warts, are more difficult to differentiate. Appendix 3, Table A3.2 lists specifics about perinatal infection.

Symptoms of STDs: The symptoms and illnesses caused by STDs vary depending on the specific infection, the age of the child or adolescent, and the site of the infection. Adolescent girls are often asymptomatic (without symptoms). Appendix 3, Table A3.2 describes the most common manifestations of STDs.

Which children should be tested for STDs? The majority of abuse victims will not have an STD. Because many STDs cause no symptoms, however, tests are often done during the medical evaluation to exclude a silent infection. Some examiners will test all alleged victims for STDs, whereas others limit testing to those whom they believe are at increased risk for infection, such as those with

- Vaginal or urethral discharge
- Rectal pain or discharge
- Genital ulcers, sores, or warts
- A history of abuse by multiple perpetrators or by a perpetrator with high-risk behaviors (intravenous or crack drug use, prostitution, multiple partners, or a history of STDs)
- A history of prostitution
- A sibling or household contact who was diagnosed with an STD
- A history of, or physical signs of, vaginal or rectal penetration
- A diagnosis of any other STD
- An age of 13 years or older
- An inability to follow up at a later time if symptoms develop

Testing the alleged perpetrator for STDs: If the sexual abuse victim has been diagnosed with an STD, the alleged perpetrator should be tested to determine if he or she also has the infection. Interpret this information cautiously. If the alleged perpetrator has already received treatment, the tests may be negative. If the tests are positive, the information will support the allegations of sexual abuse, although a definite connection linking the alleged perpetrator to the victim cannot be made. Tests for HIV, syphilis, and hepatitis will always be positive, even after the alleged perpetrator has received medical treatment.

Tests used to diagnose STDs: In cases of suspected sexual abuse or assault, it is critical that the tests used to diagnose STDs are recognized as "gold standards." Only those tests listed in Appendix 3, Table A3.2 should be used.

Treatment of STDs: In all cases of alleged abuse, appropriate diagnostic tests must be obtained before treatment is given. Treatment may be given, however, before a definitive diagnosis is made. In other situations, no presumptive treatment should be given.

- Prepubertal children without symptoms should not be treated unless an STD is diagnosed using a gold standard.
- Adolescents have a greater risk of infection and complications. Presumptive treatment may be indicated.
- A physician should evaluate within 72 hours any victim who has been assaulted by an HIV-positive perpetrator to ascertain whether HIV prophylaxis is indicated.
- Hepatitis B vaccination should be provided to all victims who are not already immunized.

Follow-up for children diagnosed or tested for STDs:

- If a STD has been diagnosed, some physicians will request a follow-up evaluation in 2 weeks. If testing for syphilis, HIV, or hepatitis, the physician may order repeat testing during a 6-month period.
- Children who develop symptoms of a STD after the initial evaluation should be seen for follow-up.

- Victims who are evaluated within 1 week of an assault and who have an increased risk for an STD may require follow-up testing.
- Victims immunized for hepatitis B may require follow-up vaccinations.

Pitfalls to avoid in the diagnosis of STDs in children:

- Some tests for STDs are inaccurate. These tests will be positive when in fact no infection exists. Only those tests listed in Appendix 3, Table A3.2 or other gold-standard tests should be used.
- Identification of an STD requires an adequate sample, careful specimen handling, and a qualified laboratory. False-negative and false-positive cultures and tests can occur if errors are made.
- Decisions regarding the likelihood of abuse should not be made based on preliminary or presumptive STD diagnoses. Wait for the final diagnosis.
- Some STDs cannot be diagnosed immediately after sexual assault or abuse. Appendix 3, Table A3.2 specifies the incubation time for each STD.
- Adolescents who are sexually active may have an STD that they acquired through consensual sex.

■ Further Reading

American Academy of Pediatrics. (1997). Sexually transmitted diseases. In G. Peter (Ed.), *Red Book: Report of the Committee on Infectious Diseases* (24th ed., pp. 108-116). Elk Grove Village, IL: Author.

Finkel, M. A., & DeJong, A. R. (1994). Medical findings in child sexual abuse. In R. M. Reece (Ed.), *Child abuse: Medical diagnosis and management*. Philadelphia: Lea & Febiger.

42

How Do I Interpret Results of a Child Sexual Abuse Examination?

What Conditions May Be Mistaken for Sexual Abuse?

■ *Robert A. Shapiro*

■ *General Principles*

Normal examinations are common after sexual abuse. Most children who have been sexually abused will have normal physical examinations, including children who report vaginal or anal penetration. The finding of a normal examination does not mean the child was not abused.

Facts about the hymen:

- Every girl is born with a hymen.
- Hymens vary in shape and size among individual females.
- The hymen changes significantly during puberty.
- After puberty, bleeding from hymenal injury may or may not occur during first-time intercourse.

The examiner is searching for physical changes that may be the result of sexual abuse. Injuries to the genitalia and anus may occur during sexual abuse. Chronic (old) sexual abuse may cause changes different from acute (recent) abuse. Sexual abuse may transmit sexually transmitted diseases (see Chapter 41, this volume).

Puberty changes the appearance and size of the genitalia as well as the examiner's ability to diagnose injury. Enlargement of the vaginal opening and redundancy (folds) of the hymen can prevent injuries from vaginal penetration or make them more difficult to recognize.

Superficial genital and anal injuries often heal quickly. If there is a delay between the time of the abuse and the examination, minor trauma that may have resulted from the abuse will no longer be present. The amount of time needed for an injury to heal varies. Deeper injuries require more time to heal, as do injuries that are not able to heal because of reinjury.

Tanner staging: The stages of puberty can be described with the Tanner Scale. Tanner Stage I describes the genitalia prior to the onset of puberty. Tanner Stage V describes the genitalia after puberty is complete. Stages II, III, and IV are intermediate stages.

Clock references in the sexual abuse reports: Many examiners refer to locations near the genitalia and anus using a "clock face" analogy. Therefore, the top-center location is referred to as "12 o'clock," "3 o'clock" refers to the area 90 degrees to the right of 12 o'clock, and so on.

■ *Anatomy*

Familiarity with certain anatomical structures and terms helps one interpret medical examination reports. The following is a brief overview of the more commonly encountered terminology:

Female Genitalia

- *Labia:* the lips surrounding the vaginal opening
  - ☐ There are two sets of labia: the labia major (outer set), and the labia minor (inner set). After puberty, the labia enlarge and more completely cover the opening of the vagina.
- *Urethral meatus:* the opening of the urethra from the bladder to the exterior through which urine passes
- *Hymen:* a membrane that partially covers the opening of the vagina
  - ☐ The hymen may be thin or thick, may cover most of the vaginal opening or very little of it, and varies in shape. Terms used to describe the appearance of a normal hymen include crescentic (crescent shaped), annular (round), redundant (folded), estrogenized (thickened), and septate (two openings).
- *Introitus* (hymenal opening): the opening in the middle of the hymen
  - ☐ Objects entering the vagina first pass through the introitus. Hymenal injury from vaginal penetration often occurs at the introitus.
- *Vagina:* a tubular structure inside the body, bordered by the hymen at the outer end and by the cervix internally
- *Posterior fourchette:* the area of mucosal skin at which the labia minora meet (opposite end to the clitoris)
- *Fossa navicularis:* the area of mucosal skin between the posterior fourchette and the hymen

Male Genitalia

- *Glans:* the tip of the penis surrounding the urethral opening
- *Prepuce* (foreskin): tissue that covers the glans in uncircumcised males
  - ☐ The prepuce is mostly removed during circumcision.
- *Phimosis:* adhesion of the prepuce to the glans

The Anus

- *Anus:* the opening of the rectum between the buttocks
- *Sphincter:* the muscles that surround the anus
- *Anal verge:* the area between the external and internal anal skins
- *Rugae:* folds of skin that radiate outward from the anus

■ Interpretation of Normal and Nonspecific Examinations

Most children who have been sexually abused have normal or nonspecific physical examinations. Some of these normal and nonspecific findings are described in the following sections. These findings are clearly not proof of sexual abuse but may be present in children who have been abused.

Normal or Nonspecific Prepubertal Female Genital Findings

- *Bumps, tags, or mounds:* small protrusions on the hymenal edge
- *Clefts:* interruptions of the normally smooth hymenal edge
  - □ They are most commonly found along the midhorizontal plane of the hymen at the 3 o'clock and 9 o'clock positions. When present below this horizontal line, they may indicate healed injury.
- *Redness, vaginitis, and discharge:* can be due to poor hygiene, infection, bubble bath, and other causes
- *Intravaginal ridges or columns:* normal folds of the vaginal wall
- *Periurethral bands:* support-like bands of tissue radiating from the urethral meatus
- *Increased vascularity of vestibule or hymen:* more than the usual number of blood vessels within these tissues
- *Posterior fourchette friability:* tendency of the posterior fourchette mucosa to bleed easily

◻ This finding seems to occur more often in children who have been abused, but it can also be seen in nonabused children.

- *Labial adhesions:* joining of the labia minora
  ◻ In some children, chronic labial irritation from sexual abuse may be the cause of the adhesions, but this finding is very nonspecific.

- *Large hymenal opening:* suggestive of vaginal penetration
  ◻ One cannot conclude, however, that vaginal penetration has occurred unless specific signs of hymenal trauma are also present. No conclusion regarding sexual abuse should be made based on the size of the vaginal opening alone.

Normal or Nonspecific Pubertal Female Genital Findings

- *Redundant, fimbriated hymen:* During puberty, the hymenal tissue becomes thicker and redundant (folded), the opening into the vagina becomes larger, and the hymenal tissue becomes more elastic and less sensitive to touch. The mucous covering the vaginal walls becomes less prone to injury from abrasion. Folds in the hymen make examination difficult, and distinguishing folds from injury can be challenging.

- *Vaginal discharge:* Although discharge can be normal, it may also indicate infection.

Normal or Nonspecific Anal Findings

- *Fissures, excoriation, redness:* may be seen after sexual abuse but there are other causes
- *Anal tags:* protrusion of tissue at the 6 o'clock or 12 o'clock midline positions
- *Diastasis ani:* smooth anal skin at the 6 o'clock or 12 o'clock midline positions
- *Increased skin pigmentation and thickened anal skin folds*
- *Venous congestion:* pooling of blood in the veins around the anus
- *Gaping (wide open) anus:* only normal if stool is present in the distal (end) anus

■ *Interpretation of Abnormal Examinations That Reveal Trauma*

Trauma may or may not indicate sexual abuse. Some types of trauma are nonspecific, whereas others indicate that sexual abuse has most likely occurred.

Prepubertal Female Genital Trauma

- Acute injuries to the genitalia cause bruising, lacerations (tears), abrasions (scrapes), and inflammation (redness, tenderness, and swelling): Most of these injuries heal quickly without leaving any lasting signs to be found on later examination. Acute genital injuries are always suspicious for sexual abuse, particularly when the trauma includes the hymen. Accidental trauma usually involves the labia or the mons pubis or both.
- Findings that indicate healed vaginal penetration: Note that the legal definition of *penetration* may include contact with the external genital structures, such as the labia, posterior fourchette, and fossa navicularis. *Vaginal penetration* in this chapter refers to internal, vaginal penetration.
  - □ Absent or significant defect of the posterior hymen (should be confirmed by examining the child in the knee-chest position):
  - □ Hymenal laceration or scar
- Findings that may indicate vaginal penetration
  - □ Enlarged hymenal opening: "enlarged" sometimes difficult to define
  - □ Decreased amount of hymenal tissue
  - □ Irregularities, notches, and clefts of the posterior hymen

Female Pubertal Genital Trauma

Signs of vaginal penetration can be more difficult to recognize, or may be absent, in the adolescent. New hymenal tears and signs of acute injury are indications of recent vaginal penetration. Transections (complete interruptions or breaks) in the hymen are present in some virginal adolescents but are more commonly seen in sexually active and sexually abused girls. Consensual sexual activity does not typically cause genital bruising, abrasions, or swelling.

Male Genital Trauma

Findings that indicate recent injury include swelling, abrasions, bruises, lacerations, and bites. Acute injury is always suspicious for sexual abuse.

Anal Trauma

- Findings of acute anal injury include bruising, lacerations, abrasions, and swelling. Most of these injuries heal without leaving any lasting signs. Acute injury is always suspicious for sexual abuse.
- Scars may result from deep lacerations after sexual abuse and will be visible long after the abuse occurred. Skin tags away from the midline of the anus may indicate healed injuries.
- Chronic sexual abuse may result in funneling (loss of subcutaneous fat around the anus), changes in the anal skin, and decreased sphincter muscle tone. Decreased tone is defined as >20 mm of anal dilation with no stool in the distal anus.

Trauma Outside the Genital and Anal Areas

Injuries to a child's breasts, throat, mouth, or other areas may occur following sexual abuse. Specific injuries from oral gags or binding of the extremities may be found.

■ Common Questions With Answers

- What types of sexual abuse are consistent with normal examinations?
  - □ Oral contact, digital fondling, genital rubbing, vaginal penetration after puberty, rectal penetration, partial or attempted vaginal penetration, and penetration that has had time to

heal are all types of sexual abuse consistent with normal examinations.

- The child describes penetration, but the exam is normal. How can this occur?

  □ The prepubertal child who describes vaginal penetration may have experienced the pain of partial or attempted penetration but may not have been penetrated past the hymen. Although the child describes penetration, because she could not "see" the extent of penetration and has no experience to be able to differentiate between full vaginal penetration and attempted or partial penetration, her impression may be that she was penetrated. If pressure is exerted against the hymen, most girls will experience pain. Note that, in many states, the legal definition of penetration does not require vaginal penetration.

  □ The pubertal adolescent may show no physical indications of vaginal penetration after sexual intercourse. In many adolescents, the hymenal opening is large enough and has sufficient elasticity to accommodate an erect male penis without tearing.

  □ Rectal penetration often results in no signs of injury. The rectum of many children can accommodate an erect male penis without injury, particularly if lubricated.

  □ In general, trauma after penetration is more likely if the victim was young, physical force was used, the penetration was deep, the victim was uncooperative, the perpetrator used no lubrication, or all these. Penetration with larger objects is more likely to result in injury than penetration with smaller objects. Repeated penetration is more likely to result in injury than single penetration.

- Can the number of abuse episodes be determined by exam?

  □ Not usually. If evidence of chronic anal abuse is present, multiple episodes of abuse occurred. Vaginal injuries do not reliably differentiate between single and multiple episodes of abuse.

- When did the injury occur?

  □ If the injuries are acute (redness, swelling, tenderness, fresh abrasions, or tears), the examiner may reliably identify the injury as relatively recent, most likely having occurred within a few days of the examination. Dating injuries within hours or to specific days is usually not possible.

- Why does one examiner's report differ from another's?
  - □ Examination findings may differ when (a) acute injuries heal between examinations, (b) one of the examinations was not optimal because the child was uncooperative, and (c) the skill levels of the examiners differ. Examiners with expert training will provide a more accurate and informative examination.

■ Conditions That Mimic Sexual Abuse

- *Nonspecific vaginitis:* many causes, including poor hygiene, bubble bath, antibiotics, nylon underwear, and bedwetting
- *Vaginitis:* many causes, including pinworms, streptococcal infection, and fungus infection
- *Vaginal foreign bodies:* may cause bloody, foul-smelling discharge; often caused by residual toilet paper in the vagina
- *Perianal strep infection:* presents with anal bleeding and redness
- *Lichen sclerosis:* hourglass-shaped area of hypopigmented skin surrounding the anus and genitalia, often with blood blister and other skin changes; bleeding common
- *Straddle injuries* (accidental trauma): abrasions, bruising, swelling of the labia; occasionally, may involve the introitus
- *Urethral prolapse:* urethra protrudes past the urethral opening and presents with a bloody, or blood-tinged, swollen lump around the top of the introitus
  - □ Often, the urethral origin of this mass cannot be easily recognized, and it may be mistaken for trauma.

■ Further Reading

Botash, A. S. (1997, May). Examination for sexual abuse in prepubertal children: An update. *Pediatric Annals, 26*(5), 312-320.
Hymel, K. P., & Jenny, C. (1996). Child sexual abuse. *Pediatrics in Review, 17*(7), 236-249.

43

How Do I Evaluate Suspected Sexual Abuse in the Adolescent Female?

■ *Joyce A. Adams*

Young girls who have started their menstrual periods are considered to be adolescents, even if they are younger than age 13. In addition to needing an examination to search for signs of injury, evidence of sperm or semen, and signs of sexually transmitted disease, adolescent girls suspected of having been sexually abused must also be screened for pregnancy.

When a girl has gone through puberty, her genital tissues change. The hymen becomes thicker and much more elastic, with folds and flaps of tissue that allow the hymen to be stretched out without tearing. It is common for an adolescent girl who has had sexual intercourse to have a perfectly normal hymen. The idea that the hymen always tears with intercourse is a myth.

■ *When Is an Examination Necessary?*

An adolescent who reveals that she has been the victim of incest or forced sexual contact with someone other than a family member should always be asked to describe when the last sexual contact occurred. The urgency of obtaining an examination will depend on her answer. If the victim describes ejaculation, the

Table 43.1   Timing of the Examination, Tests, and Treatment

Time Since Last Assault	Exam	Signs of Injury	Sexually Transmitted Diseases	Sperm or Semen
Less than 72 hours or pain or bleeding	Immediate	Possible	Treat	Test for
72 hours to 2 weeks	As soon as possible	Possible	Test	Possible
More than 2 weeks	Recommend	Unlikely	Test	Will not find

examination must be immediate so that forensic tests for sperm, semen, and other materials can be obtained.

If the victim describes pain in the genital or rectal area, or bleeding from the vagina or rectum, the examination must also be done immediately. Signs of sexually transmitted diseases can be seen as early as 3 days after a sexual contact (gonorrhea) and as late as 1 or 2 years (genital warts). If tests are done for syphilis or HIV, these must be repeated in 6 months because it can take this amount of time for the infection to be detected with a blood test.

If the sexual assault involved touching only, oral genital contact, or intercourse with lubrication or drugging of the victim, it is very unlikely that any signs of injury will be found. Table 43.1 provides guidelines for when the examination should be done and what tests or treatment might be given.

■ *Other Factors in Obtaining the History*

In addition to determining when the assault occurred and whether the victim is experiencing pain, bleeding, or discharge from the vagina, it is also necessary to determine whether an adolescent girl has previously had intercourse. If she has previously had sex, any "chronic" changes found on examination could have been caused by past abuse or by consensual sex. If a sexually transmitted infection is found, and the sexual assault was within 2 days of the examination, the infection was not caused by the assault but, rather, was already present from a previous contact.

Adolescent girls have many different reactions to sexual assault and may not appear to be as upset as the interviewer might think they should be. Denial of feelings is very common among adolescents, and it may be days, weeks, months, or even years before the full impact of the sexual abuse is felt by the teenage girl. The criteria for judging the validity of an adolescent girl's description of sexual abuse are the same as those for a younger child: Is it a clear, consistent, detailed description? Did the history come out spontaneously? Are there changes in the girl's emotional state and behavior that may have started near the time the abuse is said to have begun?

■ Overall Assessment

After the child's statement and past medical and sexual history have been obtained, the examination has been conducted, and all the laboratory results have been received, the information can be used to develop an overall assessment of the likelihood of abuse. Table 37.1 (Chapter 37, this volume) offers an approach to integrating all the information. Often, unless the victim describes pain or bleeding from the sexual assault, the girl's examination will show few or no signs of injury. The history from the teen of what occurred is the most important evidence of abuse; this applies to adolescents and to younger children.

■ Further Reading

Ernoehazy, W., & Murphy-Lavoie, H. (1998). Sexual assault. In *Online Textbook of Emergency Medicine,* 1998. Available at http://www.emedicine.com/emerg/topic527.htm

44

When Does Sexual Play Suggest a Problem?

■ *Barbara L. Bonner*

This chapter briefly reviews what is viewed as normal or expected sexual behavior in children and when sexual play between children becomes problematic and requires intervention. Note that in some families any sexual behavior, such as masturbation, may be seen as problematic or unacceptable, even though the behavior is generally viewed as normal.

■ *Normal, Expected Sexual Play in Children*

Normal sexual play includes behaviors such as playing doctor, playing house, imitating intercourse clothed, looking at or briefly touching other children's genitals, sexual talk and jokes, sexual games, and masturbation. Normal sexual behavior

- Is exploratory and spontaneous
- Occurs occasionally between peers or siblings who are of similar age, size, and developmental level
- Is not accompanied by strong feelings of anger, fear, or anxiety
- Is controlled by adult intervention or increased supervision

Should these children be referred for assessment or intervention? Typically, these children are not referred because this behavior is within normal limits and can be controlled through appropriate adult supervision.

■ Problematic Sexual Behavior in Children

Problematic sexual behavior includes behaviors such as oral, vaginal, or anal intercourse; other sexual behaviors considered inappropriate for children; and behaviors that continue to occur after adult intervention to stop the behavior. Problematic sexual behavior

- Is forced, coerced, or aggressive in any way
- Is physically harmful to a child
- Scares or frightens a child
- Occurs between older and younger children, usually 3 or more years apart; between a child and animals; or between children who do not know each other well
- Is compulsive, such as masturbation
- Is not expected for the child's age or developmental level

When should these children be referred for additional evaluation? When children show problematic sexual behavior, it is recommended that they be referred to a mental health professional who has experience with sexual behavior problems in children for an assessment and possible treatment for the child and caregivers.

The following factors may be related to problematic sexual behavior in children:

- History of sexual abuse
- Exposure to sexual behavior through videos, movies, magazines, or observing adult sexual behavior
- Other affective and behavioral problems in children

Note that many children show problematic or aggressive sexual behavior who do not have a known history of sexual abuse. It is important that caregivers and professionals use caution when interpreting sexualized behavior in children as a sign of sexual abuse.

■ *Appropriate Professional and Caregiver Reaction to Sexualized Behavior in Children*

Do not overreact to sexual behavior in children:

- Most sexual behavior in children is categorized as normal.
- Most children will stop the inappropriate behavior if they are told rules (discussed later) for their behavior, are closely supervised, have mild restriction if they break one of the rules (time-out or early bedtime), and are praised or rewarded for appropriate behavior.
- Make immediate referral to a mental health professional if problematic sexual behavior occurs.

■ *Suggestions to Reduce Problematic Sexual Behavior in Children*

- Increase adult supervision.
- Refer for professional intervention.
- Tell children rules about sexual behavior.
- Reward children for sexually appropriate behavior (e.g., "Good for you! You followed the sexual behavior rules today").
- Eliminate sexually stimulating television, videos, and exposure to adult sexual activity.
- Do not allow children to bathe or sleep with other children or adults.
- Do not allow nudity in the home.
- Distract children with other activities, such as puzzles, games, or drawing.
- Give children appropriate affection.
- Increase children's physical activities, such as riding bikes, shooting baskets, jumping rope, or skating.

■ *Suggested Sexual Behavior Rules for*
Children With Problematic Sexual Behavior

1. It is OK to touch your private parts when you are alone. (It is also acceptable to use the name of the genitalia, such as penis or vagina, instead of "private parts.")
2. It is not OK to touch other people's private parts.
3. It is not OK for other people to touch your private parts.
4. It is not OK to show your private parts to other people.
5. It is not OK for your sexual behavior to make other people uncomfortable.

■ *Further Reading*

Bonner, B. L., Walker, C. E., & Berliner, L. (1998). *Final report on children with sexual behavior problems: Assessment and treatment.* Washington, D.C.: National Clearinghouse on Child Abuse and Neglect (phone: 800-394-3366).

Friedrich, W. N., Fisher, J., Broughton, D., Houston, M., & Shafran, C. R. (1998). Normative sexual behavior in children: A contemporary sample. *Pediatrics, 101*(4), e9.

Lamb, S., & Coakley, M. (1993). "Normal" childhood sexual play and games: Differentiating play from abuse. *Child Abuse and Neglect, 17,* 515-526.

Part IV

INITIAL
ASSESSMENT

Section E:
Psychological
Maltreatment

45

How Do I Determine Whether a Child Has Been Psychologically Maltreated?

■ *Marla R. Brassard and Stuart Hart*

■ *Assessment of Psychological Maltreatment*

Psychological maltreatment is identified through observations and reports of caregiver behavior. Knowledge of the forms of psychological maltreatment described in Chapter 6 (this volume) and their embodiment in state or provincial law provide guidance in identifying psychologically abusive caregiver behaviors (see Table 6.1).

Caregiver Behavior

If possible, a professional should observe the caregiver suspected of psychological maltreatment and child interacting. Observations should be done on several occasions to obtain a representative sample of caregiver-child behavior and to detect chronic behavioral patterns. Psychologically maltreating parents may be continually critical and derogatory, threaten to abandon their child (e.g., "Do that once more and it's foster care"), place age-inappropriate demands on their child (e.g., telling a 2-year-old to go into the kitchen and get cigarettes and matches for a guest), or ignore a crying, frightened, or upset child. Single observations have limitations because some parents may not behave in their typical manner. Reported observations by one caregiver of the other, or by relatives or acquaintances, in most cases will bring suspected cases under consideration. These original reports should be carefully and thoroughly explored. Interviews with the caregiver and child, records review, collateral reports from siblings, neighbors, relatives, school and day-care personnel, and others can provide useful information.

The professional should know his or her state's statutory requirements for reporting psychological maltreatment. Some states with a lower threshold may require only documentation of psychological maltreatment. Other states also require evidence of mental harm, including observation rating forms, extensive review of other professionals' contacts with the child and family (e.g., school, day care, and health personnel), and a psychological evaluation.

Child Behavior

Child behavior can suggest that psychological maltreatment has occurred. Psychologically maltreated children may act afraid or wary of, angry with, or largely ignore their caregiver, whereas adequately reared children are often comfortable and confident in their caregiver's presence. A child's behavior alone, however, is not sufficient to substantiate a case. Mental injuries in children may be caused by many factors, such as mental illness, mental retardation and autism, and psychological trauma that is unrelated to caregiver behavior. Children with these problems, however, can also be psychologically maltreated. Ruling out other explanations for problematic behavior may be done by knowledgeable caseworkers who are familiar with adequately cared for children with mental illnesses, developmental delays, and trauma.

How do you identify mental injuries in children and adolescents? Meeting criteria for "severe emotional disturbance" as defined under the federal Individuals with Disabilities Education Act (34 Code of Federal Regulations 300.7) or a mental disorder in the *Diagnostic and Statistical Manual* (DSM-IV; APA, 1994) meets the definition of mental injury in most states. Severe emotional disturbance is a condition in which a child exhibits one or more of the following symptoms during a period of time that adversely affects functioning at home or school: (a) an inability to learn that cannot be explained by intellectual, sensory, or health factors; (b) an inability to build or maintain satisfactory interpersonal relationships with peers and other adults; (c) developmentally inappropriate behaviors or feelings in normal circumstances (e.g., not benefiting from a parent's presence when distressed); (d) a general pervasive mode of unhappiness or depression; and (e) physical symptoms or fears associated with personal or school problems.

Level of Severity

To determine the level of severity of the psychological maltreatment, the following useful guidelines can be used: (a) How intense, extreme, and chronic is the behavior? (b) To what extent is the child-caregiver relationship permeated by the maltreatment? (c) How many forms of psychological maltreatment are occurring? (d) Are there other people in a child's life that buffer the effects of the psychological maltreatment? (For example, a close relationship with the father may protect a child from a verbally abusive mother.) (e) What is the importance of appropriate caregiver behavior in relation to the child's developmental needs? (For example, a caregiver who interacts with an infant only to feed or change diapers, ignoring needs for interaction and warmth, places the child at significant developmental risk.) (f) To what extent is there probable evidence that the child has been harmed by the caregiver? For example, a marked lack of interest in the world may be probable evidence of harm because depressed, passive behavior is often seen in emotionally neglected infants and very infrequently in other infants. Continuation of this pattern of behavior will inhibit emotional and cognitive development.

Finally, evaluators should consider a family's community context and its economic, social, and cultural circumstances when assessing caregiver behavior. Parents do not always have control over adverse conditions that may be influencing their ability to parent and their child's ability to cope. For example, homelessness and living in a poor, violent neighborhood will likely have an adverse impact on both quality of care and child development despite the caregiver's best efforts. Sometimes, psychologically abusive care is maximized because of poverty; the effect on the child, however, is the same. Some clinicians argue that although some inner-city families use a lot of yelling at their children and other harsh parenting tactics, this behavior does not constitute abuse. However, research shows that children of all economic, ethnic, and racial backgrounds in the United States are harmed by psychological abuse. Regardless of socio-cultural context, if a child is being psychologically maltreated or a child is suffering mental injury suspected to be due to psychological maltreatment, investigation and appropriate intervention should occur. The investigation and the intervention for psychological maltreatment should not be mediated nor eliminated out of respect for socio-cultural context.

■ *Questions to Ask Caregivers, Neighbors, Relatives, and Older Children*

The following are examples of questions to ask caregivers, neighbors, relatives, and older children:

In the past month, how often have you done (or have you seen [name of caregiver] do) the following?

- Swore at the child or called him or her a swear name
- Called the child demeaning names, such as stupid, loser, or lazy
- Threatened to kick the child out of the house or send him or her away or to foster care
- Threatened to hit or spank a child but didn't do it
- Blamed an adult's drinking, marital, or mental health problem on the child
- Acted too busy to pay attention to the child
- Ignored a child's request to be helped when he or she was crying, hurt, or frightened
- Failed to show needed/desired affection to the child (kisses, hugs, and playful gestures)

■ *Further Reading*

American Psychiatric Association. (1994). *Diagnostic and statistical manual of mental disorders* (4th ed.). Washington, DC: Author.

American Professional Society on the Abuse of Children (1995). *Practice guidelines on the psychosocial evaluation of suspected psychological maltreatment in children and adolescents.* Chicago: Author.

Hart, S. N., Brassard, M. R., & Karlson, H. (1996). Psychological maltreatment. In J. Briere, L. Berliner, J. Bulkley, C. Jenny, & T. Reid (Eds.), *The APSAC handbook on child maltreatment* (pp. 72-89). Thousand Oaks, CA: Sage.

O'Hagan, K. (1993). *Emotional and psychological abuse of children.* Toronto: University of Toronto Press.

46

In What Circumstances Is a Child Who Witnesses Violence Experiencing Psychological Maltreatment?

■ *Ronald Zuskin*

Psychological maltreatment is a term with various legal definitions. All children who witness domestic violence are affected by it but not to a level that constitutes psychological maltreatment. The effects of witnessing domestic violence are not clearly correlated with the frequency, intensity, severity, and duration of the violence; instead, the effects of witnessing violence are assessed by the extent to which the child suffers from witnessing it. Research suggests that the following factors influence the degree to which witnessing violence affects children:

The child's age. A general rule of thumb is that the earlier the child witnesses domestic violence, the more severe the effects are likely to be. An atmosphere of domestic violence early in life can harm the child's capacity for attachment. The mother's endangered availability may affect the child's social bonding for a lifetime. Age 8 has been identified as a watershed year for the harmful effects of witnessing domestic violence. Children younger than age 8 experience developmentally appropriate egocentricity. They feel culpable when their parents fight—as if the fighting was their responsibility, and they were responsible for stopping it. Witnessing domestic violence gives young children a message about themselves—not the parents. An attack on a caregiver creates a biological fight-or-flight reaction in children, as if they were being attacked. Extreme physiological arousal can have profound effects on the child's brain and personality. After age 8, children are more likely to experience witnessing domestic violence as their parents' problem rather than their own. They are capable—physically and psychologically—of distancing themselves from the situation. To assess the impact of domestic violence, note the age at which the child began witnessing domestic violence in addition to the current age. This may help account for effects that seem extraordinary.

The child's developmental stage. Closely related to age, the effect of witnessing domestic violence will vary depending on the child's stage of development. It is known that when children expend energy to defend themselves from the experience of trauma, their development can be distorted or delayed. Learn about the child's developmental stage when the witnessing of domestic violence began, and consider the child's current stage of development. Are there delays apparent? Does the child show signs of difficulty, such as global mistrust, chronic shame, or crippling guilt that may reflect harm from having been exposed to domestic violence earlier in development?

The child's gender. Males are much more likely to identify with the aggressor. That is, they reduce the distress of watching a batterer hit the victim by seeing how useful hitting can be or by identifying the reasons for hitting. They are likely to become violent toward others, particularly those of the same sex as that of the victim. Males typically externalize the effects of witnessing violence into verbal and physical explosiveness, defiance and oppositional behaviors, and delinquent acts. They try to gain control of an unpredictable world through provocation. Females are more likely to be socialized into a passive role to "keep the peace." They are likely to internalize the effects of witnessing violence. Depression, withdrawal, and other psychological or physical symptoms can result. They try to control a dangerous world through compulsive caretaking. These effects are not as clear-cut along gender lines as they once were.

The child's role in the family. Children in roles that are more central to the violence, such as scapegoat, caretaker, and peacemaker, may be harmed more than children whose roles are more peripheral to violence, such as the hero, the mascot, or the lost child.

It is important to note that the child's age, developmental level, gender, and role in the family interact in complex ways to mediate the effects of witnessing domestic violence. We cannot assess the possible psychological maltreatment of a child on the basis of the nature of the violence alone. We must examine the consequences evidenced in the development and behavior of each individual child, keeping in mind the four factors that affect the outcome of witnessing violence.

From research, it is known that violence does breed violence. Children who are abused and neglected are much more likely to grow into delinquent teens, adult criminals, or adults with problems of violence in relationship. Research strongly suggests that witnessing violence can pose the same risks to children in the family, which result from being victims of physical abuse or neglect.

It is critical to be aware of the legal definitions of emotional maltreatment in your area. Local departments of child and family services, the police, or parent and child advocacy organizations will be able to inform you. If you have concerns about something that might constitute emotional maltreatment, consulting with screeners at the local child protective services agency can be of invaluable assistance. The law does not guarantee children optimal parenting, but it does protect children from extremes of emotional and psychological torment. When the frequency, intensity, severity, duration, or all these of domestic violence in the home produce the type of age-, stage-, gender-, and role-related problems that you might anticipate in children who witness domestic violence, then you are likely to be viewing the effects on vulnerable children of witnessing domestic violence in the home.

■ *Further Reading*

Barnett, O. W., Miller-Perrin, C. L., & Perrin, R. (1997). *Family violence across the lifespan: An introduction.* Thousand Oaks, CA: Sage.

DePanfilis, D., & Brooks, G. (1989). *Child maltreatment and woman abuse: A guide for child protective services intervention.* Washington, DC: National Woman Abuse Prevention Project.

Jaffee, P. G. , Wolfe, D. A., & Wilson, S. (1990). *Children of battered women.* Newbury Park, CA: Sage.

Monahon, C. (1993). *Children and trauma: A guide for parents and professionals.* San Francisco: Jossey-Bass.

van der Kolk, B. A., McFarlane, A. C., & Weisath, L. (Eds.). (1996). *Traumatic stress: The effect of overwhelming experience on mind, body, and society.* New York: Guilford.

Widom, C. S. (1992, October). The cycle of violence. In *National Institute of Justice: Research in Brief.* Washington, DC: WIJ.

Part IV

INITIAL
ASSESSMENT

Section F:
Risk Assessment
and Safety Evaluation

47

How Do I Assess Risk and Safety?

■ *Wayne Holder*

For the purposes of this chapter, *risk of child maltreatment* refers to a family situation in which child maltreatment is likely to occur or recur. *Risk assessment* is a thorough study that results in a judgment about the likelihood of child maltreatment. Many agencies require an assessment of risk at two points in time: (a) as part of an initial assessment to determine whether a family is in need of child protective services (CPS) (because a risk of maltreatment is identified) and (b) to determine whether CPS intervention can be terminated (because risk factors have been reduced). The process of risk assessment considers the family unit, family or other household members, and the relationships and interactions of the family members. Regardless of the model used to assess risk, the following information is always relevant:

- *Child maltreatment:* This should include a description and explanation of the events associated with the maltreatment; physical and emotional manifestations present in the child; the precise actions and behaviors of the caregivers believed to be responsible for the maltreatment; frequency, chronicity, and duration of any maltreatment; and circumstances such as parental attitude, response to the allegation, and explanation of the events and effects associated with the alleged maltreatment.

- *The child:* This should include a full consideration of all the children in a family—age and vulnerability, development, health, temperament, and functioning (cognitive, physical, emotional, and social).
- *The caregivers:* The assessment should consider general functioning (cognitive, physical, emotional, and social), mental health status, substance use, life management, coping and problem-solving capacity, social relationships, and history of all adults in a caregiving role.
- *Parenting:* The assessment should identify the relationship of the caregiver to the child (e.g., parent, relative, and friend of parent) and focus on understanding methods of discipline; parenting approaches, attitudes, sensitivity, expectations, knowledge, and skill; the parent's understanding of child development; and the nature of the parent-child relationship (attachment), empathy, and support of the child.
- *Family functioning:* The assessment of family functioning considers how the family unit works internally, how family members relate and interact, and how the family interacts with the outside world. Specific issues include demographics (that could create stress), family structure, culture, communication, affection, relationships, decision making, integration into the community, and support networks.

■ The Process of Gathering Risk Assessment Information

The family is the primary source of information. In accordance with local confidentiality policies, you may also gather or confirm information by talking with extended family members, friends, neighbors, and professionals involved with the family. Most workers prefer to begin information collection with the child based on the child's location and the potential need for protection. Whatever the order of interviewing, remember to demonstrate respect for the caregivers' authority in the family.

Your general approach in risk assessment interviews should be characterized by respect for the family, genuineness, empathy, and being specific and concrete. A risk assessment interview has a ripple effect quality. Your entry into the home is like a pebble that is dropped in the water. You introduce yourself and the agency and establish the basis for your presence by briefly reviewing the CPS report. You ask for cooperation to assist you to become informed about what is happening in the family. The first ripple occurs when you center your attention on the caregivers and their feelings and concerns rather than focusing on the report. They begin to reveal to you who they are and what the family is like. The second ripple occurs when you meet the child and learn about the child's functioning and indications of maltreatment. The third ripple occurs as you inquire about the parents' view and understanding of their child. Subsequent ripples emerge as you learn about the adults, how the family operates, parenting, stresses, strengths, and so on. This is a balanced approach to collecting information compared to focusing most of your attention on a maltreatment incident. As the ripples circle out from where you begin, you will find that returning to address the reported maltreatment circumstances and events in detail seems more natural and produces less denial and avoidance.

■ *The Process of Analyzing Risk Assessment Information*

How do you assess risk? *Assessing* is assigning weight (significance) to information. When you analyze the information you have collected, you should determine what information is significant by judging the extent to which it contributes to or explains the risk of maltreatment. The following are practical steps for assessing risk:

1. Collect information using risk-related interviews.
2. Organize information by the categories previously provided.
3. Determine whether you have sufficient and believable information, including obtaining collateral information as needed.

4. Assess. Assign significance to each category of risk factors. Various models have specific ways to assign significance (e.g., rating or giving scores and anchoring as low, moderate, or high). It is important to determine whether something you know about the family contributes to placing a child at risk.

5. Draw a conclusion. By grouping significant information into an overall picture of the family, you produce a meaningful conclusion about the risk of maltreatment. You illustrate individual and family functioning, patterns of behavior, events, interaction, and stresses to establish the rationale for the likelihood that maltreatment will occur without intervention. You justify your judgment. This is done by specifically identifying why you believe the information is significant.

■ Assessing Safety

A child may be unsafe when a family situation involves family conditions that are out of control, can be expected to occur (be displayed) immediately, and likely will have severe effects for a child. A safety assessment refers to the application of a method to identify the presence of threats to a child's safety within the family or home. It is important to always be concerned with safety; a formal safety assessment, however, is necessary at specific times in the life of a case: (a) receipt of a referral, (b) first contact with a family, (c) conclusion of the initial assessment, (d) establishment of the ongoing service plan, (e) case review, and (f) case closure.

From the definitions, it is clear that risk of maltreatment and concern for child safety (or threats to child safety) are not the same. Therefore, two distinct assessment approaches are needed. Children may be at risk of maltreatment at some point in the future but be safe from the likelihood of immediate threats of severe harm. Evaluating safety requires exploration of safety influences—that is, a risk factor that is operating at a more intense, explosive, immediate, dangerous, threatening level. Therefore, all safety influences are risk factors, but not all risk factors are safety influences.

You consider safety when you meet with the family face-to-face. You also evaluate safety when you conduct assessments or reviews during the life of the case (e.g., investigation and case assessment). You should be concerned with safety from two perspectives: (a) Is the child in danger right now (currently)? and (b) Might the child be in danger within the near future (next 30 days)?

How do you assess current danger? Search for *danger-loaded influences,* which are family situations, behavior, emotions, persons, physical circumstances, or social contexts operating in isolation or together in ways that create a current, immediate (now), and significant threat to a child's safety. These family conditions are transparent and easily identified. Examples of danger-loaded influences include hitting and hurting a child in the present, head and face injuries, premeditated maltreatment, bizarre cruelty, young children left alone unsupervised, and the parent being intoxicated or unable to perform parental duties. Because danger-loaded influences are operating in the present and because the threat is obvious and imminent, response and action must be immediate.

To assess child safety related to the next 30 days, a more complete picture of the family based on your risk assessment is necessary. Safety influences are specific behaviors (e.g., a parent is violent), specific emotions (e.g., a parent is too depressed to care for her child), specific situations (e.g., a family resides in condemned housing), or specific states of mind (e.g., a parent perceives the child in extremely negative terms). You assess safety by observing the family; listening for expressions of concern about safety; collecting risk-related information; analyzing risk information to identify safety influences; and qualifying safety influences by applying the criteria based on control, immediacy, and severity. Assessing safety is not about establishing proof or completing an empirically based prediction of what might occur. Assessing safety is grounded in (a) being well informed; (b) using prudence, reason, and logic to analyze information; and (c) being conservatively guided to ensure child safety while being respectful of parents' rights.

When assessing risk of maltreatment and threats to child safety, it must be remembered that an assessment tool is only an adjunct to effective decision making. Furthermore, predicting future human and family behavior is sufficiently difficult that one should overestimate concern to ensure the best interest of the child.

■ *Further Reading*

Doueck, H., English, D., De Panfilis, D., & Moote, G. (1993). Decision making in child protective services: A comparison of selected risk assessment models. *Child Welfare, 72,* 441-452.

Holder, W., & Corey, M. (1994). *Safety analysis through family evaluation.* Charlotte, NC: ACTION for Child Protection.

48

How Do I Consider Cultural Factors When Assessing Risk and Safety?

■ *Sheryl Brissett-Chapman*

Formal risk assessment is a structured process designed to ensure consistency with knowledgeable standards and protocols and to support the worker's decision-making process. To apply it effectively, we must also understand the potential impact of our intervention response on diverse children and family systems. What does it really mean to go beyond a "gut" instinct to acquire essential knowledge about the level of childhood vulnerability in families who are fundamentally different from oneself? How can we truly understand the ways in which diverse families (a) nurture and protect their children, physically and emotionally; (b) recognize and prioritize child endangerment situations and provide protection to avert child injury of any kind; (c) organize themselves, and others in their family or social network or larger community, to directly and consistently provide care for their children; and (d) socialize and discipline their children, teaching them how to live in the world with other people and comply with laws and community practices. In an increasingly mosaic society, how does the worker effectively recognize the relevancy of innumerable cultural distinctions and the respective impact on both the worker and the family's perceptions of the child welfare mission, the family's functioning, community interactions, and, ultimately, the child's physical and developmental status or overall well-being?

Unquestionably, it is a complicated but unavoidable task to accommodate cultural considerations when conducting protective risk assessment. The worker must understand the dynamics of difference in cultural groups that have experienced systematic discrimination or extreme environments (e.g., poverty, violence, oppression, segregation, exploitation, and war). It is equally important that the worker is mature enough to actively engage in a continuous journey of professional development, which involves minimally the following:

- Self-evaluation regarding one's own cultural values and professional motivation
- Openness to personal scrutiny and the conscious avoidance of assumptions and stereotyping
- Recognition and management of unconscious biases and emotional attachment to ignorance and falsehood about others who are different
- Reliance on an overall healthy personal mental mind-set and related helping approaches (even when the use of authority is involved, such as removal of a child from the parent)
- Natural and genuine interest in the unique lifestyles and worldviews of the families being served, requiring the use of various resources, to gain enhanced skills in assessing unacceptable or detrimental outcomes for children or both

It is no simple matter to combine cultural self-awareness and understanding of the cultures of others with the volatile and urgent child protection agenda. Nevertheless, this balance must be achieved if the worker intends to enable the family, the community, and other members of the expanded professional team to work in partnership to ensure that every child receives a safe, nurturing, and good enough childhood.

■ *The Importance of Culture*

Child welfare scholars have documented differences in affective, attitudinal, and behavioral patterns of different groups, noting that these distinctions can be seen in the varying approaches to the socialization of children. The worker must remain mindful of these potential differences while generally working under severe time constraints and often with a parent or family system involuntarily involved in the child welfare system. Cultural differences influence the way in which families interact with outsiders, cooperate with institutions and authority, perform parenting functions, and cope with trauma and hardship or success and accomplishment.

When balancing specific child maltreatment safety and risk screening activities with the validation of the cultural lens of the family, the worker's goal is to engage the family so as to gain essential and accurate information about the child's immediate status and well-being as well as the family's capacity to appropriately support the child's critical development (see Chapters 9 and 20, this volume). The scenario that follows typifies the worker's need to actively integrate the culture factor in this process:

Nikki arrived at the emergency room with her 7-year-old twin daughters. On medical examination, it was determined that both children had contracted gonorrhea. When the worker arrived, she easily gained the history from the two shy girls. For the past 2 years, Nikki had lived with her children and her boyfriend, who paid all the bills and leased their apartment. Every Sunday afternoon, he allowed Nikki to shop for food while he cared for the girls on his only day off from construction work. During this time, the girls alternated taking baths and having forced intercourse with the boyfriend. The children never reported the abuse to their mother because, as the more assertive child reported, "We called the police whenever daddy beat up our mommy, but the police *never* came!"

When Nikki discovered that the children would be removed on an emergency basis until their safety needs were ensured, she experienced an emotional crisis, which shattered her defenses. The worker used this opportunity to review questions that had been answered earlier. Initially distrusting and self-protective, Nikki had denied having any immediate family in the area, stating "They're back in North Carolina." Sensing her enormous anxiety in the hospital setting, the worker took Nikki to the cafeteria, bought her some coffee, and shared with this distraught African American parent the worker's own experiences with helping families who had migrated from North Carolina.

The worker asked, "Are you sure you don't have any folks here? It's very unusual that a young mother would come north with no people here!" Nikki broke into a new flood of tears. She shared that she did have an aunt and several cousins here but that they were angry with her for living with a man, unmarried, and they did not want to visit her. She had run away from her children's father because he had been incarcerated for murder in a street brawl in North Carolina and tried to control her activities from the state prison through his friends. She was too proud to take welfare assistance and possessed only a fifth-grade education. She only knew how to pick tobacco and sharecrop. She was still intimidated by the city, and now she was both fearful of the boyfriend and isolated from her family.

By avoiding prejudgment and stereotyping, the worker in this scenario was able to authentically engage the mother during the disclosure of child sexual abuse. The worker also recognized the cultural resiliency in the young woman. Although she had suffered from her selection of mates, failed to protect her daughters, appeared to be subordinate in all her relationships, and had been reared in a racially harsh and unsupportive community, she took pride in her children, was highly attached to them, and was willing to work closely with a professional to get them back. The path to reunification took 9 months. This seemingly passive, dependent parent (a) participated in therapy for herself and in conjoint and family therapy with her daughters, who were angry due to the lack of protection; (b) advocated for subsidy to obtain her own apartment; (c) obtained a court restraining order when her boyfriend threatened her in the neighborhood; and (d) began to seek work with help from her family, who forgave Nikki once they recognized that she was growing and changing. Considerably more acculturated to an urban environment, Nikki became adequately empowered to avoid abusive relationships, became more self-sufficient, and, most important, provided critically important protection for her children while modeling self-love and care and benefiting from a culturally specific reliance on an extended family system.

■ *Challenges to Incorporating the Culture Factor*

There are significant obstacles to accommodating cultural considerations when assessing the risk of child maltreatment or its recurrence. Most child protective service systems are generally overextended and underfunded. The worker's caseload usually does not encourage taking time to adequately engage families and their support systems or to seek clarification or pertinent information that may not be readily available or apparent due to cultural differences. The worker's most formidable task is to manage specific cultural differences that drive both the worker's and the family's expectations of child safety and well-being; only then can an effective contract be realized that ensures the child protection mission. Indeed, although there may be considerable agreement regarding when a child, minimally, is safe or thriving, there are innumerable ways to approach this goal.

■ *Getting Across the Culture Chasm*

In summary, the worker who recognizes that the acknowledgment of cultural differences is an opportunity for making certain that children are adequately nurtured and cared for is more likely to be perceived as "real" or authentic by families who are battling a variety of life challenges. The worker is more likely to gain the data needed to assess both the level of risk and the intensity and nature of the professional intervention needed, including obtaining the family's "buy-in" and commitment to change. The "culturally competent worker brings intellectual and emotional stamina to the rigors demanded in effective risk assessment.

There is no single menu for integrating culture into the risk assessment process; the worker, however, should routinely consider the following factors:

- The family's cultural identification
- How family members wish to be addressed
- The family's perceptions of the mainstream institutions or the dominant culture
- Their experiences with other professional helpers or authorities
- Clarity regarding language and meanings in verbal and nonverbal communication
- Perceptions of substance abuse and family violence and their impact
- Perceptions of the responsibilities of adults and children in the extended family and community network
- Perceptions of the impact of child abuse or neglect
- Perceptions of discipline practices, including corporal discipline and child supervision issues
- Perceptions of family response to acute stressors, chronic stressors, losses and betrayal, and discrimination
- Family accomplishments and the sense of empowerment and success

Culturally competent risk assessment involves a professional use of self, which reflects a high respect and regard for the cultural lifestyles and values of others. Culturally competent risk assessment is not a form or a checklist, and it does not eliminate the need for high-level thinking and reasoning. Emphasis should be placed on weighing risk with strength, assessing child safety and child status, and generalizing the application of cultural strengths to parenting concerns. When risk assessment practices reflect the integration of knowledge, skill, and an open mind-set, functional "bridges" are built across the cultural chasm—bridges that bring together responsible adults with a shared perspective. Children then find safety, stability, true permanency, and empowering support.

■ *Further Reading*

Brissett-Chapman, S. (1997). Child protection risk assessment and African American children: Cultural ramifications for families and communities. *Child Welfare, 66,* 45-63.

Kanda, M., Orr, L. A., Brissett-Chapman, S., & Lawson, T. S. (1993). Intentional injury. In M. Eichelberger (Ed.), *Pediatric trauma: Prevention, acute care, rehabilitation* (pp. 557-567). St. Louis, MO: Mosby Year Book.

49

How Do I Ensure a Maltreated Child's Safety in the Home?

■ *Wayne Holder*

Once you have assessed that a child is unsafe (see Chapter 47, this volume), there are essentially three ways to keep the child safe in his or her own home: (a) A nonoffending parent or adult ensures the child's safety; (b) the offending person vacates the home, and assurances exist that no return will occur; and (c) a safety service plan ensures the child's safety.

■ *Safety Ensured by Nonoffending Parent*

Consider a nonoffending parent or another adult who resides in the home as a resource for in-home safety management. You can use the following items to evaluate the nonoffending parent's or other adult's potential to be protective:

- Must be willing to provide protection and understand why protection is necessary
- Must understand the nature of the protective responsibility, what specifically will be required, and personal responsibilities

- Must be physically able with respect to meeting the demands for caring for and protecting the child, including health, mobility, strength, stamina, and senses
- Must not be fearful of or intimidated by the offender
- Must possess adequate physical prowess and courage to face up to the offender
- Must be emotionally stable and calm
- Must possess sufficient cognitive capacity
- Must be able to follow instructions and the specific details that form the safety plan
- Must be able to perceive circumstances accurately and recognize danger

When evaluating an adult other than the child's parent as an in-home safety resource, you can consider the degree of "closeness" as a yardstick. Judge closeness by the following:

- Whether the person resides or could reside in the home most of the time on a daily basis
- How long the person has been involved with the family
- How close the association (familiarity and interest) is with the child(ren)
- How comfortable the person is in assuming a responsible caregiving role

When assessing the ability to protect, you should evaluate the nonoffending parent's or other adult's intentions:

- Consider how convicted the person is in accepting the responsibility by asking what he or she believes about the reality of the threats, the requirements for protection, what should be done, how protection should be achieved and why he or she believes this is so.
- Search for certainty in communication, physical expressions, perceptions, and attitudes.
- Judge whether there appears to be resolve to ensure that the children are protected as evidenced by appropriate emotion (concern to indignation about the danger, compassion for the children, and a driven sense of determination).

- Evaluate on what basis this person establishes his or her commitment to protect the child.

An effective indicator of the ability of a nonoffending parent or other adult to provide protection to a child is a history of protective behavior. The previous incident in which protective behavior has been displayed should be described by the person in detail. Can the account of protectiveness be verified? Ask about cues that stimulated the person toward protective behaviors in the past. Consider how the historical circumstances compare to the current situation and the current threats. Is there evidence that this is a person who always follows through? Others may be able to advise you about the dependability of this person.

The nature of the relationship that exists between the nonoffending parent or other adult and the child can be used to assess the following:

- What is the person's viewpoint of the child generally (e.g., likeable, believable, and good)?
- What is the person's perception about the child's involvement in the safety circumstance?
- Does the person view the child as a victim or deserving?
- Who is the person allied with? The child? The offending parent?
- What is the quality of the relationship and attachment between the person and the child?
- Does the person value the child?
- How is the relationship described from both the adult's and the child's point of view?
- Does the child trust the adult?

Protective nonoffending parents or other adults typically respond assertively:

- They believe the threats are real.
- They believe the child. Although they may not have been aware of the need for protection or the presence of threats, their awareness is readily achieved.
- They are unambiguous about their acknowledgment of the need for protection.

- You may observe an emotional and behavioral response during acknowledgment (e.g., removing the offender from the home and filing charges).

Ask the person to describe a personal plan for protecting the child. Is it realistic? Does it demonstrate independence on the part of the person? After fully exploring the person's ability to protect, you should thoroughly document a plan that establishes the suitability of the person to provide protection.

■ *Safety Ensured by Offender*
   Leaving the Home

You may be able to obtain child safety within the home if the offending parent will leave. The "trick" to this approach lies in the confidence you can acquire about whether the offending person will honor the agreement and stay away from the family. Be aware that some people may suggest this option as a way of manipulating child protective services (CPS). A person could identify this alternative because he or she is adamant about having the offender gone. Parents may suggest this solution because it is a reasonable way to avoid having the child removed. Other family members may ask for this approach out of anger. (See Chapter 54, this volume, for factors to consider when making this decision.) If the plan is for the offending parent to leave, you must be confident about the motives involved and the reliability of this action:

- How believable is this person?
- What can you base your beliefs about this person on?
- Is the person able to persuasively provide you with reasons for you to believe him or her?

Your assurance that this approach will work will depend on many issues:

- Will the person be next door or several miles away?
- Can the person visit the child at places away from the home?

- Can the plan be formalized through a restraining order?
- Can a petition be filed in court to specify agreements about the offender's absence?
- What is the nonoffending parent's level of commitment to protection?
- Can other supportive parties (e.g., friends and extended family) be enlisted to be aware of and report on the success of the plan and notify CPS if the offender returns?
- What written communication is needed about the plan with key parties?
- In addition to the offending person vacating the home, what other provisions are needed (e.g., communication between parties, visitation, access, location, length of the arrangement, and supervision)?

■ Safety Ensured Through a Safety Services Plan

In many cases, it will be possible for you to manage child safety in the home with one or both parents present. When implementing an in-home safety plan, you need to clearly define what is jeopardizing a child's safety and then appropriately match a plan that will target these specific influences. After defining the threats but before matching services, you should evaluate the family and home context. The following critical questions apply:

1. Is the parent(s) willing to participate in and cooperate with an in-home plan?
2. Is the home setting calm and consistent to accommodate service providers?
3. Do you need specialized evaluations to proceed with an in-home plan (e.g., substance abuse and mental health)?

Safety services should address basic safety needs; be immediate in effect; be short term; control safety threats; be available, sufficient, and accessible; and be suitable by relating specifically to safety needs. Examples of safety services are supervision and monitoring, basic parenting skills coaching (e.g., how to mix formula), basic life and home management, crisis counseling, drug and mental health services, and health interventions.

Weekly CPS oversight is fundamental to in-home safety management and should be tailored to address the specific threats to child safety. External safety checks and alerts can be arranged with those who have frequent contact with the family. Safety contracts should be written to describe threats to safety, expectations, roles, responsibilities, tasks, and alternative behaviors or actions, such as counting to 10 when one gets angry or a parent taking a time-out.

■ *Further Reading*

Holder, W., & Morton, T. D. (1999). *Designing a comprehensive approach to child safety*. Atlanta: Child Welfare Institute.

50

How Do I Protect Children When There Is a History of Domestic Violence in the Family?

■ *Ronald Zuskin*

Protection for children in a family with a history of domestic violence relies on your interview and assessment and the arrangement of safety and protection. Intervention by any outside agency into these families may increase the danger of domestic violence toward the victim and increase the risk of maltreatment to the children; therefore, both steps must be handled carefully.

■ *Interview and Assessment*

Interviews generate the information from which you will assess risk of maltreatment and evaluate the safety of the children. In general, when you attempt to assess the risk to children,

- Do no harm.
- Increase the safety and protection of family members.
- Respect and support the adult victim's autonomy.

As standard interviewing practice,

- Interview all family members together and individually.
- Do not discuss domestic violence in conjoint interviews.
- If the topic arises in a conjoint interview, acknowledge its importance but discuss it in individual interviews.
- Begin with more neutral topics.
- Begin to address issues of past and possible current domestic violence with the adult victim.
- Use normal language (e.g., "How do people in the family get along?" and "How are disagreements handled?").
- Move from general to specific questions.
- Pay attention to verbal and nonverbal communication.
- Ask for descriptions of incidents and not judgments.
- Ask children questions (e.g., "Who makes the rules in your family?" and "In your family, who is allowed to hit whom?").
- If a victim acknowledges current domestic violence, consult with him or her about how to best handle this.
- Do not share a disclosure with the perpetrator unless requested by the victim.
- If children raise issues of domestic violence, always discuss them with the alleged victim before taking any other action.
- If the adult victim wishes to separate, help or refer him or her to develop a safety plan and arrange for legal or domestic violence assistance or both.
- Whenever information is to be shared with the perpetrator of domestic violence, inform the victim of the time and place.
- Remember that the best predictor of future violence is past violence.
- Keep in mind that a batterer who remains committed to exerting power and control over a victim who intends to or does separate can pose the risk of lethal violence to the victim and to children in the family.

Domestic violence poses increased risk and safety concerns related to maltreatment. Protecting kids means searching for possible domestic violence. Ask about the severity, intensity, duration, and frequency of the most recent incident. Inquire about the whereabouts and involvement of children during the outburst.

It is rare for the batterer to be out of control. Violence is usually the result of calculated decisions made on the part of a batterer intent on getting something and exacting a price for it. Children are most likely to get hurt unintentionally in domestic violence episodes. Infants in arms are at risk of severe injury, as are toddlers who are underfoot. Some children are tugged on by parents and suffer dislocated joints, sprains, or fractures. Older children attempting to intervene can suffer serious injury, as can children of any age who find themselves in harm's way whenever objects or liquids are thrown. All these scenarios indicate children's need for protection because these safety concerns cannot be addressed in standard child protective services (CPS) safety planning.

■ Arranging Safety and Protection

When arranging safety or protection, professionals who deal with domestic violence daily should be involved. They can supplement your assessment and provide outside resources for protection of adult victims and children who need to separate from perpetrators. Victim parents and children who are unsafe should be sheltered—as a unit if possible. If families acknowledge domestic violence but do not choose to separate, a thorough assessment of risk and safety must be completed. Specific safety factors to consider include the following:

- Stated intent to cause harm
- Rationalization of violent behavior
- Supposedly "out of control" behaviors
- Child(ren) or partner perceived in extremely negative terms
- Injuries to anyone in family that are not adequately explained
- Perpetrator lacks remorse
- Significant emotional symptoms or severe lack of behavioral control in adult victim or child(ren)

- Alcohol or other drug involvement
- Either or both parents overtly reject intervention or contact

Each of these is a red flag; two or more are early warning signs indicating the child's need for protection. A CPS safety plan addressing each concern must be in place, or the children may need to be sheltered until safety concerns are resolved. Once concerns for the children's imminent safety are resolved, children may be returned and a service plan can be implemented to decrease the risk of future maltreatment.

■ *Further Reading*

DePanfilis, D., & Brooks, G. (1989). *Child maltreatment and woman abuse: A guide for child protective services intervention.* Washington, DC: National Woman Abuse Prevention Project.

Ganley, A., & Schecter, S. (1996). *Domestic violence: A national curriculum for child protective services.* San Francisco: National Violence Prevention Fund.

Zuskin, R. (1995). *Domestic violence and child maltreatment.* Baltimore: University of Maryland School of Social Work.

51

How Do I Protect Children When Caregivers Have Chemical-Dependency Problems?

■ *Ronald Rogers and Chandler Scott McMillin*

Alcohol and drug problems are prime risk factors for child maltreatment; effective intervention and treatment of the addicted caregiver are a critical part of protecting children. Also, in such cases, child abuse or neglect often occur not only by the primary caregiver but also by associates (e.g., drug dealers and other users).

The following misconceptions about addiction make effective intervention a challenge for many professionals:

1. *The addict must want help.* Caught in a cycle of intoxication and withdrawal, few addicts are capable of making a rational decision for treatment. When they do seek help, it is usually because of a temporary shortage of funds or to avoid one of the many consequences of the addictive lifestyle, such as the loss of job or family, medical problems, and a jail sentence. Once in treatment, the addict feels better and thinks more clearly. In fact, most addicts who successfully recover entered treatment against their will. Treatment might be thought to have a cumulative effect. Miller and Rollnick (1991) described the following stages of change in working with involuntary clients: precontemplation,

Table 51.1   Stages of Change

Precontemplation	"I don't think I need to change."
Contemplation	"Maybe I do need to make a change."
Determination	"Here's how I am going to change."
Action	"I'm changing!"
Maintenance	"I need to keep what I've got."
Relapse	"I screwed up. How can I get back on track?"

Table 51.2   Stages of Change and the Counselor's Tasks

Patient's Stage	*Counselor's Tasks*
Precontemplation	Raise doubt—increase the patient's perception of risks and problems with current behavior. *Functions:* intervention, assessment, screens, education, orientation, and intake collateral interview
Contemplation	Tip the balance, evoke reasons to change and risks of not changing, and strengthen patient's self-efficacy for change of immediate behavior. *Functions:* self-diagnostic assignments, education, identify strengths, begin to give direction, time frame
Determination	Help patient to plan action. Identify resources, set goals, objectives, and contract. *Function:* treatment planning
Action	Help patient take steps toward change. Monitor treatment plan progress, give direction, and work on obstacles and defense mechanisms. *Functions:* group and individual counseling, case management, consultation, referral, monitor, revise, update treatment plan, and overcome defenses and obstacles
Maintenance	Develop strategies to prevent relapse, develop ongoing support system, and obtain feedback system. *Function:* monitor treatment competence
Relapse	Help patient reenter the process, usually at the level of contemplation or determination. *Functions:* crisis intervention, reassessment, and treatment planning

contemplation, determination, action, maintenance, and relapse (Table 51.1). Depending on the level of resistance, more than one treatment experience may be needed for someone to change his or her belief that he or she does not have a problem with drugs and raise doubt, motivate change, take action, and prevent relapse (Table 51.2).

2. *Addicts cannot quit until other problems are solved.* Although addicts blame their drug use on outside circumstances, the reality is that they cannot address their numerous life problems until the destructive pattern of chemical use has been interrupted. It is important to remember that active addiction and early recovery mimic most psychiatric diagnoses. It is usually good practice to treat the client for most psychiatric problems while at the same time addressing the addiction and drug toxicity.

3. *The addict may be able to quit without help.* Although most addicts experience periods of less intense use, the nature of addiction is to progress to more profound dysfunction. Few are able to achieve stable recovery without treatment.

As professionals, we counteract the destructive power of the addict's compulsion through the intelligent use of leverage and influence. In a situation involving child maltreatment, the professional may be able to give the caregiver a choice between accepting treatment for addiction and a loss of rights or privileges involving the child (e.g., visitation and custody). Case managers may also have considerable influence over an addict via their role in legal decisions such as termination of parental rights. The threat of a real and immediate consequence is the best way to motivate a resistant addict or alcoholic to take the initial steps toward change.

To determine the appropriate level of addiction treatment required, seek the assistance of an addictions professional at your local public or private clinic. An assessment using one of several standardized instruments will help determine the best modality based on the extent and severity of the addiction. To assess an addicted caregiver's status in treatment, ask yourself if he or she is

- Abstinent from drugs, as demonstrated by random testing
- Involved in a program of recovery, such as attending a self-help group
- Being treated appropriately for any comorbid psychiatric disorder

Home visits also help in evaluating the caregiver's recovery and the general home situation. Good treatment involves family members. Many programs provide education and counseling for family members as well as referrals to self-help programs, such as Al-Anon and Alateen or Al-Atot.

■ *Further Reading*

Miller, W. R., & Rollnick, S. (1991). *Motivational interviewing preparing people to change addictive behavior.* New York: Guilford.

Rogers, R. L., & McMillin, S. C. (1992). *Freeing someone you love from alcohol and other drugs.* New York: The Body Press/Perigee.

52

How Do I Protect Children From Hazardous Home Conditions and Other Poverty-Related Conditions?

■ *John R. Lutzker*

Home accidents pose a serious risk to young children. They are responsible for more than 90% of all fatalities and injuries to children younger than 5 years of age. Similarly, health risks can create many serious problems for young children, including infections and disease from harmful agents in unkempt homes such as fecal matter on the floor or dangerous bacteria from spoiled food. It has been suggested that virtually no injury is accidental; many can be anticipated and prevented. The job of the parent and the human service professional is to provide as safe an environment as possible for children to prevent injuries.

■ Assessment

In 1984, my colleagues and I created the Home Accident Prevention Inventory (HAPI; Table 52.1) to help professionals or parents assess the hazards in their homes. Recently, the HAPI was revised (HAPI-R). Hazards are categorized as fire and electrical,

Table 52.1   Home Accident Prevention Inventory—Revised

Poison by solids and liquids	Outlets or switches (without plates)
Medicines	Suffocation by mechanical object
Detergents and cleaners	Plastic bags
Polishes and waxes	Crib cords
Alcoholic beverages	Small objects
Beauty products	Ingestible small objects
Insecticides and rodenticides	Sharp objects
Paints and stains	Firearms
Solvents and thinners	Falling hazards
Glues and adhesives	Balconies
Petroleum products	Steps
Fertilizers and herbicides	Windows
Poisonous house plants	Drowning hazards
Fire and electrical hazards	Bathtubs and sinks
Combustibles	Buckets
Fireplaces without screens	Pools

suffocation by ingested object, firearms, solid and liquid poisons, suffocation by mechanical objects, falling, and drowning.

Examples of fire and electrical hazards include matches and cigarette lighters left on a coffee table and a missing fire screen in front of a fireplace. Small objects on the floor may lead to a young child choking. Other common problems include guns under kitchen and bathroom sinks and poisonous items, such as common household plants, cleaners and solvents, polishes and waxes, medications, and cosmetics. Balconies may have slats through which a young child could fall, and many swimming pools are not properly fenced off.

We also developed the Checklist for Living Environments to Assess Neglect (CLEAN) to help professionals or parents count items around a home that represent clutter and to assess filth such as decaying food.

■ Management Strategies

There are three treatment modes for safety and health. Counselor education, the first approach, is instruction to eliminate hazards systematically, room by room, by removing hazards such as small objects and covering electrical outlets.

For families with filthy and cluttered homes, posting photos depicting improvements in targeted rooms may help. Small incentives for gradual but systematic improvements can be useful. In one case, we posted a pie chart for a mother who could not read, with each piece of the pie representing a "satisfactory" room. When the chart was complete, the counselor baked a pie with the parent.

Counselor education is effective but time-consuming. Thus, we have also used a slide tape program and, recently, a video program.[1] The video program, which has five parts, has been very effective, particularly with minimal counseling. Parents viewing the video have shown generalization, removing hazards from rooms not yet discussed in the video.

It should be noted that the normal, healthy curiosity of children can cause them to "get into trouble" with hazards in a home. Anticipating and preventing "accidents" is key; getting angry "after the fact" makes less sense.

■ *Note*

1. The videos, the HAPI-R, and the CLEAN can be ordered at cost from Dr. John R. Lutzker, University of Judaism, 15600 Mulholland Drive, Los Angeles, CA 90077.

■ *Further Reading*

Mandel, U., Bigelow, K. M., & Lutzker, J. R. (1998). Using video to reduce home safety hazards with parents reported for child abuse or neglect. *Journal of Family Violence, 13,* 147-162.

Tertinger, D. A., Greene, B. F., & Lutzker, J. R. (1984). Home safety: Development and validation of one component of an ecobehavioral treatment program for abused and neglected children. *Journal of Applied Analysis, 17,* 159-174.

53

When Do Family Preservation Services Make Sense, and When Should Other Permanency Plans Be Explored?

■ *Kristine Nelson*

Since there is much confusion about family preservation services, it should first be made clear what they are not. Family preservation services *are not*

- simply an agency policy that states that families should be kept together whenever possible.
- simply a philosophy that holds that most children are better off in their own homes, although this is the main reason for providing family preservation services.
- any service provided to families at risk of separation through child placement.
- any service provided to intact families in their own homes.

Family preservation services *are*

- provided frequently, with at least one in-person contact a week.
- individually tailored to meet the family's stated needs.

- oriented toward specific goals developed collaboratively by the worker and the family.
- respectful of the family members as the experts on their own situation and needs.
- designed to allow children to remain safely in their own homes by building on family strengths and overcoming deficits.

■ Types of Family Preservation Services

According to standards defined by the Child Welfare League of America, family preservation services may be of the following types:

1. Intensive family-centered crisis services. Best known is the Homebuilders' crisis intervention model, which provides services intensively (several times a week during a 4- to 6-week time period) to build family skills and understanding and to meet their basic needs. Typically, workers are trained specifically in the Homebuilders' model and serve only two or three families at a time. Homebuilders' services work particularly well with families involved in physical abuse or status offenses. Other models of intensive family-centered crisis services provide approximately the same amount of service but do so less frequently and during a 3- or 4-month period. These services may include family and individual therapy as well as skill building and concrete services. They also may assist the family in working with other systems in the community, such as the schools. Longer, more systemic services work best with families in which sexual abuse or juvenile delinquency is the problem.

2. Family-centered casework services. These services are generally not in response to a specific crisis but provided to families with longer term, more chronic problems such as neglect. They may last 6 to 18 months and provide a comprehensive array of services to meet the family's many needs, often using paraprofessional aides to provide in-home services. Families who are not motivated to cooperate with services may respond best to offers of assistance in building support for the family and meeting the children's needs. They may need to be contacted persistently at least once a week for the first 3 months, and then they can

consolidate and maintain their gains with one or two contacts a month for a more extended period of time.

3. Family resource, support, and education services. These services are generally voluntary and provide a range of supports to high-risk families (day care, housing assistance, parent education, and support groups) in their own communities. They are sometimes located in neighborhood centers or schools. They may be useful to families who are not yet threatened with placement but who are at risk of future child abuse or neglect.

■ *When Should Family Preservation Services Be Considered?*

Family preservation services should be considered whenever a child may be placed out of the home or moved to a new placement—for example,

- When families are first contacted by a child protective worker: In a pilot project, placements were dramatically reduced in counties that teamed family preservation workers with child protective service workers for the initial 2 weeks of contact. In addition, families received more services and had fewer repeated incidents of child abuse or neglect.
- When there has been a recent crisis in the home that has led to child abuse or neglect: Many families reported to child welfare agencies are under severe or recent stress or both that may include loss of housing or a job; death, divorce, or separation; and an illness, accident, or the birth of another child. In these circumstances, immediate, intensive services may avert additional deterioration of the family and prevent the placement of a child. In such cases, the first consideration should be the safety of the child. Immediate threats to the child's safety, including lack of supervision for young children, serious injuries, unsafe housing, an urgent need for medical care, and continuing violence or threat of violence in the home, should be assessed and addressed by creating a safety plan.

For example, a depressed mother with several young children who is living in a shelter might be encouraged to let her mother or sister provide care for her children while she recovers her energy and finds new housing with the support of the family preservation worker. In cases of physical abuse, the use of crisis cards (suggesting alternative responses), respite care, or 24-hour access to a neighbor, family member, or family preservation worker might be sufficient to ensure safety. In other situations, another adult in the home, a family member, or a home aide may be able to provide support and supervision. A child should be removed only as a last resort, when no other arrangement can ensure his or her safety.

- In cases of sexual abuse when the perpetrator is out of the home or admitting his or her responsibility and the nonoffending caregiver is protective: In sexual abuse cases, family preservation services are provided to support the recovery of the victim and prevent removal from the nonoffending parent. If the parent does not believe the child or sides with the offender, family preservation services are not appropriate.

- Before a decision to place is made in nonemergency cases: In many cases, the danger to the child is not sudden or the result of a specific action but cumulative through lack of attention to the child's needs. In the event that longer term supportive services do not succeed in assisting the parent to provide adequate care, placement may be necessary.

- Before a decision to reunify is made: One of the most successful applications of family preservation services has been in reunifying children in placement with their families. Because decisions about permanency may have to be made within as short a time period as 12 months, even if a child is in placement, intensive services may be warranted. Intensive services during the reunification process may be followed by longer term, more infrequent services or "booster shots" to help families maintain stability. Several studies have shown higher rates of successful and stable reunification when family preservation services are employed.

- When a crisis threatens the stability of a kinship, foster care, or adoptive placement: Although family preservation services are most often used to maintain or reunify children with their biological parents, any family that is intended to be the long-term resource or permanent placement for a child should be eligible for services. Although the crisis may not involve child maltreatment, services should be provided during periods of developmental or family stress to prevent the placement from disrupting and further damaging the child.

Although child protection is recognized as the primary mission of child welfare services, family preservation can and should be a compatible goal to meet the child's long-term and short-term needs. Family preservation services, however, should not be considered if the child's safety cannot be ensured, even with intensive services (for further information on child safety, see Chapter 49, this volume).

■ *Further Reading*

Child Welfare League of America. (1989). *Standards for services to strengthen and preserve families with children*. Washington, DC: Author.

Henggeler, S. W., & Borduin, C. M. (1990). *Family therapy and beyond: A multisystemic approach to treating the behavior problems of children and adolescents*. Belmont, CA: Brooks/Cole.

Kaplan, L., & Girard, J. L. (1994). *Strengthening high-risk families: A handbook for practitioners*. New York: Lexington Books.

54

How Do I Decide Whether to Remove the Alleged Offender or to Remove the Child?

■ *Barbara L. Bonner*

This chapter reviews the factors to consider when making a decision whether to remove a child or an alleged offender from a home. It is currently recommended that the alleged offender be removed rather than the child if the safety and well-being of the child cannot be ensured in the home. It is also recommended that, whenever possible, removal decisions be made as part of a multidisciplinary team approach to case management.

■ *What Factors Should Be Assessed in Determining the Necessity for Removal?*

Although it is not known exactly which of the following factors places a child at increased risk, careful consideration should be given to each factor. When several factors are present, a child is considered to be at risk, and removal should occur—typically of the alleged offender.

1. *Child factors*
   Safety of the child and other children in the home;

age of the child; younger children more at risk in cases of physical abuse (In cases of sexual abuse, a child of any age is considered at risk if an alleged adult offender is in the home.)

Vulnerability due to mental or physical disabilities

Basic needs not being met (e.g., food, shelter, and clothing)

2. *Factors related to the abusive behavior* (These factors apply to all forms of maltreatment.)

Frequency, duration, and severity of current and past abuse

Lack of plausible explanation of how injury, incident, or situation occurred

Lack of appropriate supervision

Intent to harm the child (i.e., difference between intent to harm and intent to discipline or punish)

3. *Nonoffending parent factors*

Uncooperative with child protective services (CPS); unwilling to follow treatment plan

Does not believe the child's report

Blames the child for the abuse

Believes and attempts to protect the alleged offender

Consistent problems in overall level of functioning

History of past abuse or neglect of children

Lack of satisfactory utilization of past services

History of childhood abuse or current spouse abuse

Use of drugs or alcohol

Highly dependent, psychologically or economically, on the alleged offender

4. *Alleged offender factors*

History of past abuse of children

Inability to control behavior, such as history of spouse abuse, substance abuse, or serious mental health problems

Ongoing access to the child

Denial of the reported behavior

History of intimidating nonoffending parent or child

Lack of parenting knowledge, skills, and motivation to learn

5. *Other family factors*

Condition of the home hazardous

Lack of social support network, such as extended family, friends, or religious organization

High level of family conflict or stress, such as birth of child or loss of housing or benefits

Other family pressures on the child to recant

■ What Are the Typical Effects of Removal on the Child?

1. Effects can range from minimal to severe based on numerous factors, such as the severity and duration of the abuse, the child's overall adjustment, other family members' responses, the familiarity and stability of the placement setting, and the nonoffending parent's belief and support of the child. (Note: The belief and support of the nonoffending parent continue to be crucial factors in the child's short-term and long-term adjustment.)
2. The initial effects are usually mild to moderate behavioral (aggression and anger) and affective (fearfulness and depression) responses.
3. Over time, in stable placements most children adjust satisfactorily.
4. Some children continue to have highly problematic behavior; it is likely, however, that this is due to a combination of the removal, the past abuse, and other psychological factors.

■ What Are the Potential Effects of Removing the Alleged Offender?

1. Child

Potential positive effects: The child feels believed and supported by the nonoffending parent; has less disruption in his or her everyday routines, such as school, friends, and day care; and feels safer in the home.

Potential negative effects: The child feels guilty, may be blamed by family members, and may change the report of abuse.

2. Nonoffending parent

   Potential positive effects: Removal can indicate that professionals believe the child, reinforce the parent's role as protector of the child, emphasize the seriousness of alleged offender's behavior, and reduce conflict of parent choosing between child and alleged offender.

   Potential negative effects: Nonoffending parent may punish or put pressure on the child to change the abuse report, feel guilty, have fewer economic resources, and be blamed or punished by the alleged offender and other family members.

3. Alleged offender

   Potential positive effects: Removal can indicate the seriousness of the behavior, reflect that professionals believe the child, result in an admission, and lead to seeking treatment.

   Potential negative effects: The alleged offender may become more defensive and angry, less cooperative with CPS, and less likely to financially support the family.

■ *How Do I Make the Decision?*

It is recommended that information from other agencies, disciplines, and professionals be considered in a multidisciplinary case staffing when removal decisions are made.

> *Removal of the alleged offender:* The alleged offender should be removed if the child's safety and well-being in the home cannot be ensured.
>
> *Removal of the child:* The child should be removed when the nonoffending parent does not believe the child and is not capable or willing to protect the child from additional abuse.

■ *Further Reading*

DePanfilis, D., & Scannapieco, M. (1994). Assessing the safety of children at risk of maltreatment: Decision-making models. *Child Welfare, 73*, 229-245.

Pellegrin, A., & Wagner, W. G. (1990). Child sexual abuse: Factors affecting victims' removal from home. *Child Abuse and Neglect, 14*, 53-60.

55

How Do I Assess the Risk of Maltreatment in Foster Care and Kinship Care?

■ *Wayne Holder*

Prior to placing a child, you assess for risk of maltreatment in foster care or kinship care by gathering and analyzing sufficient information that emphasizes strengths and resources while illuminating risk factors and concerns. There are practical differences in assessing foster parent applicants and kinship situations. Foster parent applicants offer their services. Their offer does not necessarily involve a particular child. They do not know a child's family. You seek out kinship care arrangements. Kin know the child, may have a relationship with the child, and may have formed specific perceptions about the child. They know the child's parents. Both kinds of families are predisposed to bring their values, attitudes, and biases to the caregiving situation, some of which may be ill informed.

Information collection should include face-to-face interviews with the family, adults individually, the family's own children individually, and collateral sources. A child's parents may have important information to offer about the kinship family.

Your information collection approach is different from a child protection services risk assessment interview. You are seeking a resource on behalf of a child. Nothing has been alleged against the prospective foster or kinship family. The introductory message emphasizes (a) the importance of the quality of homes providing care to children, (b) the need to study that which contributes to acceptable care for children in placement, (c) the opportunity for prospective caregivers to gain a greater understanding of the commitment they are being asked to make, and (d) the importance of determining what positives the family has to offer to the placed child. The assessment should determine the suitability of the family for a placement.

As in assessing a child's own family, there are certain areas within the kinship and foster family system that must be evaluated, including the following:

- How does the foster or kinship family's own child(ren) function?

- How do the adult caregivers function generally? Consider the adults' relationships beyond the family (e.g., in the neighborhood, with extended family, and at work).

- How do the adult caregivers function as parents? Assess the caregivers' general parenting toward their own children. Explore issues of discipline. Be informed about the parenting history, knowledge, and expectations for children generally. Screen for any reports of maltreatment or history of maltreatment on the kinship or foster family among its own members.

- How does the kinship or foster family function (without the placed child)? Assess the involvement of the extended family.

- How do the kinship or foster family parents view birth parents that maltreat or place their children? Specifically, how does the kinship family regard the related birth parents?

- What are the demographics of the kinship or foster family? Consider stress and resources.

- What attitudes, motivation, and commitment exist in the kinship or foster family among all members (adults and children) to accept and include the placed child in the family? How is the decision made? Who is included in the decision?

- What reasons are provided for becoming a family for the placed child? Is there variation in feeling among family members (particularly adults) about accepting the child?

- What do the adults expect from this placement?
- How has this family prepared for the placement?
- How are adult caregiver expectations for their own children similar to or different from their expectations of the placed child? Assess to what extent children are valued in the family and how this is expressed.
- What is the nature of attachment among family members? Look for closeness, acceptance, understanding, expressions of endearment, demonstrations of affection, and supportive communication. Assess whether this same behavior is present or possible with the placed child.

Once the child has been placed, continuing risk assessment considers the following:

- What is the level of acceptance of the placed child into the family? Notice whether the placed child is included in family routines and life. Examine family interaction. Determine the child's given place in the family: Does the child have a physical identity (a place or a chair)? Is the child fully or selectively involved? Does all communication include the child? Does the family share equally with the child?
- Are the kinship or foster parents' expectations for the placement and the child being met?
- Are the kinship or foster parents satisfied with the arrangement?
- How do the kinship or foster parents explain their parenting expectations, style, and responses to the placed child? How do the parents compare these to those of their own children, and what is their rationale?
- What specific perceptions of and attitudes toward the placed child do the kinship or foster parents hold (negative, superficial, individualized, or accurate)?
- What are the kinship or foster parents' attitudes about, opinions of, and relationship to the placed child's parents and family?
- Have the circumstances or composition of the family changed in any way since placement?

- What does the child report? Listen for acceptance into and involvement with the family or exceptions or differences between how the family deals with its own children and the placed child. You must be discriminating with respect to a placed child's need to cast the family in a negative light because of his or her own adjustment difficulties with the situation.

- How is the child (physically, emotionally, socially, and behaviorally)? Is the child's condition a result of (a) the care received in the child's own home, (b) the adjustment to the new home and family setting, or (c) possible mistreatment by the kinship or foster parents?

- What are the attitudes and perceptions that the placed child has about the care situation? Identify specific feelings the child has about family members, being placed away from home, being with kin, being with strangers, and so on.

- What expectations does the child have for this family situation? Are these realistic? Do they set the child up? Do they stimulate positive or negative reactions from family members (and caregivers specifically)? Do they result in the child behaving in challenging and difficult ways?

- What are the similarities and differences between the placed child and other children in the family? Consider details about the children in the home and examine how the placed child is either different or viewed as different in ways that provoke mistreatment. Examine adjustment in the home and changes in the child since placement occurred.

- How has family functioning been affected since placement?

Part V

FAMILY ASSESSMENT

Section A: Emphasis on the Child

56

How Do I Assess Child and Youth Behavior?

■ *Becky Frink Sherman and E. Wayne Holden*

Behavior is the outward expression of what we think and feel. Children are often unable to express their thoughts and feelings in words; therefore, they show us their inner selves by acting out and showing us what is going on in their minds. As professionals, we need to be aware of this and learn to watch and "listen" to what a child is telling us. Usually, children do not even realize what they are communicating and therefore may not be able to explain themselves if questioned about their behavior.

As children grow and develop over time, their behaviors and how they express themselves also change. To better understand what a child is expressing through his or her behavior, we must be aware of each child's developmental level and life circumstances. With this knowledge, we are in a better position to know whether or not the child's behavior is of concern or if it is normal at his or her age and life circumstance. For example, throwing a tantrum is quite normal for a 2-year-old, but if a 10-year-old tantrums at the same level, we would be more concerned and would need to investigate why a 10-year-old needs to express himself or herself in such a manner. Is it because the child's mother is depressed and the only way the child can gain the attention he or she needs is by tantruming? Before trying to "fix"

■ 273

the child, we always need to examine more closely the child's environment to better understand why a child is acting out.

■ General Categories of Behavior Problems

Internalizing

Internalizing disorders are based on behaviors and feelings that are more inwardly directed. Because children with internalizing disorders are often not disruptive to others, these children can be overlooked and not referred for appropriate help. Anxiety and depression are the most common internalizing disorders in children, although often maltreated children experience posttraumatic stress disorder. In children, it can be difficult to identify these disorders because they exhibit many symptoms differently than adults so that a depressed child may appear very different from a depressed adult. The following is a list of some symptoms that may be normal in the short term but may be of concern if they persist or if a child experiences many of these at once: agitation, nightmares, avoidance of activities or people, difficulty falling or staying asleep (insomnia) or hypersomnia (sleeping too much), difficulty concentrating, hypervigilance, irritability, being easily fatigued, poor appetite or overeating, low self-esteem, and feelings of hopelessness.

Externalizing

Externalizing disorders are based on behaviors and feelings that are outwardly directed and generally easily observable. The behaviors associated with these disorders are often disruptive to others and therefore are addressed more quickly than internalizing disorders. Therefore, it is important for professionals to be watchful of all children in their care because many children with internalizing disorders are not identified and therefore continue to suffer alone while the children with externalizing disorders receive much attention. Girls tend to be internalizers, whereas boys tend to be externalizers. The most common externalizing disorders in children are attention deficit hyperactivity disorder and a group of disorders of acting-out behaviors—disruptive behavior disorder, oppositional defiant disorder, and conduct disorder. Behaviors associated with externalizing disorders include difficulty sustaining attention to tasks or play activities, not listening when spoken to, difficulty organizing tasks and activities, easily distracted, often forgetful in daily activities, fidgeting with hands and feet or squirming in seat, leaving seat in classroom, talking excessively, having difficulty awaiting turn, bullies or threatens others, physically cruel to people or animals, playing with or starting fires, stealing, and destroying property.

It is important to note that in children depression and anxiety, disorders we normally think of as internalizing disorders, are often exhibited through externalizing behaviors. A child who is acting out in school (e.g., throwing objects and getting into fights) may actually be depressed, although he or she does not appear depressed in the same way as an adult would appear (e.g., sluggish and sad). It is important to refer children with such problems to mental health professionals for additional evaluation.

■ Assessment

To obtain the best sense of a child and a child's behavior, one should gather information in a variety of ways: (a) direct observation of the child, (b) reports from caregivers, and (c) the use of objective screening measures. For any of these methods, it is recommended that the caregiving professional observe the child in different settings and make inquiries of multiple informants. It is important to speak to the child, parents (both, if possible), teachers, and any other adult involved in the care of the child. Children often act differently in various environments, and therefore each informant may have distinct or even contrasting views of the child. These methods are discussed further as follows:

Observation: When observing a child, the goal is to learn more about the child's behavior, and therefore it is important to examine how the child interacts with others (especially peers and significant adults), what frustrates or stresses the child (recess, math, transitions from one activity to the next, etc.), and how the child copes with frustration and stress (does the child withdraw, become aggressive, or become agitated?).

Caregiver report: This is an interview with the caregiver in which the caregiving professional is trying to gain as much information about the child's behavior as possible.

Screening measures: The most common screening measures used to assess children's behavior include the Child Behavior Checklist and the Conner's Rating Scales. These measures have both parent and teacher forms. Each questionnaire lists a range of problematic child behaviors that may be grouped into an overall set of problem scales (e.g., attention problems, social problems, and anxious or depressed). If enough items in a group are checked by the informant, the child is said to be exhibiting significant problems in that area.

■ Referrals

When to Refer

When a child's behavior, internalizing or externalizing, interferes with a child's functioning (e.g., peer or family relationships, academic functioning, emotional well-being, and physical health), it is recommended that the child be referred for additional assessment. For example, when a child is acting out in school and therefore is unable to focus on his or her work and is not achieving as expected, the child should be referred for a psychological evaluation and perhaps psychotherapy. When a child's behavior changes dramatically, such as when a child who is generally outgoing suddenly becomes very withdrawn and shy, a referral should be considered.

To Whom to Refer

There are many professionals who work with behavior problems in children. In an outpatient setting, a child may be referred to a clinical social worker, a psychologist, or a psychiatrist. Often, schools have their own counselors who may be able to work with the child. If a child needs a complete psychological evaluation, the child should be referred to a psychologist because psychologists are the only professionals trained to do a full battery of psychological assessments. If the problem behavior is exhibited by a physical symptom, such as headaches, stomachaches, enuresis, and encopresis, the child should be referred first to the primary care physician to rule out physical causes for the behavior.

■ *Further Reading*

Mash, E. J., & Terdal, L. G. (Eds.). (1997). *Assessment of childhood disorders* (3rd ed.). New York: Guilford.

57

How Do I Assess Child and Youth Development?

■ *Becky Frink Sherman and E. Wayne Holden*

The term *child and youth development* is a very broad one. For the purpose of this chapter, *development* refers to the child's cognitive, educational, motor, and language development as well as the development of adaptive behavior (see Appendix 4). Children who have experienced trauma of any type (be it physical, sexual, or emotional abuse or physical or emotional neglect) often show signs of delayed development. In fact, it is almost expected that a maltreated child will demonstrate difficulties in at least one area of development, although no specific effects of maltreatment have been observed. The difficulties may not be due directly to the maltreatment; rather, the problems may be related to the troubled environment that is associated with maltreatment and in which the child lives. A child who has been neglected may lag behind other children of the same age in motor and language development, or a child who has been abused may act out or be unable to focus in school, leading to academic problems. As a caregiving professional, one can have a significant impact on the life of a child by learning more about development and understanding when to refer a child to the appropriate professional to further evaluate and treat if necessary.

The following section describes each area of development, the measures commonly used to evaluate each area, and possible screening tools that can be used by professionals, with only brief instruction.

■ *Areas of Development and Assessment Measures*

Cognitive development: refers to a child's cognitive or intellectual abilities, commonly referred to as intelligence quotient (IQ). A cognitive evaluation assesses what a child is capable of doing rather than what he or she is currently achieving. Cognitive abilities generally assessed are a child's ability to problem solve, how a child thinks about or understands his or her world, how and what a child understands what is said to him or her, and how and what a child is able to communicate to others. The most common cognitive assessment measure for children is the Wechsler Intelligence Scale for Children-Third Edition. Screening measures are not recommended due to their serious limitations.

Educational development: refers to what a child is learning or his or her level of achievement in school. An educational evaluation assesses what the child is actually doing or achieving as opposed to what he or she is capable of doing (as described previously). A child is diagnosed with a learning disability when he or she is not achieving at the level expected given his or her cognitive abilities (IQ). An educational evaluation generally assesses the main areas of schooling, such as mathematics, spelling, reading, and writing. Measures commonly used to assess educational development include the Wechlser Individual Achievement Test and the Woodcock-Johnson Psycho-Educational Battery-Revised. The Wide Range Achievement Test-Third Edition is a frequently used screener.

Motor development: refers to how a child is developing in terms of gross motor skills (sitting, standing, and walking) and fine motor skills. Children attain motor developmental milestones within an age range. For example, children begin to walk between 9 and 18 months of age. Common measures used to assess a child's motor development include the Bayley Scales of Infant Development-Third Edition (BSID-III) and the Denver Developmental Screening Test-Revised (DDST-R).

Language development: refers to how a child is developing in terms of his or her language acquisition. For example, children generally imitate new words by 12 months of age and combine words into short sentences by approximately 24 months of age. Common measures used to assess a child's language development include the BSID-III, the Bayley Infant Neurodevelopmental Scale, the Early Language Milestones, and the DDST-R.

Adaptive behavior: refers to how a child functions in the day-to-day world. Skill areas included in adaptive behavior assessments are communication, socialization, motor, and daily living skills. A common measure used to assess a child's adaptive functioning is the Vineland Adaptive Behavior Scales for Children.

■ Referrals

When to Refer

In general, if the caregiving professional has questions or concerns about a child's development, the professional should not hesitate to call the primary care physician and inquire as to whether the child should be evaluated. Specifically, if a child fails a screening exam, is exhibiting significant difficulties in school, fails to attain developmental milestones, or appears significantly "slower" than other children, a call to the primary care physician is warranted.

To Whom to Refer

Children generally need to be assessed by a primary care physician before referral to a specialist. It is helpful to the physician to provide as much information about the child as possible. If the child's parents are unavailable, and if the physician does not have prior information on the child, the caregiver accompanying the child should have a detailed medical history of the child, such as birth history, birth weight, birth complications, neonatal history, ages of developmental milestones, hospitalizations, serious illnesses or injuries, allergies, current medications, and family history of illnesses. Information should also be provided to the physician regarding the developmental area of concern. The physician will examine the child, and if additional evaluation is necessary, the physician should refer the child to the appropriate specialist. Possible specialists include a psychologist for cognitive functioning, an educational specialist or psychologist for educational functioning, a speech and language pathologist for speech development, a physical therapist or occupational therapist for motor development, and a psychologist for behavior and emotional problems.

■ Further Reading

Aylward, G. P. (1995). *Manual for the Bayley Infant Neurodevelopmental Screener.* San Antonio, TX: Psychological Corporation.

Bayley, N. (1993). *Manual for the Bayley Scales of Infant Development* (2nd ed.). San Antonio, TX: Psychological Corporation.

Coplan, J. (1983). *Manual for the Early Language Milestone Scale.* Tulsa, OK: Modern Education Corporation.

Frankenburg, W. K., Dodds, J., Archer, P., Bresnick, B., Maschka, P., Edelman, H., & Shapiro, H. (1992). *Manual for the Denver II.* Denver, CO: Denver Developmental Materials.

Parker, S., & Zuckerman, B. (Eds.). (1995). *Behavioral and developmental pediatrics: A handbook for primary care.* New York: Little, Brown.

Schor, E. L. (Ed.). (1993). *Caring for your baby and young child: Birth to age 5.* New York: Bantam.

Shelov, S. P., & Hannemann, R. E. (Eds.). (1996). *Caring for your school-age child: Ages 5-12.* New York: Bantam.

Wechsler, D. (1991). *Wechsler Intelligence Scale for Children* (3rd ed.). San Antonio, TX: Psychological Corporation.

Wechsler, D. (1992). *Manual for the Wechsler Individual Achievement Test.* San Antonio, TX: Psychological Corporation.

Wilkinson, G. S. (1993). *Manual for the Wide Range Achievement Test-3.* Wilmington, DE: Jastak.

Woodcock, R., & Johnson, W. B. (1989). *Manual for the Woodcock-Johnson Psycho-Educational Battery-Revised.* Allen, TX: DLM–Teaching Resources.

58

How Do I Assess Child and Youth Emotional States?

■ *Becky Frink Sherman and E. Wayne Holden*

The emotional experience of a child or adult is one of the most complex aspects of human existence. It is also one of the most fragile. At the most basic level, emotions consist of private internal sensations that can be experienced and described only by the individual. Emotions experienced internally, however, influence all other aspects of behavior and thought, resulting in observable changes that reflect different emotional states. For example, children from the preschool period onward can label the internal sensations associated with experiencing anger, and it is usually relatively easy for adults to identify the outward, behavioral manifestations of anger in the typically developing child. During development, both the internal and the external aspects of emotions change significantly as the ability to regulate emotional expression matures. This developmental process can be easily disrupted by traumatic or stressful incidents in a child's life and by the absence of appropriately supportive and nurturing relationships with parents or caregivers. When this occurs, children display emotional disturbance that can have a profound negative impact on their ability to successfully negotiate life's challenges.

Children who are maltreated are at particular risk for developing emotional problems. Negative and traumatic experiences with adult authority figures or the absence of nurturing relationships with caregivers or both create a variety of problems. As a result, these children are likely to display anxiety, depression, anger, or all three and to have limited capacity for recognizing different emotional states, regulating their emotions, and effectively integrating these emotions into their experience. Due to their lack of adequate development in the emotional arena, direct discussions with these children regarding emotional experience may yield little useful information. The strong effects of emotions on all other areas of functioning become useful in this situation. Maltreated children with emotional disturbance will display observable changes in their behavior that are the key to identifying the underlying emotional disturbance. For example, overly anxious children may withdraw from others and have difficulty sustaining social interactions, angry children may display oppositional or defiant behavior, aggression, or both, and depressed children may appear to be overtly sad and fail to initiate activities with others. The range of behaviors displayed, however, can be large and confusing when attempting to link behavioral changes to underlying emotional states.

■ *Evaluation*

There is no one agreed-on method for evaluating children's emotional state. This is complicated by the fact that clear standards for distinguishing normal from abnormal emotional functioning and expression do not exist. In this situation, it is important to obtain reports from several individuals in a child's or adolescent's life before reaching a conclusion about the presence or absence of an emotional disturbance. When there is agreement across settings and among important individuals in a child's life, concern is increased that an emotional disturbance is present and creating problems in the child's life. In addition to your own professional observations, important individuals to include in this assessment are parents, teachers, siblings, and other adults who interact with maltreated children. Each individual may be somewhat biased in his or her personal perspective, but moderate agreement between individuals is strong evidence that a problem exists that needs professional attention. Observation from multiple perspectives is the most valid and reliable method for evaluating children's emotional and behavioral status.

■ *Referral*

It is important to make appropriate referrals for additional assessment and possible treatment when an emotional disturbance has been identified in a maltreated child. Delayed or avoided treatment leads only to more chronic problems that may be more difficult to treat later. Resources for evaluation and treatment of emotional disturbance include mental health professionals, such as social workers, psychologists, and psychiatrists. Mental health clinics in the community and hospitals are good sources to locate these resources. In addition, local school systems can provide some resources because they are required by law to evaluate and provide services for emotional disturbance, even for preschool children. No matter what system is used for additional assessment and intervention, it is important to use advocacy and case management skills to continue to access appropriate services for emotionally disturbed children and youth.

Direct methods used by professionals for assessing child and adolescent emotional state include interviews with children and self-report scales, such as the Children's Depression Inventory, State-Trait Anxiety Inventory for Children, and the Youth Self-Report form of the Child Behavior Checklist. Difficulties with interviews have been discussed previously: Children with emotional disturbance may not be able to effectively communicate their emotions. Self-report scales can be easy to administer and very useful in the evaluation of adolescents. A problem with self-report scales is their limitation with children younger than age 10 in whom the ability to identify and self-report emotions is not fully developed. Indirect methods for assessing child and youth emotional state include projective tests such as drawings, sentence completion tests, storytelling in response to pictures, and interpretation of inkblot responses. These latter methods require substantial clinical training and experience for accurate administration and interpretation. Even with these skills, the usefulness of these methods for evaluating children younger than age 10 is uncertain.

Emotional state is one of the most complex aspects of children and youth to accurately evaluate and treat. The ability to identify emerging emotional problems and provide early intervention, however, is critically important to preventing chronic, long-term emotional disturbance and substantial disability. Given the high risk of emotional problems as a result of maltreatment, professionals working in this field should be particularly attuned to identifying these children and assisting them to overcome emotional difficulties.

■ *Further Reading*

Mash, E. J., & Terdal, L. G. (Eds.). (1997). *Assessment of childhood disorders* (3rd ed.). New York: Guilford.

59

How Do I Recognize and Assess Common or Important Mental Health Problems in Children?

■ *David J. Kolko*

■ *Mental Health Effects of Child Abuse*

Recommendations for assessment of the clinical functioning of maltreated children are guided by studies that identify the effects of abuse. Several studies provide useful information about various consequences of abuse and on a range of appropriate instruments (see Kolko, 1996). Suggestions for assessing some common mental health problems are described in this chapter.

■ *General Assessment: Considerations and Issues*

Whenever possible, it is useful to collect information across a range of topics from multiple sources, including child victims and their siblings, caregivers and other adults in the home, teachers, clinicians, and records. These efforts may complement one another in highlighting different aspects of the precursors to or impact of the abusive experience or both (e.g., risk factors, clinical symptoms, and impaired functioning). Such information may not only clarify the child's functioning but also serve as outcome indicators (targets) to help document the impact of intervention on a child's adjustment (e.g., medical status, social and developmental stimulation, behavior management, and education).

The use of different methods may enhance the overall utility and accuracy of the assessment. Although most information is obtained from parent interviews, it may also be collected using child self-report instruments, structured diagnostic interviews, and behavioral observation or ratings. The inclusion of multiple informants, measures, and assessment methods may help develop the most accurate and comprehensive understanding of an individual case to guide an appropriate intervention.

■ *Assessment of Specific Problems*

Many maltreated children have problems with physical aggression and violent behavior, among other conduct problems, that may lead to delinquent or even criminal activities. These problems may manifest as physically coercive acts (e.g., fighting and cruelty), persistent defiance (e.g., authority conflicts), or antisocial behaviors that are concealed or "covert" (e.g., lying and stealing). It is important to evaluate the frequency, severity, and duration of such problems using parent or teacher questionnaires, such as the Child Behavior Checklist (CBCL; Achenbach, 1991) and its associated measures—the Teacher Report Form (TRF) and the Youth Self-Report. These scales assess diverse behavioral and emotional symptoms and social competency (social skills). Other questions might examine the child's involvement in verbally and physically aggressive behaviors (e.g., fighting and weapon use). It may be helpful to obtain more specific information by asking parents about the frequency and severity of individual behaviors (e.g., fighting, stealing, and lying) within the past week.

Symptoms of hyperactivity and, specifically, attention deficit hyperactivity disorder, often manifest as problems with attention, impulse control, and overactivity. Generally, children receive the diagnosis before the age of 7. Questions should be asked of teachers and parents about the severity of these types of problems relative to that of other children of the same age and developmental level (e.g., "How excitable or impulsive is your child?" and "Is he easily distracted?"). It is important to assess the effects of the perceived hyperactivity at school and at home. If this concern is raised, evaluation by a pediatrician or mental health professional is recommended.

Problematic social behavior and poor interpersonal skills include poor peer relations and negative peer behaviors, limited peer involvement and initiations during play sessions, and social isolation. Specific social skills can be evaluated individually (e.g., "How well does he maintain conversations . . . use polite language?"), and peer relationships can be evaluated using the previously mentioned scales (e.g., CBCL and TRF) or a few key questions (e.g., "How many close friends does he have?" and "How often does he get involved in social activities?"). Teachers can help supplement an interview with behavioral observations during social activities (e.g., recess).

Problems with self-esteem, depression, and anxiety, which have been documented in high-risk samples, can be assessed during child or parent interviews. Often, child interviews may elicit feelings of sadness, a sense of lost pleasure in previously enjoyable activities, feelings of hopelessness or distortions about oneself or one's future, or all these, which should prompt additional evaluation of suicidality (ideation, intent, and plans). Specific items useful to evaluating severity of depressive symptoms include the child's level of sadness, loss of interest in preferred activities, irritability, physical complaints and loss of energy or weight, guilt, and negative perceptions of oneself, the world, and the future. Problems with anxiety may be manifested by frequent worries, multiple fears, physiological symptoms related to anxiety, and avoidance of specific situations or people.

Posttraumatic stress disorder (PTSD) and related reactions are important targets for clinical treatment that merit careful diagnostic interviewing. Questions about scary events in the child's life can determine whether a significant stressor has been experienced and, if so, the severity of any resulting symptoms (e.g., hyperarousal and numbing). Certain instruments evaluate the severity of these reactions, primarily in sexually abused children—for example, the Children's Impact of Traumatic Events Scale-Revised (Wolfe, Gentile, Michienzi, Sas, & Wolfe, 1991) evaluates the severity of problems in four areas (e.g., PTSD-intrusive thoughts), and the Trauma Symptom Checklist for Children (Briere, 1996) assesses depression, anxiety, posttraumatic stress, dissociation, anger, and sexual concerns. These measures may help to determine the severity of specific problems following a physically abusive or traumatic experience.

A child's mental health problems may be related to parent-child conflict and family problems, which may be important to evaluate from the child's perspective. These problems often are reflected in hostile comments, lengthy arguments, and threatened or actual physical altercations as well as reduced cohesion and support among family members. Assessment can ascertain perceived positive and negative characteristics of the parents and family. Maltreated children may reside in families characterized by limited parental supervision and positive discipline and inconsistent or excessive use of harsh discipline, highlighting the need to assess the caregiver's use of different management practices. Other questions can supplement what is known about the family's level of conflict and hostility or punitivenesss. Observations of family interactions in the home may be especially helpful to identify targets for intervention.

Of course, it is important to also determine positive family influences. Thus, questions should be asked about the level of children's social support from different sources (e.g., family, teacher, and peers). Finally, aspects of the family environment, such as warmth, cohesion, supportiveness, and expressiveness (e.g., "How often do you do things together?"), are important to assess. Understanding the family's relationships, activities, and structure provides a helpful perspective regarding family influences on the child's behavior.

■ *Further Reading*

Achenbach, T. M. (1991). *Intergrative guide for the 1991 CBCL/4-18 YSR and TRF profiles.* Burlington, VT: University of Vermont, Department of Psychiatry.

Briere, J. (1996). *Trauma Symptom Checklist for Children.* Odessa, FL: Psychological Assessment Resources.

Kolko, D. J. (1996). Child physical abuse. In J. Briere, L. Berliner, J. A. Bulkey, C. Jenny, & T. Reid (Eds.), *APSAC handbook on child maltreatment* (pp. 21-50). Thousand Oaks, CA: Sage.

Wolfe, V., Gentile, C., Michienzi, T., Sas, L., & Wolfe, D. A. (1991). The Children's Impact of Traumatic Events Scale: A measure of post-sexual-abuse PTSD symptoms. *Behavioral Assessment, 13,* 359-383.

60

What Preventive Pediatric and Dental Care Should Children and Youth Receive?

■ *Charles I. Shubin*

Preventive pediatric and dental care for children and youth is the keystone of efforts to ensure their health and well-being. By ensure that such preventive care is received, problems can be detected early and thus dealt with more effectively and efficiently. The maintenance of an accurate record of a child's well child care, in addition to illnesses, such as in a medical passport, helps ensure that maltreated children receive appropriate care. The ability of children to reach adulthood healthy and prepared for the world they will face depends on such efforts.

■ *Pediatric Preventive Care*

Well child visits: scheduled at 1, 2, 4, 6, 9, 12, and 18 months and 2, 3, 4, 5, 6, 8, 10, 12, 14, 16, and 18 years. These visits include the following:

- *Health history:* initial and interval, personal, family, and social
- *Developmental screening:* to detect children at risk for or already showing developmental delays; usually uses a

tool such as the Denver Developmental Screening Test-Revised

- *Mental health screening:* to detect behavioral or psychosocial difficulties or both, including school problems and family violence, involving children or adults or both
- *Comprehensive physical examination:* "head to toe," includes screening for evidence of abuse, neglect, or both, and for growth
- *Vision and hearing screening*

Laboratory and other tests

- *Hereditary diseases* ("PKU" [phenylketonuria] test): at birth and repeated as needed
- *Lead and anemia:* at 9 to 12 months and yearly as needed according to behavior, examination findings, and environment from 2 to 6 years—more often as results dictate
- *Cholesterol screening:* as indicated by family history
- *Tuberculosis:* by needle test only ("Mantoux test") and not multipuncture test ("Tine test") if high risk by history of exposure to active tuberculosis or other risk factors (e.g., HIV positive)
- *Sexually transmitted diseases:* if sexually active or 16 years or older

Immunizations: as recommended by the American Academy of Pediatrics Committee on Infectious Diseases and the U.S. Public Health Service Advisory Committee on Immunization Practices. This schedule changes periodically.

Health education and anticipatory guidance: Health education focuses on specific problems (e.g., asthma). Anticipatory guidance involves age-appropriate advice and counseling concerning anticipated concerns and health and developmental issues, including discipline (e.g., discussing the increasing mobility and curiosity of toddlers and how best to manage them).

■ Dental Preventive Care

Regular dental visits: every 6 months starting at age 3 years or earlier if there are problems. Dental preventive care includes the following:

- *Oral screening examinations:* searching for cavities, malocclusion (need for orthodontics), and other abnormalities
- *Fluoride and sealant applications:* as recommended
- *Oral health education:* includes the following:
    - □ Advice on brushing and flossing
    - □ Diet education, especially dietary fluoride: not letting babies sleep with bottles of milk or juice
    - □ Dental injury prevention education, especially use of mouth guards

■ Summary

Although the previous discussion provided the recommendations for preventive pediatric and dental care for all children and youth, those that have been or are being maltreated, especially neglected, may not have had the recommended care and thus need "catch-up" visits. In addition, additional health problems in these children may require more than the routine visits. An appropriate catch-up schedule should be planned.

61

How Do I Assess a Child's Health Status?

■ *Howard Dubowitz*

Health includes physical, emotional, and dental status. Primary health care screens children for potential problems so as to intervene early and prevent problems from occurring. It is thus important to assess whether the child has a pediatric and a dental provider, and whether adequate care has been received (see Chapter 60, this volume). The following are of special interest:

- Are immunizations up to date?
- Were vision and hearing screens OK?
- Were there any concerns regarding development or mental health?
- Were other problems noted (e.g., anemia, lead poisoning, and sickle cell disease)?

The previous information may be available from the child and parent, but contact with the primary health care provider should provide useful information. If adequate primary care has not been obtained, there may be important gaps (e.g., immunizations), making it difficult to be sure of the child's health status.

If health problems have been identified, one needs to know the following:

- The cause(s)
- Its severity (e.g., how often does it affect the child?)
- How it affects the child (e.g., can the child play sports, go to school, and do most things?)
- What treatment is needed
- Is the treatment being fully implemented? (If not, why not?)

Some problems are minor (e.g., occasional ear infections) and need limited care; others are more serious and have lifelong implications (e.g., diabetes). It is important to recognize that the same disease can affect children very differently; for example, asthma can be a daily problem or cause symptoms every few years. Therefore, it is necessary to understand how the condition affects the child. It is useful to know the extent to which the treatment enables the child to function well, free of symptoms. For example, medications may fully control a seizure disorder, allowing the child to do most things. It should be recognized that physical problems may affect emotional health and vice versa. Mind and body are surely connected. Thus, serious and chronic diseases raise concerns about a child's mental health. Much of this information may be available from the child and parent, but clarification with the health care provider is recommended.

Health problems may not have been identified, especially if health care has been inadequate. Screening can be done by asking the child and parent whether they have any health problems:

For children: "Is there anything about your health or body that bothers you?"

For parents: "How would you rate your child's health— excellent, good, fair, or poor?"

"Fair" or "poor" are red flags that additional evaluation is needed. There are several brief questionnaires that professionals can use for assessing children's behavior (see Chapter 56, this volume). Sometimes, health problems can be observed (e.g., a disfiguring burn and a sad, withdrawn child). Caseworkers and other professionals can play a valuable role by recognizing possible health problems that need additional evaluation.

A child's functioning reflects his or her health status. The following are some useful questions:

Regarding physical health:

- Can he or she perform developmentally appropriate activities of daily living (e.g., dress himself or herself and climb stairs)?
- Can the child play sports?
- Can the child attend school regularly?

Regarding emotional health:

- How does the child get along with others—at home, at school, and in the neighborhood?
- Is behavior a problem in any of these settings?
- Does the child appear happy, secure, sad, withdrawn, and so on?

Regarding dental health:

- Does the child have a toothache?
- When was the last time the child saw a dentist? (After age 3, the child should be checked every year.)

Such questions provide a screening of a child's functioning and health status. Possible problems will often require additional evaluation.

The previous picture may be drawn mostly by talking with the child and parents. Talking to the child's health care provider, however, is strongly recommended. Other professionals (e.g., teachers and therapists) may also add valuable information. Caseworkers might explain that their work includes ensuring that children are being adequately cared for. Caseworkers may also have concerns or information that are important to convey to health professionals. Periodic communication between caseworkers and health care providers is valuable, with the frequency tailored to the specific circumstances. By sharing information and working collaboratively, children's health and interests are best served.

Children involved with child protective services, especially those who have been in substitute care, may have had health care from multiple providers. It can be extremely helpful if the caseworker collects information from those who have been substantially involved, particularly primary care providers, to develop a relatively complete record of the child's health. This does require a considerable effort to first obtain the names of health care providers from the family, and in some instances permission to contact them, but it can be very worthwhile. Several states have implemented "health passports" as a medical record for children in foster care to have a comprehensive view and to improve the health care of these high-risk children.

62

How Do I Assess a Child's Social Support System?

■ *Ross A. Thompson*

The support that children receive in their natural social networks contributes significantly to treatment outcomes when children are victims of maltreatment and to the prevention of future abuse or neglect because social support offers children many human resources. Social support provides counseling and emotional nurturance that are important to psychological healing. Also, it provides access to information, services, and material assistance that children may need. Children are unlikely to be aware of possible therapeutic aid, social services, or school support, or to ask for and obtain such assistance, without the help of adults. Social support may be instrumental in developmental remediation and skill acquisition, particularly in areas in which psychosocial growth is impaired by abuse or neglect. Supportive adults can serve as substitute attachment figures, for example, and contribute to improving social skills deficits and damaged self-esteem. Social support networks are also important to the prevention of future maltreatment, especially as adults assume responsibility for monitoring children's well-being. For these reasons, understanding children's social support networks (especially from the child's perspective) is an important therapeutic and preventive goal.

An important step in understanding children's social support networks is appreciating the nature of the networks and how they change with development:

- Children's social networks are less extensive than those of adults, especially early in life when their primary social relationships are within the family. Even after their social networks have expanded with day care, preschool, and primary and secondary school relationships, the family remains central to social support. Although this is a problem when family life is abusive or traumatizing (although siblings can be supportive), it is important to remember that during most periods of early life children also have relationships outside the home in day care or school, with extended family members, in neighborhood activities, or in after-school programs. Identifying where a child perceives that social support might be found outside the home is important.

- Children's social networks overlap with those of their parents. Family friends, neighborhood associations, extended family relationships, and church and recreational contacts are shared by parents and offspring. Moreover, parents are often mediators of their children's social networks through their willingness to plan, schedule, and arrange transportation for offspring. Thus, social support to children often must occur indirectly through their parents.

- The support that children perceive from others changes with age. Extended kin are always important, and they become increasingly so throughout childhood. Peers become increasingly important in adolescence. After school begins, teachers and pediatricians are occasionally regarded as supportive, and day care teachers are often attachment figures for younger children.

What is the best way to assess children's perceptions of their support systems? In general, a two-step process is required: (1) assessing the breadth of a child's social network (i.e., who is the child regularly in contact with?) and (2) assessing how supportive these people are from the child's perspective. It is also often helpful to distinguish different forms of support (e.g., emotional nurturance, instrumental or material aid, advice or counseling, affirmation, and protection).

Depending on the child's age, various approaches can be considered. Specific questions can be used to probe the kinds of support older children experience in different relationships (e.g., "Are there people to whom you talk about really important things?" and "Are there people who make you feel good or special?"). A series of concentric circles can be used to "map" younger children's perceptions of their closeness to various people in their networks (with the innermost circle representing "people who are most close and important to you" and so forth). Once the breadth of a child's support network has been identified, ranking procedures can be used to indicate the one or two people who are most important to the child when help is needed. Sometimes, simple and straightforward inquiries (e.g., "If you needed help, who would you ask?") can accomplish the same goal. Visual aids (such as a schematic thermometer with increasing levels indicating how much emotional support, companionship, and tangible assistance children believe they receive from specific people in their networks) can be especially helpful with younger children. Also helpful would be a walk around the child's neighborhood and other familiar settings coupled with specific questions about who the child knows, what kinds of experiences he or she has shared with these partners, and who would the child turn to if he or she needed help. There are also standardized questionnaires and rating instruments that can be used with older children (Belle, 1989).

■ *Further Reading*

Belle, D. (Ed.). (1989). *Children's social networks and social supports.* New York: John Wiley.

Salzinger, S., Antrobus, J., & Hammer, M. (1988). *Social networks of children, adolescents, and college students.* Hillsdale, NJ: Lawrence Erlbaum.

Thompson, R. A. (1995). *Preventing child maltreatment through social support: A critical analysis.* Thousand Oaks, CA: Sage.

63

How Do I Assess a Child's Behavior Related to Separation and Visitation?

■ *Caroline L. Burry*

Visitation with their birth family is a core service for children in out-of-home care. Many foster parents and group care providers report that children present challenging behaviors before, during, and after visitation. Therefore, assessing children's behavior related to visitation is critical in permanency planning. This chapter provides examples of typical behavioral problems related to visitation, underlying feelings and issues to explore, and strategies to use in assessing these behaviors and issues.

■ *Typical Behavioral Problems and*
  Underlying Feelings and Issues to Explore

It is important to individualize children who are in care and understand that they have their own histories and needs. There are some behaviors, however, that commonly occur with regard to visitation and separation, and it is helpful to be prepared to assess for these. For instance, many children have sleep problems, such as bed-wetting or nightmares. Possible feelings and issues to explore regarding these sleep problems include that the child is regressing because of anxiety, "being bad" in the hope of being returned to the birth family, or showing signs of posttraumatic stress. Another typical behavior is clinging. The child who clings may be grieving losses or may be regressing to an earlier developmental stage.

Hostile behaviors, both physical and verbal, are very common in children at visitation times. When hostile behaviors are seen, it is useful to consider whether the child might be expressing feelings of anger or feelings of loss. Both anger and loss are powerful and scary feelings for children—and for adults—so it is not surprising that these are sometimes expressed in behavior.

Another possible issue to be explored is whether the child is attempting to cause the foster parents to reject him or her in hopes of being returned. Finally, posttraumatic stress should again be considered.

Many children in care act inconsistently. For instance, sometimes they may have mood or behavioral swings. Possible underlying issues for these behaviors include uncertainty about the future, confusion, and lack of trust.

Many foster parents have indicated that they are very challenged by children who lie and steal. These behaviors may be related to children's hopes that, if they misbehave, they will be returned. These behaviors could also indicate anger, lack of trust, or low self-esteem.

Some foster children are overly affectionate. This may be assessed as regression to an earlier developmental stage due to anxiety or to wanting to be seen positively. Other foster children may be described as pseudomature; they seem old beyond their years. These children may be trying to assert some control in their lives, may be fearful of getting close emotionally to the foster parents, may be rejecting the need for birth parents, or may be reenacting previous roles played in their birth families.

Finally, it is also common for foster children to run away or act withdrawn at times of visitation. When children run away, they may be depressed, feel overwhelmed, or be trying to assert some control over their lives. When children act withdrawn, they may be feeling hopeless, depressed, or having posttraumatic stress symptoms.

■ *Factors to Consider in Assessing*
  Behaviors and Their Related Issues

The first factor to consider is the child's age and developmental stage. Younger children tend to express feelings through behavior. Because most children lose some developmental ground with removal and placement, some difficult behaviors may be interpreted as less challenging when the children are considered as being at earlier developmental stages. Even children who appear overcompetent may actually be pseudomature. Second, consider the child's placement history. Multiple placements mean multiple losses and tend to exacerbate behavioral problems. Finally, consider the child's loss and grief experiences. Children who have had more losses are likely to show more behavioral extremes.

■ *Strategies for Assessing Behaviors*
  and Their Underlying Issues

Several strategies are useful in assessing behaviors and their underlying issues with children in care. First, it is helpful to give children clear permission and entitlement to have and express feelings. Second, caregivers and workers should help the child express feelings in a safe way. When children are acting out, they are often attempting to express feelings but may put themselves and their relationships at risk. Finally, there are several tools that may be helpful with children in care. For instance, the "Life Book" can be used to review a child's history and discuss feelings and events. Younger children may respond to speaking about feelings with a play phone or through play therapy. Many children can express feelings about issues through making collages and other art projects. Older children can sometimes write about their feelings in journals or letters.

■ *Further Reading*

Fahlberg, V. (1991). *A child's journey through placement*. Indianapolis, IN: Perspectives Press.

Part V

FAMILY
ASSESSMENT

Section B:
Emphasis on
Parents and Caregivers

64

How Do I Assess a Caregiver's Personal History and Its Meaning for Practice?

■ *John Curtis McMillen*

■ *A Case*

Mrs. R. is a single 22-year-old mother of three children, boys ages 6 and 4 and a 2-month-old girl. A neighbor alleges that the boys are unkempt, unsupervised, and approach strangers for food. At an initial unannounced visit on a summer day, a child protection worker found Mrs. R. watching TV inside a sparsely furnished apartment with the baby asleep next to her on the couch. Mrs. R. stated she was unaware of the where-abouts of her boys, who were found outside playing together. When questioned, the older boy reported he last ate yesterday evening and last bathed several days ago. The younger boy did not respond to questions. Mrs. R. said he rarely talked and knew only a few dozen words. For food, Mrs. R. had only three cans of soup in the apartment. She reported she was breast-feeding the baby. Mrs. R. denied any drug or alcohol use but reported she had been feeling "down" for several months and that she knew she had not been caring well for her family. The child protection worker took the family to a nearby food pantry, helped Mrs. R. make a doctor's appointment for the baby, and scheduled a time the next day to talk further with Mrs. R. Mrs. R. said she would welcome additional help.

■ *The Caregiver's History*

Information about the parents' past can provide valuable clues about the kinds of interventions that will best help them protect their children. Ideally, a child protection worker will complete a thorough social assessment and history of each family, including a thorough history of each parent or caregiver. It has been said that if one does not know what to do with a family, one has not done a thorough assessment. Important aspects of a caregiver's history include special events in childhood, relationships with caregiver's parents and extended family, and health, romantic, employment, education, and legal history.

A helpful way to gather this information is to draw a family genogram with the family. The genogram is a visual depiction of the family tree with some additional vital information, such as important dates, employment, brief personality descriptions, and a visual depiction of who gets along with whom. A limited genogram of Mrs. R.'s family is shown in Appendix 6. Details on how to draw a genogram are provided by McGoldrick and Gerson (1985).

The genogram allows you to learn a great amount about a family in a short time and provides a reason to ask important questions about personal history. If used correctly, it also helps build a working relationship with parents. Parents may be pleased to have been assigned a child protection worker who has taken the time to understand their social reality. By the time the genogram is completed, confusing parent and child behaviors may make sense when seen in the context of personal history.

An advantage of the genogram is that it forces the child protection worker to specifically ask about the parent's relatives, relationships with romantic partners or other parents of the children, and families. Thus, the child protection worker is not only assessing family history but also the social support available from family members and potential placement resources if needed later. Regarding Mrs. R.'s family, she has a sister who may serve as a placement resource and a source of support, but in general she is isolated from her family.

Many aspects of a parent's past can affect how he or she cares for his or her children. Many of these can be assessed while drawing the genogram. After drawing major parts of the family tree, you can ask specific questions about employment, education, health, and whether any of the family members depicted have a history of substance abuse, mental illness, sexual abuse, family violence, or criminal activity. Search for troubling events from the parent's past that may have impeded the parent's development and led to his or her parenting difficulties. Because some of these topics are sensitive, you might want to practice beforehand a respectful but concrete way to ask about them, avoiding stigmatizing words. Because one source of Mrs. R.'s parenting difficulties may be her possible depression, she should be asked about a family history of depression. Instead of asking about "depression," however, she should be asked a specific question about whether there are others in her family who have a history of being "sad or blue" for long periods of time. Mrs. R's genogram shows some familial alcoholism (a brother), no sexual abuse, and a maternal family history of depression. Also note that her father died when she was 3 years old. The family history increases suspicion that Mrs. R. may be suffering from an underlying depression that may have preceded her difficult situation. The fact that her father died when she was young may suggest a family upheaval in her childhood that affected her mother's ability to parent her at a crucial time in her development.

For parents struggling to care for their children, one should explore memories of how they were cared for when they were children. Does Mrs. R. remember being hungry and there being no food to eat? At what age was she allowed to go unsupervised? For other families, questions about how the parent was disciplined might be the most crucial. Mrs. R.'s genogram shows that she does not believe her mother did a good job raising her. She felt neglected and uncared for and remembers being teased at school for having dirty clothes. This might suggest to a worker that Mrs. R. has never learned how to supervise children and that her family may not be supportive in helping her make parenting changes.

Do not feel compelled to find a "smoking gun" in a caregiver's past. Child maltreatment is caused by multiple factors. It is a myth that every maltreating parent has been maltreated.

■ *It Is Not What Is in Your History*
But, Rather, What You Think About It

Be careful how you interpret the information you obtain about a family member's history. None of us are doomed to repeat the mistakes of our parents. Research on a variety of family problems has concluded that most people who experience a problem in their family of origin do not re-create the same problem in their family of creation, although they are at greater risk than others of doing so. In other words, most children of alcoholics do not become alcoholics, although they are at a greater risk of becoming alcoholics than those people who did not have a parent who was an alcoholic.

Research rooted in attachment theory suggests that parents who can think about their difficult childhood experiences coherently, and who talk about the negative ways in which they were affected by their parents' actions, often raise securely attached children. In other words, parents who understand their history can work to ensure better environments for their children.

■ *Signs That Caregivers Understand*
Their Painful Histories

- Express how they were harmed by maltreatment received as children: These parents may recognize how their children are being harmed.
- Talk about how they wished things would have been different when they were children: These parents may be willing to make changes in their own lives to help their children.
- Motivated to avoid mistakes of own parents: For example, some children of alcoholics purposefully abstain from alcohol so that their spouse and children avoid the horrors they experienced. If Mrs. R. can express what it was like to feel neglected by a depressed mother, she may be more likely to seek help for her own depression.

■ *Red Flags That Suggest a Caregiver's*
Past Is Hindering the Ability to Parent

- Not being able to talk about painful childhood experiences: These parents may deny or avoid thinking about the maltreatment their children are receiving because acknowledging their children's pain may mean having to acknowledge their own.
- Denying that the maltreatment they experienced as children had any effect on their development: These parents may think that their children will be unaffected by the maltreatment they are receiving.
- Idealizing a perpetrator of abuse: If parents overlook their parents' troubling behaviors, they may be willing to overlook their own.
- Excusing the behavior of an adult who mistreated them or saying that they deserved the maltreatment they received: These parents may be willing to excuse the behavior of other perpetrators, or they may distort their current situation to think that their children deserve the maltreatment they are receiving.

Parents exhibiting the previous behaviors may benefit from psychotherapy to help them process their childhood experiences and see how these have had an impact on their development and the parenting of their children. Unfortunately, parents who deny or distort their history may also be the most resistant to treatment. They may fear confronting a painful past. It may be helpful to point out, as concretely as possible, the effects that current behaviors are having on the development of their children.

■ *Further Reading*

McGoldrick, M., & Gerson, R. (1985). *Genograms in family assessment.* New York: Norton.

65

How Do I Assess a Caregiver's Parenting Attitudes, Knowledge, and Level of Functioning?

■ *Sandra T. Azar and Champika K. Soysa*

The key to effective service planning with parents is a careful assessment of their attitudes, knowledge, and level of functioning, as well as the other intrapsychic and behavioral disturbances and contextual factors that may interfere with the use of skills of parents. This information facilitates targeting treatment, monitoring progress, and adjusting services as needed. It also allows for documentation of final outcomes that are useful for decision making (e.g., termination of parental rights, reunification) and for examining more general program effectiveness. *Assessment of attitudes and behavioral skills in specific domains of parenting* (e.g., medical care knowledge and the ability to provide cognitive stimulation) and of *cross-domain capacities* (e.g., interpersonal problem solving, perspective-taking) are needed.

Before discussing specific techniques, a brief discussion is needed regarding professional resistance to conducting assessments (e.g., concerns that it will damage the relationship; needs will be identified that cannot be handled, such as suicidality; and lack of progress will be used against them or their agency). Some concerns may have validity, but others may not. For example, appropriate assessment can help a parent to feel listened to and empowered (telling you their needs). It can also allow the worker to more easily ask questions about personal issues (e.g., "this is on the form"). In addition, it is easy to omit important areas when dealing with families in crisis. A carefully constructed assessment plan can ensure this does not occur. Most important, it improves our ability to set the most useful goals for families, to assess our work, and to help parents see their own progress. Table A7.1 in Appendix 7 provides tips for how to do assessment in a "relationship"-building way.

A framework (i.e., the areas crucial to assess) is needed to structure the selection of the assessment method(s). The assessment of level of functioning refers to what parents do in various domains (e.g., how they diaper an infant, carry out discipline of a 4-year-old, or deal with a teenager's violating a curfew). In contrast, assessment of attitudes and knowledge has more to do with the foundation of information and beliefs on which a parent draws to perform the functions of parenting. For example, parents may try to keep teenagers at home to listen to their problems, instead of letting them be with peers, because they believe this is what teenagers *should* do. Also, they may spank a 3-year-old for not staying out of their way when they are in a bad mood, if they believe that 3-year-olds are capable of perspective taking.

Given the heterogeneity of parental deficits, it is difficult to provide a single assessment strategy. Capacities to complete basic survival tasks, handle emergencies, and provide for a child's developmental needs require attention. Common areas that require attention are noted in Table A7.2 of Appendix 7, and methods for collecting this information are outlined in the following sections.

■ Informal Interviews and Observations

In talking with parents, one should pay careful attention to their spontaneous narratives regarding children for indicators of *disturbed attitudes or beliefs regarding both their children and their role as parents*. Examples of distortions in such narratives include

- Assumptions of mind reading (e.g., "He *knew* I was tired.")

- Evidence of attributional biases (e.g., "He's that way—he's selfish" and "She knew it would get to me.")
- A sense of low self-efficacy as a parent (e.g., "She thinks she's boss" and "He thinks I'm stupid.")
- Indications of spillover of negative affect from other relationships (e.g., "He's just like his father—no good!")

When questioning a parent regarding problems with his or her child (e.g., crying, tantrums), a set of specific questions can also sometimes uncover distortions in the parent's perceptions. For example, a parent might be questioned in the following way regarding his or her response to a tantrum:

Worker: All mothers get upset at tantrums, but for all mothers it is different. What about it was the hardest part for you?

Mother: He thinks he's boss.

Worker: What about being a mother of a child who thinks he's boss is the hardest part for you?

Mother: He thinks I am stupid.

Worker: Feeling that way must be awful! Are there other people who make you feel this way?

Mother: He's just like his father. He was always calling me "dummy"!

For this mother, her history with men and low sense of self-efficacy emerge in difficult transactions with her son. These might be dealt with in addition to providing skills on how to handle tantrums.

In visits with families, informal observations can be collected on the quality of parent-child interactions. Recording of behaviors across visits may identify patterns of responding that are problematic (e.g., poor stress management, inability to negotiate conflict, failure to identify safety risks, and little use of positive approaches). During interactions, questions regarding parents' beliefs and thought patterns can also be solicited (e.g., "I just saw Johnny have trouble with following your commands. Why do you think that is?").

■ *Structured Assessments*

Although informal interviews and observations can be useful, structured methods can provide a broader and more thorough coverage and, in some cases, norms against which to measure the meaning of parents' responses. Interview protocols, self-report instruments, and formal observational schemas exist for many of the domains noted in Table A7.2 in Appendix 7. Some cautions are in order, however. Most have limited psychometric data (e.g., norms, versions in different languages, and validity data with large samples and with diverse sets of parents). Given that parents involved with child protective services (CPS) are also under legal constraints, they may not respond honestly. Also, if parents have lost child custody, the lack of contact may affect their responses. Finally, our ability to predict future violence has been questioned. Nonetheless, the available methods can provide a useful starting point.

Promising approaches exist, including self-report measures for parenting beliefs and knowledge, measures of problem-solving capacities, and ones assessing cognitive distortions regarding children (although the latter are less well developed) (see Appendix 7 for sample measures). Many have subscales measuring domains of parenting and the level of child risk. Some have norms on parents who have been involved with CPS.

Behavioral protocols exist that might be adapted for observations of parent-child interaction (Marsh, 1991; Appendix 7). There are several ways to approach these observations (e.g., home vs. clinic setting; structured vs. "naturalistic" interactions). Specific common aversive child-rearing and child care situations can be presented, and parents can be asked to enact them with their children or role-play how they typically handle these situations. Both their thinking in the midst of such difficulties and weaknesses in their strategies can be examined. The situations you present may vary with the developmental level of the child (e.g., feeding, handling of noncompliance, supervision, disagreements with partners, and problems with teachers). Care must be taken to obtain an adequate sample of interactions. Indices of parental behavior derived from single, short samples (e.g., 45 minutes) may not be stable, even over short time spans (Wachs, 1987). In contrast, data collapsed over many observations may have greater stability and thus may provide a more accurate assessment of typical patterns of interactions (e.g., from 5 to 9 hours of sampling across four or five sessions). Sampling behavior across multiple contexts (e.g., child care, play, teaching) and at high-risk (e.g., dinner hour) and low-risk times may also be important. The validity of such observations when parents have been apart from their children for lengthy periods of time or under legal constraints (termination of parental rights proceedings) might be questioned.

■ Neglect Issues

Neglect is an important area of assessment. It should include direct parenting judgment and behavior (e.g., handling of emergencies) and indirect choices that parents make regarding the environment in which they raise their children (e.g., home safety) (Appendix 7). For the latter, caution must be used because poverty often determines whether parents do in fact have choices.

■ Assessment of Parent Resources and Liabilities and Critical Contextual Factors

Parents may also have skill deficits that interfere with treatment or other problems that interfere with the optimal use of their parenting capacities. For example, literacy is needed to read prescription labels or to use parent education materials; thus, an assessment of basic reading and writing is important. Psychiatric problems can also interfere with parenting (e.g., depression), and using screening instruments can determine treatment needs (see Appendix 7 for sample measures).

Parenting involves a match between the parent's capacities and the child's needs. Thus, an assessment of child functioning may be useful. Common screening instruments can be administered, and referrals can be made as needed for more detailed evaluations. Broad-spectrum and narrowband (e.g., attention problems, trauma) screening instruments are available. Because parents may distort their child's difficulties, it is best to obtain reports from teachers and others familiar with the child.

Parents function best under low contextual stress and with high levels of positive social support. Thus, assessing these two contextual factors is crucial. The number and type of stressful events (e.g., daily hassles vs. life events) and the parents' perception of the intensity of these events need to be considered. Selecting instruments that fit parents' social class and life circumstances is important. Assessing social support includes collecting data on the size of parents' social networks, the amount of contact, the valence (positive or negative) of that contact, and the satisfaction with the support provided. Potential instruments are listed in Appendix 7.

■ *Cultural Context*

In performing evaluations, variation in cultural practices should be considered. For example, high parental control may be viewed negatively in one culture but signify caring in another. Culture may also influence the meaning of social cues (e.g., children turning eyes downward when speaking to adults may be mistakenly seen as fear when it may signify respect). (For additional information, see Chapters 9, 20, 48, and 71, this volume.)

■ *Further Reading*

Mash, E. H. (1991). Measurement of parent-child interaction in studies of maltreatment. In R. Starr & D. A. Wolfe (Eds.), *The effects of child abuse and neglect* (pp. 203-255). New York: Guilford.

Wachs, T. D. (1987). Short-term stability of aggregated and nonaggregated measures of parental behavior. *Child Development, 58,* 796-797.

66

How Do I Assess the Care of Children With Major Medical Problems?

■ *Prasanna Nair*

All children with chronic health problems must have an identified source of primary medical care. To assess whether the care provided is adequate, the worker must first be aware of the needs of the child. Talking with the child's primary care provider will clarify the child's condition, needs, and treatment as well as impressions of how the family is coping. The family's perception of the situation can then be assessed. Identifying barriers to care helps guide appropriate intervention.

■ Newborn

1. Infants who are premature, low-birth-weight, or both

   - Infants delivered before 37 weeks of gestation are called premature.
   - Infants who weigh 2,500 grams (5 lbs 8 oz.) or less are low-birth-weight infants and may be appropriate (weight) for gestational age or small for gestational age. Records

from the nursery should indicate into which category the baby should be classified.

- Very-low-birth-weight infants weight less than 1,500 grams, usually due to prematurity, and are likely to have more problems related to growth and development.
- Weight gain: Is infant receiving adequate feeding, vitamins, iron, and fluoride?
- Development: Is infant receiving regular assessment of development and hearing?

2. Drug-exposed infants

- Babies exposed to narcotics, such as heroin and methadone, *in utero* can have withdrawal symptoms, which can be mild to severe, lasting from a few days to several months (neonatal abstinence syndrome).
- Mild symptoms can be managed without medications by providing a quiet environment, dim lighting, swaddling (tightly wrapping), and frequent small feedings if infant has vomiting.
- If medications are needed, close follow-up by the physician is needed until the infant is weaned off medication.
- Neonatal abstinence score is a scale used to measure the severity of withdrawal.
- Weight gain should be checked at least weekly until the infant shows an adequate weight gain.
- Parenting ability and mother-infant bonding must be assessed, and the mother should be referred to a drug treatment program.

3. Fetal alcohol syndrome

- Infants are small for gestational age and may have facial abnormalities, heart defects, delayed development, and mental deficiency varying from borderline to severe.
- Growth and development must be monitored and appropriate referrals made early to infant stimulation programs if needed.

4. Infant born to HIV-positive woman

- Ensure that infant is receiving primary care in a program that is up-to-date with current recommendations for diagnosis and treatment of HIV infection.
- Check if the infant is receiving AZT every 6 hours during the first 6 weeks of life.
- After 6 weeks, the infant needs Bactrim for PCP prophylaxis 3 days per week until discontinued by physician.
- Infant's HIV and immune status must be closely monitored with tests for HIV infection (RNA viral load, DNA polymerase chain reaction, HIV cocultures, and P24 antigen) and T cell (CD4) counts.

■ Chronic Illnesses

Asthma

Asthma is a common chronic lung disease with the following characteristics:

- Airways are hyperresponsive (i.e., very sensitive). They react to different stimuli or triggers.
- Triggers include cold air, exercise, allergens (cat dander, dust mites, and mold), irritants (smoke, sprays, and strong smells), and infections.
- Airways are inflamed—that is, the airway linings are swollen.
- Airways become narrow, and breathing becomes difficult.
- There is often a family history of asthma or allergies.

Good health care is crucial for a child with asthma. Although it is usually easily treated, it can be severe and life threatening. Health education is extremely important:

- Parents and older children must understand what is meant by "asthma," its environmental controls, the triggers for the affected child, how different medicines work, and how to use home peak flow monitoring.

- Proper use of peak flowmeters will help them identify early stages of airway obstruction and determine if treatment is working.
- Ensure that the family is referred to an appropriate asthma education program. Poorly treated asthma is one of the most common reasons for preventable hospitalizations.

Cerebral Palsy

Cerebral palsy (CP) is a nonprogressive condition of posture and movement, often associated with abnormalities of speech, vision, and intellect, resulting from a defect or lesion of the developing brain. The needs of children with CP are as follows:

- Children with CP need a comprehensive approach to care, which should include physical and occupational therapists, a developmental psychologist, a speech pathologist, a social worker, a primary health care provider, and educators. Interdisciplinary teams offer the best approach.
- Children need physical and occupational therapy early to limit the effects of abnormal muscle tone and to prevent contractures.

■ *Further Reading*

Berger, S. P., Holt-Turner, I., Cupoli, J. M., Mass, M., & Hageman, J. R. (1998, June). Caring for the graduate from the neonatal intensive care unit: At home, in the office and in the community. *Pediatric Clinics of North America, 45*(3), 701-712.

National Asthma Education Program Information Center, Bethesda, Maryland, provides sources for information on various aspects of asthma (phone: 301-951-3260; website: *http://beWell.com*).

American College of Allergy, Asthma and Immunology. (1997). *The guidelines for diagnosis and management of asthma.* Arlington Heights, IL 60005 (phone: 1-800-842-7777).

Liptak, G. S. (1998, February). The child who has severe neurological impairment. *Pediatric Clinics of North America, 45,* 123-144.

67

How Do I Assess a Caregiver's Strengths and Treatment Needs?

■ *Marsha K. Salus*

A ssessing the strengths and needs of caregivers is a joint process that requires establishing rapport with caregivers as the critical first step to gathering information needed to ensure the child's safety and to help the caregivers change the behaviors or conditions that are related to the risk of maltreatment. Child protection agencies tend to be problem focused. As a result, many workers focus on identifying, categorizing, and labeling what is wrong with parents, their weaknesses, and their limitations. It is clear that all human beings have strengths. Workers must determine these by examining the whole person. They must identify the behaviors or conditions of the caregivers that must change to reduce or eliminate the risk of maltreatment, and they must also search for the caregivers' strengths that will provide the foundation on which change can occur.

■ *Domains of Information*

The domains of information gathering necessary to identify the caregivers' strengths and treatment needs include the following:

- *Physical health:* Are the caregivers physically healthy? Do they have any illnesses or conditions that may impact their ability to provide care and nurturing for their children?

- *Psychological functioning and emotional expression:* Are the caregivers emotionally healthy? Do they have a good self-concept? Are the caregivers likable and honest? Are the caregivers able to express love and affection to their children? Do they have any psychological problems, and, if so, what is the extent of these problems? Do they have good coping skills? Are they able to control their feelings, thoughts, and impulses?

- *Cognitive functioning:* What are the caregivers' levels of intellectual functioning? Do they have any limitations that may impact on their care of the child? Are the caregivers able to accurately assess the situations in which they find themselves? Do the caregivers have insight? How would you describe the caregivers' problem-solving abilities?

- *Social functioning and interpersonal relationships:* Do the caregivers have positive and healthy relationships with adults (family and friends) outside the home? Are the caregivers able to form trusting relationships with others? How would you characterize the nature of the caregivers' relationships? Are they characterized by openness, help, and support?

- *Childhood history:* Did the caregivers grow up in nurturing and loving environments? Were the caregivers' childhood experiences fraught with trauma, abuse, or deprivation?

■ Identifying the Caregiver's Strengths

The fundamental skills of identifying, respecting, and making use of people's strengths and resources must be emphasized in the assessment of caregivers' strengths and treatment needs. By searching for strengths and abilities, the worker is identifying something powerful in the caregivers as well as something often neglected. The following strategies can assist in identifying caregivers' strengths:

- Move beyond the behavior contributing to the risk of maltreatment and search for the purpose or positive intention behind it. Workers must believe that all behavior is purposeful, it meets a need in the individual, and it has healthy intention behind it. For example, a father who was physically abused injures his 4-year-old son, who has been diagnosed with attention deficit hyperactivity disorder and engages in destructive and aggressive behavior. The father loves his son and is trying to control his son's behavior so that he will develop into a healthy functioning adult.

- Discuss the caregivers' interests, likes, and abilities. Listen to how the caregivers talk about everyday things. Ask what they do for fun. Thoroughly examine all parts of the caregivers' lives to find hidden strengths.

- Find out the caregivers' hopes and dreams. Ask them what they want out of life. Ask them where they would like to be in 5 years. Ask about what they hope for their family and their children.

- Caregivers who abuse or neglect their children or both have often survived abuse, neglect, trauma, or deprivation as children and many other difficulties as adults. Therefore, determine what personal qualities they have that helped them survive.

- Everyone has had times in their lives when things were going well. Ask parents the following: "Think of a time when things were going well. What was different? How would you describe what was different this morning when you didn't have a drink?" This helps identify abilities successfully used in one situation that could be used to address other problems. (For more examples, see Chapter 19, this volume.)

■ Determining What Behaviors or Conditions the Caregivers Must Change

Determining what must change to reduce or eliminate the risk of maltreatment requires an analysis of the information regarding the caregivers' physical health; their psychological, social, and cognitive abilities; and their history. The purpose of the analysis is to answer the following questions:

- Which of the caregivers' behaviors or conditions are contributing to the risk of maltreatment? (The intent is to move beyond the symptoms.)
- What do the caregivers need to do to change the behaviors or conditions? For example, in a case of sexual abuse, the nonoffending mother may need to work through her own victimization to fully meet her daughter's need to be believed and emotionally supported.
- How pervasive is the problem? How many aspects of the caregivers' lives do the problems or conditions affect?
- How serious is the problem?
- How long has the problem been occurring?
- Are the caregivers capable of changing the problem or condition?

■ *Summary*

To identify caregivers' strengths, workers must first believe that all human beings have strengths. It is the worker's role to help caregivers discover the strengths they can tap into to help them change the behaviors or conditions that contribute to the risk of maltreatment.

■ *Further Reading*

Holder, W., & Mohr, C. (Eds.). (1980). *Helping in child protective services.* Denver, CO: American Humane Association.

Saleebey, D. (Ed.). (1997). *The strengths perspective in social work practice.* New York: Longman.

Wolins, S. J., & Wolins, S. (1993). *The resilient self.* New York: Villard.

68

How Do I Assess a Caregiver's Motivation and Readiness to Change?

■ *Diane DePanfilis*

All human beings are motivated to meet basic needs. Clients frequently differ in their state of readiness or eagerness to change, however. Also, their readiness to change may fluctuate from one time or situation to another. Motivation is clearly linked to the degree of hope that change is possible. Part of our role in assessing motivation is to foster hope through the development of a helping relationship (see Chapter 8, this volume). Thus, although this chapter is concerned with assessing motivation, it is also about enhancing motivation.

How do we know when caregivers are motivated to change? Is it because they agree that they need help? Is it because they attended a parent education class? Is it because they appear to be distressed by their current situation? The degree to which clients are ready to change varies over time and has been described as following a pattern:

1. Precontemplation: not seeing any need to change
2. Contemplation: considering change but also rejecting it
3. Determination: wants to do something about the problem
4. Action: takes steps to change
5. Maintenance: maintains goal achievement
6. Relapse: recurrence of some earlier problems

This chapter provides a brief outline of areas that will inform the practitioner's assessment of a client's readiness to enter into, continue, and adhere to specific change strategies.

■ *Assessing Comfort With the Status Quo*

Although occasionally families come to us through a self-referral, most of the time our first contact with a family occurs because someone else was concerned and made a referral. Thus, information suggested about the engagement process (see Chapters 7 through 12, this volume) must be considered before we can make an accurate assessment of a caregiver's comfort with the status quo. The best strategy for assessing the degree of comfort with the status quo is to help all family members talk about their daily lives and their degree of satisfaction with their current situation. Part of our goal is to raise doubt "that everything is OK" and help caregivers recognize the consequences of current behaviors or conditions that may contribute to maltreatment. Although they may not initially listen to you as an outsider, they might be convinced when they hear their children talk about how scared they are when they are left alone at night.

■ *Assessing the Degree of Hope That the Situation Can Be Different*

As suggested previously, motivation is very much affected by hope. It is important that we assess the client's hope that the situation can be different by what they say, by what we observe, and by what they do. It is also important that we recognize that sometimes clients are incapacitated by conditions that need to be addressed first (e.g., depression). It is easier to pursue a goal (even if one is unhappy with the status quo) if one has faith that the goal can be achieved. One method to encourage hope is to follow the suggestions offered in Chapter 19 (i.e., help family members identify the exceptions). For example, sometimes families need considerable help to remember the times when things were better or to create a picture of what their life could look like with fewer stresses and strains. Sometimes it is difficult to convey hope that things can be different because clients have had negative experiences with formal systems and cannot imagine that a worker could actually want to work with them, not against them. Nevertheless, to engage in change that can be sustained, hope must be part of the equation, even if one of the motivating factors at first is the wish that we "get out of their lives."

■ Assessing Motivation and Values

To sustain change, goals must be consistent with a person's values and culture, and we should not try to impose our values on others (see Chapter 20, this volume). Sometimes, however, we may be able to offer a broader vision of ways of being. For example, if having a clean house is not something the caregiver thinks is very important, it may be necessary for the worker to understand what value the caregiver may have that may reinforce a goal to keep a child's environment healthy (e.g., "Every time one of the kids get sick, everyone ends up getting sick. I know it's no fun taking care of sick kids all of the time"). Also, if the caregiver dropped out of school in the eighth grade, he or she may not believe that to succeed in life children should do well in school. To construct goals that will be achieved, we need to better understand our clients' values and beliefs. Family members are the best source of this information.

■ Assessing Whether Wants and Goals Are Realistic

A very important role that we play in the assessment process is understanding what the caregiver wants to change and whether this view of the future is realistic and achievable. Some caregivers want to work on goals that exceed their capacity (e.g., seek career goals that are beyond their personal aptitude). Other caregivers might suggest goals that are beyond the sphere of influence of the caregivers and the worker—for example, interest in their children having no contact with their father ever again). If there is nothing to suggest that the children are unsafe when they are with their father, it is unrealistic that this goal could ever be achieved. We want to encourage self-determination, which fosters motivation; we do not want to contribute to a caregiver's failure, however, by knowingly developing plans that are unrealistic.

■ *Assessing Strength of Motivation*

Sometimes, caregivers express an interest in change, but because their view of the problem is different from ours, they may not have the willingness or skills to fully engage in the process. For example, a caregiver might state,

> It is OK if you see my daughter, Malinda, so she learns how *not* to talk back to me, but I really don't have any time for this stuff. . . . I have to hold down two jobs plus take care of these kids and the house.

Alternatively, a caregiver might say, "I'll do whatever that court order says, and then I want my kids back but I don't have time to go to the school and talk with Eugene's teacher." Part of our goal in the assessment process is to assess not only what a caregiver says he or she is willing to do but also what he or she is unwilling to do. Sometimes, when we detect weak motivation, it may be because of a disparity in one of the other assessment areas (e.g., the caregivers feel OK with the status quo, do not really have hope that things can be different, are being asked to do things that are inconsistent with their values, or have unrealistic ideas about how things can be better).

■ *Summary*

Motivation is much more than compliance with a court order or service plan. Even if a caregiver acknowledges the need for help, we may observe ambivalence or actual avoidance of the difficult tasks required to actually change long-standing behaviors or conditions. As noted in Chapter 11, caregivers that are the easiest to work with may actually be less motivated to change. Caregivers who initially react negatively to our intervention (see Chapters 10 and 11, this volume), however, may have the most potential to change. Assessment of motivation is complex and begins with the first contact and continues throughout the change process.

■ *Further Reading*

Hepworth, D. H., Rooney, R. H., & Larsen, J. (1997). *Direct social work practice.* Pacific Grove, CA: Brooks/Cole.

Miller, W. R., & Rollnick, S. (1991). *Motivational interviewing.* New York: Guilford.

Prochaska, J. O., & DeClemente, C. C. (1982). Transtheoretical therapy: Toward a more integrative model of change. *Psychotherapy: Theory, Research, and Practice, 19,* 276-288.

Prochaska, J. O., DeClemente, C. C., & Norcross, J. C. (1992). In search of how people change. *American Psychologist, 47,* 1102-1113.

69

What Do I Need to Know About Care Needs and Parenting Capacity in Caregivers With HIV or AIDS?

■ *Prasanna Nair*

Currently, the most common life-threatening diagnoses in a young adult are HIV infection and cancer. The general facts presented in this chapter regarding HIV infection may be helpful when you are dealing with an HIV-positive caregiver. AIDS is caused by HIV. Being infected with HIV does not mean that the person has AIDS. Also, AIDS is a syndrome that develops when the immune system is no longer able to function effectively in preventing illnesses that the body can normally resist.

Signs of AIDS in Adults

Early signs are nonspecific and can include swollen glands, tiring easily, weight loss, fever, night sweats, and diarrhea. The most common AIDS-associated condition in both women and men is a serious lung infection called *Pneumocystis carinii* pneumonia.

Women and AIDS

- Women are usually the primary caregivers of their children, and illness related to HIV or AIDS can affect their ability to care for their children because of hospitalizations, debilitation, and central nervous system disease.
- Early diagnosis of HIV is important: The only way to determine if a person is infected with HIV is with a blood test. Survival time for women is shorter than that for men because women often are not diagnosed early and therefore do not receive treatment early. Compared to men, HIV-infected women have less access to care and poorer use of health care resources.
- Domestic violence, homelessness, and lack of social support for women may be important factors. Therefore, it is important to identify infected women as soon as possible and enroll them in a comprehensive health care program.
- The following are common problems in women with AIDS: esophageal candidiasis (yeast), herpes simplex virus, esophagitis, bacterial pneumonia, vaginal infections, pelvic inflammatory disease, and menstrual irregularity.

Life Expectancy

Average time between infection with HIV and onset of clinically apparent disease is approximately 10 years. A small percentage of infected individuals die within months following infection, and approximately 5% have no signs of disease even after 12 years. With the new multiple-drug treatment, life expectancy is expected to increase considerably.

Health Care Needs

All HIV-infected individuals must have primary health care provided by staff knowledgeable of HIV and AIDS.

New Advances in Treatment of HIV Infection

Major advances in assessing the severity of HIV infection and in treatment have occurred. Tests such as the viral load have shown how high levels of virus correlate with worsening clinical course. Patients with AIDS have a larger amount of the virus than do asymptomatic patients. Decrease in viral load due to treatment is strongly correlated with improved clinical outcome.

Current Recommendations for Treatment

The current recommendations are based on the very poor prognosis of untreated HIV. The HIV virus can becomes resistant to antiviral drugs, especially if the drugs are not taken as recommended, requiring excellent compliance with treatment. Therefore, the long-term suppression of viral growth and preventing resistance can only be achieved with combinations of medications, known as "highly active antiretroviral therapy."

- Effective antiviral treatment should be introduced before extensive immune system damage has occurred.
- Viral load monitoring is an essential tool to determine the risk of disease progression and response to antiviral therapy.
- A combination of antiviral drugs should be used to suppress HIV replication to below detection level by sensitive viral load tests.
- Education and support should be provided to patients to achieve compliance with complicated treatment using combination antiviral therapy.

Counseling and Support

Knowledge that one is infected with HIV is emotionally devastating to most individuals and often to the family. Stresses experienced by affected families include the following:

- Separation, grieving, loss (e.g., placement of children in substitute care, loss of function, and death), and depression
- Stigma, guilt, ostracism, and secrecy

- Disclosure of diagnosis to family, children, and friends
- Alteration of caregiver's lifestyle, plans, finances, and housing needs
- Intense involvement with medical systems, hospitalizations, handling numerous appointments, problems in obtaining medications, and making medical decisions that may be life threatening
- Child care, especially as the caretaker's illness progresses
- Legal guardianship and permanency planning
- Behavior problems in children
- Issues related to death and dying

When the caregiver has AIDS, professionals need to be aware of the previous issues and be able to help families deal with them by:

- Providing ongoing assessment and counseling of psychosocial needs of the parent or caregiver and children
- Helping parents plan for the future care of their children and make preparations for themselves
- Accessing resources for legal help with issues of temporary placement during an acute exacerbation of the illness and later with permanency planning
- Considering the needs of the whole family
- Coordinating efforts with other agencies (Usually, these families are involved with multiple agencies.)

Strategies helpful in coping with a life-threatening illness include:

- Problem focussed support—for example, providing help with financial, legal, medical, issues of disclosure, and child behavior problems
- Mental health services dealing with acceptance, reducing isolation, and promoting family functioning and self-reliance
- Religion (formal religious supports and private prayer)
- Skills to communicate with the health care system and social service agencies
- Social support groups
- Family therapy
- Respite care

Caregiving Capacity

The initial impact of learning of HIV infection is devastating to most individuals. Depression, denial, anger toward the person who is the probable source of HIV infection, and feelings of shame, guilt, and fear of abandonment or violence are common. The latter makes disclosure difficult; therefore, issues of confidentiality are important when dealing with other family members. Providing emotional support and referral to medical and other professionals experienced in the care of HIV-infected individuals is crucial. Assessment of the mother's or caregiver's ability to care for children should be ongoing. Even when a mother is ill, with support she can continue caring for her healthy children but she may need special help if a child is also HIV infected and is on multiple medications. If a parent is becoming sick, plans should be discussed regarding future care of the children, such as drawing up a formal legal permanency planning document. If the parent needs hospitalization, help in arranging interim care for children will be needed.

■ Resources

Educational materials on HIV and AIDS can be obtained free from the following resources:

Department of Health and Human Services, *Guidelines for use of antiviral agents in adults and adolescent patients with HIV infection.* Clearinghouse: phone: 1-800-438-5231
    Website: *http://www.cdcnac.org.*

National AIDS Hotline, *Basic facts about AIDS*: provides information about AIDS support groups, clinics, and other help you can get in your area (phone: 1-800-342-AIDS).

Clinical trials: Much has been learned in a short time about how to help people living with HIV. New drugs are needed, however, because the virus easily develops resistance. When a drug is tested in people to determine if it is safe and whether it helps them to become healthy, these research studies are known as clinical trials. Information about these studies is available from AIDS Clinical Trials (phone: 1-800-874-2572).

Part V

FAMILY
ASSESSMENT

Section C:
Emphasis on Families

70

How Do I Assess the Strengths in Families?

■ *Diane DePanfilis*

A strengths-based orientation to child protection practice provides the opportunity to develop or build on existing competencies needed by the family to respond to crises and stress, to meet needs, and to enhance the functioning of the family system. Uncovering strengths, however, cannot be accomplished in a simplistic manner, just as using a checklist to assess risk cannot capture the interrelationships among factors that increase the likelihood of maltreatment. Strengths are not isolated variables but, rather, form clusters and constellations that are dynamic and interrelated. Research on family strengths has identified a core set of 12 qualities that help families cope with stress and meet the needs of their members. This chapter reviews each quality and considers how each of these areas of assessment may be relevant to child protection practice. As you review these areas, you will notice the interrelationships among them.

1. A belief in and commitment to promote the well-being and growth of individual family members and that of the family unit: Is this a family in which all members reside in the same household but each member comes and goes, or are there strong connections between members? When important decisions need to be made, do they talk over the implications

of the decision for each member? If there are strong alliances between family members, individuals may be able to be counted on to follow through with safety and treatment plans that benefit other members.

2. Appreciation for the small and large things that individual family members do well and encouragement to do better: Similar to the first quality, if individuals are proud of each other, then they will be more likely to support each other to fully participate in a plan that will reduce the risk of maltreatment. Ask each member to talk about the positive qualities of other members. What makes them particularly proud? How do they show or convey that positive feeling? How often do they feel they take each other for granted? It is important to remember that when caregivers feel unappreciated, this may lead to negative interaction or withdrawal from caregiving responsibilities.

3. Concentrated effort to spend time and do things together, no matter how formal or informal the activity or event: Ask family members to talk about how they spend time together. Even if they spend time pitching in together to do household chores, there is a supportive quality to this activity versus the case in which a family's members spend time in the same household but not together. Ask what they like to do for fun as a family. Even when things are difficult, if the family works to do things together, individuals are less isolated and more able to cope with stress.

4. A sense of purpose or agreement that permeates the reasons and basis for continuing in both bad and good times: What happens when the family faces a problem? Do family members "stick together," or do they blame each other for their troubles? If family members say they will be home at a certain time to help with the evening meal, do they follow through or do they let each other down if they get better offers? Even families who stick together in their negative reaction to intervention possess a quality that we can build on.

5. Common agreement among family members regarding the value and importance of assigning time and energy to meet needs: What do family members agree about? How do they come to agreement on issues that are most important?

Because we know that conflict occurs when families do not have ways to develop a consensus among members, this is an important area of assessment.

6. The ability to communicate with one another in a way that emphasizes positive interactions: Are family members able to share concerns and feelings with each other in productive ways? When there are disagreements, do family members listen to all sides of the story? This area of assessment is especially important in families for which domestic violence is a concern.

7. A clear set of family rules, values, and beliefs that establish expectations about acceptable and desired behavior: Do family members agree about how each member is expected to behave? Does everyone have the same understanding about family rules? In the absence of this quality, families may have conflict because rules are unclear. Furthermore, families who clearly do not hold consistent values and beliefs may be more likely to neglect the needs of some members.

8. A varied repertoire of coping strategies that promote positive functioning in dealing with stressful life events: Do family members have ways to keep their mind off their worries? Are they able to keep things in perspective and take things one at a time? Do they have others to turn to for support? Being overwhelmed with stress can result in withdrawn behavior and possibly neglecting the needs of children or in exploding, which could result in family conflict or abuse.

9. The ability to engage in problem-solving activities designed to evaluate options for meeting needs and obtaining resources: Are family members able to talk together about problems and arrive at solutions, or do problems multiply or seem to occur repeatedly without long-term solutions being developed? In families that seem to live in constant crisis, and as a consequence the care of children is compromised, this is a particularly important area of assessment.

10. The ability to be positive and see the positive in many aspects of their lives, including the ability to view crisis and problems as an opportunity to learn and grow: Do family members have the view that something good can be found in

everything? Do they express hope for the future? If so, it should be much easier to engage the family in a partnership that reduces the risk of maltreatment.

11. Flexibility and adaptability: Do family members have a history of helping each other when something goes wrong? Does everyone pitch in to find a solution to a problem? When families have the capacity to adapt to unexpected circumstances, relationships between members are less likely to break down, and children are more likely to be nurtured and supported.

12. A balance between the use of internal and external family resources for coping and adapting to life events and planning for the future: In times of need, does the family first try to find solutions on their own? Are they able to recognize when they need to access outside resources? These are skills we try to build through our intervention.

Although it is unlikely that most families will show evidence of strengths in all these areas, it is important that we examine areas in which strength does exist. Examples of assessment instruments (without copyright restrictions) to assess family strengths, resources, and social supports are provided in Appendixes 8 and 9.

■ *Further Reading*

Dunst, C., Trivette, C., & Deal, A. (1988). *Enabling and empowering families*. Cambridge, MA: Brookline.

Dunst, C., Trivette, C., & Deal, A. (Eds.). (1994). *Supporting & strengthening families*. Cambridge, MA: Brookline.

71

How Do I Conduct an Ethnographic Interview to Learn About the Family's Culture?

■ *Julia Rauch*

■ *What Are Ethnographic Interviews?*

Ethnographic interviews are tools for learning about another culture from an "insider's" point of view. The core concern is with the meaning of actions and events to culture members.

■ *What Is Culture?*

Culture can be defined as learned values, beliefs, and behaviors of a defined group of people. The group may be as small as a family or as large as a continent. Cultures differ in many ways (e.g., child-rearing practices, ways of resolving conflicts, and interpersonal communication).

Larger cultures, such as a nation's, have cocultures. Cocultures share features of the larger culture but are also distinctive. The United States has several cocultures—for example, African American and Japanese American. In addition, many recent immigrant groups are maintaining their native cultures (although in the future they may evolve into cocultures). Thus, the United States has a dominant culture, cocultures, and other cultures.

Worker and client culture and coculture differences are a major barrier to effective services. Culturally unaware workers may be ineffective. They may misjudge a situation or provide culturally inappropriate services or both. Ethnographic interviewing may help you to overcome cultural barriers and become more effective.

■ How Do Ethnographic Interviews Compare With Other Interviews?

Like all interviews, ethnographic interviews have a purpose; have beginnings, middles, and ends; and use standard interviewing techniques. Ethnographic interviews differ from other interviews in specific purpose (interviewer learning), focus (culture), and participants' roles (learner/teacher). They are more like friendly conversations than formal interviews. The interviewer actively expresses appreciation (e.g., "I'm learning so much from you" and "I never heard about 'hot' and 'cold' diseases before"). Change-oriented interview techniques are not used.

■ What Do I Want to Know?

Try to learn about child welfare-related topics that will be helpful to you. Possible topics are family composition, structure, and processes; child-rearing beliefs and practices; attitudes and behaviors toward human service agencies; and helping resources used by culture members. Because your time is limited, you will need to prioritize your topics.

For your chosen topics, brainstorm possible questions. For example, regarding families you might want to know who belongs to the family, who is involved in child rearing and in what way, what child behaviors are defined as acceptable and unacceptable, how children are disciplined, and who speaks for the family in its contacts with the outside world. What else might you want to know?

■ What Should I Ask?

What you want to know and what you ask in the interview are not the same. People are generally unaware of significant aspects of their culture and unable to answer abstract cultural questions. Some concepts, such as role, may not be known or understood. Some languages do not even have a word or concept equivalent to culture.

Ethnographers usually focus on daily life by asking descriptive questions. One approach is to ask a person to describe a typical day. Using this approach, one can explore more fully an identified topic when it is mentioned by the interviewee. Another approach is to ask about a specific type of interaction or episode—for example, "Tell me about the last time your son was disrespectful." Try to obtain rich descriptive detail, for example, by asking the parent to describe a recent incident and who was involved, when and where it occurred, what happened, why he or she thinks her son was disrespectful, and how he or she responded to the son.

"Disrespectful" is an example of a cover term. *Cover terms* are words or phrases that literally cover a range of cultural ideas and meanings. Sometimes, cover terms stand out because they are unfamiliar to you. At other times, they will be familiar terms that mean dfferent things to you and your client. For example, you and a client may not mean the same thing by "good child" and "bad child." Cover terms can literally "uncover" a wealth of cultural information if explored. When you do an ethnographic interview, you will need to balance following your interviewee's lead and cover terms (he or she is the expert) with structuring the interview to meet your learning needs.

▪ Whom Can I Interview?

You can use ethnographic interviewing techniques with clients, other members of the culture, or people who are knowledgeable about the culture.

▪ How Do I Prepare for an Ethnographic Interview?

Prepare by identifying what you want to know and writing possible questions. Both are tools to help you listen for topics that you might want to ask about in greater detail. Identified topics can also help you to jump-start the interview if it lags. Decide whether you want to ask the person to describe a typical day or a type of episode. Choose the approach that you think will make your interviewee most comfortable. You may want to list your topics on a small index card.

To set the stage, admit your ignorance to your potential interviewee, express interest in finding out what life is like for him or her (or other culture members), ask the person to be your teacher, arrange to meet in a mutually comfortable setting, and agree on a time and time limit for the interview. Most important, relax. Remember that ethnographic interviews are friendly, interesting conversations. Enjoy your learning!

■ *Further Reading*

Fetterman, D. M. (1989). *Ethnography step by step*. Newbury Park, CA: Sage.

Leigh, J. W. (1998). *Communicating for cultural competence*. Boston: Allyn & Bacon.

72

How Do I Assess Family Functioning?

■ *Vanessa G. Hodges*

Family functioning is an elusive concept that has many dimensions and is defined differently based on theoretical principles and racial and cultural identity. Some practitioners view attributes such as family adaptability (the ability to change roles, rules, and relationships to cope with environmental and personal stressors) and emotional bonding of family members as critical dimensions of family functioning. Other practitioners view family problem-solving abilities and communication skills as critical dimensions. Irrespective of the theoretical perspective, the purpose of assessing family functioning is to learn how families manage typical daily living activities and to determine whether these activities satisfy the needs of individual family members and the family as a whole.

Assessments of family functioning evaluate environmental, cultural, social, physical, and psychological functioning of its members. The primary difference between family assessment and individual assessment is a focus on the entire family as a unit as opposed to focusing on a single individual within the family. Given that family needs vary considerably depending on developmental levels of family members, community assets, and access to cultural, financial, material, and human resources, it is important for practitioners to evaluate both family strengths and needs in each of these areas. Ultimately, interventions will focus on developing and strengthening the family's capacity to meet its members' needs.

This chapter outlines four primary attributes of healthy family functioning: Connections, Assets, Relationships, and Environment (CARE). These attributes capture both internal family interactions and transactions between families and larger systems. It should be noted that practitioners may not formally assess each of the CARE dimensions. Family problems, severity of crises, and family composition will help set priorities.

■ *Connections*

Connections are the first element in the CARE assessment of family functioning. This assesses family access to resources and supports outside the household, including extended family members, neighbors and friends, schools, employers, health and mental health services, religious institutions, recreational activities, and other community groups and organizations. Social support systems generally help in the following ways: supplying food and clothing, lending or giving money, assistance with health or mental health needs, and providing emotional support, help with job hunting, child care, transportation, recreation, use of telephone and appliances, and ethnic and cultural activities.

Connections are an important component of family functioning. The reciprocal nature of social support makes it especially appropriate for families with limited resources. Goods and services may be exchanged, making families feel less like they are receiving charity than asking for help. All families need resources outside of the family unit to function optimally. During the assessment, practitioners collect information on the types of formal resources available in the community (public transportation, public safety, recreational and educational resources, and health and mental health services) and informal resources (relationships with friends, extended family, and neighbors). This element of family assessment is especially pertinent to families of color. Racism, discrimination, and poverty require many families of color to depend on each other to meet daily needs by sharing meals, child care, and a home.

■ *Assets*

This element of the CARE protocol focuses on skills and abilities that enable healthy family functioning, including parenting skills, knowledge of child development and age-appropriate expectations, and problem-solving abilities.

Parenting and Child Development Knowledge and Skills

Caregivers are the most important and influential people in young children's lives. An evaluation of healthy family functioning must include data on the caregiver's parenting knowledge and skills. In addition to assessing the degree of affection, emotional bonding, physical care of a child, and discipline techniques, the ability of caretakers to teach children skills and to set limits must also be assessed. Parents must understand the developmental and cognitive abilities of children at various ages because these dictate what children are able to do. For example, parents of 3-year-olds cannot expect them to make their beds perfectly. Three-year-olds are unable to understand the steps involved in making a bed, and they do not have the fine motor abilities to do so. Other important parenting skills to assess include competence in establishing rules and setting limits, structuring time and activities, ignoring inappropriate behaviors, and rewarding and punishing behaviors.

Although assessment of parental roles is important, it is crucial to also assess attitudes and perceptions of children. For example, do children show respect for parents? Do they follow instructions? Do children have shared activities and companionship with parents? Are children involved in age-appropriate family decision making and problem solving?

Problem-Solving Skills

Families are constantly faced with unexpected emergencies, obstacles, and problems. Occasionally, these problems are significant, and at other times they are minor. Irrespective of the type of problem, a family's ability to systematically strategize, generate solutions, and select a plan increases the likelihood of satisfactory resolution. Healthy families have a process for solving problems, which generally prevents impulsive and emotional reactions to problems.

■ *Relationships*

This CARE element assesses relationships with other household members, communication patterns, and roles and their effect on relationships between family members. The nature and quality of relationships with family members can be a key factor in assessing family functioning. Families that have a strong sense of identity and connectedness, share common values, beliefs, rituals, and cultural traditions, interact with each other in warm and affirming ways, and express warmth and affection toward each other are likely to be able to draw on these resources during crisis periods. Family members who are isolated from each other, maintain troublesome communication patterns, feel little pride or sense of "oneness" as a family group, or have weak bonds and little commitment to each other, however, are much less likely to pull together during stressful times. Particular attention should be given to assessing a family's cultural identity, pride, and relationship to ethnic community resources and services. Having a strong racial identity and practicing cultural rituals and traditions can help sustain families through difficult times.

Communication

Open communication is the most important characteristic in healthy family functioning. Practitioners must carefully attend to both verbal and nonverbal communication because messages are often incongruent. For example, tone of voice and facial expression might send a different message than words. Although verbal and nonverbal messages are essential, the most important component of communication is listening. Assessing if family members speak for themselves or depend on others to speak for them gives clues to inappropriate communication patterns and to power relationships within the family. Practitioners should observe and inquire about typical communication patterns among family members.

In addition to communication patterns, it is important to assess relationships (subsystems) within the family, including parent or caregiver subsystems, parent-child subsystems, and sibling subsystems. Commitment, bonding, and conflict are important variables to consider.

Roles

All family members perform specific roles to maintain relationships in families. These roles help to maintain the stability of the family and are often gender based and stereotypical. For example, women routinely perform roles such as caregiver, nurturer, child care provider, disciplinarian, cook, house cleaner, and relational roles such as wife, girlfriend, lover, partner, mother, grandmother, sister, and friend. Children also stabilize the family by playing roles such as scapegoat, passive child, perfect child, rebel, troublemaker, comedian, and studious child. The ability to perform several roles and to move in and out of these roles fluidly is crucial.

It is critical to assess family roles because roles tend to be complementary. For example, if one parent is strict, the other tends to be lenient, and if one child is quiet and passive another tends to be boisterous and assertive. Complementary roles reinforce each other. When assessing the significance of roles in families, it is important to understand that people tend to become established in their roles and find it difficult to change because other family members expect that behavior. Family members may find themselves stuck in certain roles while at the same time hoping others will change.

■ Environment

This is the final element of the CARE protocol, and it assesses the home environment and sufficiency of resources to meet the daily living needs of family members. This element assesses economic resources (source, stability, and adequacy of income) and tasks for basic living. For example, workers should assess the safety and adequacy of current living arrangements, including space, basic household provisions (furnishings, toilet, bathing, cooking, and sleeping), management of household chores, and regularity and adequacy of meals.

■ *Conducting an Assessment of Family Functioning*

Practitioners use multiple sources of data when collecting information for family assessments, including informal observation, interviews, paper-and-pencil measures, and standardized measures. The following are resources and suggestions for collecting data to assess family functioning:

CARE Interview Questions

Connection

- In what ways are you and your family connected to other members of the community?
- Does your family participate in any religious, cultural, or ethnic community groups or organizations?
- Does your family experience any special risks or benefits from living in the community?
- What types of help do you give and receive from your family and friends?

Assets

- How do you discipline your children? Does the discipline work for the short term? Long term? How do you know it is working? Which method of discipline do you believe works best?
- How do you manage your children when you are frustrated with their behavior?
- When you are faced with a difficult problem, how do you go about solving it? Who is involved in the decision? What happens if your plan fails? Are all problems solved this way, or do you solve some problems differently?

Relationships

- How would you describe your relationship with other family members? (Relationship)
- How well do family members communicate needs and expectations? (Communication)

- How well do your children get along with each other? Are they able to work out their problems without your intervention? Give me an example of a conflict they resolved successfully? Unsuccessfully?
- Tell me about your daily routine. Start at the beginning of the day and tell me who does what? (Roles)
- Is your family's problem related to someone failing to perform an expected role? Why is the role important? What would happen if the person never performs the role? (Roles)
- Which members belong in the family (family members may be biological, adoptive, or close friends as long as they are considered family members)?

Environment

- Is income sufficient to support your family (pay rent and utility bills and supply necessities such as food and clothing)?
- Do you worry about your financial situation?
- What are the daily and weekly household chores?
- Who participates? How are those assignments decided?
- Does the family eat meals together? How often?

Paper-and-Pencil Tools

Ecomap: A graphic representation of a family's connection to social resources. The ecomap uses circles to depict social resources and symbols (dotted lines, broken lines, etc.) to represent the nature and strength of the relationship.

Genogram: A graphic representation of three or more generations of family members. The genogram can also include information about intergenerational relationships, occupations, religious background, family roles, and racial and cultural background.

Standardized measures

Index of Family Relations (Hudson, 1992): Twenty-five-item, rapid-assessment instrument measuring the severity and magnitude of relationship problems in families. Each item is rated on a 7-point scale (1, "None of the time"; 7, "All of the time").

■ *Further Reading*

Geismar, L. L., & Camasso, M. (1993). *The Family Functioning Scale: A guide to research and practice.* New York: Springer.

Hartman, A., & Laird, J. (1983). *Family-centered social work practice.* New York: Free Press.

Hudson, W. W. (1992). *The WALMYR Assessment Scales scoring manual.* Tempe, AZ: WALMYR.

McPhatter, A. R. (1996). Assessment revisited: A comprehensive approach to understanding family dynamics. In J. Rauch (Ed.), *Assessment: A sourcebook for social work practice.* Milwaukee, WI: Families International.

73

How Do I Assess a Parent-Child Relationship?

■ *Maureen M. Black*

A clear and responsive parent-child relationship forms the basis for healthy personality development as children learn to communicate their needs and desires and to respond to the demands of others. Parent-child relationships play such an important role in children's development that they can protect or buffer children against the threat of a hostile environment, such as poverty or community violence. In optimal circumstances, the parent-child relationship is characterized by a balance in which parents and children take turns signaling and responding to one another. Communication is clear because each adapts to the rhythm style of the other and to the demands of the situation. For example, a mother's response to a crying child varies depending on whether she thinks the cries signal hunger, pain, or fatigue.

In maltreating families, parent-child interactions are often distorted and marked by signals that lack clarity, misperceptions of signals, inconsistent responses, or responses that are not appropriate. Thus, maltreatment may occur when a parent misperceives the child's cries and responds either by withholding basic caregiving needs (neglect) or by hitting the child "to make him stop crying" (abuse). Similarly, parents who are depressed or overwhelmed by their own mental health needs may be unable

■ 353

to communicate clearly, may not "hear" their child's cues, or may view their actions or inactions toward the child as being justified.

Children also vary in their capacity to communicate with their parents. For example, children who are ill, premature, or temperamentally challenging may be less able to communicate clearly. An analysis of parent-child interaction is important in the evaluation of maltreatment, but it does not necessarily yield an explanation regarding the reason for the distortion.

Parent-child interaction is often assessed through three methods: (a) self-report from the parent or child, (b) report from another source (nurse, teacher, social worker, etc.), or (c) direct observation. Self-report often includes an interview with the participants about the interaction. Questions may be directed to the parent or child (usually individually and in private) and address their perceptions of the quality of the interaction. Report from another source is assessed by interviewing a third party about the interactions observed between the parent and child. Direct observation occurs when the parent and child are observed interacting with one another.

Although evaluations of parent-child interaction are often directed toward parents and their infants or toddlers, parent-child interaction is a critical issue throughout children's development and should not be limited to the early years. Evaluations should be directed toward both parents and children rather than focusing exclusively on parental behaviors, and they should include information about the context. For example, if a child has been ill or a family pet has died, interactions may not be typical. In addition, evaluations should consider multiple contexts. Children and parents may have little difficulty communicating with one another in low-stress situations in which there are few demands, such as free play, but they may have difficulty in situations that are potentially stressful, such as mealtimes or separations.

Observations of interactions may be conducted in the home, during health care visits, or in other settings (e.g., during a meal, playing a game, reading a book, and waiting for a visit). The following questions are synthesized from existing protocols of parent-child interactions and can be used to guide observations or interviews:

Position

- Are the parent and the child positioned so they are comfortable? In the case of a young child, does positioning provide adequate support?
- Are parent and the child able to see and hear one another?

Setting

- Is the environment free from distractions (noise and activity) that may disrupt the parent and the child?
- Are the parent and the child dressed appropriately for the setting?
- Are the parent and the child clean and adequately groomed?
- Are the demands of the situation (i.e., what's expected) clear?

Parent and Child: Clarity of Cues and Comments

- Do the parent and the child direct clear and coherent comments to one another?
- Are comments or instructions from the parent to the child consistent with the child's developmental level?
- Does the child use words or actions to attract the parent's attention (rather than misbehaving)?
- Does the parent praise the child after he or she has done something positive?
- Does the parent prepare the child for new events or activities?

Parent and Child: Responsivity

- Do the parent and the child look at and attend to one another periodically (as opposed to ignoring one another or attending to other activities)?
- Do the parent and the child "listen" to what the other says or watch what the other does (or does each respond only if the other person is loud, forceful, etc.)?
- If one person makes an error, does the other person correct the error respectfully (as opposed to laughing or making a disparaging comment)?
- If one person exhibits distress, does the other person offer comfort or support?
- If one person makes a request, does the other person acknowledge the request?

- Is the child responsive to the demands of the situation (as opposed to being disruptive or misbehaving)?
- If the child is disruptive or misbehaves, does the parent discipline the child without disparaging the child's character, evoking guilt, or physically forcing the child? Does the child end the disruptive behavior?

Parent and Child: Affect

- Do the parent and the child have affectionate expressions (as opposed to neutral or hostile expressions)?
- Do the child and the parent smile or laugh in response to something positive?
- Are comments between the parent and the child affectionate and respectful (as opposed to hostile or exclusively directives)?
- Does the child cope with new events or activities without becoming distressed or withdrawn?
- If the parent praises the child, does the child look appreciative or happy?
- Are conflicts resolved with mutual respect?
- Is the overall tone of the interaction positive and mutually respectful?

■ Further Reading

Barnard, K., Hammond, M., Booth, C., Bee, H., Mitchell, S., & Speiker, S. (1989). Measurement and meaning of parent-child interaction. In F. J. Morrison & C. E. Lee (Eds.), *Applied developmental psychology* (Vol. 3, pp. 39-80). San Diego: Academic Press.

Black, M., Hutcheson, J., Dubowitz, H., Berenson Howard, J., & Starr, R. H. (1996). The roots of competence: Mother-infant interaction among low-income, African American families. *Applied Developmental Psychology, 17,* 367-391.

Casey, P. H., Barrett, K., Bradley, R. H., & Spiker, D. (1993). Pediatric clinical assessment of mother-child interaction: Concurrent and predictive validity. *Journal of Developmental and Behavioral Pediatrics, 14,* 313-317.

74

How Do I Assess the Treatment Needs of Children Affected by Domestic Violence?

■ *Ronald Zuskin*

■ *General Considerations*

Because domestic violence and child maltreatment are closely correlated, all cases of child maltreatment should be assessed for possible domestic violence. If domestic violence is discovered in a family, it is important to remember that all children are indirectly affected by domestic violence in the family, whether they are maltreated or not. Each child in the family should be assessed for the possible effects of domestic violence. The effects on children of exposure to domestic violence vary widely. Common sense may lead one to believe that the severity of a child's response to witnessing domestic violence is correlated with the severity of the violence that he or she has witnessed, but this is not so. The child's age, developmental stage, gender, and role in the family interact with the nature of the violence he or she has witnessed to heighten or to mitigate the effects of witnessing violence. All assessments are of unique individual children in specific family situations. Assessment of the child's treatment needs involves knowing what to examine (assessment criteria), where and how to examine (assessment process), and how to interpret the information (treatment planning).

■ *Assessment Criteria: Distress Versus Trauma*

Some experts suggest that all children who experience sudden, unexpected, and overwhelming situations that include high physiological arousal and affective constriction, such as witnessing domestic violence, will experience distress. The following are signs of distress:

- Coping ability is temporarily overwhelmed.
- Defenses are used flexibly.
- Acute posttraumatic stress disorder (PTSD) responses are evident.
- Personal and environmental resources can be accessed.
- Outlets for expressive responses are used.
- Dynamic play occurs in therapy.
- Memories of distressing events are specific.
- A sense of control is regained in a timely way.
- The distressing event is experienced as something that happened.
- The implicit or actual threat to a child's "being" is resolved.

When physiologic arousal and affective constriction are intense and chronic, trauma results. The following are signs of trauma:

- The child's coping ability is chronically overwhelmed.
- Defenses are rigid and become part of the child's personality structure.
- Chronic PTSD responses and fragmentation of personality are evident.
- The child is isolated from personal and environmental resources.
- The child shows defensive symptomatology or acting-out behaviors or both.
- Play in therapy is static or repetitive, lacking thematic movement.

- The child has vague or no explicit memories of traumatic events (reenactments).
- The child has a debilitating and pervasive sense of loss of control.
- Traumatic events are experienced as self-defining ("I am bad" or "I am a troublemaker").

Traumatized children have incorporated the violence they have witnessed into their sense of themselves. These children display persistent (longer than 1 month) symptoms or acting-out behaviors that cause them emotional disturbance or impairment in important areas of functioning that may include:

- Reexperiencing the traumatic events via intrusive thoughts or feelings, recurring dreams, flashbacks, and distress or reactivity to cues similar to the traumatic events
- Avoiding thoughts, people, and places that remind children of the traumatic events as well as difficulty in recalling aspects of the trauma
- General numbing of responsiveness, reducing interest and participation in significant activities, restricted affect, and a sense of doom or limited future
- Evidence of increasing arousal demonstrated in sleep problems, irritability, outbursts out of keeping with provocation, hypervigilance, concentration problems, and heightened startle response

■ *The Assessment Process*

Assessment is a process of sampling information from different sources in different circumstances. Direct and indirect interviewing, observation, testing, and using collaterals are assessment methodologies. Direct interviewing involves speaking to individuals directly about issues. The child and family are primary sources of information. Extended family, substitute caregivers, educators, and others involved with the family can provide collateral responses to direct questioning. Indirect interviewing refers to techniques that allow assessment criteria to surface in response to inquiries that are not directly related to family violence. Indirect inquiry is important because children and family members may not always be forthcoming about family violence. Instead of asking directly about incidents, indirect questioning focuses on more general family issues, such as rule making, decision making, and family relations, in an attempt to bring assessment criteria to the surface in nonthreatening ways.

Observations of family members interacting in office or at-home setting in dyads, with peers, and in the family group can yield assessment criteria unavailable via interview. Arranging visitation, structured or unstructured parent-child play, caregiving opportunities, discussions, and home visits provide the assessor an opportunity to gather information about assessment criteria through observation.

A variety of tests, interview questionnaires, and other written or interview protocols may yield additional assessment information. Child and adult attachment inventories, developmental assessment tools, personality assessment tools, and family interaction and relationship assessment tools can all yield information. Currently, however, there is no one assessment tool that specifically assesses the treatment needs of children who witness family violence.

■ *Interpreting Treatment Needs Based on Information Generated During Assessment*

The assessment process generates information that can be compared to the framework provided by assessment criteria. Using these criteria, the assessor can determine if the child appears to be more or less distressed or traumatized. Distressed children can benefit from relatively short-term treatment. Treatment of choice involves guaranteeing their safety, activating existing personal and environmental resources, and giving them the opportunity in therapy to identify, express, and work through upsetting experiences. This may occur in group or short-term individual therapy. Traumatized children are likely to require long-term intervention and, perhaps, special circumstances to help them monitor and manage self-defeating or explosive behaviors. In general, traumatized children need

- To move from unpredictable danger into reliable safety
- To integrate trauma by reconstructing and assimilating the "trauma story" with acknowledged affect and memory
- To move from isolation to reconnection of thoughts to feelings and past experiences to the present and to connect to a community of supportive relationships

■ Summary

In summary, assessment of the treatment needs of children who witness domestic violence requires familiarity with criteria related to distress and traumatization, use of a variety of methodologies to obtain relevant information, and the determination of the best course of treatment based on clinical judgments regarding the assessment information.

■ Further Reading

Brohl, K. (1996). *Working with traumatized children: A handbook for healing*. Washington, DC: CWLA Press.

Jaffee, P. G., Wolfe, D. A., & Wilson, S. K. (1990). *Children of battered women*. Newbury Park, CA: Sage.

Monahon, C. (1993). *Children and trauma: A guide for parents and professionals*. San Francisco: Josey-Bass.

Rauch, J. B. (Ed.). (1993). *Assessment: A sourcebook for social work practice*. Milwaukee, WI: Families International, Inc.

van der Kolk, B. A., McFarlane, A. C., & Weisath, L. (Eds.). (1996). *Traumatic stress: The effect of overwhelming experience on mind, body, and society*. New York: Guilford.

Vernon, A. (1993). *Developmental assessment and intervention with children and adolescents*. Alexandria, VA: American Counseling Association.

75

How Do I Assess the Likelihood of an Intervention Succeeding?

■ *Vanessa G. Hodges*

When practitioners begin working with families, the anticipated outcome depends on the goals of the treatment program or social work services; in all cases, however, practitioners begin services with great anticipation of positive outcomes. This chapter identifies family and worker factors that hinder or facilitate successful outcomes. An accurate assessment of these factors will assist workers and families in developing realistic expectations and meaningful intervention plans.

■ Worker Factors

Engaging and motivating families are important qualities in successful interventions. Family commitment to intervention plans is largely based on the worker's ability to "join" the family. Joining is the most critical initial task of family intervention and is the foundation of future success with families. It refers to a family's sense of connection to the social worker. A practitioner's ability to enhance connections with families by demonstrating understanding, instilling hope, showing respect, and expressing genuine care and concern contributes to successful outcomes. Families who believe that they can benefit from interventions and have a clear sense of the goals, objectives, and outcomes are much more likely to invest energy, time, and commitment to the therapeutic process.

Another worker quality that facilitates successful outcomes is the ability to balance family problems, needs, and stressors with strengths, resources, and assets. Families may feel hopeless if all interactions with workers focus on problems and deficits. A worker who has skills in acknowledging, validating, and affirming family strengths, resources, and needs facilitates the likelihood of achieving positive outcomes with families.

■ *Family Factors*

A family's likelihood for succeeding depends on the family's insight into their problem, prior involvement with child welfare services, overall family stress, and available resources and assets. Although a family's ability to recognize and articulate their own strengths helps reinforce interventions and increase the likelihood of successful outcomes, family strengths will not be discussed in this chapter.

A family's insight into their own environmental stressors (e.g., eviction, loss of job, and serious illness) and personal stressors (e.g., marital conflict, gross neglect, substance abuse, and domestic violence) helps in assessing the likelihood of a successful intervention. A family that can understand and identify environmental and personal stressors contributing to a family crisis is much more likely to be able to problem-solve and to change behaviors to increase family stability.

Prior involvement with child welfare services is another important factor in assessing the likelihood of success. Families previously involved with child welfare may be discouraged, believing that family conditions will never change; they are not likely to engage in services or to be motivated to change. Families who have experienced positive involvement with child welfare assistance, however, may be more likely to be motivated, hopeful, and ready to become actively involved in services again.

A third factor for assessing the likelihood for successful intervention is an assessment of the overall family stress. Families experiencing severe stress are often not able to focus and engage in a therapeutic alliance with workers. For example, families coping with addiction, mental illness, or a chronic physical illness, coupled with the day-to-day responsibilities of managing a household and child-rearing responsibilities, may not be able to actively engage in treatment.

Finally, a family's resources and assets may contribute to treatment outcomes. Availability and access to transportation, adequate and safe housing and neighborhoods, employment-related stress, marital conflict, inadequate health care, and racial, gender, or sexual discrimination may affect a family's outcome.

■ *Further Reading*

Downs, S. W., Costin, L. B., & McFadden, E. J. (1996). *Child welfare and family services: Policies and practice.* White Plains, NY: Longman.

Holman, A. M. (1983). *Family Assessment: Tools for understanding and intervention.* Beverly Hills, CA: Sage.

Patterson, J., Williams, L., Grauf-Grounds, C., & Chaow, L. (1998). *Essential skills in family therapy from the first intervention to termination.* New York: Guilford.

Part VI

SERVICE PLANNING

76

How Do I Match Risks to Client Outcomes?

■ *Diane DePanfilis*

Part of the assessment process (See Part V, this volume) involves prioritizing among the most significant risks or treatment needs. As a bridge to the process of treatment planning (see Chapters 78 and 79, this volume), client outcomes should be identified that will indicate that the risk of maltreatment has been adequately reduced and the effects of maltreatment satisfactorily addressed. With the passage of the Adoption and Safe Families Act of 1997, child welfare agencies are designing their intervention systems to measure the achievement of outcomes. At the program level, there is consensus that child welfare outcomes can be grouped into four categories: child safety, child permanence, child well-being, and family well-being (functioning). Indicators that reflect aggregation of existing data usually measure achievement of program outcomes. For example, the percentage of children who do not experience recurrence of maltreatment could be set as an indicator for child safety. (See Chapter 77, this volume, for a discussion of these broader child welfare program outcome areas.) Although these indicators may be appropriate measures of success at a broad program level, targeting outcomes at the client level involves a more precise process for evaluating the degree to which an individual family makes specific changes. The purpose of this chapter is to illustrate the connection between risks identified during the family assessment and client outcomes that become the focus of treatment planning and service delivery.

■ What Is a Client Outcome?

Client outcomes are positive results for individuals and families that indicate that both risks and effects of maltreatment have been reduced. Client outcomes relate to the most critical risk influences identified in a family, which require child protection intervention or treatment. Outcomes include targeted change in behavior, conditions, perceptions, attitudes, skill, functioning, and feelings. The focus could relate to the child, the parents or other caregivers, the family system, or the environment because all these are related to the risk of maltreatment. Depending on the complexity of the family situation, short- and long-term goals can then follow that indicate incremental movement toward the ultimate achievement of client outcomes. (See Chapter 79, this volume, for a discussion of how to establish measurable goals.)

■ Matching Risks to Client Outcomes

To match risks to outcomes, characteristics must be apparent (e.g., a mother's use of drugs) that are amenable to change. Client outcomes must be measurable, understandable, and pertinent to child protection services intervention.

There may be many risk influences in a family, each of which could be matched to a client outcome. The purpose of family assessment, however, is to set priorities based on an understanding of the risks that create the most concern or vulnerability for children. The following sections provide examples of matching risks to client outcomes related to children, parents or other caregivers, the family system, and the environment.

Child-Level Client Outcomes

Child outcomes could relate to targeted change regarding a child's behavior, development, emotional state, mental health, physical health, educational achievement, peer relations, or com-

Table 76.1   Child-Related Risks and Possible Client Outcomes

Sample Child-Related Risk	*Possible Client Outcome*
Acting-out behavior (e.g., refusing to listen and throwing temper tantrums)	Behavioral control (e.g., management of impulses and practices breathing exercises when feeling stressed)
Developmental delays (e.g., language delays)	Improved development (e.g., child's language ability increases to within correct range for age)
Withdrawn, isolating behavior	Increased social interaction (e.g., more positive mood and involved in at least one age-appropriate activity)

Table 76.2   Caregiver-Related Risks and Possible Outcomes

Sample Caregiver-Related Risk	*Possible Outcome*
Depression (e.g., feels sad, which affects capacity to wake children for school and to take care of basic needs)	Emotional control (e.g., improved outlook, increased energy, and hope that things can be different, leading to meeting children's basic needs)
Problems managing child's behavior (e.g., uses inconsistent strategies to respond to temper tantrums and refusals to cooperate)	Child management skills (e.g., appropriate discipline strategies)
Drug addiction (e.g., long-term use or abuse and addiction that lead to leaving children alone)	Recovery from addiction (e.g., evidence of recovery that leads to meeting basic needs of children more often, and even during relapses appropriate arrangements are made for the care of the children)

munication skills. Examples of child-specific risks and possible client-level outcomes are provided in Table 76.1.

Parent or Caregiver Outcomes

Caregiver outcomes can relate to multiple dimensions (e.g., the caregiver's perspective of his or her childhood history, motivation to change, mental health functioning, parenting attitudes and knowledge, problem-solving capacity, impulse control, stress management, communication skills, social skills, and financial management skills). Examples of caregiver-specific risks and possible client-level outcomes are provided in Table 76.2.

Table 76.3   Family-Related Risks and Possible Outcomes

Sample Family-Related Risk	Possible Outcome
Poor communication (For example, mom believes her kids do not talk to her, and the kids believe mom never listens.)	Better communication skills (For example, family members have one time daily when they "check in" with each other, and they use skills to "check out" whether they clearly understand each other.)
Role reversal (For example, the oldest daughter performs most of the child care tasks for younger brothers and sisters, dad is too busy working two jobs, and the daughter is doing poorly in school.)	Appropriate role performance (For example, the family develops a new schedule to reduce the amount of time the daughter spends on child care, the daughter participates in one age-related activity, and the family does one fun thing together each week.)
Domestic violence (For example, adults in the household use violence to resolve conflict, the father makes all the decisions, and the children are fearful and cannot bring other children into the home.)	Improved conflict management and decision-making skills (For example, adults say they want to stay together; when stress is high, dad leaves the house for at least 10 minutes; and the family holds meetings weekly to make family-related decisions.)

Family Outcomes

Examples of family-focused outcomes include aspects of family functioning that will help the family "pull together" to manage stresses and difficult times. For example, intervention can target changes in communication among family members, roles and relationships, family rules and expectations, balance of responsibilities, and aspects of social support within the family. Examples of family-specific risks and possible client-level outcomes are provided in Table 76.3.

Environmental Outcomes

Because child maltreatment is the consequence of risks that are outside of the family, some outcomes are focused on environmental factors, although adults and others in the community may need to be engaged to achieve them. Environmental outcomes

Table 76.4   Environmental-Related Risks and Possible Outcomes

Sample Environmental-Related Risk	*Possible Outcome*
Condemned housing (e.g., no heat or running water, children diagnosed with lead poisoning, and numerous safety hazards for young children)	Adequate housing (e.g., family establishes a safe household and caregivers develop financial management skills and problem-solving skills to avoid eviction)
Social isolation (e.g., family recently immigrated from Vietnam, lost contact with extended family, and language barriers)	Social support (e.g., family "adopted" by local church, caregivers given child care respite while they attend English classes, and children enrolled in Head Start)
Neighborhood violence (e.g., neighborhood "taken over" by drug markets, streets littered with numerous needles and other hazardous waste, gunshots at all times of day and night, and mother trying to maintain recovery)	Neighborhood safety (e.g., family relocates to new neighborhood in the process of economic development and renewal, children have a park in which to play (with supervision), mom close to day treatment center, and children walk to new school)

include a safe and healthy household; adequate furnishings, heat, and running water; social support from the neighborhood, extended family, and friends; and a safe neighborhood. Examples of environmental risks and possible outcomes are provided in Table 76.4.

■ *Summary*

To achieve program-level outcomes of child safety, permanence, child well-being, and family well-being (functioning) (see Chapter 77, this volume), intervention and treatment must first be targeted toward client outcomes. Assessments should help to identify the key outcomes, which can then be used to guide treatment planning (see Chapters 78 and 79, this volume). Assessment protocols and standardized measures used during the assessment can also be used at later stages of intervention to measure the achievement of outcomes. Targeting outcomes promotes a shift to focus on strengths and positive intervention. It provides greater clarity and understanding for the worker-family partnership in respect to the final desired result that is expected.

■ *Further Reading*

Holder, W., & Roe Lund, T. R. (1995). Translating risks to positive outcomes: Outcome-oriented case management from risk assessment information. In D. DePanfilis, D. Daro, & S. Wells (Eds.), *The APSAC advisor special issue on risk assessment* (Vol. 8, pp. 20-24). Chicago: American Professional Society on the Abuse of Children.

77

What Outcomes Are Relevant For Intervention?

■ *Mark Courtney*

P rovision of child welfare services has long been guided by various "best practice" standards, but ultimately the quality of practice must be judged by the outcomes achieved for children and families. A variety of outcomes are relevant for child protective services intervention. They can be loosely grouped into four categories: child safety, child permanence, child well-being, and family functioning. Although all four are important, federal and state laws emphasize child safety and permanence, and these two outcomes are often used in global evaluation of agency or system performance. In contrast, at the individual case level, child welfare workers usually attempt to achieve child safety and permanence through efforts to ensure child well-being and improve family functioning. For example, to achieve child safety and permanency through family reunification, a child welfare worker might help parents to learn alternative, nonviolent methods of resolving family conflict and thereby help improve family functioning.

■ *Child Safety*

Protecting a child from additional harm due to maltreatment by caregivers is the foremost purpose of child protective services. This is true whether a child's family is receiving intensive in-home family preservation services or the child is living in out-of-home care. When decisions regarding whether to remove a child from parental care, place a child in a particular out-of-home care setting, or return a child to his or her home must be made, the caseworker should seriously consider the likely impact of the decisions on child safety. Some indicators of child safety include an absence of maltreatment of children

- In families receiving ongoing in-home child protective services
- During family visits associated with family reunification planning
- In families formerly open to child protective services
- In ongoing out-of-home care

■ *Permanence*

Although maintaining a constant focus on child safety, child welfare services interventions are also aimed at maintaining or creating permanent living arrangements and emotional attachments for children. This is based on the assumption that stable, caring relationships created in the context of a family are essential for healthy child development. Thus, great emphasis is placed on keeping children with their families or reunifying children in out-of-home care with their families whenever possible.

In recent years, the increasing importance of family continuity in guiding child welfare practice has been reflected in the growth of foster care, adoption, and legal guardianship by kin of children placed in out-of-home care. When children cannot be returned home and no appropriate kin are available to care for them, nonrelative adoption is generally the permanency goal of choice.

Placement stability is a key outcome for children in long-term out-of-home care. In addition, efforts should be made to place such children and youth in the least restrictive, most family-like setting possible.

Child-level indicators of permanence include the following:

- Positive relationships between the child and members of the child's family, including extended family and fictive kin, are maintained.
- The child lives in the least restrictive environment appropriate to the child's special needs.
- The child experiences a stable placement in out-of-home care.
- To the extent that there is a reasonable possibility that the child may not be able to return to parental care, efforts are made to explore other permanency options for the child (e.g., long-term kinship care, adoption, and guardianship).
- A permanent home is found for the child who does not return to his or her home in a timely manner.
- The child given a "permanent" placement is able to remain there until reaching adulthood.

Some program-level indicators of permanence (or the lack thereof) for children who come in contact with the child protection system include the following:

- The proportion of children whose families receive child welfare services who are able to remain safely in their homes
- The proportion of children who are removed from their homes who are able to safely return home
- The proportion of children who cannot live with their parents who are placed in long-term, stable living arrangements with kin or adopted by nonrelatives
- The rate of disruption of guardianships and adoptions
- The number of placement changes experienced by children in long-term out-of-home care

■ Child Well-Being

Although child welfare practice focuses on safety and permanency for children, the general well-being of children who come in contact with the system must also be taken into account, particularly for children in out-of-home care. The limited time frame in which child welfare services intervention occurs with most families calls for humility regarding the capacity of such services to improve child well-being, although this should not be used as an excuse for failing to appropriately attend to the wide array of children's needs. At a minimum, child welfare practitioners should attempt to ensure that children involved with child protective services are functioning within "normal" bounds, or moving in measurable ways in that direction, in the following areas:

- Physical health
- Mental health
- Positive relations with peers
- Supportive relationships with adults
- School attendance and performance
- For older youth, the capacity for independent living

This requires that children's health, mental health, and educational needs be assessed in a timely manner and that preventive and treatment services are provided when warranted. In general, professionals should seek to ensure that necessary services are made available to all maltreated children whose well-being suffers as a result of the consequences of maltreatment (e.g., mental health and other behavioral problems).

■ Family Functioning (Well-Being)

Families must be able to function at a basic level if they are to provide safe and permanent environments in which children can be raised. In particular, parenting must be done in a manner that is safe for children. Parenting occurs in a very complex context, however, that includes some or all of the following influences: family history, other members of the immediate family, extended family, neighbors, employers, schools, human services, cultural norms, and the economy.

On the one hand, child welfare practitioners cannot be expected to focus on optimal family functioning or to single-handedly solve the myriad social problems facing families today. On the other hand, they cannot ignore the fact that child maltreatment occurs in families, and that attempts to ensure child safety, permanence, and well-being will often require that families function differently than they have in the past. Thus, intervention with families will usually be directed at improving family functioning in one or more of the following areas:

- The level of conflict and violence between family members
- Parenting knowledge and skills
- The ability of family members to use formal and informal supports
- The ability of the family to be self-sufficient in terms of income, basic housing, access to health care, and so on

■ Recognizing Trade-Offs Between Outcomes

In an ideal world, efforts to achieve the outcomes described previously would be thoroughly compatible with each other, and there would be no need to worry about prioritizing one over another. In reality, the child protection worker is often faced with the need to weigh one goal against another, with the ultimate decision about which goal to favor having important potential consequences for the parties involved.

For example, in many cases the worker knows that there is risk to the child posed by returning him or her from out-of-home care to the care of parents who, although seemingly rehabilitated, were abusive in the past. The worker knows, however, that the child and parents are strongly attached to each other and wish to be reunited. An exclusive focus on child safety might lead the worker to recommend against sending the child home. In contrast, an emphasis on promoting permanence might lead the worker to favor family reunification. In the aggregate, a primary focus on child safety leads to a larger number of children remaining in out-of-home care, whereas a similar commitment to promoting permanence through family preservation increases the risk of children being maltreated by their parents. In other words, with respect to permanence and child safety there is no way to maximize one outcome without running the risk of not maximizing the other. Moreover, there are risks to child safety, well-being, and permanence associated with virtually any course of action, including placing children in out-of-home care. Child welfare workers should consider such risks and trade-offs as they decide which avenues to pursue in their work with children and families, keeping in mind that their foremost priority should always be child safety.

■ *Further Reading*

McDaniel, N. C., & Alsop, R. (1998). *Fifth National Roundtable on Outcome Measures in Child Welfare Services* [Summary of proceedings]. Englewood, CO: American Humane Association. (See also the proceedings of previous American Humane Association meetings on outcome measurement in child welfare.)

78

What Is Strengths-Based Service Planning?

■ *Vanessa G. Hodges and Peter J. Pecora*

In child protective services, in which initial safety assessment and longer term risk assessment are the primary focus of the initial intervention, employing a strengths perspective in services planning may be difficult, but it is essential. Strengths-based planning provides a more balanced and comprehensive view of the family, allows for the selection of more feasible interventions, and is more likely to elicit family investment in the service plan.

Strengths-based planning involves a purposeful focus on identifying child, family, and community strengths or resources that could be employed to help address the situation as well as "protective factors." These protective factors include the constellation of individual, family, and community characteristics that positively alter a person's response to a predisposed maladaptive outcome.

Including strengths in service planning poses special challenges to practitioners who are unfamiliar with the cultural diversity in families of color. Families of color often have different family structures, child-rearing practices, gender and family roles, and relationships to community. Failing to accurately assess these cultural differences might yield an incomplete assessment of the family, especially as it relates to family strengths. Lack of resources related to poverty might also obscure a practitioner's ability to identify strengths. Misunderstanding a cultural norm or a consequence of poverty as evidence of abuse or neglect could lead to removing the child from the home and the accompanying social and emotional losses for the child and family.

■ Incorporating Strengths Into Assessment and Service Planning

Assessment and service planning should address both the characteristics that place children and caregivers in jeopardy and the characteristics that may provide resources and supports to them (Table 78.1). The challenge is to determine how to integrate and interpret strengths to increase the accuracy of assessments and to create a feasible service plan on which members of the family can agree.

Table 78.1   Strengths- and Risk-Based Planning Factors

Strengths-Based Factors	Risk-Based Factors
Personal coping	Child risks
Protective factors	Family risks
Family strengths	Environmental risks
Cultural strengths	Other risk factors
Environmental supports	

■ Major Strengths and Protective Factors to Consider

Strengths and protective factors can be classified into three general categories: individual characteristics, family characteristics, and supportive significant others, including facets of the community. The following are examples:

Individual Factors

- Personal attributes: high self-esteem, academic achievement, assertiveness, quality of adjustment to single-parent household, health status (healthy during infancy and childhood), activity level (multiple interests and hobbies, participation, and competence), and disposition (good-natured, precocious, mature, inquisitive, willing to take risks, optimistic, hopeful, altruistic, and personable)

- Cognitive skills: able to focus on positive attributes and ignore negatives; intellectual abilities
- Self-concept: high self-esteem and internal locus of control
- Perceptive: quickly assesses dangerous situations and avoids harm
- Interpersonal skills: able to create, develop, and nurture or maintain supportive relationships with others, including being able to give and receive love and affection; communicates well (oral and written); assertive; ability to relate to both children and adults
- Strong racial identity: exhibits racial pride; strongly identifies with ethnic group through clubs, organizations, and political and social change movements

Family Factors

- Supportive family milieu, including personal relationships with parental figures, cohesiveness, extensive kinship network, nonconflictual relations, structure (rules and household responsibilities for all members), and family relational factors (coherence and attachment and open exchange and expression of feelings and emotions)
- Parental factors: supervision and monitoring of children, a strong bond to at least one parent figure, a warm and supportive relationship, abundant attention during the first year of life, and parental agreement on family values and morals
- Active extended family: fictive or blood relatives that are active in the child's life; provides material resources, child care, supervision, parenting, and emotional support to the child

Community and Other Supports

- Church or religious affiliation: belongs to and actively participates in a group religious experience; faith and prayer

- Close attachment to the ethnic community: resides in the ethnic community of choice; easy access to ethnic resources, including social services, merchants, and media (newspaper); and demonstrates a commitment to the ethnic community
- External support system: extended family in close proximity, positive relationship with one or more teachers, involvement of birth parents who are not married or living with each other, availability of male role models, and supportive social environments of the community

■ Case Examples

A caseworker may be very concerned about the safety of a child who is frequently truant from school because he or she is distracted and accosted by dropouts in the neighborhood while walking alone to school. Although drug trafficking and gang activity might place a neighborhood at risk of violence, stable, long-term residents and a tight informal support network can also exist in the same neighborhood and should be identified as strengths. The service plan might be developed with the family, extended family, and neighbors so that someone could be enlisted to help walk or drive the child to school on most days.

In another situation, children having trouble engaging in school and with tutors might instead be provided with a volunteer to help them excel in an athletic or artistic area because it has been shown that this can "free up" energy and build self-confidence for academic work. Similarly, some staff members create service plans that involve tutoring initially to a child's strengths rather than addressing the child's weakest academic areas to build self-confidence and energy for other improvements.

■ Conclusion

Although strengths have a clear role in the intervention planning process, it is unclear how they influence child and family outcome in the presence of and interaction with risk. This chapter identified how individual, family, and community strengths and protective factors can inform service planning.

■ *Further Reading*

Garmezy, N. (1985). Stress resistant children: The search for protective factors. In J. E. Stevenson (Ed.), *Recent research in developmental psychopathology* (pp. 213-233). Oxford, UK: Pergamon.

Hodges, V. (1994). Assessing for strengths and protective factors in child abuse and neglect: Risk assessment with families of color. In P. J. Pecora & D. J. English (Eds.), *Multi-cultural guidelines for assessing family strengths and risk factors in child protective services.* Seattle: University of Washington, School of Social Work/Washington State Department of Social Services.

Rutter, M. (1990). Psychosocial resilience and protective mechanisms. In J. Rolf (Ed.), *Risk and protective factors in the development of psychopathology.* New York: Cambridge University Press.

Note: See also Appendix 8 for supplemental references.

79

How Do I Develop Measurable Goals and Objectives That Match Client Intervention Outcomes?

■ *Peter J. Pecora*

■ *Components of Case Planning*

Three major components pertain to professional case planning in child protective services: (a) assessments (child and family intake assessment and periodic case review and assessment); (b) identifying case goals or outcomes using the agency mission for children and families, identifying case goals for a particular child, parents, or family that are outcome oriented, and identifying indicators that mark the progress toward case goals; and (c) intervention methods (development of the service plan, including case resources, case methods, and services provision). The role of the assessment and intervention methods are described in other chapters in this volume; setting case goals is the focus of this chapter.

■ *Developing Measurable Goals and Objectives in the Context of the Agency Mission*

An outcome is an end state that is desired (see Chapters 76 and 77, this volume). In assessment and case planning, one must be able to specify the desired short-term and intermediate outcome(s) by keeping in mind the core components of the agency mission (e.g., child safety, permanence, child well-being, and family functioning), identifying with the child and parents the most essential outcomes to be achieved, and creating the goals and indicators that form the milestones that must be reached along the way.

How should one translate the assessment information into a set of manageable, short-term, and intermediate (if appropriate) case goals? First, the worker must have a frame of reference, which provides a starting point in analyzing child and family functioning and indicates what needs must be met. This question is best answered by using initial safety and ongoing risk assessments (see Chapters 47, 48, and 55, this volume) and by using assessments of the child, parent, or family by placing them in a developmental range, both by age and by observation of their behaviors. Then, the worker and family set case goals that link to the assessment of the child or family. The following are examples of case goals, with general outcome domains included in parentheses:

1. Mary will improve her behavior in the school shown by reducing physical fights and stealing from students by April 15, as measured by teacher reports (child well-being/functioning).
2. John will improve his school attendance by next month (child well-being and functioning).
3. Mary's relationship with her husband will improve by January 1 so that violent disagreements are noted only one or two times per week by both parents (child safety and family functioning).
4. Veronica will be returned to her birth mother by December 15, and no incidents of maltreatment will be observed within 6 months (child safety and permanence).

In summary, case goals should be clear, specific, measurable, related to key risk factors, developed with the child or caregiver, expressed in the form of an observable end state, consistent with the child's particular developmental strengths and needs, time limited, realistic in terms of being able to be improved or affected by the anticipated intervention, and appropriate to the social and cultural circumstances of the child and his or her family.

■ *Further Reading*

Traglia, J. J., Pecora, P. J., Paddock, G., & Wilson, L. (1997). Outcome-oriented case planning in family foster care. *Families in Society, 78*(5), 453-462.

80

What Is Concurrent Planning, and How Do I Do It?

■ *Caroline L. Burry*

■ *What Is Concurrent Planning?*

Concurrent planning means working toward reunification of children in care with their birth families while concurrently formulating an alternative plan for permanency. Concurrent planning requires that foster families are also approved and prepared to adopt if adoption becomes necessary. The overall goal is early permanence for children; this is consistent with the federal law guiding placements—the Adoption and Safe Families Act of 1997.

Although it may seem confusing to work in two directions at the same time, concurrent planning works because it is based on the following core beliefs: Children need safe, stable homes with continuous relationships; the number of moves for children should be minimized; and birth families should be supported in changing to meet the needs of their children within in a reasonable time frame.

■ *When Is Concurrent Planning Appropriate?*

Concurrent planning is appropriate when reunification is likely but you have concerns about possible barriers, such as parental addiction, so that you want to have the "safety net" of another permanent family in place. Concurrent planning is less likely to be appropriate when you are dealing with highly motivated birth parents with a very high likelihood of reunification. Also, concurrent planning is not appropriate when adoption is clearly the plan.

■ *What Do I Need to Do Before Beginning to Use Concurrent Planning?*

- As you begin concurrent planning, it is important to plan to maintain current, clear case documentation in measurable, behavioral terms and consult regularly with legal staff to ensure that statutory requirements are met.
- Conduct targeted recruitment of, specialized training of, and ongoing support for dually prepared foster or adoptive parents.

■ *What Are the Steps in Concurrent Planning?*

- Assess birth families thoroughly and early for the appropriateness of using concurrent planning in the process of working together.
- Select foster or adoptive parents. Some will be relatives; the availability of kinship or adoptive parents should be assessed during the initiation of child protective services intervention so the identified families can be prepared as quickly as possible.
- Prepare birth families to work together toward the goal of early permanence; be direct with them about the consequences of not following through with treatment or reunification plans.
- Set short but reasonable time goals in treatment plans, and use a team approach involving child welfare agency staff, community helpers, birth parents, and foster or adoptive parents to work on goals, including providing therapy, case management, and mediation services. There should

be ongoing close monitoring and assessment in making interim and final decisions.

• During concurrent planning, work with children intensively to help them deal with their feelings about separation and possible reunification or adoption.

81

How Do I Use Family Meetings to Develop Optimal Service Plans?

■ *Lisa Merkel-Holguin*

Since the early 1990s, many U.S. public and private child welfare agencies have been organizing family meetings to capitalize on the family's strengths and wisdom to develop service plans for their maltreated children to ensure their well-being and safety. This approach is called family group decision making (FGDM).

■ *What Is Family Group Decision Making?*

FGDM provides families, including extended relatives (e.g., grandparents and cousins), perpetrators, victims, and others considered by the family as important to their lives (e.g., tribal elders, clergy, neighbors, and fictive kin), with a process to make decisions that protect and ensure the safety of their maltreated children. Two of the best-known examples are family group conferences (FGC) and family unity meetings (FUM). The FGC model was first developed and legislatively mandated in New Zealand in 1989, and the FUM model was developed in Oregon in 1990. Most U.S. communities are implementing family group conferencing processes.

■ *What Philosophies Are Embodied in FGDM?*

FGDM is rooted in strengths-based, family-centered, and com-munity-based philosophies. A strengths-based approach helps professionals to recognize and build on a family's expertise, wisdom, and history. Family members know their strengths, weaknesses, and unspoken secrets—knowledge that can be help-ful in formulating plans that better protect children. Family group decision making recognizes and mobilizes the broader commu-nity to provide supports and resources to families during and after the development of a plan.

■ *What Are the Benefits of This Process?*

Because there has been limited evaluation on FGDM in the United States, the results of this approach are equivocal. None-theless, FGDM appears to have some positive benefits for both families and child welfare professionals, including these:

- Increased willingness of family members to support and accept the services provided because they were central to developing the service plan
- Improved relationships between professionals and family members, increasing the satisfaction and decreasing the isolation of professionals
- Maintenance of family continuity and connectedness through an increase in the number of kinship placements
- Reduction in reabuse rates and substantiated cases of abuse and neglect, an outcome demonstrated in England and Canada

■ *When Is FGDM Used?*

New Zealand's legislation mandates that FGCs be held in cases in which an investigator has determined that a child or young person is in need of care or protection. In most U.S. communities, FGDM is being implemented on a voluntary basis in cases of child abuse and neglect and juvenile delinquency offenses. Although a philosophical underpinning of FGDM is that all families can benefit from this process because it includes the healthier functioning members of the family, many U.S. communities have decided not to use this process in cases that involve child sexual abuse and domestic violence.

■ What Is the Process?

Holding a family meeting appears to be a simple concept. The process, however, is more complex. In traditional service planning processes, caseworkers gather and evaluate information and work with the family to determine goals and make decisions. Although involving the family in developing service plans has always been good practice, FGDM, particularly the FGC model, adds an additional step. It puts families in charge of making decisions about their children. Communities in the United States commonly use four phases when implementing family meetings.

Phase 1: Referral to Hold an FGDM Meeting

Typically, a public child welfare agency social worker refers a case to another professional, called a coordinator, who is responsible for arranging the family meeting. In most U.S. communities, coordinators are employed by either the public or the private child welfare agency implementing the FGDM initiative.

Phase 2: Preparation and Planning

Unlike case staffings, organizing a family meeting requires the coordinator to spend time preparing the extended family network and other attendees for the meeting. The coordinator should remain neutral during this and the other phases of the family meeting. The success of meetings depends on how well the families are prepared for the actual event. Coordinators will need to do the following:

- Work with family members to clarify the goal of the meeting
- Invite family members to the meeting
- Ensure the emotional and physical safety of victims and perpetrators attending the meeting
- Define and communicate participants' roles

- Manage unresolved family issues
- Coordinate logistics for the meeting

Sometimes, the people who are not immediately thought of as "family" can play the most significant role in decision making and service planning. New Zealand's legislation provides the coordinator with the authority to invite to the meeting any individual within the extended family network who can provide support to or be a resource for the family. Although the intent of family meetings is similar in the United States—to widen the circle of family and others, thus including healthier components of the family system—because of confidentiality laws, in certain states the parent typically controls who is invited to a meeting. In some communities, parents are asked to sign a voluntary consent form that allows the coordinator to contact anyone who fits within that parent's definition of family. Certain individuals may not be included in the family meeting, including those who have a history of violence and children typically under the age of 10. Individuals who are not invited to attend the family meeting may be asked to prepare written, videotaped, or audiotaped statements that are shared at the meeting.

Phase 3: The Family Meeting

This is often considered to be the crux of the process, but all the activities before and after the actual event greatly impact the outcome of the meeting. The meeting process, independent of the model used, involves professionals sharing information about the case and families making decisions about how their children can be cared for and protected.

Meetings that use the FGC model provide family with time to have discussion and make decisions in private. Therefore, all professionals, service providers, and other nonfamily members leave the room, and the family formulates their service plan that they then present to these individuals. In the United States, communities have constructed a check-and-balance system, which provides a limited number of professionals and family members to veto the plan if it does not keep the children safe.

The last stage of the family meeting involves using the family's decision to develop the service plan and case monitoring process. The individuals participating in the family meeting typically volunteer to help carry out the service plan. For example, they may be willing to support the family by providing day care for the children or by driving family members to appointments.

Phase 4: Follow-Up

At the meeting's conclusion, a plan is constructed to review and monitor the case. During the family meeting, family members and service providers agree to their roles and responsibilities for implementing the plan, which assists the monitoring process. Sometimes, when the service plan generated from a family meeting does not work, the coordinator, caseworker, or a family member will ask for another meeting.

■ How Do Family Meetings Differ From Involving the Family in Traditional Service Planning?

A family meeting can be a powerful event. At the beginning of the meeting, children's caregivers commonly have feelings of shame, isolation, and embarrassment. The meeting process can reverse these initial feelings, whereby at the end of the meeting families feel empowered and supported. Through balancing power differentials and capitalizing on a family's commitment to its members and functioning, family meetings can positively transform, even for a short period of time, the way families operate.

Because families involved in the child welfare system are not regularly included in making decisions about the care and protection of their children, family group meetings offer a new way to engage families in service planning. If agencies use the FGC model, which provides families with private time to make their decisions without interference or guidance from professionals, child welfare practice can be radically transformed. Families know from the responsibility they are given and the trust that is placed in their ability to make decisions that they have a critical role to play in service planning. They become more than just partners of the professionals in service planning. Instead, through family group decision-making processes, they become the primary decision makers.

■ *Further Reading*

Hudson, J., Morris, A., Maxwell, G., & Galaway, B. (1996). *Family group conferences: Perspectives on policy and practice.* Monsey, NY: Willow Tree Press.

Merkel-Holguin, L. (1998). Implementation of family group decision making in the U.S.: Policies and practices in transition. *Protecting Children, 14*(4), 4-10.

Merkel-Holguin, L. (with Ribich, K.). (in press). Family group conferencing: An "extended family" process to safeguard children and strengthen family well-being. In E. Walton, P. Sandau-Beckler, & M. Mannes (Eds.), *Family-centered services and child well-being: Exploring issues in policy, practice, theory, and research.* New York: Columbia University Press.

82

How Do I Involve Fathers?

■ *Geoffrey Greif*

Although the involvement of fathers in the family has increased greatly during the past generation, many fathers are still relatively uninvolved with regard to child care and other critical functions. In some neighborhoods, only a fraction of families even have fathers in the homes. Fathers have historically been breadwinners, leaving child care to the mothers. Mothers have often been comfortable with this arrangement and have been known to encourage such a division of responsibilities. Professionals have joined in this "conspiracy," perhaps reflecting their own view of a diminished role of the father. As a result, children often do not have the benefits of their fathers' input. How does one reach out to the father who has been marginalized by society, by the mother, and by himself? If there is no father available, how can other potential father figures be included? Specific steps can be taken by agencies and professionals to increase fathers' involvement in the lives of their children.

■ Inclusion

Agencies and professionals must believe in the value of the inclusion of fathers. Without including them, the family is broken into pieces. In some families, fathers are the power source and can sabotage whatever plans are put into place.

■ Communicate Inclusion

This value must be communicated to families in multiple ways. Are posters in the agency reflective of fathers being a part of families? Do intake workers expect fathers' participation as a matter of course? Is the father often assumed to be the problematic person in family relationships? Do the books in the agency offices have "father" (or grandfather) in the title? It is not enough to believe that fathers (or uncles, male friends, and grandfathers) are important. It must be demonstrated in ways that families can see.

■ Understand the Father's Discomfort

Fathers often feel uncomfortable talking about feelings and sharing what may be considered family secrets. Airing "dirty laundry" is discouraged in many cultures. Most fathers who are interviewed about their families have no familial role models for doing so. If they are asked how they feel, fathers (and men) say what they think. Asked to be expressive, they become directive and opinionated. If a father feels uncomfortable with the situation, he may shut down or not attend sessions.

■ Act Appropriately

Many specific approaches are valuable. The professional needs to encourage the father's involvement and treat the father as one of the experts on the family. The following statements can be helpful:

- "Kids do a lot better when caring dads are involved."
- "I like to think of parents as experts on their children. You know your child much better than me. What do you think will work to help out this situation?"

The family should be given concrete and goal-specific tasks to achieve. Leaving the family to "talk things out" may not be specific enough for many fathers. For example, you could state the following:

- "I want you to spend 10 minutes each night reading to little Sammy."
- "When would be the best time for you and Sally to see each other? Can you decide right now how that is going to happen?"
- "Let's give mom a break between 6:30 and 7:00 each night so you can get to know the children better. During that time, I want them to pick out games for you all to play."

Finally, look for ways to enhance the competence of the father that do not depend on the mother's involvement. This could include saying the following:

- "It sounds like you handled that situation on your own, like an expert."
- "The children are really responding to your parenting style well."

Not all fathers should be included in family interviews. When the father has been a perpetrator of abuse and shows no genuine signs of remorse or wanting to change his behavior, supporting the other family members and involving more responsible father figures may be appropriate.

83

How Do I Develop a Collaborative Intervention Plan With the Kinship Network?

■ *Maria Scannapieco*

Relative caregivers are different from foster caregivers in that they view themselves as the authority on what is best for the child(ren). This is a unique aspect of working in kinship situations that should be nurtured. Children are placed with kinship caregivers in primarily three ways: as a diversion from out-of-home care, as a type of foster care, or as a means of ensuring family preservation or reunification. These programs are defined as follows:

- *Diversion:* If a report of abuse or neglect has been substantiated and the child has been assessed as not being safe in his or her own home, kin are sought out prior to the state taking custody of the child. In these circumstances, the relative takes custody of the child and, if the state determines it to be necessary, the state will provide protective supervision. In this way, the child welfare system remains formally involved with the kinship care network. Protective supervision is the least intrusive option of court-ordered child welfare services.

- *Foster care:* Children who are in the custody of the state and placed with kinship caregivers should be considered children in out-of-home care. Even when the caregivers are receiving welfare payments instead of federal foster care funding, these children are in the custody of the state and not their family. The state is ultimately responsible for the child's protection and well-being, and the caregiver does not have primary legal responsibility in these circumstances.

- *Family preservation or reunification:* Family preservation services may be provided to relative caregivers at two different times to meet two distinctive program goals: (a) at the time the child enters the kinship home as a diversion to foster care and (b) at the time of family reunification to meet permanency planning goals. Both options are similar to protective supervision, but they differ in the intensity of services provided.

No matter how children enter kinship care, it is essential to assess the kinship caregiver. Children remain in kinship care for longer periods than children do in foster care. Therefore, it is critical that at the time of placement the child welfare worker performs a concurrent assessment that measures not only the appropriateness of the home to meet the immediate needs of the child but also the permanency needs.

The assessment of kinship homes requires attention to two sets of factors:

- Those associated with the first use of any home for child placement, including parenting and family aspects, matters of safety and protection of children, and physical environment (see Chapter 55, this volume)
- Those associated with selecting a permanent placement for particular children (including attachment, permanence, and kinship)

Across all the previously discussed factors, kinship placement raises issues that are substantially different from those of traditional foster care, suggesting that each criterion for assessment must be adapted for use with kinship homes.

■ *Collaboration Models*

Family Group Meeting

Probably one of the most quickly proliferating practice concepts is that of family group decision making, and collaboration is the essential component of this practice model (see Chapter 81, this volume). Kinship family meetings give the child welfare worker a vehicle of true collaboration with the kinship network that allows all parties to develop an intervention plan that ensures the child's safety, permanence, and well-being. No matter at which point along the child welfare service continuum (diversion, out-of-home care, or family reunification) the child enters kinship care, the intervention plan needs to address the issues of safety, permanency, and well-being. In all these programs, the family meeting is a mechanism for collaborative intervention planning.

The following are important elements of this model:

- Family meetings are called if a child welfare agency performs an initial assessment and determines that a child is in need of care and protection.
- Family members who are currently or could potentially play a role in the child's life attend the meeting. This may include the child's parent(s), extended family members, close friends, godparents, and others whom the family defines as family.
- The child welfare worker, teachers, psychologists, and other professionals who are working with the family also typically attend the meeting.
- Parents can limit participation by other family members.
- The meeting setting is amiable and provides an opportunity for all members to feel comfortable to express their thoughts and feelings.
- The family brainstorms options for the care and protection of the child by identifying strengths of the different family members and the community. Permanency options with the highest degree of success are identified.
- Children are given an opportunity to give input about where and with whom they want to be.

- Child welfare workers mediate the decision-making process by helping the family develop a plan for the child to ensure the child's safety and well-being.

Family meetings, no matter the configuration, have been found to reduce out-of-home placement and increase placement of children in their same ethnic, racial, religious group, or all three. The family is empowered to make decisions and, with the child welfare worker, establish a collaborative intervention plan with which they are comfortable and invested in accomplishing. This practice concept is culturally sensitive and is proving to be quite effective in addressing the well-being of the child and family.

Caregiver Meeting Model

It is not always feasible to conduct a family group meeting for determining the best permanency option for a child. Often, family members refuse to participate, a parent may be incarcerated, or families cannot meet because of geographical limitations. The "caregivers" should include the parent(s), the current person caring for the child, and kin who may be potential caregivers for the child. The child welfare worker must apply the same collaborative principles as those used in a family group meeting:

- Viewing the caregiver as a colleague
- Working with the caregiver versus on the caregiver
- Sincerity and clearness about the choices and consequences with all caregivers
- Keeping the focus on the risk of harm to the child and permanence

Caregiver meetings are one-on-one meetings with each caregiver and the child welfare worker. The meetings are designed to educate and explore options with the caregivers, such as termination of parental rights, adoption, and guardianship, as a basis for shared decision making toward a permanent plan.

The worker then needs to synthesize all the information he or she has received from the various kin and negotiate the best plan of action. In light of the emphasis on concurrent permanency planning (see Chapter 80, this volume), the child welfare worker and the caregivers should establish a primary and secondary permanency plan.

■ *Further Reading*

Berrick, J. D., Needell, B., & Barth, R. P. (1995). *Kinship care in California: An empirically based curriculum.* Berkeley: University of California, Berkeley, Child Welfare Research Center.

Scannapieco, M., & Hegar, R. L. (1996). A nontraditional assessment framework for kinship foster homes. *Child Welfare, 75*(5), 567-582.

Wilcox, R., Smith, D., Moore, J., Hewitt, A., Allan, G., Walker, H., Ropata, M., Monu, L., & Featherstone, T. (1991). *Family decision making, family group conferences: Practitioners' view.* Lower Hutt, New Zealand: Practitioners' Publishing.

84

What Do I Need to Know to Plan Effectively Across Child Welfare Programs?

■ *Richard L. Norman*

In many agencies, a "child welfare system" may be more accurately described as an organized linking of child welfare programs with differing philosophies and practices. In these circumstances, case management becomes an 800-pound gorilla with an attitude!

As a "front-end" process, the child protective services (CPS) assessment and evaluation information must efficiently cross internal agency boundaries to be useful. The CPS worker must receive this information from a complex web of people, programs, and overlapping service systems in the agency to ensure its use for effective intervention. To accomplish this, the worker must first recognize and then understand the dysfunctional modes of agency operation that distort communication and can block or sidetrack the worker's intervention planning efforts. The worker can also use key people, role awareness, and specialized communication to succeed.

The four dysfunctional modes of agency operation are the blind mode, the underdeveloped mode, the rejecting mode, and the conflicted mode. The following examples of the dysfunctional modes illustrate how the modes produce communication that works against intervention planning:

- Blind: "This client is a schizophrenic!" Technical or procedural language, or both, in effect conceals the determination of useful practical client realities.
- Underdeveloped: "You have been in this unit for a year and you don't know pediatricians that are expert at sex abuse physical exams." There is no reliable method of saving and sharing critical information.
- Rejecting: "So they get a recording instead of a person, at least we know who called!" The emphasis is on agency responsibility to receive messages as opposed to responsiveness.
- Conflicted: "Who cares if they know the family history? I'm making the decisions now." Conflict minimizes information flow between programs, and clients fall between the cracks.

If dysfunctional modes are examples of "what" to look for as potential barriers to intervention planning, then identification of key people in facilitating roles is an example of "who" to look for as potential barrier busters across systems. Key people can be identified by their role-based authority and modeling of good practice. Also, key people have the power to bring people together for collaboration.

The following are vehicles of communication available for use in offsetting the dysfunctional modes and engaging key people for effective intervention planning:

- Protocol: a planned approach to complex case situations
  - ➤ Prevents trial-and-error responses by new workers
  - ➤ Enhances communication within and between units
  - ➤ Links practice wisdom to intervention

- Staffing: two or more persons discuss the situation to aid decision making
  - ➤ Identifies holders of "practice wisdom" for consultation and so on
  - ➤ Prevents isolation of inexperienced workers

■ *Further Reading*

Compher, J. V. (1987). The dance beyond the family system. *Social Work, 32,* 105-108.

Part VII

INTERVENTION

Section A:
Emphasis on the Child

85

What Types of Mental Health Treatment Should Be Considered for Maltreated Children?

■ *Mark Chaffin*

D o all abused children need therapy? What type of therapy works best for maltreated children? How long should it last? Who should provide it? To answer these questions, this chapter provides a general discussion of why maltreated children may need mental health services, how professionals can decide which children need services and which do not, and how different treatment approaches can be matched to the specific presenting symptoms of each child.

■ *Do All Maltreated Children Have Mental Health Problems or Need Therapy?*

Sometimes, children are sent to therapy simply because they have been abused. It is not correct to assume, however, that abused children always need therapy any more than it would be to assume that all children who have suffered automobile accidents need stitches. In both cases, some will need the particular treatment and some will not. Abuse or neglect are not mental health disorders. They are events in children's lives. Whether a child has a mental health disorder is determined by the child's symptoms rather than the events the child has experienced. Although the child's abuse history is important in the child's treatment, and may be a major focus of treatment, it is symptom status and not history that determines whether treatment is needed and, if so, what type. Because symptoms may or may not be readily apparent, it is important that an assessment be conducted by a qualified provider who is familiar with child maltreatment. The following characteristics seem clear regarding the relationship between abuse or neglect and mental health symptoms:

- Abuse or neglect significantly increases the risk for mental health symptoms.
- Although risk is increased, not all abused or neglected children necessarily have symptoms related to their maltreatment. One third or more of children have minor symptoms or none at all. There is no evidence that children without symptoms need extensive treatment.
- The types of symptoms that maltreatment can cause vary with the types of maltreatment, and they vary widely from one individual child to another. Although maltreated children may share some common characteristics, ultimately each child may be affected in unique ways.
- Maltreated children often have other mental health symptoms that are unrelated to their maltreatment or that may predate their maltreatment. For example, an abused child may have attention deficit or hyperactivity that was not caused by the abuse but may still need treatment.

■ What Should Be Done to Determine If Mental Health Services Are Needed?

The process of determining what symptoms are present and what treatment is needed is called *assessment*. Although some maltreated children may not need therapy, it is advisable that all maltreated children be assessed by a qualified mental health professional to determine their need for services and which services are appropriate. Assessment is the critical first step and should be a routine service in all cases unless the child is already receiving treatment. Assessments should be performed by a licensed mental health professional specializing in children or adolescents and with experience and training in evaluating and treating maltreated children in particular. The professional might be a child and adolescent psychiatrist, a child or pediatric psychologist, or a licensed clinical social worker who specializes in abuse and neglect. Workers and parents should ask mental health professionals about their credentials, areas of specialization, and training before making a selection.

The assessment will usually involve an interview with the child and the child's parents or guardians and conversations with the child's social worker, schoolteacher, and others. It also may involve psychological testing, although testing is not necessary in most cases. A psychologist may conduct testing to help answer specific questions that remain unanswered after an interview. Testing is not a "crystal ball," however, and it is not necessary to process every child through a battery of tests on a routine basis. Because abuse often occurs in the context of family or social problems, the assessment should examine these areas, if possible. When referrals are made for assessment, it is important for workers to be very clear and very specific about what they want to know from the assessment. Ask direct questions such as the following: (a) Does this child have a significant need for mental health services? (b) If so, what specific types of services are most indicated? (c) How long would treatment be expected to last? and (d) Who, in addition to the child, should be involved? Workers should expect to receive specific and practical answers to their questions.

■ *If Treatment Is Needed, What*
  Type Is Most Appropriate?

Assuming there is a need for mental health treatment, what type of treatment is best? Should it be group or individual therapy? Should it be long term or short term? Should it include parents? What approach should be used? Currently, it is not possible to clearly answer these questions because research on this topic has only recently begun. Also, the child's individual assessment will provide the most important guidance. Table 85.1 provides general guidelines for treatment selection decisions.

Many of the treatment approaches described in Table 85.1 are short term (i.e., approximately 12 sessions) and have been shown to be associated with significant improvements in major symptom areas. Most professionals agree that, if needed, treatment should be initiated as soon as possible, including during the crisis period often precipitated by disclosure and investigation. Parental involvement in treatment is generally desirable, and for some types of treatment (e.g., behavioral parenting programs for acting-out behaviors) it is absolutely required. Even when children are in therapy for depression or anxiety, parent involvement has been found to be helpful. Workers should be cautious of therapists who routinely refuse to meet with parents or routinely refuse to discuss the child's therapy with parents or workers.

Studies show that, on average, most abused children are seen for approximately 12 sessions. It is less clear whether longer term treatments are necessarily associated with more improvement, although they may be required for more severe cases. Also, a general guideline is that one type of therapy focused on the child's main problem is often as good as or better than multiple therapies. "Polytherapy," or shotgun approaches, should be avoided. Support groups or brief educative programs may be appropriate and may have some preventive benefit, even for asymptomatic children. Also, note that sometimes no therapy or periodic monitoring alone is appropriate. Periodic monitoring might be conducted by a qualified mental health professional. Monitoring might also be conducted by workers or informed and supportive caregivers. If workers or parents have questions about monitoring, the professional who assessed or treated the child can generally provide individualized specific advice.

If treatment is needed, children should get it. Although this sounds simple, many workers know it is not. Simply making a referral for service does not ensure that the service is actually received. Assistance may be needed in scheduling appointments, transportation, arranging child care, or securing payment. Assistance may be needed to maintain motivation. Also, workers need to closely monitor clients' attendance, progress, and satisfaction with services.

Table 85.1   Mental Health Treatment Approaches for Maltreated Children

Approach	What Is It?	When May It Be More Appropriate?	When May It Be Less Appropriate?
Exposure-based therapy	Gradually recounting aspects of upsetting events and coping with them until they become less upsetting	Frequently used for posttraumatic stress symptoms and other anxiety symptoms	Children with behavior problems or acting out; children who are not symptomatic or are improving spontaneously
Cognitive therapy	Replacing negative beliefs and attitudes (such as self-blame or distrust) with more adaptive thinking patterns	Well supported for a variety of problems, especially depression	Children with behavior problems or acting out
Behavioral parent training	Teaching parents specific skills to improve relationships and implement effective discipline with their children	Children with behavior problems or acting out	Posttraumatic stress disorder symptoms or depression
Support groups	Groups of children with common experiences providing mutual support and encouraging positive change	Relatively well-functioning children with minimal to moderate symptoms or as an adjunctive treatment; may be used as a preventive treatment	Severely disturbed children, children who are unable to fit in socially, or severely depressed or avoidant children
Pharmacology	Directly changing brain chemistry using medication	Attention deficit and hyperactivity or serious mental disorders such as psychosis	Less severe problems or problems that are environmental or social
Long-term relationship-based or dynamic therapy	Using the relationship with the therapist to change emotional regulation and relationship patterns	When short-term approaches have failed to yield results	Children who are responding to short-term therapy or are improving spontaneously or younger and less verbal children
No therapy with or without periodic monitoring	Having children return for periodic check-ups at intervals of several weeks to several months	Children who have few or no symptoms or children who are improving on their own and seem to have good social support	Children with serious symptoms or children who seem to be getting worse

86

What Are Effective Strategies to Address Common Behavior Problems?

■ *Barbara L. Bonner*

This chapter reviews typical behavioral and affective problems seen in abused and neglected children. Effective strategies to suggest to parents and foster parents are described, and recommendations regarding when to refer children for mental health intervention are presented.

■ *What Are Typical Problems and Effective Strategies to Help Abused and Neglected Children?*

1. Typical internalizing problems are anxiety, fearfulness, depression, and low self-esteem. These children may appear sad, withdrawn, frightened, or lonely. They may have problems sleeping and eating.

   Suggestions for caregivers

   • Encourage children to draw or talk about their feelings.
   • Engage the child in activities such as skating, cooking, playing with Play-Doh, riding bikes, and painting.

- Rock the child in a rocking chair; read the child a bedtime story each night.
- Praise the child for being "brave," being a "big boy" or "big girl," and trying new activities.
- Reassure the child that he or she is safe.

2. Typical externalizing problems are aggressive behavior and oppositional or defiant behavior. These children can be aggressive with other children, adults, animals, or property. They may be uncooperative, defiant, and take a negative stance repeatedly. They will test your patience and can be difficult to manage.

Suggestions for caregivers

- Remember that behavior changes slowly with many ups and downs; over time, children can improve their behavior.
- Expect children to test the limits, and be patient when they do.
- Draw firm behavioral lines for what is acceptable behavior (e.g., "Kicking is not allowed at our house").
- Keep your voice neutral but firm.
- Discuss issues with the child before saying "no" because the word "no" often acts as a trigger for aggressive or oppositional behavior (e.g., "Let's see how we can work this out").
- Praise children when they control their behavior.
- Give the child two choices (e.g., "You can lower your voice, or you can go sit on your bed for a few minutes").
- Tell the child what to do in a positive way (e.g., "Keep your hands in your pockets for a few minutes. That's the way; good for you!").

3. The following are other childhood problems that may be present in maltreated children:

Enuresis: This is wetting in the daytime or persistent nighttime wetting after age 5. Children may regress to earlier childhood behaviors, such as wetting the bed, when abuse occurs or when they are removed from their home. This is not unusual because it may occur with nonabused children in a new setting.

Suggestions for caregivers

- Treat the behavior as one that is "normal" that will stop over time.
- Encourage the child to use the toilet just before bedtime.
- Praise the child on dry mornings.
- Restrict fluids in the evening.
- Use pull-ups at night with young children who are agreeable.

Encopresis: This is soiling in children older than age 4. Children may become constipated due to changes in their diet or surroundings, or children may be hesitant to use the toilet in a new setting, resulting in soiling. In some cases, children may have difficulty controlling their bowel movements as a result of sexual abuse.

Suggestions for caregivers

- Set a regular time for the child to sit on the toilet for a short period each day.
- Increase the amount of fiber in the child's diet.
- Praise the child for clean days.
- Encourage the child to use the toilet by giving him or her a sticker or star.
- Talk to the child's pediatrician.

Attachment disorders: Children may not have a positive attachment or closeness to their primary caregivers. They may be withdrawn or "detached" from new caregivers, or they may quickly form an inappropriately close attachment to new adults; both of these attachment forms can be problematic.

Suggestions for caregivers

- Show the child appropriate affection, such as giving the child a hug and rocking the child in a rocking chair.
- Discourage or limit inappropriate affectionate behavior by the child, such as repeated kissing of adults or children.
- Encourage the child to be a member of your family while he or she lives with your family.
- Be clear that the child may not live with your family forever.

- Allow the child to call you "mom," "dad," or a special name such as "Momma B."

Academic problems: Children may have difficulty adjusting to a new classroom and teacher. Their performance at school can be affected by other problems discussed in this chapter. Because children attend school for several hours each day, a satisfactory adjustment in this setting is very important.

Suggestions for caregivers

- Discuss the child's strengths and problems with the teacher before the child joins the class; ask the teacher to notify you immediately if problems occur.
- Request the teacher assign a "buddy" to help your child.
- Assist the child with assignments each day on a regular basis.
- Read to the child every night at bedtime.
- Praise the child for working hard at school.

Attention deficit disorder (ADD) or attention deficit with hyperactivity disorder (ADHD): Children who have persistent inattentiveness, an inability to concentrate, and high levels of physical activity may have ADD or ADHD. Abused children with high levels of anxiety or posttraumatic stress disorder, however, may appear to have ADHD due to their agitated or disorganized behavior. This differentiation should be made by a mental health professional or physician with training and experience in this area.

Suggestions for caregivers

- Decrease the amount of highly stimulating videos, movies, and TV viewed by the child.
- Have realistic expectations about a child's behavior in a new setting.
- Establish a structured routine for the child.
- Show the child how to do normal tasks, such as brushing his or her teeth or making his or her bed.
- Rock the child daily to help him or her relax.
- Teach the child to take deep breaths to slow down.

- Remind the child in a positive way, "Let's see your slow turtle walk in the house."
- Designate a place for the child to go for a few minutes for him or her to "slow down" that the child does not view as punishment.

Posttraumatic stress disorder (PTSD): Some children have symptoms of PTSD, such as recurrent, unwanted memories or dreams of the abuse; persistent avoidance of thoughts or feelings about the abuse; or persistent symptoms of increased arousal, such as irritability, sleeping problems, and difficulty concentrating.

Suggestions for caregivers

- Assure the child that he or she is in a safe place.
- Anticipate stressful situations and prepare the child ahead of time.
- Distract the child with activities such as drawing, skating, and playing ball.
- Eliminate frightening or violent TV, videos, and movies.
- Allow the child to talk about the abuse if he or she chooses to do so.
- Use the suggestions discussed for attachment disorders and ADD and ADHD.

■ When Should a Child Be Referred for Assessment and Treatment?

1. A child should be referred before
   - The child's problems have clearly escalated
   - The caretaker is highly frustrated with the child's behavior
   - The child's placement is in jeopardy

2. A child should be referred when the problems
   - Do not respond to the suggestions discussed previously
   - Persist longer than 6 to 8 weeks
   - Appear to be getting worse
   - Interfere with his or her functioning at school or at home

■ *What Treatment Interventions*
  Are Effective With Children?

Effective treatment strategies
  • Usually involve the caregiver and the child
  • Encourage the child to label and talk about his or her feelings
  • Teach children coping strategies to deal with stressful situations
  • Encourage the caregivers to focus on the positive aspects of the child's behavior
  • Focus on improving the caregiver-child relationship

The following specific treatment strategies have been determined to be effective for abused children:
  • Cognitive-behavioral approaches are highly effective, particularly with sexually abused children and their parents.
  • Parent-child interaction therapy is a highly effective approach to reducing severe behavior problems in children ages 2 to 7.
  • Play therapy approaches can be useful with young children.

■ *Further Reading*

Adams, C., & Fruge, E. (1996). *Why children misbehave and what to do about it*. Oakland, CA: New Harbinger.

Hembree-Kigin, T., & McNeil, C. (1995). *Parent-child interaction therapy*. New York: Plenum.

Morris, R. J., & Kratochwill, T. R. (1998). *The practice of child therapy* (3rd ed.). Boston: Allyn & Bacon.

87

How Do I Help Children Adjust to Out-of-Home Care Placement?

■ *Brenda Jones Harden*

Facilitating children's adjustment to out-of-home placement is in many ways a precarious venture. Children are biologically equipped to develop intimate relationships with their first parents, particularly their biological parents. When they are moved to another family, their attachment systems are challenged in a way that may affect their relationships throughout the life span. Thus, this chapter accepts the premise that it is inherently stressful for any child older than 6 months of age to adjust to a new home environment.

Therefore, the goal of the child welfare practitioner is to support the child to develop the best relationship possible with the out-of-home care provider. This is important whether the permanency goal is a return home or adoptive placement. A child's potential move to another family should not be used as a reason to inhibit the child's attachment to the current caregivers. Because a child's placement is contingent on many factors, it is difficult to predict the timing and circumstances of a move. More important, if a child has felt the comfort and support of one attachment relationship, he or she is much more able to be open to another.

In keeping with this goal, practitioner strategies to facilitate children's adjustment to out-of-home care should most often include the foster parents. Regular parent-child activities (e.g., the parent follows the child's lead and engages in activities that the child selects) are crucial and should be supported by the child welfare practitioner. In fact, caseworker visits to the homes should routinely incorporate these parent-child activities. The following are strategies that child welfare workers and foster parents can use to support children in out-of-home care:

Techniques for fostering emotional connections between children and substitute caregivers

- Individual quiet time between the foster parent and child on a daily basis
- Caregiving routines that are nurturing and responsive (e.g., make dressing for school a time when the foster parent can comment on how nice the child looks)
- Foster parent attunement to the child during periods of vulnerability (e.g., when the child is tired, afraid, or frustrated)
- Conversations between the foster parent and the child that allow the child to express feelings without fear of judgment or reprisal
- Foster parent "holding" of the child through challenging experiences (e.g., academic pursuits, visits with biological parents, and meetings with caseworkers)

Techniques for facilitating the adjustment of children to out-of-home care

- Understanding the child's regression to an earlier developmental period, which is often part of the child's way of coping with placements
- Accepting the child's attachment to biological and former foster parents (e.g., allowing the child to keep a picture of them visible), acknowledging but not overfocusing on the child's past, and refraining from negative descriptions of the child's former parents
- Being empathic to the sadness the child may feel at being separated from former parents

- Supporting the child's visitation with the biological parents by accepting his or her tendency to regress or act out following visits and assuring him or her of a safe place in the foster home
- Having discussions with the child about the reasons for placement and permanency plans
- Helping the child to use language, play, art, music, and other developmentally appropriate modes to express his or her feelings about the placement
- Finding many opportunities to provide the child with praise and self-esteem boosts
- Respecting the child's need to withdraw from family and to spend time alone
- Understanding the emotional root to the child's behavior problems and providing structure, rules, and consequences for misbehavior in a caring and nonpunitive manner
- Providing the child with a safe way to act out, such as writing about his or her negative feelings or hitting a stuffed animal
- Knowing when assistance for a child's adjustment problems should be sought in the form of consultation with the caseworker or psychotherapy for the child and family

Techniques for facilitating transitions between placements

- Creating a life book that chronicles the child's history and incorporates the child's perceptions of his or her placements and earlier experiences
- Having a small, quiet family celebration of the child's entry into the new home
- Meeting of the caseworker, the new family, and the child (if preschool-aged or older) regarding the culture of the new family (e.g., rules, values, activities, and schedule); creating concrete reminders for the child regarding the family culture (e.g., create a story and put reminder list in the child's bedroom or on the refrigerator door)
- The selection of nonthreatening names for the new parents with the child (e.g., if the child calls the biological

mother "mommy," another name could be given to the foster mother)

- Immediately placing pictures and belongings of the child throughout the house, taking a family picture with the child in it, and involving the child in family rituals and activities
- Allowing the child to grieve the loss of the former parents by giving him or her space and support to feel sad and angry
- Identifying a "transitional object" for the child (i.e., a concrete, psychologically meaningful object to remind the child of the positive aspects of a former familial relationship)
- Frequent visits for the child with the new family, with duration of the visitation period contingent on the child's developmental period (shorter for young children and longer for adolescents); if possible, first visit should occur in the child's current home
- If possible, meeting between current and former caregivers to discuss the child's preferences and dislikes, caregiving routines the child experienced, disciplinary strategies that worked, and any major events for the child
- Ideal transition entails the former parent psychologically "handing over" the child to the new parent via an appropriate good-bye and well-wishing

As child welfare practitioners seek to support children through various placements, it is important that they consider the following issues: (a) Any move is traumatic for children, particularly during specific developmental periods (e.g., 6-36 months) and in specific circumstances (e.g., if the child is very attached to the biological parent); (b) the strategies used to facilitate adjustment should be determined by the needs of the individual child and consistent with the developmental period of the child (e.g., a transitional object for a young child may be a stuffed animal, whereas for an adolescent it may be an old pair of sneakers); (c) the memory of former parents should be supported for children in ways they can tolerate; (d) the child needs many outlets for expressing negative and positive feelings about each parent; and (e) the trauma that accompanies moves can be diminished by proper planning of visitation, preplacement meetings between caregivers, and establishment of supports for the family and child prior to placement. Employing the previous approaches cannot eradicate the pain that children will inevitably feel when they must move, but it may facilitate their adjustment to the out-of-home care they experience.

■ *Further Reading*

Brodzinsky, D., & Schechter, M. (1990). *The psychology of adoption.* New York: Oxford University Press.

Falhlberg, V. (1991). *A child's journey through placement.* Indianapolis, IN: Perspectives Press.

88

How Do I Help Children Maintain Cultural Identity When They Are Placed in Out-of-Home Care?

■ *Sheryl Brissett-Chapman*

Whenever a child protective services worker or a law enforcement official deems that a child is not safe in his or her immediate family environment or is in imminent danger of abuse or neglect, emergency child removal and placement is considered. Generally, if resources cannot be found to quickly alter the situation, and reduce the risk, the child is separated from the parent(s) and placed with relatives or in the foster care system. Such separation is always costly in terms of child development and family functioning, and it should occur only when the child's prominent need for safety is jeopardized. Separation reinforces a child's sense of impermanence and diffuses identity, potentially contributing to (a) a lack of attachment to the adult caregiver(s), (b) a decreased sense of self-worth, (c) inability to trust others, (d) emotional and intellectual delays, (e) diminished ability to cope with normal developmental stresses, and (f) hopelessness. Culture represents the lens through which we all understand what is unacceptable child rearing and what is child protection. Certainly, culture plays a role in ameliorating the potentially negative impact of out-of-home placements and enhancing the benefits for the child, his or her family, and the community.

■ *Culturally Competent Programs and Practices*

Culturally competent organizations are most effective in supporting out-of-home placements due to their recognition of the need to recognize the cultural and ethnic diversity of the client population that the agency serves. Indeed, the organization's policymakers or governing boards ensure a process for developing and updating a mission that reflects a commitment to the population served, recruiting diverse staff, and evaluating policy and program directions with input from individual representatives of the different cultures or ethnic groups. The importance of cultural identity for all clients is valued.

Children who are placed in out-of-home care require a program that engages its staff and nonrelative caregivers in training regarding cross-cultural communication, culturally diverse family customs, and conflict resolution. Program outcomes should be evaluated to determine whether there are differential results for different cultural or ethnic groups. Case plans should consider the availability of community resources and should be formulated in settings that are most comfortable to the family (i.e., home, neighborhood facility, or church).

■ *Practice Issues*

Ultimately, direct service staff should recognize opportunities for accommodating the cultural dimension in all aspects of out-of-home placements. The following sections present typical areas warranting close examination by the worker. These areas represent opportunities for celebrating differences and cultural identity, as a resource for enhancing the benefits of the placement, while reducing secondary risk factors due to separation. The worker should include these in his or her assessment of the biological family, and assume the responsibility for ensuring that the relative or foster placement accommodates the child's culturally specific values and experiences to the extent possible.

Matching

Unfortunately, often children are placed in emergency situations, and little time is available for matching them with the initial placements. It is important to recognize that children placed in new settings must adapt rapidly to new ways of "how we are *here*." Ultimately, when a child is placed in out-of-home care, he or she needs a great amount of love, forgiveness, reasonable structure, support, and stimulation. Matching is also critical, however, because diverse cultural groups (i.e., families, institutions, or communities) have different values and rhythms. It is important to consider cultural ramifications in the match because of the vast differences in lifestyles; recreational and leisure activities; religious orientation, practices, and spiritual needs; and general interests. Relative and nonrelative caregivers should be screened for their recognition of the differing values that might be relevant to the child and his or her biological parents.

Caregivers who are intolerant or judgmental serve only to create divided loyalties for the child and to undermine possible reunification. Adoptive parents who are culturally insensitive are at risk for disrupting placement at the onset of adolescence, when the child's autonomy allows the cultural difference to become apparent or realized. Unfortunately, culturally incompetent caregivers may alienate a child from his or her own racial or ethnic identity, thus creating new challenges in the adult years. Good matching is good practice and produces stable placements, which can survive crises and promote continuity of care for highly vulnerable children.

Grooming

This aspect is often minimized, but it is an important consideration. Hair texture and style, clothes, colors and trends, nail care and jewelry, and actual skin care all reflect racial and ethnic considerations. A common complaint of African American professionals is the number of children in cross-cultural placements whose skin is not oiled or whose hair is washed too frequently or left unbraided. Some cultural groups, however, value bright colors and place great emphasis on vibrant and distinctive clothing, even for males.

Food

Food has symbolic and nutritional benefits. Children in out-of-home placement are nurtured emotionally and sustained by food that is familiar to them and reflects their cultural heritage.

Celebration and Mourning

Various cultural groups express joy and grief in different ways. For some families, the death of an elder becomes an opportunity to celebrate and "party." For others, death is received briefly and very solemnly: The dead are buried the day after death. For even others, death is viewed as something to be respected and is a natural conclusion of life. The family must come from afar and gather to reaffirm its ties and anticipate the next loss. For some, weddings and graduations may result in family members traveling afar in some groups and celebrations lasting for several days. Children in out-of-home placement should be supported in maintaining their family and cultural ties, especially with regard to reunions of any type. Minimally, these children should be allowed a preference.

Health Care

Different cultural groups have had different experiences with the health care system. Linguistically isolated populations, for example, have limited access in English-speaking systems and often feel disempowered. Other groups are distrusting of a health care system that may be perceived as "experimenting" with poor people, providing inferior services, or withholding care. Children in out-of-home placement may be vulnerable to a history of minimal contact with medical professionals for the previously discussed reasons. Parents and caregivers may be suspicious of medications (e.g., psychotropic). When there is an emphasis on prevention or behavior management, children may be perceived as "bad" and not needing medication; medication may be viewed as dependency forming or harmful. Efforts should be made to negotiate these issues and should include a high degree of attention to health education.

Discipline and Advocacy

Discipline is a controversial issue in low-income ethnic minority communities because parents may be more inclined to employ corporal discipline when rearing children. Children in out-of-home placement may be more accustomed to physical controls being imposed on them and may view this type of discipline as "caring"; caregivers, however, are typically prohibited from using such discipline. In fact, the child protection worker may have identified physical discipline as a risk factor that contributed to the removal of the child under the category of neglect. Another substantial reason why children of color are often removed involves inadequate supervision. There are cultural variations regarding the age and the conditions under which children are old enough to take care of themselves or supervise another child. Caregivers need to recognize that the biological parent who uses corporal discipline is not necessarily abusive or uncaring. Certainly, this attitude should not be communicated to the child in care.

Sexuality

This is another characteristic that indicates cultural differences in the socialization of children. Issues include nudity, type of attire, sexual language, sexual exploration, dating, and peer sexual contact. For the child in out-of-home placement, there is a need for the worker to understand the family's handling of these issues and to support the foster parent in providing transitional clarity for the child in adjusting to the different "rules" in the new setting.

Spirituality

One of the most prominent community institutions in cultural minority communities is the church or the mosque. Although children may not have formal religious training when placed, and their parents may not be active worshippers, deep-rooted spiritual beliefs may be an essential aspect of their background. Supporting the child's spiritual growth and development in placement is possibly the most effective strategy for helping him or her to cope with the trauma of separation, and its accompanying sense of abandonment, and to gain hope. Religious institutions in the community become a resource for this effort, but the child should never be forced into a fully involuntary experience.

■ *Summary*

In summary, children in out-of-home placements require a total organizational approach to optimally maintain their cultural identity. Culturally competent organizations creatively challenge themselves to address the unique needs of all children while promoting the children's sense of "peoplehood" and cultural identity.

■ *Further Reading*

Brissett-Chapman, S., & Issacs-Shockley, M. (1997). *Children in social peril. A community vision for preserving family care of African American children and youth.* Washington, DC: CWLA Press.

89

What Kind of Pediatric Care Should Abused and Neglected Children Receive?

■ *John M. Leventhal*

Studies have shown that abused and neglected children often suffer from a variety of physical, developmental, and emotional problems that need attention. These problems may be due to the maltreatment (e.g., seizures from shaken baby syndrome) or the inadequate care provided by the family (e.g., delays in immunizations). An approach to providing care to these children is to consider the following levels of pediatric care:

- Health screen
- Comprehensive health evaluation
- Ongoing health supervision

■ *Health Screen*

Although some children are placed in foster care directly from a health care facility (e.g., a child who is placed after evaluation and treatment of a broken femur), many other children enter foster care without a recent medical examination and should receive a timely medical exam (within 3-5 days). This exam can be done by the child's pediatrician, the pediatrician for the foster family, or a special clinic set up for this purpose. It is very helpful to gather as much information on the child's past medical history as possible from the family and from primary health care providers. It is best to avoid arranging for these exams in the local emergency department.

The purpose of the health screen is to evaluate the child for

- Signs of abuse (e.g., new or healed bruises or burns)
- Health problems that need treatment (e.g., an ear infection or a sexually transmitted disease)
- Health problems that are contagious (e.g., head lice)
- Urgent, serious mental health problems (e.g., suicidal thoughts) (Ideally, this assessment should be done by a mental health professional.)

■ Comprehensive Health Evaluation

An abused or neglected child (either living at home or placed in foster care) should have a comprehensive evaluation to develop a treatment plan that includes the child's health and mental health needs. If the child is in foster care, the child protective service (CPS) agency has the responsibility of ensuring an appropriate evaluation.

The evaluation might be performed in a specialized foster care clinic in which the child is evaluated by a multidisciplinary team that might include a pediatrician, a developmental specialist (for children younger than 5 years of age), a mental health expert, and an educator. Alternatively, the pediatric exam can be conducted separately and the child referred to appropriate services in the community.

The pediatric evaluation focuses on the child's

- Immunization status
- Growth
- Abnormalities on physical exam (e.g., findings of past sexual abuse)
- Vision and hearing screen
- Developmental abnormalities (e.g., delayed language)
- Behavioral problems (e.g., bed-wetting or soiling)
- Progress in school

- Need for dental care
- Need for screening tests (e.g., for anemia, lead, or tuberculosis)

When abnormalities are detected, it is important that the child receive appropriate services (e.g., referral to an ear, nose, and throat specialist for chronic ear infections and a specialized preschool program for children with language delay). Often, recommended services are not obtained; CPS has a valuable role in ensuring that the child receives necessary care.

■ *Ongoing Health Supervision*

Abused and neglected children, like all children, need ongoing health care to provide immunizations, periodic physical examinations and screening, and treatment of chronic health conditions such as asthma. In addition, maltreated children and their families need careful monitoring in the following areas:

> *Growth:* Many children, particularly those who have been neglected or have suffered from nonorganic failure to thrive, grow well in foster homes. Documenting these changes in growth can be important when making decisions regarding whether the child should continue in placement or be returned to the biological family.
>
> *Development and behavior:* Advances in the child's development and improvements in the child's behavior usually indicate a good adjustment in foster care. Persistent abnormalities may indicate the need for more intensive services for the child. The new onset of a behavioral problem or the recurrence of an old problem may suggest new stresses, such as the beginning of unsupervised visits with the biological parents. The pediatrician can help document a child's response to such visitations and help facilitate counseling if indicated.
>
> *Parenting:* Providing nurturing care to abused and neglected children who often have serious emotional or behavioral problems can be particularly challenging, even to the most skilled foster parents. The pediatri-

cian can help determine whether foster parents are providing adequate and appropriate care. If foster parents are struggling to provide such care, the pediatrician can provide advice and referrals for counseling, notify CPS, advise an alternative placement for the child, or all three.

Signs of maltreatment: Children in foster care often feel safe to talk about the maltreatment that they have suffered in their biological homes. The pediatrician can examine the child related to these disclosures or refer the child to the appropriate specialist. Children can be abused, neglected, or sexually abused in foster care or during visitations with parents. Pediatricians can be helpful in evaluating new statements by the child, new symptoms (e.g., vaginal discharge), or new injuries.

■ *Further Reading*

Szilagyi, M. (1998). The pediatrician and the child in foster care. *Pediatrics in Review, 19,* 39-50.

Part VII

INTERVENTION

Section B:
Emphasis on the
Parent or Caregiver

90

How Can Parenting Be Enhanced?

■ *Sandra T. Azar and Monica H. Ferraro*

Enhancing something assumed to be as *basic* as the capacity to parent is fraught with difficulties, from helping parents to acknowledge the need for help to shifting well-ingrained patterns of interpersonal responding. This chapter focuses on both process issues and the active strategies needed to produce parental change. For the former, we outline professional skills and special issues when dealing with multistressed parents. For the latter, we discuss both how to change how parents think about children's behavior and their development and a set of skill areas needed to enhance parenting: life skills, cognitive stimulation and child management, anger and stress management, and basic child care (e.g., home safety and hygiene).

■ Process Issues and Special Problems

There are special problems you will likely encounter in establishing rapport and working with parents. First, in many cases, parents are involuntary clients and may resent being told what to do by an "expert." They may also fear that you will assume a blaming stance and view them as "bad parents." It is important to balance your expertise with empowering parents. You need to create an environment in which parents believe that you and they are a team. They are the experts on their children, whereas you have firsthand experiences based on work with large numbers of parents and children. It is important to stress that you understand that being a parent is a hard job, and that you will help them find ways to make their job easier. Starting with a problem area that they find the most difficult will enhance motivation for them to work on problem areas you suggest. Praise positive steps parents make, no matter how small. You want to embody a model of the strategies you will be teaching them for use with their children. The following are basic tips that are useful:

1. Listen! Listen! Listen some more before you intervene.
2. Do not set yourself up as an expert—stay low-key.
3. Emphasize the positive (build on what parents have done well).
4. Let parents know that you do not view them as bad (e.g., "You really are trying hard to help your son").
5. If you do need to criticize, do it in "normative" terms (e.g., "Lots of parents think that works, but . . ").
6. Use adult analogies to make your points (e.g., to explain rewarding children, you could state, "If you worked all day making a nice dinner for your boyfriend and afterwards he didn't say anything, would you do it again?")
7. Be concrete in your explanations and have parents explain them to you or demonstrate what you have suggested they do.
8. Use gentle humor to make a point and praise generously.

Parents are often multistressed. Mastering new skills requires continuity and consistent practice. It is difficult to teach parents to be consistent with their children when their own lives are not stable. Relapse is common and maintaining gains requires including a relapse prevention component (i.e., developing a plan for how they will get "back on track" if they slip into old patterns). Because families live from crisis to crisis, it is also difficult for treatment to remain goal directed. Crises need to be addressed but should be used to illustrate skills being trained. For example, if a parent is having trouble with her landlord, communication and problem-solving skills that are being directed toward working with her children can be used (e.g., role-playing how to talk to the landlord and identifying the problem and potential solutions). Later, these same strategies can be linked to child rearing.

A final set of concerns involve professional strains (e.g., conflicts of values, potential for having unrealistic expectations of parents and ourselves, and difficulties with holding adequate as opposed to optimal parenting as a goal). Dealing with violence also means working in a context of risk (e.g., reporting abuse and potential for direct and vicarious trauma to professionals). It is helpful to work in teams to deal with these issues.

■ *Deciding Whether Parenting*
  Is What Should Be Targeted

Parents can have multiple problems that interfere with treatment (e.g., substance abuse and psychiatric diagnoses) that might need resolution first or to be treated simultaneously with parenting work. Cognitive limitations also present challenges. Targeting more basic skills (e.g., math for shopping and increasing literacy to read medicine labels) and breaking material into very small steps are helpful.

■ *Practical Issues*

A practical decision is whether to conduct work in the office or home setting. The office allows freedom from distractions and may be the only option if the child is in foster care. Problems with office visits include the requirement that parents have the skills and resources to negotiate getting to the office and greater concerns that they are being evaluated when they are in this setting. Home visits may be preferable. They have the added benefits of naturally occurring child misbehavior with which to work and potential for greater generalization of learning because this is the natural setting of parenting. The disadvantage is the greater potential for interruptions and chaos that may interrupt the flow of work. If an office is used, a setting that has a "home-like" quality will place the parent and child at ease. There should also be "props" for creating parenting dilemmas (e.g., messy play materials) and opportunities (e.g., books). Ideally, the room should have a one-way mirror with a potential for "cueing" new responses (e.g., bug-in-the-ear transmitter, a device that looks like a hearing aid, to communicate with parents through the mirror).

Another decision is whether to do individual or group work. The benefits of groups are many (e.g., parents learn by comparison, it is easier for parents to see a problem when it is another parent's, parents listen to each other more than they do to professionals, parents begin to see that some problems are inherent in stages of development rather than their children being "bad," and parents feel less alone). Groups may be less useful for cognitively limited parents. Also, group work needs to be combined with individual work to refine parents' skills, identify misapplication of techniques, and monitor child risk. Support groups are useful for low-risk parents in cases in which stress is producing the parenting deficits (e.g., Parents Anonymous), whereas moderate and high-risk parents need skills training and education groups in addition to support. (For an example of a parenting group program, see Azar, 1989).

■ The Targets of Enhancement

Parenting involves thinking (e.g., problem solving, appropriate labeling of child behavior, and perspective taking) and doing (e.g., appropriate discipline). Both aspects need to be addressed (see Chapter 65, this volume, for an assessment model). Basic intervention strategies include *didactic instruction, modeling new responses, role plays,* and *providing feedback.*

Work on understanding and interpreting child behavior includes the following:

1. *Increasing knowledge regarding developmental norms and basic care* (e.g., identifying when a rash is in need of a physician's care): This is best done through demonstrations and concrete examples (e.g., an exercise in which parents are asked to perform a task they cannot do, such as fix a carburetor, to help them understand what its like for children; role-playing emergencies).
2. *Challenging unrealistic expectations regarding children and misattributions* (Appendix 7, Table A7.3) using cognitive restructuring, which includes teaching parents to do the following:

- Recognize that their thoughts about situations and others affect their mood and behavior (e.g., believing their child is "out to get them" makes it harder to stay calm and teach their child).
- Generate their own "personalized" cognitions in problem situations using role plays and questioning (e.g., "All moms find tantrums hard, but what about them is the most upsetting *for you*? What goes through your head?").
- Challenge dysfunctional or self-defeating cognitions (e.g., "Is he really doing this on purpose?" and "Do you really think other mothers can do this?"). Demonstrating children's lower capacities can also be useful.
- Replace them with more appropriate "self-talk," such as "He's only 2. He doesn't know any better" or "I am doing the best I can."

3. *Helping parents to see their role in children's learning.* This involves explaining the impact of modeling, reinforcement, and punishment on their children's behavior. It is important, for example, to teach the parents that parental attention can actually increase negative behaviors (e.g., giving in to tantrums in the grocery store) and increase appropriate behaviors (e.g., "Why did he learn to be toilet trained? Because you gave him attention when he tried. Your attention is his 'paycheck'!").

4. *Training parents in the steps of problem solving,* including problem identification, alternative solution generation, and evaluating outcomes

In addition to changing thinking, parents need behavioral skills. These vary with development—from skills as basic as how to feed and diaper infants to more complex skills such as negotiating curfews with teens. A component analysis of the steps of the skill needs to be done and factors that interfere with use identified. The following are examples:

1. *Child management skills training* is useful to widen parents' repertoire beyond negative ones (e.g., yelling and physical punishment) (see Appendix 7, Table A7.4). Parents should be trained in the use of positive techniques (use of rewards to increase appropriate behavior; distraction). (For more

information regarding child management skills training, see Becker, 1971; Appendix 7). Parents also need discrimination training (e.g., matching the type and level of response to the nature of the misbehavior and how this changes with children's development).

2. *Anger and stress management* often need to be learned before other parenting strategies can be carried out well. Although direct assistance can address contextual stresses (e.g., financial help and marital work), training in managing stress and anger is also essential. This involves three steps. First, parents need to identify triggers for anger and stress. Through questioning their examples of stressful times (e.g., "What caused the stress or anger?" "How did you feel?" "What were you thinking?" "What did you do?" and "How did your child or others react?"), a pattern of "hot" issues or events that set off a parent and his or her unique set of "warning" signs can be identified. The latter can include physical responses ("I feel a tightening in my stomach") and cognitive responses ("I say to myself, 'Why me? It's not fair!' " or "He's doing this on purpose! He wants me to look bad.") Relaxation skills (e.g., deep muscle relaxation) or "better" self-talk (e.g., "It feels like he's trying to get to me, but he's just tired.") can then be taught.

3. *Neglect issues* are among the most difficult to address. Skill areas include home safety, hygiene, emergency skills, budgeting and nutrition, medical care skills, and supervision skills. As noted previously, breaking skills down into small steps and working on each is essential. For example, programs exist in which parents are trained to scan their home and identify and rectify safety risks (e.g., uncovered outlets). First, someone models this task, and then the parents attempt to do so. Spot checks are then made to help them maintain safety. Emergencies can be staged and the problem solving and behavioral responses modeled for them. (See Appendix 7 for references to the work of Tymchuk and Lutzker and colleagues.)

4. *Work on increasing social support* is also important to help reduce stress through the provision of information, concrete help, and feedback. Social skills training may also be useful (e.g., role plays of asking another parent for coffee), as can support groups (see Chapter 92, this volume).

■ *Further Reading*

Azar, S. T. (1989). Training parents of abused children. In C. E. Shaefer & J. M. Briesmeister (Eds.), *Handbook of parent training* (pp. 414-441). New York: John Wiley.

Becker, W. C. (1971). *Parents are teachers*. Champaign, IL: Research Press.

91

What Interventions Are Available for the Nonabusive Parent?

■ *Mark Chaffin*

A
lthough the service needs of abused children and abusers are generally acknowledged, the service needs of non-abusive parents may be easy to overlook. In fact, non-abusive parents have sometimes been blamed rather than helped. Nonabusive partners may be either men or women, although most research and discussion have focused on nonabusive mothers, particularly in sexual abuse cases in which they are sometimes labeled as "unprotective," "unsupportive," or "in collusion with the abusive parent." For example, it has been suggested that some women may actually seek out and marry child molesters based on some presumed (and unproven) unconscious psychopathology, possibly related to their own abuse history. In particular, mothers in incest abuse cases have been viewed with suspicion at best or contempt at worst. It is often assumed that they secretly knew about their child's abuse and condoned it. The available research suggests that few of these stereotypes are true for the majority of nonabusive parents. Most tend to believe and support their children. Few are aware of, let alone condone, sexual abuse. There are only slightly higher rates of childhood sexual abuse for mothers in incest families than other women. Also, nonabusive partners as a group have no typical personality profile or demonstrable psychopathology.

It is clear, however, that nonabusive partners are commonly and understandably upset or even in crisis after abuse has been reported in their family. In sexual abuse cases, abuse is often hidden and secretive. Disclosure can be an acute emotional shock for the nonabusive parent, who may react with disbelief, guilt, fear, panic, anger, confusion, emotional numbness, or a mixture of all these emotions. In some cases, the nonabusive partner may be the victim of domestic violence from the abuser and may feel paralyzed to act or may fear for her own welfare and that of her entire family. Occasionally, women who have been repeatedly victimized and dominated may seem helpless to act at all. In most of these circumstances, the correct types of services can help.

Two types of services are important: services designed to benefit the nonabusive parent directly and services for the children and family that include the nonabusive parent as a participant. Services designed to benefit nonabusive parents directly might include the following:

- Protective services, such as protection from partner violence, shelter services, or other services designed to ensure physical safety: This is a critical first step in any work with nonabusive parents.
- Concrete supports, such as child care, employment, temporary assistance to needy families, housing, and transportation services: These might be needed in cases in which the abusive parent is the primary breadwinner for the family and has left the home or should leave the home.
- Social supports, such as parent support groups, supportive therapy, home visitation, or other interventions designed to create supportive social networks: Parents may also be encouraged to use whatever natural support systems might be available and helpful, such as friendship networks, church or clergy, and family.
- Mental health services, such as therapy groups or individual therapy: These services manage problems related to the emotional upset or turmoil often associated with disclosure.

It is critical to recognize that nonabusive parents may need the previously discussed types of help for their own sake. Also, the interests of the abused child and the other children in the family are fostered by providing these services. Research has shown that when nonabusive parents are functioning better, their children function better. Similarly, it is important to include nonabusive parents in their children's services. Research has demonstrated that, in general, therapy for abused children works better when the nonabusive parent is included as an integral part of the treatment. If possible, the nonabusive parent should be included in referrals for assessment and treatment.

Finally, it is important to remember that nonabusive parents not only are acutely upset but also are caught between many conflicting demands. They may feel responsible for the welfare of both the abused child and other children in the family or for the welfare of their abusive spouse with whom there may be a strong or ambivalent attachment. Nonabusive parents commonly receive unsolicited and conflicting advice or demands from friends, family, spouse, child protective services, therapists, ministers, and professionals. It is important that workers avoid arguing, lecturing, or pressuring nonabusive parents at this point. Advising should be kept to a minimum. Workers should avoid blaming or labeling the parent as "unprotective" or "unsupportive." This can have the unintended effect of creating an adversarial relationship between the parent and the agency that may become permanent. Better results can be obtained by first establishing a nonjudgmental and supportive relationship, listening carefully and empathetically, and attempting to help the nonabusive parent make a healthy and empowered decision about the parent's children and family on his or her own. Although this cannot be accomplished in all cases, a patient and supportive approach often yields the best outcomes.

92

How Can I Help Parents and Caregivers Develop Social Skills and Make Positive Connections to the Community?

■ *Ross A. Thompson*

Families at risk for child maltreatment are often multi-problem families. The association between child maltreatment and socioeconomic distress (including unemployment, poor housing, and welfare reliance) means that high-risk families are frequently stressed by their living conditions. Child maltreatment is also associated with domestic violence, substance abuse, residential mobility, neighborhood dysfunction, parental emotional problems, and other difficulties. In addition to these life stresses, high-risk families are often socially isolated within their communities, lacking strong relational ties to neighbors, family, friends, coworkers, or others who could provide assistance.

Because of these characteristics, assistance to high-risk families often includes efforts to better integrate family members into supportive social networks. Strengthening social support is believed to have many advantages for the treatment and prevention of child maltreatment. Social support offers emotional sustenance to parents that can assist in their coping with the frustration, anger, or anxiety associated with difficult life conditions. It can provide the basis for exchanging advice, referrals, material aid, or other resources that enable families to function more successfully. Social support can contribute to an increase in parenting competence and skills in household management, financial planning, and even job performance. It also contributes to community networking and connections to agencies and services that can aid family members. Social support also provides opportunities for others to monitor for suspected child maltreatment. For all these reasons, strengthening parents' social skills to better integrate them into the community and reduce their social isolation is viewed as an important strategy for stress reduction and for preventing and treating child maltreatment.

■ What Is Social Isolation?

How is social support accomplished? One must first have an understanding of what is meant by the "social isolation" of high-risk families. When families are described as socially isolated, this typically means that they have infrequent contact with extended family, neighbors, friends, and others in the community. Their social networks are thus small and limited. It is not always true, however, that family members feel lonely or isolated or perceive that friends or kin are unsupportive or unhelpful. Sometimes they do. In other cases, however, parents feel considerable emotional support from the limited number of people with whom they associate, even though these relationships are ineffective in reducing their abusive behavior (this sometimes occurs when family or friends are hesitant to challenge a parent's treatment of offspring and instead act reassuringly or minimize the seriousness of harm in an effort to act supportively). Sometimes, parents deliberately limit the size of their social networks to people who share their values and orientation to child rearing. Therefore, strengthening positive community ties for treating or preventing child maltreatment requires more than merely increasing the size of the family's social network. It also requires strengthening relationships that family members perceive as emotionally supportive and that contribute to changing harmful parental practices.

■ *Reasons for Social Isolation*

It is important to understand why troubled families become socially isolated. Several reasons have been identified in studies of high-risk families:

- Parents may isolate themselves from neighborhood and kin contacts because they recognize that their behavior is inappropriate, and they seek to escape detection.
- Family members may be stigmatized and ostracized within their neighborhoods and extended family because of their atypical behavior. Families may be stigmatized because of how children are treated but also for other reasons, including domestic violence, poverty, substance abuse, mental illness, social incompetence, and delinquency.
- Family members may fail to create or maintain social connections because they are too exhausted by stressful life circumstances to expend energy on sociability or because asking for assistance may be experienced as humiliating or demeaning.
- Family members may become socially isolated because of limited social competence: They lack the skills for initiating new relationships with others and maintaining these connections through positive reciprocity, warm sociability, and mutual assistance.
- Families may live in communities that are dangerous, depleted, or dysfunctional in the "human capital" they have to offer in activities, resources, or relationships. Social isolation thus reflects a response to difficult neighborhood conditions.

Social isolation in troubled families may have diverse origins, and it is necessary to understand these before developing strategies for strengthening social support.

■ Strengthening Positive Community Connections

The following are some approaches to consider:

- *Normalize the need for social support:* Sometimes support is neither sought nor maintained because the need for it is unrecognized. Assistance in recognizing the potential benefits of social support, which everyone needs, can be a valuable first step.

- *Assess community resources for social support:* Within the social networks of family members, where are potential sources of support and community integration? Do extended family members live nearby? Are workplace associates possible candidates for assistance? For children, do teachers, counselors, and peers at school offer opportunities for social integration? Are neighbors available, constructively interested, and capable? Do family members have interests or skills that offer opportunities for new, positive relationships with others who share their interests? An assessment of the family's needs and personal resources, as well as those of the community, is essential.

- *Coordinate formal and informal assistance:* Formal sources of support are professionals such as social workers, counselors, physicians, school personnel, clergy, and others who have been trained to provide assistance to troubled family members. Informal sources of support include neighbors, extended family members, coworkers, classmates, and friends who lack professional training but are often the first to whom family members turn for assistance. It is important not only to identify potential sources of support but also to coordinate these sources for the family, such as asking clergy to enlist assistance from the religious community, asking a school counselor to talk to teachers about a child's needs, or asking a physician to make referrals to needed social services for the family. In doing so, the specialized roles assumed by different support agents in a family's social network can be used, and the collective contributions of these sources are strengthened by their coordination. It is important, however, to avoid overwhelming family members by enlisting too many supportive agents on their behalf.

- *Bridge access to community connections:* It is sometimes true that socially isolated family members have little knowledge of community resources and few means of accessing those resources. It may be necessary, therefore, not only to inform parents about agencies, community groups, and programs that would benefit them but also to provide transportation, assist in making and keeping appointments, and bridging access in other practical ways.

- *Improving recipient reactions to assistance:* Sometimes, receiving help can be experienced as humiliating or denigrating, and aid might be rejected because of feelings of indebtedness or failure. Positive community connections are instilled when assistance can be accepted constructively, and this often occurs when assistance is reciprocated (e.g., the recipient is enlisted to help needy others), occurs in contexts that reduce stigma, and is accompanied by efforts to reduce dependency and strengthen self-reliance.

- *Strengthening social skills:* Strengthening social skills in troubled family members is not easy, especially because social skills deficits are often tied to broader family problems (e.g., substance abuse and emotional problems). Nevertheless, the motivation to establish meaningful relationships with others, improve communication skills, learn to reciprocate assistance offered by others, reduce defensiveness, and strengthen conflict-resolution capabilities should be goals of efforts to improve positive community connections through strengthened social skills.

- *Assisting sources of social support:* Helping needy families can be exhausting, especially for informal helpers with no professional training. Thus, efforts to assist those who can support family members, such as through informal counseling of extended family members or neighborhood networking, can strengthen their contribution to improved family functioning.

■ *Further Reading*

Cochran, M., Larner, M., Riley, D., Gunnarsson, L., & Henderson, C. R. (Eds.). (1990). *Extending families: The social networks of parents and their children.* New York: Cambridge University Press.

Melton, G. B., & Barry, F. D. (Eds.). (1994). *Protecting children from abuse and neglect.* New York: Guilford.

Thompson, R. A. (1995). *Preventing child maltreatment through social support: A critical analysis.* Thousand Oaks, CA: Sage.

93

What Treatment Is Recommended for Sexual Abuse Perpetrators?

■ *Melissa McDermott*

Sexual perpetrator treatment is not a "cure"; the goal of treatment is to teach a perpetrator how to identify, intervene, and control his or her sexually abusive behaviors and strategies used to entrap the victim(s). The true clients in perpetrator treatment are past and potential victims of the identified perpetrator; community safety is of the utmost importance.

■ *General*

A sexual perpetrator will not change his or her behavior (self-correct) without external intervention, which includes treatment and pressure from the judicial system. The perpetrator's internal motivation greatly enhances the prognosis but is typically not present at the onset of treatment. Perpetrators should be mandated by criminal or juvenile court to participate in, not just attend, treatment. Also, a period of incarceration can further motivate a perpetrator. The sanction of consequences besides therapy can help motivate a perpetrator. Treatment should be a collaborative effort. Through an interdisciplinary approach involving child welfare, probation, treatment, and polygraph, a perpetrator can be held accountable by using both internal and external controls measures.

Perpetrator treatment is of a long duration. Typically, the perpetrator should have, at a minimum, 1½ to 2 years of intervention. The perpetrator can learn his or her pattern of offending and strategies by which to control such behaviors and at the same time be managed by a system that is concerned about public safety and victim protection.

■ *Treatment Provider Qualifications*

The treatment provider should have an advanced degree in a human services field from a fully accredited institution. Furthermore, he or she should receive continuing education in sexual perpetrator-specific interventions through attendance at regional and national conferences and a thorough review of the current research. Preferably, the professional should have a minimum of 2,000 hours of direct experience with sexual perpetrators. The professional should provide sexual perpetrator-specific treatment and not general counseling.

■ *Psychosexual Evaluation*

A perpetrator should receive a psychosexual evaluation prior to entering treatment. This evaluation, which includes a detailed social and sexual history, provides treatment recommendations and determines the best means of intervention for the individual. It can identify the individual perpetrator's level of risk and can be used as part of a presentence investigation.

■ *Treatment*

A sexual perpetrator's behavior is the product of decisions that he or she has made. It is not a spontaneous action; thus, the intervention must be a cognitive-behavioral relapse prevention program. Cognitions are thought processes that are part of all intentional behaviors. Relapse prevention is a self-control program that was originally developed in the addictions field and modified for sexual abuse perpetrators. It assists perpetrators in identifying and coping with behaviors that could lead to relapse or reoffense. Relapse prevention teaches perpetrators internal self-management skills and plans for an external supervisory component. It also provides a framework within which a variety of behavioral, cognitive, educational, and skills training approaches are taught to perpetrators to recognize and interrupt the chain of events that could lead to reoffense.

■ *Treatment Modalities*

Treatment should involve individual and group therapy and, in some cases, marital and family sessions. Group therapy has become a preferred modality of intervention because it provides an atmosphere of affirmation, confrontation, and socialization from both therapists and other perpetrators. Furthermore, group therapy interrupts two of the elements needed to maintain sexual abuse—isolation and secrecy. Individual therapy is beneficial in the beginning of treatment and as a supplement to group sessions. In cases of incest, marital and family sessions should occur when reunification is probable. Family sessions should not be provided, however, until all members of the family are entrenched in their individual treatment and the professionals believe the sessions will be of benefit rather than possibly harming any of the family members.

■ *Treatment Goals*

The focus of treatment is to assist perpetrators in asserting control over their sexually abusive behaviors. This management will need to continue throughout their life. The perpetrator must acquire motivation not to reoffend. This is assessed through his or her investment and participation in treatment and willingness to attempt new life patterns.

Taking responsibility for one's behavior is pivotal to relapse prevention. Perpetrators need to hold themselves responsible for the sexual perpetrations and thinking errors, divulge the grooming behaviors and actions of all sexual perpetrations (initial referral and others), identify their own triggers and warning signs, combat denial in its numerous forms, and demonstrate the capability to reduce and manage deviant sexual urges and fantasies. The perpetrator must also identify his or her individual cycle of offense, develop a protection plan, and share the plan with those who will act as an external control (e.g., parents and spouse). Treatment should also include development of victim empathy, the acquisition of appropriate social skills, improvement of life-style behaviors, and the development of healthy sexual expression and values.

■ Other Interventions

To complement cognitive treatment, the polygraph, plethysmograph, arousal gauges such as the Abel Screen, psychopharmacologic interventions, or all these should be used. These interventions are not used in place of treatment but, rather, as an adjunct to treatment. Furthermore, treatment programs should choose which external device will be used to monitor the perpetrator's deviant fantasies and behaviors.

The polygraph can elicit information regarding thoughts, arousals, and behaviors. There are three types of examinations: sexual history, specific issue, and monitoring. The sexual history examination focuses on the perpetrator's sexual history and his or her victimizations, perpetrations, and consensual encounters. The specific issue examination addresses specific allegations, behaviors, events, or all three. The monitoring examination is a periodic examination of the perpetrator's compliance with treatment, probation, child welfare, or all three.

The plethysmograph is an assessment of sexual arousal and provides objective data regarding sexual preferences. It can assist in monitoring changes in patterns of sexual arousal. The plethysmograph measures erection response to sexually explicit slides and audio sexual material.

The Abel Screen is a computer-driven instrument. Through self-report, the perpetrator acknowledges his or her sexual preferences to slides of various stimuli presented. This is supplemented by a comprehensive questionnaire that the perpetrator completes that addresses the sexual and paraphiliac history.

Psychopharmacologic intervention and medications can assist in the management of sexually abusive and violent behaviors. Medications such as antidepressants, antipsychotics, anticonvulsants, antianxiety agents, antiandrogens, and stimulants can be advantageous to sexual perpetrators' intervention. Such intervention should not be routinely prescribed to all perpetrators but rather used on an individual basis.

■ *Visitation*

Because child safety is a priority in perpetrator intervention, in cases of incest the sexual perpetrator should be removed from his or her residence. Removal of the perpetrator is more suitable than removal of the children. The exception to this practice is when the nonoffending parent will not protect the children. Likewise, the perpetrator, incestuous or extrafamilial, should be restricted from having access to and unsupervised visitation with any children.

Supervised visitation should be authorized only when all family members have successfully engaged in treatment and the perpetrator has demonstrated the ability to control his or her deviant thoughts, arousal, and behaviors. Contact should not be recommended unless the child's therapist has determined it to be in the best interest of the child, and the nonoffending parent's therapist can conclude that the nonoffending parent can provide appropriate supervision.

■ *Reunification*

Reunification should be determined only by the interdisciplinary team when the perpetrator and all the family members have successfully completed the intervention(s). Perpetrators are always at risk to reoffend; approximately 20% do so.

Although family preservation impacts the professionals' interventions, the child's protection should remain at the forefront of decision making. The individual perpetrator's recovery and risk should be factored heavily into the decision for reunification.

■ *Further Reading*

Association for the Treatment of Sexual Abusers. (1997). *Ethical standards and principles for the management of sexual abusers.* Beaverton, OR: Author.

English, K., Pullen, S., & Jones, L. (1997). *Managing adult sex offenders in the community—A containment approach* (National Institute of Justice Research in Brief). Washington, DC: U.S. Department of Justice.

Knopp, F. H. (1984.) *Retraining adult sex offenders: Methods and models.* Orwell, VT: Safer Society Press.

Marshall, W. L., Laws, D. R., & Barbaree, H. E. (Eds.). (1990). *Handbook of sexual assault: Issues, theories, and treatment of the offender.* New York: Plenum.

National Institute of Justice. (1997). *Child sexual molestation: Research issues.* Washington, DC: U.S. Department of Justice.

Quinsey, V. L., Lalumiere, M. L., Rice, M. E., & Harris, G. T. (1995). Predicting sexual offenses. In J. C. Campbell (Ed.), *Assessing dangerousness: Violence by sexual offenders, batterers, and child abusers.* Thousand Oaks, CA: Sage.

94

What Treatment Is Recommended to Address Physically Abusive Behavior?

■ *David J. Kolko*

S tudies of treatment or intervention in the area of child physical abuse (CPA) have generally examined alternative approaches to modifying an adult's abusive or coercive behavior (National Academy of Sciences, 1998). Most of the treatment models for CPA consider the importance of parental behavior and the reciprocal influences between parents and children. Indeed, interventions in this area often target the caregiver given the expectation that adult behavior change will result in improved child functioning and protection. The importance of parental involvement in treatment is based on studies that have identified specific parental or adult factors related to abusive behavior, such as social isolation, parental distress, and poor parenting skills or child development knowledge. Furthermore, clinical impressions and outcome studies suggest the benefits of parent-directed treatments, such as individual parent counseling and education, parent support groups, family therapy, and in-home services. These interventions may promote abilities to inhibit abusive behavior and minimize the psychological effects of abusive interactions. Of course, parent-directed methods to eliminate abusive behavior need to be supplemented with child-directed services (Kolko, 1998).

■ *Common Problems and Intervention Approaches*

Adult-directed interventions often emphasize parent training in various psychosocial skills, such as the use of contingency management procedures, nonviolent discipline, and self-management procedures together with clinical or support services (e.g., self-help groups and child development information). Parent training using cognitive-behavioral techniques has been associated with improvement in both parent (e.g., child abuse potential and depression) and child (e.g., behavior problems).

Anger

Problems with anger management have been reported in many abusive parents. To address this problem, parents can be taught anger management skills to replace hostile or negative behavior with more positive and constructive strategies. This usually involves identifying the internal and external "triggers" of anger, examining and challenging the types of distorted or exaggerated thoughts that may precipitate angry responses, teaching progressive muscle relaxation (e.g., push down on the arm of a chair for 5 seconds and then relax), and recommending alternative "coping self-statements" (e.g., "I'm in control, not my child") or other responses to enhance self-control when angry. More general stress management skills may be needed to minimize negative emotional reactions to the parent's adverse circumstances. Teaching empathy is a related method that may enhance a parent's ability to appreciate alternative perspectives regarding a problem situation. Thus, both emotional and cognitive change methods can be used to improve self-control. These skills can be taught on an individual and group basis. Training involves coaching, role plays, and subsequent performance feedback.

Impulse-Control Problems

Impulse-control problems can be addressed using anger-control procedures, but parents may also need to learn more prosocial methods for solving problems that minimize impulsive responses. Several skills may be taught in solving specific problems: Parents should be taught to (a) identify goals, (b) clearly

define the problem, (c) stop and think about the problem carefully, (d) generate alternative solutions, (e) evaluate each solution, (f) pick one solution to implement, and (g) make revisions
based on the result. Each step can be applied to deal with specific
problems identified by the parent (e.g., child defiance and aggression). Practicing with different problems on a regular basis may
help the parent develop a routine for solving problems in a
constructive, nonaggressive fashion.

Harsh or Punitive Discipline

The next target for treatment involves providing parents with
alternatives to punitive discipline. Initially, one can ask all family
members, not just the parent, to comply with a "no physical force
or discipline" contract. Specialized training in appropriate parenting techniques, such as effective discipline and child management, is commonly used to enhance parental control and use of
more appropriate discipline (Schellenbach, 1998). Such training
may teach parents how to attend to their children appropriately
while ignoring disruptive behavior, praise or reinforce their good
behavior (e.g., say something nice after the behavior), withhold
privileges (e.g., identify a problem behavior, determine what may
be withheld, warn the child before the privilege is withheld), and
administer time-outs following inappropriate behavior. An example is the removal of a child from an enjoyable activity for a brief,
specified amount of time. Once skills training has been conducted, specific home programs can be developed to target
individual child and family problems. Treatment may be facilitated if both general principles and specific techniques are taught
to help parents learn how to generalize their disciplinary skills to
new problems. Both individual and group approaches have been
determined to be effective in teaching alternative discipline skills.
Many clinical programs have parenting groups that provide
in-depth instruction in the application of specific behavior management skills, and there are many publications describing these
parenting skills in basic, friendly language.

Social Isolation and Skill Deficits

Given deficiencies or problems in social competence, it is
often important to enhance the interpersonal or communication

skills of abusive parents. For example, parents have been trained and then coached to listen to and communicate appropriately with their children, validate their experiences, and encourage their children's sociability. Assertive skills are helpful when parents' responses to stressful situations are submissive or passive or aggressive (e.g., stating one's position and making requests to initiate or stop a behavior). Such interventions have also taught appropriate steps to solve interpersonal problems, such as identifying one's goal, generating solutions, and then evaluating the positive and negative consequences of each proposed solution.

Family Dysfunction and Stress

Practitioners may determine that training in the previously discussed areas can be effectively conducted in various contexts, such as individual, parent-child, and group settings; in some instances, however, parallel child and parent treatment may be helpful. Coercive parents who need to develop more positive relationships with their children and to learn appropriate parenting techniques may benefit from "coaching" sessions that offer feedback during or after observed parent-child interactions. In addition to learning new skills, some parents may benefit from involvement in family and social support interventions that address dysfunctional family processes, such as teaching their family how to communicate positively or to strengthen extrafamilial contacts. In a recent study, parent treatment addressed their perception of the child's abuse experience, risk factors for abuse, stress management, anger control, child development, cognitive distortions and therapy, nonviolent discipline, and home programs (Kolko, 1996).

Other services may be appropriate for the entire family, such as advocacy with local agencies or services, life skills training, home management and safety, and social support interventions, some of which address problems in the parent-child relationship and the parent's attachment to the child (Schellenbach, 1998). Sometimes, general but relevant information may be helpful to the family, such as that on self-management (e.g., decision-making and observation skills), health and safety (e.g., taking medicines and home and community safety), and parent-child interaction skills (e.g., playing together). Helping parents attend to family issues may help them better promote their children's adjustment and development, which may minimize the likelihood that parents will exhibit abusive behavior.

■ Other Treatment Options and Considerations

Parental treatment or counseling may help parents control abusive behavior and support their children in coping with the effects of abuse. Effective treatment often involves teaching psychological skills that enhance social or adaptive competence and directly address parental symptoms or related psychiatric dysfunction. It is also important to recognize the potential benefits of including other family members in treatment on improving family outcomes and relationships. In general, studies of parent-directed treatments have reported beneficial outcomes on parental control or coercive behaviors, parental distress, family relations and cohesion, and child behavior. These goals may be promoted when interventions incorporate these components in the context of ongoing family work.

Regardless of the types of service provided, efforts to enhance treatment engagement and compliance may influence the likelihood of a positive treatment outcome. As such, child protection services workers are encouraged to routinely monitor the effects of treatment to understand client response and to identify clinical obstacles to improvement. Families presenting with serious parental or family dysfunction and frequent violent behavior may require referral for more intensive clinical services. Indeed, many parents who participate in treatment may still not show sufficient improvement or even a positive response to intervention. Only careful treatment planning and monitoring can maximize the likelihood that parental interventions will minimize their abusive behavior and promote the welfare of their children.

■ Further Reading

Kolko, D. J. (1996). Individual cognitive-behavioral treatment and family therapy for physically abused children and their offending parents: A comparison of clinical outcomes. *Child Maltreatment, 1,* 322-342.

Kolko, D. J. (1998). Interventions for children. In P. K. Trickett & C. J. Schellenbach (Eds.), *Violence against children in the family and the community* (pp. 213-248). Washington, DC: American Psychological Association.

National Academy of Sciences. (1998). *Violence in families: Assessing prevention and treatment programs.* Washington, DC: National Academy Press.

Schellenbach, C. (1998). Child maltreatment: A critical review of research on treatment for physically abusive parents. In P. K. Trickett & C. J. Schellenbach (Eds.), *Violence against children in the family and community* (pp. 251-268). Washington, DC: American Psychological Association.

95

What Is the Most Effective Treatment for Depression?

■ *David Corwin*

D epression is a serious psychiatric illness characterized by feelings of sadness and hopelessness that may be accompanied by poor appetite or overeating, changes in sleep, low energy or fatigue, low self-esteem, poor concentration, difficulty making decisions, and recurrent thoughts of death. As a psychiatric diagnosis, it is called dysthymic disorder in its milder form and major depressive disorder (MDD) in its more severe form. The public health importance of MDD is underscored by how life threatening it is and its commonness. As many as 15% of its sufferers die by suicide. Current lifetime prevalence of MDD among woman is estimated to be between 10% and 25% and from 5% to 12% for men. Conditions that may be confused with MDD because of shared symptoms include normal grieving, various medical conditions, and substance abuse disorders.

Recognizing depression is particularly important because treatment can dramatically decrease the suffering of depressed persons. Effective treatments include behavioral, cognitive, and interpersonal psychotherapies; antidepressant medications; and electroconvulsive treatment.

Regardless of which treatment is initially selected, studies suggest that only 45% to 55% of depressed outpatients will respond to initial treatment. Therefore, it is important that depressed patients be closely followed and not given unrealistic expectations of a certain and swift cure.

There is no single treatment that is most effective for all cases of depression. The first step toward effective treatment is a careful diagnostic evaluation that matches the patients' needs to the most appropriate available treatment. After treatment is initiated, the patient's progress should be monitored and the treatment adjusted or changed, as needed, in a timely manner. Once depression is recognized, suicide assessment and prevention are a priority. (See Chapter 23 for information on screening caregivers' dangerousness to themselves or their children.)

■ Psychotherapies

Time-Limited Psychosocial Therapy

Interpersonal (IPT), cognitive (CT), and behavioral (BT) psychotherapies have been specifically developed and studied with depressed patients. Each has demonstrated effectiveness on a level similar to that of antidepressant medication.

IPT focuses on improving a depressed person's relationships with others, and CT seeks to change negative thoughts. BT begins with an assessment of the relationship between identified problems, underdeveloped skills, and the depressive symptoms. A stepwise plan for treatment is developed, and desired behavior change is socially reinforced as the behavior is gradually shaped in the desired direction.

Psychodynamic Therapy

Psychodynamic therapy uses psychoanalytic theories and principles developed by Freud and many others. Although not as well researched as cognitive-behavioral and interpersonal therapy for depression, it is believed that some depressed patients may benefit from this approach, which focuses on unconscious conflicts, depleted self-esteem, and problems related to early life experiences with caregivers.

Abuse-Focused Therapy

Abuse-focused therapy addresses various problems, including depression and relationship difficulties, often associated with childhood abuse experiences. Like psychodynamic therapy, with which it shares an emphasis on the importance of early life experiences, abuse-focused therapy for depression has not been subjected to many controlled research studies. There are many different approaches to abuse-focused therapy, some of which incorporate cognitive-behavioral and interpersonal therapeutic techniques.

■ Biological Treatments

Antidepressant Medication

Current antidepressant medications include several different classes of drugs that act on brain messenger chemicals involved in mood regulation and response to stress. These classes of drugs are the monoamine oxidase inhibitors, tricyclic antidepressants, and the selective serotonin reuptake inhibitors, of which Prozac is the most famous and widely prescribed. There are other medications, including stimulants and anticonvulsants, that may also be useful for treating some depressions.

Electroconvulsive Therapy

Despite its negative portrayal in popular media, electroconvulsive therapy (ECT) remains an important treatment for severe depression, especially for medication-resistant or medication-intolerant patients. Technical advances, including the use of general anesthesia, muscle relaxation, oxygen administration to patients before inducing convulsions, brief pulse duration, unilateral electrode placement, and seizure monitoring, make the current ECT a safer and more acceptable treatment for severe depression than earlier ECT methods.

■ Combined Therapy

There is little evidence that one mode of treatment is markedly superior to other modes described previously for the initial treatment of depression. Combining a properly selected and skillfully conducted psychotherapy along with appropriate antidepressant medication may offer broader treatment for the many symptoms and problems associated with depression and is often the best approach for severe and chronic cases of depression.

■ Screening Questions

The following questions are derived from the Beck Depression Inventory, a well-researched instrument for measuring the presence and severity of depression. The more "yes" responses and clear descriptions of these symptoms a client gives, the more likely it is that he or she is depressed and should be referred to a mental health care provider.

- Have you been feeling sad or hopeless?
- Have you been feeling more negatively about yourself?
- Have you been crying more than usual?
- Have you recently lost interest in other people or things you used to like to do?
- Has your sleeping, appetite, or energy level changed?
- Have you had any thoughts of harming or killing yourself?

Because depression is a common, disabling, and potentially fatal illness, child protective workers who screen clients and find indicators of depression should refer these individuals to mental health care providers.

■ *Further Reading*

American Psychiatric Association. (1994). *Diagnostic and statistical manual of mental disorders* (4th ed.). Washington, DC: American Psychiatric Association.

Beck, A., Steer, R. A., & Brown, G. K. (1993). *Beck Depression Inventory II manual.* San Antonio, TX: The Psychological Corporation. (phone: 800-211-8378)

Gabbard, G. O. (1995). *Treatments of psychiatric disorders* (2nd ed.). Washington, DC: American Psychiatric Press.

96

What Interventions Are Most Effective in Addressing Domestic Violence?

■ *Ronald Zuskin*

■ *"Political" Aspects of Intervention*

The use of power in any relationship politicizes that relationship. During the past two decades, legislation has been influenced by the grassroots activism of women advocating for the protection of women from physical and sexual abuse by their intimate male partners. Feminist theorists accentuate societal tolerance and support for male violence toward women. Efforts to raise societal awareness of woman abuse has resulted in increased awareness of battering and abusiveness by women toward men, by partners in same-sex relationships, and by couples in dating relationships. Since the late 1970s, all states have implemented laws and services affording victims of domestic violence protection and support. Victims of violence usually seek treatment voluntarily, most often bringing their children for treatment with them. Because domestic violence affects children of all ages, interventions must consider their service needs. Batterers are more likely to be in treatment as a result of some form of legal involvement that requires their participation in treatment, usually for a time-limited period.

■ *Traditional Approaches to Intervention*

Cognitive and psychoeducational treatment comprise traditional approaches to intervention with family violence. Providing information about the dynamics of domestic violence, providing instruction about legal options, raising consciousness about nonviolence in relationships, and providing anger management are examples of such approaches. Multimodal treatment, which includes individual and group therapy, is used. Treatment must focus on topics germane to domestic violence. Scant research exists to definitively support specific treatment approaches. Couples' therapy is generally contraindicated because it is viewed as a potential threat to the victim of domestic violence. Recent literature emphasizes the importance of safety as the precursor for genuine therapeutic intervention. All intervention should begin with assessment (see Chapter 74, this volume). Traditional approaches to additional intervention with the adult victim (in child welfare contexts—usually the mother), the child(ren), and the batterer or abuser are as follows:

Intervening with the adult victim (usually the mother)

- Support the woman's autonomy to the fullest extent possible.
- Provide information about legal and clinical services that support safety, separation, and change.
- Address and engage family, community, and social resources.
- Understand that interventions are cumulative, and failed separations may precede a lasting one.
- Describe any apparent connections between domestic violence and its effects on children.
- Inform the mother of safety concerns regarding children and the reality of alternatives for the family.
- Offer suggestions free from judgments, especially for mothers who do not separate—there may be very good reasons why they do not.
- Refer the mother to domestic violence treatment centers, and encourage her participation in groups with other

battered women to help raise her awareness of domestic violence issues and gain insight into her situation.

Intervening with children

- Provide a referral to group counseling with children of similar age and circumstance.
- Focus treatment on labeling feelings (especially anger), building safety skills, gaining support from others, understanding the dynamics of family violence as appropriate to age level, and relief of perceived responsibility for having caused or for having to end the violence.
- Individualize assessment and treatment for symptomatic behavior, particularly provocative or aggressive behaviors, compulsive caretaking, posttraumatic stress disorder, and excessive fears or anxieties.

Intervening with batterers and abusers

- Provide immediate protection for adult victim and children, including using legal sanctions (arrest, probation, imprisonment, etc.), supports, and safety planning (ex parte).
- Modify and monitor abuses of power and control as well as physical and sexual battery.
- Assess and provide appropriate treatment for alcohol and other drug problems.
- Provide professionally led, structured, long-term group therapy with other batterers and abusers.
- Carefully monitor progress with regular reporting to appropriate authorities.
- Promote self-assessment of violent behavior, development of personal responsibility for nonviolent relating, and relapse prevention—all keys to successful outcomes.
- Refrain from showing too much caring, which is perceived as weakness and invites manipulation.
- Focus on concern for the effects of his behavior on his goals for himself, his wife, and family.

■ Implications for Child Welfare

Staff should be familiar with the indicators of domestic violence and be capable of safely conducting initial screening and assessment interviews. Batterers are likely to resist the intervention of professionals or agencies or to appear to comply on the surface. Many batterers have threatened their adult victims by telling them that child welfare intervention will lead to the placement of their children. Women need to be reassured that family preservation is a guiding principle for child welfare service delivery. Child welfare staff need to recognize that their intervention, especially pressure on the woman to separate, may increase the risk of violence to the adult victim and the children to dangerous, even lethal, levels. If the mother elects to remain with a man who abuses her, this may be a realistic recognition of the dangers that separation would pose for her and her child(ren). This should not automatically be viewed as inherently neglectful on her part. The family unit to be considered for preservation is the mother with her children. In situations in which the batterer expresses remorse, accepts full responsibility for his behavior, has worked in therapy toward change and relapse prevention, and has demonstrated a commitment to nonviolence in relating, it may be possible to consider preservation or reunification of the entire family unit. It is critical to partner with domestic violence professionals and agencies in the community as soon as domestic violence has been identified.

■ Further Reading

Dutton, D. G. (1998). *The abusive personality: Violence and control in intimate relatioships.* New York: Guilford.

Jaffee, P. G., Wolfe, D. A., & Wilson, S. K. (1990). *Children of battered women.* Newbury Park, CA: Sage.

The link between child abuse and domestic violence. The role of depression and alcohol. Treatment outcomes for spouses who batter. (1997, Spring). *Virginia Child Protection Newsletter, 50,* 1-14.

Walker, L. E. A. (1994). *Abused women and survivor therapy.* Washington, DC: American Psychological Association.

Zuskin, R. (1995). *Domestic violence and child maltreatment.* Baltimore: Univesity of Maryland School of Social Work.

97

What Are the Treatment Options for Parents With Alcohol or Other Drug Problems?

■ *Ronald Rogers and Chandler Scott McMillin*

A ddiction treatment has four main goals:

1. To educate the addict or alcoholic about the nature and dynamics of addiction: This replaces the addict's myths and misconceptions about addiction with accurate information.
2. To encourage self-diagnosis as an addicted person: Once the addict views him- or herself as sick and in need of treatment, motivation and compliance increase.
3. To involve the addict in an ongoing program of treatment and self-help: Addiction is chronic and requires continued supervision and relapse prevention.
4. To encourage the recovering addict to assume personal responsibility for his or her recovery: Addicts must renounce their long-standing practice of blaming outside forces or circumstances for their drug use.

Treatment modalities for addictions include the following:

> *Detoxification* involves medical care during the period of acute withdrawal. Depending on the severity of withdrawal, detoxification may occur in a hospital, in a community clinic or residential setting, or on an outpatient basis under a physician's supervision. Detoxification may be a short-term process (e.g., for alcohol) or an extended one (e.g., for methadone).
>
> *Inpatient rehabilitation:* Once the staple of addiction treatment, extended inpatient rehabilitation stays have been dramatically reduced by managed care. Currently, such stays are ordinarily confined to cases with complicating factors, such as comorbid severe psychiatric disorders.
>
> *Intensive outpatient* involves structured, multiple-hour therapy sessions, usually several evenings per week, for a month or longer.
>
> *Partial hospitalization or day treatment* are alternatives to inpatient rehabilitation that require daily attendance for a variety of therapeutic activities until the parent is stable enough to enter outpatient counseling.
>
> *Outpatient counseling* involves ongoing treatment, usually weekly, for an hour or more.
>
> *Long-term residential programs* are for those requiring continued structure and supervision to maintain recovery.

Treatment modalities for addictions include medical care, psychoeducation, individual counseling, addictions case management, group therapy, discharge planning, family education, relapse prevention education, and exposure to self-help fellowships. Most addiction clinicians prefer a cognitive-behavioral approach based on the premise that addiction is a chronic and progressive disorder requiring prompt intervention and ongoing treatment.

■ The Double-Abuse Group

Addicted caregivers present additional challenges to the child protection professional. Most addiction treatment programs do not adequately address the complex nature of child maltreatment. Likewise, most groups oriented to child maltreatment are unprepared to effectively address chronic addictive behavior. As a result, the addicted caregiver "falls through the cracks" in both systems.

To avoid this problem, we recommend "double-abuse groups," in which the members are selected for their involvement in child maltreatment and drug or alcohol abuse and the leader is skilled in the treatment of both. This makes the group homogeneous on two levels, promoting honest self-disclosure and support and positive bonding regarding the larger task of double recovery.

Our double-abuse groups meet once weekly for 2 hours during a 16-week period. Client defenses are remarkably similar for both disorders. Many begin in severe denial of one or both problems. Other common defenses include the following:

- Rationalization: "I was under stress" (which excuses my drug use/neglect of my child).
- Externalizing: "I wouldn't have slapped the child/gotten loaded on drugs if my wife hadn't made me so angry."
- Minimizing: "My drug use/child abuse wasn't as bad as they said."
- Undoing: "No matter what I do, I always make it up to the child later."

The group setting permits the leader and the other members to isolate and confront these defenses effectively.

Although outcome studies are incomplete, anecdotal reports from the first double-abuse group have been promising. A year after completion, there were no reported cases of additional child maltreatment, and 80% of the parents appeared to be in stable recovery from addiction.

■ *Further Reading*

Rogers, R. L., & McMillin, C. S. (1992). *Freeing someone you love from alcohol and other drugs.* New York: The Body Press/Perigee.

Zuskin, R., & DePanfilis, D. (1995). Working with CPS families with alcohol and other drug problems. *APSAC Advisor, 8*(1), 7-12.

Part VII

INTERVENTION

Section C:
Emphasis on the Family

98

What Do I Need to Know About Family Therapy?

■ *Geoffrey Greif*

Family therapy is a way of working with people that views the interactions among family members as contributing to and maintaining individual and family dysfunction. Child maltreatment is a sign of family dysfunction. In part, maltreatment may occur because family members have been unable to set proper boundaries between themselves, negotiate the handling of new developmental stages, or cope with external demands (loss of job, crowded living conditions, etc.). The treatment of choice for child maltreatment may be family therapy. Family therapy, based on a systems approach, considers the child and the other family members as being linked, with each family member's behavior affecting everyone else's. Within this context, assessment of the whole family is crucial in understanding the experiences of the child. Also important, interventions must be designed that include the whole family.

Family therapy is often more thorough than individual therapy because the assessment process includes more people. It can be carried out more quickly than individual therapy because more people are involved in seeking a solution to the family problems. Finally, it is often more effective because interventions affect more people.

■ *Treatment*

Once a decision is made about which family members to include in treatment (it may not be possible to include everyone due to scheduling conflicts, refusal to come for treatment, or the deleterious influence that a family member may have on the family), the following approaches may be attempted:

> *Positive reinforcement:* The therapist actively reinforces the behaviors that are appropriate to the needs of the family; through this process, self-esteem is built.
>
> *Insight:* Family members are helped to understand their own behavior and how this behavior has led to difficulties in the family.
>
> *Parent education:* The family learns both alternative methods of interacting and appropriate developmental expectations for children.
>
> *Appropriate boundaries:* The therapist emphasizes that when parents and children are overly close or overly distant, problems develop.
>
> *Reframe:* The family is taught a new way of thinking about their situation that can lead to other options for behavior. Families often start treatment with a fixed view of themselves and benefit when this view is changed.
>
> *The therapeutic relationship:* The therapist connects with the family. No intervention will be successful unless the professional has established a working relationship with the family members.

Family therapy in cases of abuse can be a powerful method of assessment and treatment. It is strongly recommended when family members are willing to work together to solve the problem and are able to discuss past mistakes. It is not always appropriate, however. If a child is afraid of a parent or if there is a high level of secrecy or denial in the family, family therapy can be counterproductive. Individual or group therapy are recommended in such cases.

99

How Can I Support Biological Families After a Child Has Been Removed From Their Care?

■ *Anthony N. Maluccio, Robin Warsh,*
and Barbara A. Pine

Working with the biological families of children placed in foster care is becoming more complex because child abuse and neglect of children by their parents have increased dramatically due to societal problems such as unemployment, poverty, family violence, drug abuse, alcoholism, and homelessness. As the challenge of helping children in foster care and their families has thus intensified, there is throughout the country evidence of creative and potentially effective efforts by social workers to support biological families. This chapter reviews the key components of these programs.

■ *Focus on the Family*

The first and foremost component in service delivery is a family-centered orientation—that is, considering the birth family as the central unit or focus of attention. Such an orientation involves in particular the following:

- Placing the child in a foster home or residential setting that is close to the family—geographically and culturally and racially
- Making case decisions that help strengthen parent-child relationships and maximize the potential for eventual reunification of the child with his or her family
- Maintaining and supporting ongoing and regular contacts between the child and the parents and other members of the immediate family as well as the extended kinship network
- Helping the children to understand the events that led to placement and to reestablish a relationship that better meets their needs for safety and nurturance
- Supporting the parents in their efforts to cope with their own life challenges and enhance their own functioning

■ *Mobilizing Parental Motivation*

When faced with separation from their children and the threat of losing their parental rights, many parents can be helped to become motivated to work on their problems and accomplish reunification with their children. Strategies that have been found to be effective in this connection include the following:

- Identifying and building on the parents' concern for and attachment to the child
- Clarifying for parents the real threat of termination of parental rights
- Facilitating the family's ongoing involvement with the child through a range of creative means
- Providing supports to the parents as human beings who are entitled to help in their own right
- Using the child's placement as a therapeutic tool to promote changes in the child and family and to maintain and enhance their sense of connectedness with each other
- Showing confidence in the parents' potential to grow and encouraging them to believe in themselves and their strengths and potentialities

- Removing obstacles that interfere with parents' coping and adaptive strivings

■ *Forming a Partnership With Parents*

The family-centered focus and the emphasis on mobilizing parental motivation lead to the importance of forming a partnership among biological parents and other family members, foster parents or other caregivers, and social workers and other professionals. In particular, foster care services should involve parents and other family members as partners in the helping process as much as possible.

Although the involvement of parents is widely accepted in theory, it is difficult to implement in practice because of problems and challenges presented by parents, societal and professional bias against parents who are accused of child abuse and neglect, and organizational and service impediments such as limited funding. Guidelines for forming and sustaining an effective partnership with parents include:

- Shifting from a view of parents as being inadequate or carriers of pathology to a belief that many of them can change and grow if provided with adequate attention and help
- Viewing parents, as much as possible, as colleagues or partners in the change process
- Using tools such as the contract or service agreement to clarify the respective roles of parents and practitioners and make joint decisions about case planning and goal formulation
- Regarding foster parents and child care personnel as partners in the provision of service, as members of the service team, and as resources for parents through such means as role modeling, serving as parent aides, or providing respite care for the children

■ *Providing Comprehensive Services and Supports*

Given the multiple and complex needs of families brought to the attention of child welfare workers, another major component of service delivery is providing a comprehensive range of supports and services with respect to their basic life conditions and needs. Pertinent principles in this regard include:

- Combining "soft" services, such as counseling, with "hard" services, such as income assistance and day care
- Providing informal supports, such as parent aides, volunteers, and recreational opportunities, for parents and children
- Using parent training and other educational opportunities to help parents become more competent
- Encouraging parents to become involved in self-help groups such as Parents Anonymous, which can enhance the parents' self-esteem and parenting skills
- Supporting the parents' involvement in advocacy and social action on their behalf

■ Collaborating With Service Providers

Helping parents and children involved in foster care requires the services of several systems, especially income maintenance, law and juvenile justice, health and mental health, and education. There are successful programs in child welfare that regularly convene interagency, interdisciplinary teams for training, goal planning, and service implementation. These programs demonstrate principles such as the following:

- Facilitating coordination of services through such means as appointing a case manager
- Clarifying and delegating roles and functions of team members on behalf of each family
- Enhancing the parents' skills in dealing with representatives of diverse agencies and systems
- Evaluating and revising planning in each case through periodic meetings or consultation
- Selecting and implementing a safe, permanent plan for the child

■ *Assessing Readiness for Reunification*

In regard to implementation of a permanent plan, practitioners face the challenge of determining whether and when the child and family are ready to be reunited. Unless otherwise indicated, family reunification is regarded as the most desirable choice of permanent plan in most cases. In assessing the advisability of reunification in a particular case, practitioners and family members need to consider many critical questions, including the following:

- Have the conditions that originally led to the child's placement been satisfactorily resolved?
- Do the quality and outcome of parent-child visiting indicate readiness for reunification?
- Can the child's safety be ensured while also respecting family integrity and autonomy?
- Can the risk of returning a child to the family be balanced with the risk inherent in prolonging the child's stay in foster care?
- Can supports be put in place through the extended family or community or both to maintain the reunification?

■ *Case Example*

The following case example illustrates the principles and strategies presented in this chapter:

> Mr. Franklin's physical abuse of his wife, witnessed 3 years ago by his then 5-year-old son, Andy, resulted in a restraining order prohibiting contact between the parents. The father's visits with Andy during the next 2 years were sporadic and often unwelcomed by the boy. The mother died suddenly 1 year ago, and guardianship was given to the maternal aunt, whose rage at the father reinforced Andy's negative image of him. Following the mother's death, Mr. Franklin expressed a renewed commitment to become a part of his son's life. Andy, however, refused to see his father and would tell all who

would listen that he never wanted to see him again. Mr. Franklin then contacted a social worker for help in reuniting with his son.

Following interviews with all parties, the social worker came to view the boy's rage at his father as a wish for some form of attachment to him. She worked with the father to help him write a series of letters to Andy in which, over time, he claimed responsibility for his past actions, apologized and asked for his son's forgiveness, and expressed his love for Andy and his wish to reconnect with him. The social worker sat with Andy during the reading of each letter to help him process his feelings and clarify issues. After several months, Andy's attitude began to soften, and he asked his father, through the social worker, to address specific topics in future letters.

At the same time, the social worker met with the aunt to enhance her capacity to help Andy act on his feelings of interest in his father. In addition, the social worker contacted Mr. Franklin's mother, who had not seen Andy since the restraining order had originally been issued, and arranged for visits to begin between Andy and his grandmother.

Through the process of letter writing, Mr. Franklin came to understand how much he had frightened Andy with his fits of temper, and he was helped by the social worker to enroll in an anger management course. Initially, it was difficult for Mr. Franklin to see the extent to which his anger alienated his son; bolstered by the social worker's genuine efforts to help him reconnect with Andy, however, he came to see her as a partner and ally and began to address his own rage.

After nearly 1 year of work, Mr. Franklin and Andy have begun weekly supervised visits, which the aunt occasionally attends. This provides the social worker with the opportunity to continue to forge an alliance between these two important adults in Andy's life. Plans are under way to extend visits to full days, with the eventual goal of reunification.

■ Conclusion

To assist children and their biological families effectively, it is urgent to acknowledge their multiple and diverse needs and provide comprehensive as well as intensive services prior to, during, and following the child's placement in foster care. Most important, foster parents, practitioners, administrators, and other community representatives must collaborate so as to regard foster care placement as a part of the overall service rather than as the service—as a tool rather than as an end in itself.

■ *Further Reading*

Maluccio, A. N., Abramczyk, L. W., & Thomlison, B. (1996). Family reunification in out-of-home care: Research perspectives. *Children and Youth Services Review, 18*(4/5), 287-305.

Maluccio, A. N., Warsh, R., & Pine, B. A. (1993). Family reunification: An overview. In B. A. Pine, R. Warsh, & A. N. Maluccio (Eds.), *Together again—Family reunification in foster care* (pp. 3-19). Washington, DC: Child Welfare League of America.

Warsh, R., Maluccio, A. N., & Pine, B. A. (1994). *Teaching family reunification: A sourcebook.* Washington, DC: Child Welfare League of America.

100

How Do I Facilitate Visits Between Foster Children and Their Biological Families That Support the Goals and Objectives of Intervention?

■ *Caroline L. Burry*

The core belief underlying the importance of visitation is that consistency and high frequency of visits are predictive of successful reunification. The following are useful strategies for facilitating visitation:

- Prepare for visits: Both foster and birth parents need to know that visiting is stressful, and that children may act out behaviorally as a result of anger, grief, or other feelings. In addition, birth parents may need concrete assistance in making arrangements to visit. It is extremely difficult for children when their birth parents do not attend a scheduled visit. Children also need clarification about the "rules" for visits so that their expectations are realistic. For instance, children should be told the location and duration of visits.

- Use visits as part of ongoing assessment: Use visits to assess the quality of parent-child interaction, communication patterns, roles, rules, strengths, concerns, and overall progress. For instance, parents can plan ahead to use discipline rather than corporal punishment during the next visit and then can rate themselves on their success with this objective.

- Use visits to maintain and increase attachment: Birth parents should be encouraged to meet their children's emotional and physical needs during visitation because these activities enhance attachment.

- Use visits to help parents and children deal with their feelings: Often, it is helpful to end visits with a "review" of both birth parents' and children's feelings about the visit and progress toward reunification. Also, it may be helpful to use tools, such as life books, pictures, and videos taken during visits, to talk about feelings.

- Use visits to help birth parents practice new skills in a supportive environment: Although visitation is not the same as living together, it is important to set up visitation that, to the extent possible, approximates "real-life" parenting. For instance, birth parents could shop with their children for school supplies to practice both meeting needs and limit setting.

- Use visits to identify and reduce fantasies about reunification: Clarifying goals and objectives with birth parents and children together will help parents accept their responsibilities. Children often blame themselves for being in care and, particularly when they are younger, use magical thinking in trying to understand reunification. Like their birth parents, children will benefit from clear statements of goals and objectives in behavioral terms.

- Following visits, process the outcomes: It is important to process visits with foster parents and birth parents. For instance, after discussing a visit, you may decide to accelerate or decelerate the pace of visits, change the duration or location of visits, and so on. Also, in these discussions the foster parents and birth parents can work together to deal with challenging behaviors that the children may exhibit during or after visitation.

■ *Further Reading*

Fahlberg, V. (1991). *A child's journey through placement.* Indianapolis, IN: Perspectives Press.

101

How Do I Build Families'
Financial Management Skills?

■ *Richard Bolan*

The following is an approach to maximize emergency funding resources and build families' financial management skills:

Self-assess: To adequately support families to develop and use financial management skills, the worker must first develop empathy for the family in crisis. This involves examining his or her own feelings, attitudes, and experiences about financial crises. This is the first step to "tune in" to what the client is experiencing so that the worker may successfully engage the family to develop solutions (see Chapter 8, this volume). Regarding financial crises, families may try to deny or minimize their situations because of embarrassment. Workers can be more successful if clients perceive that they display a nonjudgmental attitude. Being self-aware is an important ingredient in this process.

Provide emotional support: Family emotional issues of concern parallel task performance and should be addressed first. Stabilization of family emotions throughout intervention should be monitored carefully and motivation to change reinforced at every opportunity (see Chapter 68, this volume).

Determine what the family wants to do to address the immediate crisis: Change cannot be forced on a family. Family-generated solutions to financial management concerns should be elicited, family strengths engaged, and intervention leveraged to resolve financial crises. Self-direction, planning, and resolution of ambivalence to change by family caregivers promotes change. Identification of partial solutions and exceptions to crisis development will assist the worker and family to engage in a solution-focused planning and intervention process. For example, what is the family's plan to address the crisis? How do the caregiver and family want to proceed? How has the caregiver resolved similar crises in the past? What partial successes can be identified? When a crisis did not occur in the past, what strategies did the caregiver and family use? What family strengths can be identified and used to meet the crisis? Who can support and assist the caregiver in the kinship and neighborhood network?

Use emergency funding resources to address immediate crisis needs: Crisis intervention skills and flexible funds are needed to calm family emotions, codirect family response to crisis, and provide immediate emergency resources. The following are questions to consider: Does your agency have an emergency resource directory? Does the directory include churches, emergency food, and shelter resources; specialty resources for new baby needs; utility resources; and cash? Have all family and extended family resources been considered by the caregiver? Are petty cash or flexible funds available?

Strengthen family motivation: Once the immediate crisis has been addressed, the focus of attention turns to strengthening family motivation for change, developing family strengths, involving family and extended family resources, and creating with family involvement an action plan to learning financial management skills and prevent recurring financial crisis. It is also important to identify barriers to success. For example, are monies being spent on drugs or alcohol? Are family members or friends taking advantage of the family when they know it is "check day"? Are dynamics associated with domestic violence presenting financial constraints because one adult "controls" the spending decisions? Are there too many persons residing in a household without sufficient financial resources to support everyone?

Develop family crisis recognition and response skills: Family crisis recognition and response skills can be developed by identifying family values and goals and by assisting the family in recognizing signs and patterning of crises. Use of crisis and value cards clarifies family needs and patterns of response. A written response action plan can be developed to detail steps to be taken to avert crisis and enlist key support.

Teach financial management and budget skills: A money planner and budget sheets can be used to identify family income, needs, undisclosed expenditures, and family priorities. The worker should teach skills in small steps and demonstrate and rehearse skills with the caregiver or family member. Repeated skill building of budget management skills, with positive reinforcement of family efforts, is required. Attention to family emotional issues and sensitivity to gender and cultural differences among families regarding money management are critical. Sample areas to explore include the following: How is money currently spent? What are the family's priorities? What income is available to the family or in need of development?

Troubleshoot the budget with the family: By troubleshooting the budget with the family, financial skills can be sharpened and additional areas of need and family strength can be developed. Once the caregiver has learned budgeting skills, help the caregiver and family to troubleshoot the budget. What types of expenses typically occur in this family that explode the budget? Holiday gifts? Kin or relationship needs? Impulse purchases? Explore with the caregiver how crises have occurred and what safeguards can be built into the budget. Provide examples of how to use weekly accounting to manage resources. Consider whether there is a need for a part-time job to increase income or whether there are ways that expenses can be reduced.

Link to additional helping resources: Linkage to a helping resource is not the same as referral. Connection of the family to family, neighborhood, and service helping resources will require assessment of the family's readiness to receive such resources and of barriers that may prevent the family linkage and follow-up to ensure that linkage has been achieved and help received by the family. What additional helping resources may this family require? How close are these resources located to the neighborhood in which the family lives? What transportation arrangements may be needed? What efforts will be needed to ensure that linkage occurs and the family receives the resources it may need to prevent an additional crisis?

Evaluate outcomes: Ask the family how they will know when their financial management skills have improved and financial stability has been obtained. As the intervention concludes, what objective outcomes can be documented? Is this because there has been no financial crisis in 2 months or because the caregiver was able to find emergency resources on his or her own? What evidence is there that the family has learned, and is practicing, financial management and self-sufficiency skills?

■ Summary

The goals in child protection practice are to support and strengthen the family, increase family resilience, ensure children's safety, and reduce the risk of out-of-home placement. To maximize emergency funding resources and build families' financial management skills, we need to work with the family to identify strengths and needs, use these strengths to formulate with the family measurable goals, develop and implement a written action plan, teach financial management skills, link to additional helping resources, and document objective outcomes achieved.

102

How Can I Best Manage the Intervention Process When Multiple Service Providers Are Involved?

■ *Charles Wilson*

For most maltreatment cases, no single agency, including the child protection agency, can meet the full range of needs of the family and child. Child protection workers play a vital role in assessing needs, finding others who can assist in building on family strengths and addressing areas of concern, and in building coalitions of helping professionals and others. These key players in the helping system may be drawn from the formal helping system of professionals, such as therapists, parenting aides, teaching homemakers, teachers, physicians, and substance abuse or domestic violence counselors, and from the natural informal helping network of family members, church members, neighbors, and others. The worker can craft a mix of interveners who, when working in concert, can have a powerful influence on family behavior. Such power, however, requires coordination. Without coordination, the mix of service providers can work at cross-purposes and even interfere with progress.

To best manage an intervention process, which involves a variety of service providers and informal helpers, the worker must determine in what circumstances information can be shared and with whom. Very conservative interpretations of confidentiality make such coordination difficult. Using agency policy and state law, the worker should determine the best way to achieve coordination. This typically involves the use of informed consent of the primary caregivers (and child, if old enough) and facilitation of planning meetings involving all involved parties.

The case plan should articulate who is involved in the service delivery process (see Chapters 78 through 83, this volume), and information from all systems (social service, education, mental health, medical, law enforcement, etc.) should be gathered and used in the case planning process. A very successful model of securing the input and perspective of all service providers and for improving coordination is to hold periodic case planning meetings to which all interested parties are invited and encouraged to attend.

■ The Case Planning Meeting

The meeting should be held at a time and place of greatest convenience to the family and key service providers. To this meeting, the family should be invited, along with all social service providers, therapists and counselors, foster parents or residential service providers, teachers for all the children, and any other formal or informal service providers. With all present, the worker can lead a frank discussion of the issues and what actions each person should take to implement the plan for safety and long-term success for the family or child or both. Participants should be encouraged to speak honestly with the client family while being respectful and ensuring that positives are also noted with any areas of concern. Such meetings must be followed up by the worker with personal contacts to test progress and to determine successes to celebrate with the family, risks that signal danger for the child or the need for revisions in the case plan, or both. Major changes in direction should be accompanied by a reconvening of the case planning team and a revised plan.

In between such meetings and when a meeting is not feasible, the caseworker must take other steps to ensure coordination. This can take the form of personal contact between the caseworker and each professional or layperson playing a planned role in the service delivery plan. Few services can be initiated and then ignored. Most plans require consistent monitoring and adjustment (see Chapter 106, this volume). The caseworker must determine with the client how each provider fits into the overall plan. These roles must be communicated, both verbally and in writing, to each service provider, and the caseworker must secure feedback from each one to ensure the service provision is proceeding as planned. Among the issues that must be evaluated on an on-going basis are progress toward desired outcomes, the cooperation of the parties, the impact the intervention on the parties, the frequency of contact, and any interaction (direct or otherwise) between the service provider and other service providers (formal or informal). On the basis of the totality of the information received from the client and service providers, the caseworker, working with the client, can adjust the plan and communicate the revised roles to the clients and each service provider.

103

What Is "Family to Family," and How Does It Support Permanency for Children?

■ *Lorelei Schaffhausen*

Responding to escalating demand and dwindling resources, in 1992 the Annie E. Casey Foundation began an initiative called "Family to Family" to improve outcomes for children and families served by the child welfare system. More than a foster care program, Family to Family provides integrated child welfare services that are family focused, child centered, and neighborhood based. While ensuring the safety of children, it focuses our work on the strengths of whole families and communities.

The following are the philosophies of Family to Family:

- Case managers are family workers, not just child workers. Engage the parents of children in foster care in the process. All families have strengths you can build on.
- Foster parents are coparents, mentors, and team members. With your support, foster parents work closely with you and the birth parent(s) in achieving permanency for the child.

- Children in out-of-home care remain in their own community. When foster care is needed, place the child with a family in his or her own community.

The following are successful Family to Family practices:

- Early intervention: If safety can be ensured, divert placement. If placement occurs, begin working with the family immediately. The crisis of placement is the opportunity for change.
- Family team meetings: Bring everyone together as soon and as often as possible to plan for what will happen. The team includes the case manager, foster parent, birth parent, extended family, the child when appropriate, and anyone else involved in the case.
- Concurrent permanency planning: Clearly delineate what needs to occur for a family to be reunited while simultaneously discussing and planning for other options (see Chapter 80, this volume).
- Aftercare involvement of the foster parents: Continued involvement by the foster parents with the child and birth family helps to stabilize reunification.

■ *Family to Family Supports Permanency for Children*

Applying the previously discussed practices reduces the number of children coming into care, achieves permanency earlier, provides a more stable pool of foster families, and decreases worker turnover. Whether your agency has formally adopted this model or not, you and the members of your team will benefit if you include the following philosophies and practices in your work:

Children

- Have reduced stress because they are not torn between two families
- Experience fewer losses (school placement, familiar surroundings, and familiar relationships)

Birth parents

- Are more involved in their child's life
- Experience less stress and anxiety by knowing, and working with, the foster parents

Foster parents

- Are more satisfied with their role when treated as professional members of the team
- Have a positive relationship with the birth parent(s) that reinforces the goal of reunification and makes it easier to let the child go home
- Report less "acting out" by the child because there is less conflict about having positive feelings for the two families

Caseworkers

- Report that shared responsibility for work and collegial relationships with foster parents reduce stress
- Report higher morale and job satisfaction

■ *Further Reading*

Welty, K. (1997). *A framework for foster care reform: Policy and practice to shorten children's stays.* St. Paul, MN: North American Council on Adoptable Children.

104

Foster and Kinship Caregivers

What Are Their Support and Intervention Needs?

■ *Maria Scannapieco*

oster and kinship caregivers are two of the most important resources in the child welfare system repository for caring for children. Individuals and families that provide foster and kinship care are essentially contributing the same services to child welfare agencies, but child welfare agencies do not provide the same resources to kinship and foster families. Kinship care homes receive less money and fewer services, and monitoring of the homes is less frequent. Child welfare programs need to provide services that are more equitable across both types of out-of-home care. Often, child welfare workers believe that kinship care families have fewer needs, but this is not supported by research. The needs of foster and kinship providers may be different, but the needs of the children in care are often similar.

In this chapter, I divide support and intervention for foster and kinship families into four categories of needs: financial, services, social support, and educational. When appropriate, a distinction is made between foster and kinship families and the different needs that each possess.

■ *Support and Intervention Needs*

Financial

Foster and kinship families may receive funding from different sources. Foster families are required to be licensed and therefore receive funding through foster care funding streams. Kinship families may or may not be licensed. If they are not licensed, they receive funding through the Personal Responsibility and Work Opportunity Reconciliation Act of 1996.

Per diem rates vary from state to state for foster care children. Foster and kinship families receiving foster care payments are allocated a designated amount per child. Families may receive more money per child if the child has special needs (e.g., HIV positive status). Kinship families that are not eligible for foster care payments may receive welfare benefits for the child. In addition, if the kinship caregiver is caring for a brother or sister or cousin in the same family, the caregiver may receive an incremental increase (not the full payment that they would receive in foster care) in her or his welfare payment based on the standard welfare increases.

Clothing

Foster and kinship caregivers need assistance in providing clothes for children, the cost of which cannot be covered totally with the per diem received by the families. Special occasions, such as proms or sporting activities, may require extra clothes. It is important that the child welfare worker assist the family in locating additional clothing resources.

Transportation

As in any family, children require transportation to and from sporting activities, school events, doctors' offices, and so on, and sometimes this requires the worker to locate transportation or assist in the transport of children. Unlike other children, foster and kinship children may have additional transportation needs that sometimes put strain on the family. Many children are in therapy or need to have visits with parents and siblings. To reduce stress on the foster and kinship families, workers should assist families in identifying transportation resources.

Services

Foster and kinship families require equal but in some circumstances different services. Compared to foster families, kinship families are poorer, usually older, single parent, and less educated. In assessing needs in kinship families, the worker has to examine the following triad: caregiver, parent, and child. Children placed in foster and kinship families often require the same services because the reasons for entering into care are comparable.

Case Management

After establishing a collaborative intervention plan with the family, the child welfare worker will have to manage and oversee the progress in meeting the objectives and goals of the permanency treatment plan. Kinship families, even more than foster families, may demand the worker to more actively act as an advocate and broker of services. Other kinship families may find that any intervention is intrusive because they view the child placed in their home as "their kin" and may believe they know what is best for the child. It is a balancing act that the worker needs to negotiate with the family, with the child's needs in mind.

The child welfare worker should also help the foster and kinship families negotiate the court system. Often, families and children are required to be present in court. It is helpful for the worker to inform the foster and kinship family about the court process and what to expect (e.g., delays).

Mental Health

Foster and kinship children come into care for similar reasons and need mental health services at similar rates. On the basis of a thorough assessment, the worker identifies what mental health resources are most appropriate for the child and assists the foster or kinship family in obtaining the service. In addition, in the case of kinship families, the caregiver may need mental health services. Often, the caregiver may be struggling with the reality of his or her child's drug addiction or status of being HIV positive.

Medical Care

Many children enter care due to neglect, and as a result they often have not received routine medical care (see Chapter 26, this volume). All children need to be evaluated to ascertain their current medical status. Families will then need support in following through on medical recommendations. Often, children enter care with special medical needs (e.g., HIV positive or other sexually transmitted disease, lice, and physical or sexual abuse injury that require immediate attention). The ultimate responsibility of the child welfare worker is to ensure that the child has received all required medical treatment.

Dental Care

The caregiver sometimes neglects dental care. Children require routine dental checkups (see Chapter 60, this volume). Because children in foster and kinship care are insured by Medicaid, families may need assistance in identifying a dentist who accepts this type of insurance. A doctor who accepts Medicaid is frequently not the family's current dental care provider and may be located further away. The worker needs to keep this in mind when negotiating with families to provide this care.

Social Support

Social support interventions provide for many of the needs that foster and kinship families present. The worker is charged with helping families assess challenges in their social network and to make the appropriate connections in their communities to address them.

Formal Social Support

The worker may be one of the most important formal social supports on which the foster or kinship family must rely. Support that the child welfare worker provides to families is fundamental.

Foster and kinship families may be very involved in their community support systems (e.g., family support services, churches, schools, and community centers); however, if they are not, or if a child presents a need not met by a current support system, the worker can encourage families to become connected with formal support systems. Social support can reduce stress, address concrete and emotional needs, and provide information to families.

Another form of formal social support that the worker may aid in providing is respite care. Respite care may be the deciding factor for families when considering taking a special needs child. It provides the needed break from what is often a very stressful situation.

Informal Social Support

Informal social supports provide emotional and tangible support to foster and kinship families. It is important for the worker to encourage families to build informal social support systems such as family, friends, and coworkers. Particularly in kinship families, informal social supports are significant. Considering that the majority of children in kinship care are from families of color and that culturally these families rely on extended family for support, the worker should support and acknowledge this as a valuable resource in kinship homes. For example, a 70-year-old grandmother may need to depend on an aunt or uncle to provide some of the care for her grandchildren.

Educational Needs

Educational planning for children is a key service that foster and kinship families require. Many children in care are developmentally delayed and require special education. The system is overwhelming at times and one that families often want aid in negotiating. The worker may need to advocate for the child to get the needed resources to meet his or her educational needs.

Individual Educational Plan

This is a formal process of assessment of the child's educational needs. The worker and the caregiver may be required to attend the meeting. The family may need assistance to understand the individual educational plan process and what they can demand from the educational institution.

Special Services

Some children will need to be placed in a special education classroom or need speech or hearing classes. The worker may need to help families demand assistance in understanding and accessing these services.

Behavioral problems of the child may also require special services and cause additional stress on the foster and kinship families. It is important that the worker facilitates a program that will help reduce the child's behavior (e.g., behavior modification program).

Training

Although in many states training is mandated for foster and kinship caregivers, the worker may want to identify areas of training needs for the families and try to find resources that meet these needs. Videos and books can often serve as part of mandated training (e.g., how to manage a particular situation). It is very supportive if the worker can aid in obtaining training resources, thus contributing to the overall well-being and functioning of the family.

■ *Further Reading*

DePanfilis, D. (1996). Social isolation of neglectful families: A review of social support assessment and intervention models. *Child Maltreatment, 1,* 37-52.

105

What Are the Unique Roles of Religious Institutions in Supporting and Strengthening Families?

■ *Lorine L. Cummings*

In the initial phase of the investigation or assessment of families, practitioners have to be aware of all potential resources available to assist families. Members of the clergy or those in spiritual leadership are often overlooked as viable supports to families. Knowing and discussing a family's religious or spiritual context or both may assist practitioners in understanding the attitudes, values, and the explicit and implicit messages that may inform a family's belief system with regard to physical punishment as a method of discipline.

Practitioners, spiritual leaders, and the client must address issues of confidentiality. If the client has identified their pastor, minister, rabbi, or priest as someone to whom information can be released, then by all means that person should be used as a resource. In the absence of formal consent, the child protective service law does allow relevant parties to meet as a multidisciplinary team during the investigation. Spiritual leaders can be invited to attend the multidisciplinary team in support of their parishioner; without a formal team, however, the practitioner needs written consent from the child's parent or guardian. Religious leaders are also bound by laws of confidentiality and cannot disclose information shared in a pastoral counseling session without written consent from the parishioner. Pastoral counseling sessions are bound by the same ethical standard as those of priest confessionals. Practitioners can request a meeting between the client and spiritual leader in which the client decides the extent of disclosure.

Many clients do not disclose the origins of their feelings regarding disciplining their children with corporal punishment. These feelings are often based on a strong religious value base or their belief that the government does not have the right to tell them how to discipline their children. Other clients may not disclose their religious affiliation because they do not want to be viewed negatively by their spiritual leaders or community.

Understanding a family's religious faith can assist the practitioner in assessing whether there is spiritual sanction for the use of corporal punishment to change behavior in children. Many clients use their religious or spiritual values as a rationale or basis for using physical discipline to punish their children. The belief for some that "sparing the rod spoils the child" is often used to justify the physical abuse of children. In the traditional Christian context, some parents may view their child's behavior as "demonic" or "satanic"—that is, the child is "full of the devil," which allows the parent to literally attempt to "beat the hell" out of the youngster. These families rarely view their child's behavior as a manifestation of family dysfunction.

Many spiritual and religious belief systems view confession, repentance, and forgiveness as essential to their followers' healing and recovery. Confession to their "God" and forgiveness from their God should lead to repentance for the behavior of harming their child. Hurting someone in most spiritual contexts is considered a "sin" for which one needs forgiveness. Forgiveness allows for reconciliation with self, individuals wronged, and community. Most religious individuals engage in some form of prayer, meditation, or spiritual ritual. For example, Christians believe that the "Holy Ghost" or "Holy Spirit" of God leads, guides, and directs them in decision making. This includes whether it is problematic to hit their child.

The practitioner's ability to connect with the family and understand their spiritual or religious frame of reference or both is important in terms of the family's disclosure. How the practitioner handles the family's expression of religious influence will dictate, to a large extent, whether the family will allow an intervention that includes their spiritual or religious leader during the investigative phase. Including a spiritual leader that the client identifies as helpful can influence the therapeutic process and offer a forum for reconciliation between the child and the family.

There are a variety of spiritual and religious institutions in communities—Protestants, Catholics, members of the Jewish and Islamic faiths, and Black Muslims. Legitimate spiritual leadership in any of these denominations must meet a minimal standard to be recognized by the community of faith to which they belong. Ordination or some formal ritual is usually a part of the process that allows for legitimate leadership. Legitimate clergy are usually involved in congregations and do not stand alone, do not rule or govern in isolation, and will not hesitate to send a practitioner information about the denomination or the particular church. The practitioner has to risk asking questions and informing the clergyperson that he or she is in the midst of an investigation in which he or she could use the clergyperson's expertise. A good way to ascertain whether a particular church or faith community will be helpful to the therapeutic process with dysfunctional families is to ask whether the church has a counseling ministry or if the church uses counseling ministries in the community. The response will give the practitioner an idea about the importance of counseling to that church.

Workers need to cultivate relationships with religious leaders in as many denominations and beliefs systems as possible so they can use these leaders as consultants when they need specific information about a particular denomination and how it functions. Many religious persons do not believe that physical punishment is inconsistent with appropriate parenting. Rather, they believe that God's authority supersedes governmental authority and allows them to use corporal punishment. Alternatives to the use of corporal punishment could involve assisting parents in identifying nonphysical ways to punish inappropriate behavior and rewarding appropriate behavior. For example, withholding privileges and use of time-outs are constructive forms of noncorporal punishment.

Pastors and leaders of religious institutions are very diverse. There is no standard response or approach that can be identified and used in assessing and interacting with those in the religious community. Practitioners must use their professional skills to assess whether they believe a particular clergy or spiritual leader can assist in providing support to a family.

Practitioners must be willing to risk themselves by entering into meaningful relationships with both clients and clergy. Although workers cannot train clergy on the finer points of the child protective service laws, practitioners can educate clergy on what constitutes abuse of children. Efforts with clergy must be viewed as a partnership in which clergy and laity come together on behalf of the family.

■ Further Reading

Payne, W. J. (1991). *Directory of African-American religious bodies.* Washington, DC: Howard University Press.

Williams, W. B. (1992). *The encyclopedia of religion in the United States.* New York: Crossroads.

Part VIII

EVALUATION
AND CLOSURE

106

How Do I Measure Risk Reduction?

■ *Dee Wilson*

■ *Theoretical Framework and Assumptions*

In general, treatment plans formulated by public child welfare agencies to protect abused and neglected children from additional maltreatment seek to reduce factors that increase the likelihood of the recurrence of abuse and neglect or increase factors that protect children from future harm or both. Some risk factors cannot be altered, either because they are matters of historical fact (e.g., a parent's history of abuse in his or her family of origin) or because these factors cannot be influenced to a significant extent by public child welfare agencies (e.g., family poverty). Many factors related to child behavior, parental functioning, the parent-child relationship, and the family's social support system, however, can and must change if children are to be safe from further maltreatment. It is the responsibility of caseworkers in public child welfare agencies to identify key risk factors that must be eliminated or reduced to prevent the recurrence of abuse or neglect or both. With the participation of parents, caseworkers must also formulate treatment plans that can be reasonably expected to result in a safer environment for children. It is also the responsibility of caseworkers to evaluate whether anticipated changes have actually occurred and are likely to be stable. In addition, it is often possible for public agencies to add to, or

■ 513

strengthen, factors that protect children from further maltreatment.

■ *Evaluating Treatment Outcomes*

It is well established that effective treatment in serious cases of child maltreatment requires several months (at least) of intensive efforts, and that the probability of a recurrence of maltreatment during the course of treatment is quite high. Social workers responsible for child protection should remember the axiom that "treatment is not protection" and be vigilant in monitoring child safety while parents are involved in various types of services. Caseworkers should not naively assume that because parents are involved in services, or have complied with court orders, that children will be safe from harm. Risk reduction cannot be measured by participation in services or compliance with court orders; it is the outcome of these processes that must be assessed.

A recurrence of abuse or neglect during treatment efforts, however, is not an indicator that treatment has failed or cannot succeed. For example, a parent may occasionally use harsh physical punishment while attempting to learn new disciplinary approaches. The parent's motivation to learn new nonabusive ways of responding to child misbehavior may actually be strengthened by a minor incident of parent-child conflict.

When children remain in the parent's home during treatment, social workers must carefully monitor child safety both to respond quickly to further child maltreatment and, if it occurs, to evaluate the extent to which risk of future maltreatment has been reduced. At the very least, incidents of child maltreatment should become less frequent and less serious when children remain in the home if treatment efforts are having a positive effect. Caseworkers should also expect to see improvements in parental functioning (including attitudes and perceptions as well as behavior) and in the way in which parents interact with and respond to their children before concluding that child maltreatment is unlikely to reoccur. A parent's ability to retain new skills or behaviors under stress is an indicator that positive changes are likely to be stable. A reversion to old habits under stress is usually a sign that additional time in services or treatment is needed to stabilize new skills or behaviors.

Table 106.1   **Proxy Measures of Change**

Positive Measure	Negative Measure
Increased empathy and responsiveness to child	Little or no empathy with child
Increased enjoyment of contact with child	Little or no enjoyment of child
Increased ability to set limits on child behavior without hitting, yelling, ignoring, or abandoning	Little or no ability to set limits on child behavior without hitting, yelling, ignoring, or abandoning
Increased reliability in keeping appointments, fulfilling promises, and visiting child	Not reliable in keeping appointments, fulfilling basic responsibilities, and visiting child
Increased recognition of past history of child abuse and neglect	Little or no recognition of child abuse and neglect
Increased contact with persons supportive of positive changes	Isolated or extensive contact with persons discouraging positive change
The absence of violence in interpersonal relationships	Recurrent violence in interpersonal relationships
Increased motivation to change following relapse	Relapse followed by abandonment of treatment program
Increased self-esteem	Low self-esteem

■ *Evaluating Risk Reduction*
  Through Use of Proxy Measures

When children are placed out of the home, caseworkers must usually rely on proxy measures of change because parents have little or no opportunity to engage in further maltreatment during this period of time (Table 106.1). In evaluating whether the risk of future maltreatment has been reduced, caseworkers should ask themselves whether the parent demonstrates increased empathy in his or her interactions with the child or children. Does the parent demonstrate increased recognition and ownership of a history of maltreatment? Has the parent become more reliable and dependable in fulfilling responsibilities, keeping promises, visiting the child, and taking care of his or her own personal needs? In the absence of concrete evidence of positive changes in personal functioning and in the parent's relationship with his or her child, caseworkers should be skeptical of claims that services

Table 106.2   Parental Attitudes Toward the Child

Positive Attitude	Negative Attitude
Parent expresses appreciation, love, and caring about child through verbal and nonverbal behavior	Parent displays little affection or regard for child
Parent demonstrates patience with and understanding of child's misbehavior	Parent blames child for personal or family misfortune
Parent expresses pride in child's development and achievements	Parent views child as embodiment of despised parent or spouse
Child is treated fairly compared to siblings	Parent attributes bad or evil motives to child
Parent demonstrates through behavior that the child's well-being is a priority	Parent demonstrates little concern for child in pain or under emotional distress
Parent forgives child following disciplinary incidents (e.g., "lets go" of anger toward child)	Parent does not let go of anger toward child
Parent perceives child accurately	Parent emotionally abuses child with insults, demeaning behavior, or comments
Parent demonstrates concern with child's physical pain or emotional distress	Parent puts own needs (or the needs of siblings) before child's needs

have reduced risk of future harm, even if parents are not currently abusing or neglecting their children or engaging in addictive behavior or both.

■ *Overall Level of Risk Following Treatment or Reunification or Both*

Many research studies have found that approximately 30% of children who are reunified with their birth families return to out-of-home care. The recurrence of abuse or neglect is only one reason why children return to foster care, but it is vital that child safety be carefully monitored following reunification. Strongly negative parental attitudes in the form of scapegoating or emotional rejection are indicators of emotional abuse and may be warning signs that physical or sexual abuse is likely to reoccur. A parent's willingness to work through a child's behavioral problems, and accompanying anger, is a positive prognostic indicator.

A parent's attitude toward a child and the parent's motivation to provide positive parenting are of the utmost importance in assessing the likelihood of future maltreatment whether children remain in the home, are placed in out-of-home care, or have been recently reunified with the birth family. Parental attitudes toward children and their motivation to provide positive parenting mediate abusive and neglectful tendencies resulting from a parent's early history of maltreatment, current psychological problems and impairments, or the pressures of the social environment. Social workers responsible for child safety need to engage in frequent discussions with parents that will reveal parental attitudes and motivation relative to the "at risk" child (Table 106.2).

Caseworkers' confidence that risk of child maltreatment has been significantly reduced is firmly grounded when (a) there is no recent history of abuse and neglect of children in the home; (b) the parent has been able to sustain changes in behavior, skills, perceptions, and attitudes that greatly reduce the risk of maltreatment; and (c) these changes include a dramatic increase of positive attitudes toward the child and a decrease in negative attitudes toward the child. The recurrence of maltreatment, even minor incidents, or relapse to negative patterns of behavior or both, combined with deterioration in the parents' attitude toward the child, warrants highly vigilant behavior on the part of caseworkers responsible for child safety.

■ *Further Reading*

Barth, R. P., & Berry, M. (1994). Implications of research on the welfare of children under permanency planning. In J. Duerr Berrick, R. Barth, & N. Gilbert (Eds.), *Child welfare research review* (Vol. 2, chap. 14). New York: Columbia University Press.

Cohn, A. (1979). Effective treatment of child abuse and neglect. *Social Work, 24,* 513-519.

Salter, A. C., Richardson, C. M., & Martin, P. A. (1985). Treating abusive parents. *Child Welfare, 64,* 327-340.

107

When Is Termination of Parental Rights and Adoption the Best Permanency Option?

■ *Thomas D. Morton*

■ *What Is Permanency?*

Permanency involves both a legal and a psychological context. For permanency to exist in the former, a family must have some form of permanent legal custody over and responsibility for a child. As long as the child is in the custody of the state, this does not exist. Although some forms of guardianship may convey legal rights to a family, not all forms of guardianship provide a basis of legal entitlements equivalent to those of natural parenthood or adoption.

The psychological context of permanency is more complicated. This requires the child to be in a relationship with a caregiver in which the child experiences a sense of emotional security derived from the caregiver's commitment to meeting the child's needs through adulthood. For most children born into a family and still living with one or both parents, this evolves through the continuity experienced in the relationship combined with the repeated nurturing provided by the parent. For children who have been involuntarily separated form their parents, the practical knowledge that this continuity can be disrupted presents new and powerful issues relative to finding and maintaining emotional security.

■ *Permanency Options*

The first permanency option is preserving the family. This can be accomplished by ensuring the safety and well-being of a child within the family, thus avoiding the placement experience. The second is accomplished through reunification. When these cannot be accomplished, the child is faced with care through adulthood in one or more state-supported placement options unless a new form of permanence can be created. The alternatives are adoption and, recently, subsidized guardianship with relatives. Like subsidized adoption, subsidized guardianship removes potential financial barriers to families taking responsibility for a child with special needs. Although relative guardianship does not equate with the legal commitment of adoption, the social commitment of a family to a child member of the family may be equally as strong. Independent living or transitioning to adult self-sufficiency from foster care is not considered a permanency option because it lacks one key ingredient—a committed relationship with an adult caregiver that has independent legal status.

■ *Termination of Parental Rights*

Children cannot become adopted without termination of parental rights. This can be accomplished through voluntary relinquishment by the birth parents or through involuntary termination of parental rights. Herein lies a dilemma. Children cannot be adopted without termination of parental rights. Not all children whose parental rights are terminated will be adopted. Hence, the probability of adoption needs to be weighed against the possibility of legal orphanhood. Because legal risks are associated with moving forward in adoption planning in situations in which parental rights have not been terminated, many argue that failure to proceed with termination is a barrier to adoption.

There are many considerations relevant to choosing to pursue termination of parental rights and adoption, including the prognosis for reunification, prospects for termination of parental rights, the child's needs, the value of current family connections, and age. The prognosis for reunification involves two considerations. First, can the family provide the protective factors and manage any threats to safety necessary to preventing future risk of harm? Second, can this be done within a time frame reasonable for the developmental needs of the child? The passage of the Adoption and Safe Families Act, in addition to similar legislation being created at the state level, has served to alter time frames and modify estimates of prognosis. Although exceptions are allowed in many cases, determinations will be required in 12 to 15 months. Such abbreviated time frames may conflict with expectations about recovery cycles in cases in which alcohol and other drugs are involved. Nevertheless, the first decision is still concerned with the feasibility of ensuring continuing safety within the birth family.

Where safety cannot be ensured within the birth family, the state usually seeks another permanency option. Increased use of relative care initially created a new dilemma: Should a child be taken away from the security of living with kin when the kinship caregivers are not willing to adopt? Forms of relative guardianship, such as those in Illinois, have provided a clear option and have also increased the number of relative adoptions.

The probability of successful termination of parental rights depends greatly on the state's laws, which provide the grounds for termination, and on the quality of the work with the family toward reunification. When family failure to make progress can be established, termination is more likely. When the agency has created case plans based on completion of treatment steps, termination may be hindered by the family's compliance with the plan even though progress is not evident. Equally important is the agency's diligent search for absent parents. When parents and other relatives are identified at child protective services intake, this is made much easier.

A third consideration is the child's needs. This is not so much a question of whether to terminate parental rights as it is of what type of resource is needed in adoption. When the child's conditions qualify the child for adoption subsidy, perceived financial risks for the adopting family may be alleviated. Every child is potentially adoptable no matter what special needs and conditions exist. Consequently, no assumption should be made that a child is not adoptable.

A fourth consideration is family connections. Where possible, adoption by a relative will keep the child within the same system of family and cultural identity. When relative adoption is not possible, openness in adoption is a consideration. Openness refers to the degree of continuing contact with birth family members. In general, placement of siblings together is preferred. When splitting sibling groups is necessary, natural connections among the children should receive consideration. When maintenance of family connections does not threaten the child's safety or present barriers to adoption, the child's emotional well-being is often enhanced by these connections.

Age is a final consideration. Many states give children older than age 14 some consideration in the adoption decision. Evidence suggests that the likelihood of being adopted declines with age. As stated previously, however, every child can be adopted, and age should not be considered a reason not to pursue termination of parental rights and adoption. What is important is that the adoption process recognize that expectations of attachment may be working against the natural developmental process of formation of an independent identity. The adoptive family's needs for claiming and attachment, if high, may be rejected by the older child. Conversely, the potential to benefit from adoption is greatest when a child is very young. Important developmental work regarding trust occurs during the first year of life. Children who spend their first years of life in multiple foster homes are more likely to experience attachment problems later. Hence, permanency-planning time frames are much more critical to the well-being of children younger than 5 years of age.

108

When Can a Child Be Safely Reunited With His or Her Family?

■ *Thomas D. Morton*

Foster care and other forms of out-of-home placement are used for many reasons. The most prevalent reason is as a safety intervention in cases of child maltreatment. Safe reunification when child maltreatment was the reason for entry into care depends on the caregiver's ability to ensure child safety and meet the child's needs for development.

■ *When Is a Child Safe?*

A child is safe when the protective factors in the child's environment are sufficient to counter any threats to safety. Current safety assessment practices have focused primarily on immediate time frames. Initial safety assessment is mostly characterized by the question "Is an immediate intervention necessary to ensure the safety of the child?" At reunification, the question is "Can safety be managed by a combination of family protective factors and less restrictive agency safety interventions?" Note that this is not the same as case closure in which the question is "Can the threats to safety and relevant risk factors be managed by the family without additional protective factors from the agency?" Assessing safety at reunification requires consideration of factors in addition to those assessed at initial intake and entry into care. Nonchangeable factors, such as history, are not practical at the time of reunification decision making.

■ *What Changes at Reunification?*

Reunification restores to the family almost all of the executive functions of parenthood. Although periodic contact will be maintained with some service providers, much of the time spent in parent and child interaction will occur within the range of privacy afforded most families. This means that the child's visibility will decline significantly, and the child's safety becomes significantly dependent on caregiver capacity to protect.

■ *Factors to Consider in Reunification*

Generally, three types of information are used to decide if reunification is possible. The first concerns the current level of threats to safety. These represent a set of indicators. Because threats to safety are primarily negative patterns of behavior within the family, they are often assessed in the context of their absence or a significantly reduced level of incidence. For example, if alcohol and other drugs have interfered with the caregiver's ability to recognize and respond to a child's needs, then a decrease in the frequency and amount of use would be an indictor of a reduced threat level (which is not the same as the threat being eliminated). For reunification to occur, threats to safety must have been reduced to a level that the family and agency can co-manage with the child in the family. This is not the same as risk reduction. A child can be at risk of a recurrence of maltreatment but still be safe.

The second type of information concerns protective factors. A parent that consistently removes dangerous objects from the reach of a toddler or arranges for a capable older sibling or an adult to watch younger children while the parent runs an errand would be exhibiting patterns of behavior that are actions of protection. The parent's ability to manage anger, use nonphysical means of control, prepare nutritious meals, keep the environment physically safe, protect a child from exploitation by others, and be alert and responsive to the child's needs are all examples of protective factors. It is not sufficient to eliminate threats to safety if sufficient protective factors are not present to counter future threats.

The third type of information concerns the existence of social supports sufficient to sustain the protective factors and inhibit the return of safety threats under crisis. A parent who has stopped using alcohol but has no support system to deal with a personal crisis may be extremely vulnerable to relapse and a new threat to safety.

In selecting criteria for decision making relative to these three classes of information, the practitioner and agency need to consider the strength of association of the criteria with the potential for harm. Most human behavior cannot be simply explained by linear and single-variable models of causation. Much human behavior results from many factors that are mutually interactive.

As a result of the Adoption and Safe Families Act enacted in 1997, the time frame for permanency decisions has been accelerated. The law gives parents less time to demonstrate changes necessary for reunification. This change in policy positively responds to the reality that time to a child and that to an adult are much different. The developmental needs of a very young child cannot wait for years while a parent makes necessary changes. Given the prevalence of substance abuse in child protection cases, however, shortened time frames conflict with current models of treatment and associated length of time to recovery. This has placed the child's needs for permanency and the child protection system's ability to treat family conditions in conflict.

Although recent census bureau data suggest that family composition is stabilizing, families remain strongly dynamic. Given the prevalence of single-parent families in the child protection system, agencies are often confronted not only with the role of a parent's current partner but also with potential problems associated with the choice of the next partner. High-profile child deaths at the hands of a new partner are causing increased community concern about child safety when a new partner (sometimes called paramour) enters the family. A temporary solution may be to consider a parent's history and potential to form relationships with violent partners as a safety factor.

Other future events are also difficult to anticipate. Loss of a job, a key member of the family, or a part of a social support network cannot be anticipated in safety assessment. Nor can interventions necessarily ensure that supports currently in place will be available for crises that occur 3 or 4 years after the current intervention.

Experience suggests that the likelihood of return to care is less when supportive services are provided for a period of time following reunification. Reunification combined with immediate case closure produce a higher rate of return to care. Some agencies are experimenting with an intensive home-based service intervention similar to family preservation services but provided immediately following reunification. Such approaches recognize that reunification is also a family crisis.

■ *Further Reading*

Adoption and Safe Families Act. (1997, November). P.L. 105-89.

Holder, W. (1998). *Family assessment change strategy*. Charlotte, NC: Action for Child Protection.

Morton, T., & Holder, W. (Eds.). (1997). *Decision making in children's protective services: Advancing the state of the art*. Atlanta, GA: Child Welfare Institute.

109

Preparing Youth for Independent Living

What Are the Best Methods for Reaching Self-Sufficiency?

■ *Maria Scannapieco*

Every year in the United States, an estimated 20,000 young persons are emancipated and leave foster care to assume independence. Many of these young adults, because of emotional and social problems stemming from maltreatment and the temporary life of foster care, are not prepared for self-sufficiency. In 1985, the Independent Living Initiative contained in Public Law (P.L.) 99-272 was adopted as part of the Comprehensive Omnibus Budget Reconciliation Act. The purpose was to appropriate Title IV-E funds for use with programs to help youth make the transition from foster care to independence. In recognition of the gap in services to adolescents in the foster care system, independent living programs (ILPs) are designed to reduce the difficulty that youth experience in the transition to independence.

Outlined in this chapter are services to youth in the foster care system preparing for independent living. ILP services either are offered to adolescents in a separate foster care unit or are integrated on an individual case by case basis. The ILPs focus on preparation for self-sufficiency after foster care by integrating services that prepare youth for employment and provide life skills training to enhance youths' ability to manage daily living. Program areas are divided into seven general areas.

■ Program Areas

Casework Services

Many of the program areas stem from the management of the case by the child welfare worker. Child welfare workers' goal is to offer intensive, relationship-based services using a task-centered and goal-oriented service model. Capitalizing on identified strengths, caseworkers promote the creation of opportunities and the encouragement and support to reach personal goals. The planning for independence is negotiated between the youth and the caseworker and includes many of the program areas discussed later.

Educational Services

Education is significantly related to independent living outcomes for youth. One of the best ways to ensure that educational needs are met is to reduce the multiple placements during the school year. If multiple placements occur, the caseworker should track the young person's educational progress. Independent living programs have an obligation to focus on what will best prepare youth for employment. Whether college preparatory or vocational courses, programs must support youth in identifying the importance of education.

Because many foster care youth require special needs education, support groups that focus on study skills and tutoring on immediate assignments are beneficial. When appropriate, peer tutoring has been found to be effective.

Employment-Readiness Programs

Using both individual and group methods, these programs focus on the skills youth need to obtain jobs. Skills focus on résumé writing, completing job applications, interviewing techniques, and decorum. Effective strategies are modeling, role playing, practicing skills such as filling out application, and "dress rehearsals."

Employer expectations and required behavior in the workplace are also subjects of employment readiness programs. Sexual harassment issues, timeliness, language, and dress code are subjects most often discussed.

Life Skills Training

The emphasis of life skills programs is on education and training and not on counseling. Life skills programs may encompass several components, but the most important are interpersonal communication skills, problem solving and decision making, self-management and control, strategies for coping with stress, and housing and financial skills:

- *Interpersonal communication skills* are those that lead to effective interpersonal relationships, and these are sometimes referred to as social skills or human relations skills. Books that outline exercises that are effective with adolescents and others that may be appropriate for some ILP participants with less well-developed skills are available. It is important to focus on both verbal and nonverbal communication skills.

- *Problem solving and decision making:* Many children in the foster care system will view life events more rigidly and see fewer options when confronted with a difficult interpersonal or social situation. ILPs work on improving the ability of youth to make and select from alternative solutions through the development of problem-solving and decision-making skills. Although there are many different models of problem solving and decision making, most entail the following components: define the problem, examine variables, consider alternatives, develop a plan, do action steps, and evaluate effects.

- *Self-management and control:* Training in self-management and control includes the following skills: self-assessment (evaluating one's own behavior to determine if it is adequate), self-monitoring (being able to monitor and be aware of current functioning), and self-reinforcement (providing one's own consequence for conduct).

- *Strategies for coping with stress:* High levels of anxiety because of maltreatment affect many children in the foster care system. This often leads to persistent stress. Methods to help youth cope with stress will enable them to focus on educational and vocational issues. Some of the more beneficial methods are relaxation techniques, imagery training, and cognitive restructuring of negative beliefs.
- *Housing and financial skills:* General skills that are taught in this area are locating an apartment, negotiating a rental agreement, performing housekeeping chores, purchasing bargains, preparing nutritious meals, and maintaining a savings or checking account. These skills are most effectively taught through the use of group methods. Hands-on practicing of these skills is key to successful development of proficiency in all areas.

Mentoring Programs

There are many types of mentoring programs; most have been found to have a positive impact on youth in attaining self-sufficiency skills. The essential component in all programs is the use of an adult volunteer who is matched with an adolescent and whose task is to help the youth make a successful transition to early adult living. The mentor takes on the role of advocate, teacher, and friend. Through working with the youth on self-esteem and skills needed to overcome peer pressure and other barriers, mentoring leads to advancement in education and job opportunities. Many mentoring programs, such as Big Brother and Big Sister, Each One, Teach One, Career Mentor Programs, and Sisters by Choice, operate in many communities.

Placement Setting

Placement setting refers to the various types of out-of-home services available to youth in the child welfare system and the number of placements youth experience. The more restrictive the setting, the longer the stay; the more placements the youth experiences, the more likely the youth will have unsuccessful outcomes at emancipation. This is an aspect of casework services that needs to be attended to throughout the time the youth is in foster care, and increased consideration should be given to placement options as the child reaches adolescence.

Some ILPs transition the youth from foster care to supervised apartment living to community apartment living. This model of emancipation services incorporates many of the program areas discussed in this chapter. Supervised apartment living programs allow the youth to "practice" self-sufficiency while still having a safety net. Creativity in these programs allows the caseworker and youth to do individual case planning to maximize self-sufficiency skills.

Social Support Networks

Emancipation from foster care can be a scary time for many youth, especially for those that have spent many years in care. Many foster care youth lack ongoing support from their own family, and a continued supportive connection with foster parents is important to their subsequent well-being and self-sufficiency. Association with former foster care youth can also be beneficial. Support groups for adolescents who are in ILPs can transition into informal social support networks. Integral to an overall case plan is the linking of youth, who are working toward emancipation, to formal and informal social support networks.

■ Further Reading

Goldstein, A., Sprafkin, R., Gershaw, N., & Klein, P. (1980). *Skill streaming the adolescent: A structured learning approach to teaching prosocial behavior.* Champaign, IL: Research Press.

McGinnis, E., & Goldstein, A. (1990). *Skillstreaming the elementary school child: A guide for teaching prosocial skills.* Champaign, IL: Research Press.

McWhirter, J., McWhirter, B., McWhirter, A., & McWhirter, E. (1998). *At-risk youth: A comprehensive response.* New York: Brooks/Cole.

110

How Do I Prepare Families for Case Closure?

■ *Esta Glazer-Semmel*

Termination refers to the process of ending your relationship with a family and helping the family to put closure on their relationship with you. It may also mark the end of their work with the agency. It is a time for remembering what you and the family did together, both what was accomplished and what may still remain to be done. It also explores the meaning of the relationship and how it feels to say "good-bye."

■ *The Personal to Professional Continuum*

None of us can always separate our personal emotions from our professional impressions. Termination is a stage of the helping process that may be especially difficult because of losses or endings that we have experienced in our own lives. It is crucial that we try to stay aware of personal feelings that our work is eliciting. Then, we can identify and use strategies to manage the feelings outside of the clinical process. Sometimes, a colleague or supervisor may need to help us identify or address these feelings.

■ *Marking Time Over Time*

In child welfare, relationships with clients are time limited. Family risks and protective factors, legal mandates and agency regulations, and assigned roles combine to define the duration. It is important to identify the time frame for the client at the beginning of the relationship. Then, you continue to help the family remember, at increasingly frequent intervals, how much time is remaining in your work together. Naturally occurring events such as holidays are helpful in marking progress toward the end of work.

■ *Types of Termination*

It is important that you and your clients are clear about what will happen when the relationship ends. Regardless of the type of termination, it is crucial that you help your clients to know where they can turn for help in the future. The following are types of termination:

1. *Termination* occurs when the end of your relationship with a family also means that there is no immediate plan for them to work with other helpers.
2. *Referral* occurs when a family will continue to work with formal or informal helpers outside of your agency. When the relationship with you has been a good one, then defining its growth as a skill that the family takes with them may ease their transition. Exploring issues related to starting new relationships and learning new systems is also important.
3. *Transferral* occurs when their time with you is ending but they will continue to work with another provider in your agency. When your relationship has been a good one, a joint meeting may help the family assign some of the positive feelings to the new helping relationship.
4. *Client discontinuation* occurs when the client unilaterally ends the relationship.

■ *The Skills of Ending*

Reviewing the Process

Talk with the family about where the relationship started, what happened during the time you worked together, and where it is at the end. Describe the ways in which family members have contributed to making the process work. Do not discount anyone's impressions, and expect different reactions from different members.

Final Evaluating

Encourage the family to celebrate their successes. At the same time, help them to decide how they may or must address remaining concerns. Identify strengths on which they can build to encourage their continued work and increase the likelihood of additional positive outcomes.

Sharing Ending Feelings and Saying Good-Bye

Each client's experience of and response to ending the relationship will be unique. Sadness and loss, anger, powerlessness, fear, rejection, denial, ambivalence, relief, and maybe even delight are some of the emotions they may feel. It is important to encourage clients to share their feelings while acknowledging their possible discomfort and, ultimately, their power in choosing whether or not to share their feelings. You must also decide what, if any, of your own feelings will be shared. Stating "I'm glad we've had the chance to work together" conveys the important message that the relationship, even if it has been a difficult one, has value.

■ *Marking the End*

When working with children, it may be helpful to complete a small project together, such as a story or picture, that they can keep as a concrete remembrance of you, the relationship, and the work they have done. Similarly, with an adult, a diary or memory book may be meaningful. As appropriate, an individualized list of resources may be helpful and reinforce the need to redirect their requests for continued help.

■ *Further Reading*

Cournoyer, B. (1996). *The social work skills workbook* (2nd ed.). Pacific Grove, CA: Brooks/Cole.

Schulman, E. D. (1982). *Intervention in human services: A guide to skills and knowledge* (3rd ed.). St. Louis, MO: Mosby.

Part IX

LEGAL AND ETHICAL ISSUES

111

What Rights Do My Clients Have to Information in Their Case Records?

■ *Dennis Ichikawa*

This chapter provides child welfare workers with general information relating to the public disclosure of child welfare agency records. State laws and procedures vary; therefore, it is important to know your own state and local laws, rules, practices, and procedures. Public disclosure requests are different from "discovery" requests. Public disclosure requests may be made by any person and may be made whether or not there is a court action. Discovery requests may be made only in the context of a legal proceeding by a party to the proceeding.

Question: Are parents[1] and children entitled to agency records that relate to them?

> *Answer:* Yes. Public disclosure laws entitle parents and children to obtain a copy of most child welfare agency records that relate to them. Not all records are released; there is a balance between the need to disclose information fairly and the need to preserve the confidentiality of records to protect the privacy rights of parents and children.

> *Exceptions:* Certain information may be "redacted" (i.e., deleted) from the copy of the record that is provided to the

parent(s). For example, typically the name and address of the foster parents will be redacted. Also, most state laws allow "referents" (people who call the agency with child abuse or neglect referrals) to request anonymity or confidentiality. There are usually special laws that relate to the disclosure of medical records, mental health records, drug and alcohol treatment records, personnel records, and HIV and AIDS status. The agency's copy of an evaluation on one parent should not be released to the other parent (unless the parent who was evaluated signs a release of information or the court orders the release). Federal law contains a general exception that exempts an agency from having to disclose information if disclosure would endanger the life or physical safety of any individual. Federal law also exempts interagency and intraagency memorandums or letters from disclosure. Some states require that when a decision is made to decline a public disclosure request, the reason(s) must be stated. The decision to decline a public disclosure request may be subject to an appeal process. Information relating to a worker's consultation with the agency's attorney is also exempt from public disclosure under attorney-client privilege.

Question: Are people other than parents (i.e., "third parties") entitled to information in the agency records?

Answer: Yes. The disclosure to third parties, however, is usually limited to only information that directly relates to them. There are three exceptions to this limitation:

- When compelling circumstances can be shown to support that the additional information needs to be disclosed because it affects the health or safety of an individual. (Notice of disclosure must be sent to the individual identified in the information.)
- When the release of additional information is made pursuant to a court order. (The court will typically review the records "in camera" [i.e., privately in court chambers] before ruling on whether or not to release the records.)
- When the third party is authorized by the parents to receive the additional information.

Question: How quickly do copies of the agency records have to be provided to the person who is requesting them?

Answer: Public disclosure requests are triggered by the filing of a public disclosure request form. Most states have laws that establish a time line for responding.

Question: Does a parent retain the right to the information even if his or her parental rights have been terminated?

Answer: No. If a request is made by a parent after his or her parental rights have been terminated, then the disclosure request does not have to be approved. (The parent may be entitled to limited disclosure, similar to a third party.)

Question: What should I do when I am uncertain if an appropriate disclosure request form has been filed or how to respond to it or both?

Answer: Whenever you have any questions about a public disclosure request, you should contact your supervisor or agency attorney or both.

■ *Note*

---

1. As used in this context, "parents" includes "legal guardians."

112

How Do I Avoid Being Sued?

■ *Rebecca J. Roe*

If one believes the negative press about lawyers, one will believe that the answer to the question "How do I avoid being sued?" is "You can't." In fact, there is little incentive for lawyers to file frivolous lawsuits—after all, one third of $0 is $0. Performing your work competently, courteously, and expeditiously reduces your chances of being sued. The following guidelines can be used:

- Be a professional, not an advocate.
- If it is not in the record, it does not exist.
- "Just the facts, ma'am."
- Explain yourself.
- Comply with internal standards and guidelines.
- Consult your supervisors where appropriate.
- Avoid bureaucratic numbness.
- Judges have immunity—use their shield.
- Do not "cop an attitude."
- There are worse things in life than being sued.

Be a professional, not an advocate. Webster's dictionary defines an *advocate* as a person who pleads another's case and a *professional* as "having much experience and great skill in a specified role." It is the job of others to be advocates; it is your job to bring experience and skill to your role. First and foremost, be objective and neutral as you gather facts and reserve judgment until you have sufficient information to form a valid opinion, conclusion, or recommendation. The clearest path to trouble is to hastily form an opinion about what happened to a child and tailor your investigation to confirm your prematurely formed opinion.

Investigate alternative explanations for injuries, and consider theories offered by parents and other professionals. Do not simply dismiss them as silly or ludicrous. Conversely, do not assume you are a human polygraph, and because you believe the parent's statement of denial you can dispense with further interviews.

If it is not in the record, it does not exist. Document every interview, even if the information gained appears unimportant or if the person says that he or she has observed nothing out of the ordinary. If, for instance, you document only interviews from people who say they saw abuse, but not those of others who deny seeing anything, your investigation will appear incomplete and biased.

"Just the facts, ma'am." Do not report opinions, interpretations, or conclusions as fact. For instance, the child stating "He touched my peepee" is not shorthand for you to state "The child reported sexual abuse." Similarly, a parent's statement, "I touched my daughter's crotch," is not a "confession" to child sexual abuse and should not be reported as such. There may be an appropriate place and time when your opinions and conclusions are relevant. When that time comes, designate them as such. Report interpretations or conclusions separately from the facts.

Explain yourself. Opinions, conclusions, and recommendations should address all the facts gathered. For instance, if several people interviewed say the parent could not possibly have abused the child but your opinion is the opposite, explain why you are discounting or are unpersuaded by the witnesses. Bias is one possibility, and lack of opportunity to observe is another.

Comply with internal standards and guidelines. It may be difficult to consistently meet standards, particularly regarding time lines. If your office manual requires three collateral contacts with neighbors, teachers, and so on, and you make only one—or none—however, the plaintiff wins round one in the upcoming lawsuit. Standards are set for a reason. Collateral information about what is occurring with a child is an invaluable method of protecting the child. Resistance to complying with standards and complaining about caseload will not going to avoid a lawsuit when the tardy information was significant. People who are going to sue you and jurors who will decide the case are not sympathetic to hearing about your caseload. Most people are busy and have many demands on their time; you are no different than anyone else. If you were rushing to remove a child from his or her home instead of interviewing an exculpatory witness, the jury will be unimpressed with your time management.

Consult your supervisors where appropriate. You should anticipate that some cases are more controversial than others. Take the time to consult your supervisor and plan a course of action for the tricky ones. Such a consultation serves multiple purposes: getting another point of view, ensuring compliance with standards, and getting the "buyoff" of your supervisors on your course of action.

Avoid bureaucratic numbness. Many lawsuits are filed because of a failure to act. A common explanation offered by workers for the failure to act is that "I did not think it would do any good to go to court this time because it did not do any good last time." This answer is not acceptable. Every situation is different, and failing to take reasonable action based on the belief that it is futile is a poor explanation. Others, including plaintiffs' attorneys and jurors, will construe your inaction as laziness, a lack of caring, or both.

Judges have immunity—use their shield. Conduct pursuant to a judge's order is almost routinely immune in civil suits. If you believe a child is being abused, take it to court. Do not decide your evidence is not sufficient to support action because some other caseworker presented some other facts to some other judge and the child was not removed. This will not be an acceptable excuse for you not to have taken your case to court. Force judges to make the decisions. Do not let them off the hook (no matter how much they complain about their workload) if you believe that action only a judge can authorize is warranted. If you have gone to court to recommend against unsupervised visitation but the judge orders the unsupervised visits and the child is harmed, you are likely immune and your conscience should be clear. If you failed to even ask for visitation limitations—because you did not want the hassle of going to court, you did not think the judge would grant your request, and so on—you will be sued (and you probably deserve it).

Do not "cop an attitude." No one disputes that a child protection services worker's job is stressful, controversial, and thankless. Some clients will be a pain—pure and simple. Do not worry about the people who threaten a lawsuit every other minute. Every attorney they approach will view them as you viewed them and will not file their lawsuit. The ones who will sue you—successfully—are the people you have treated rudely, shortly, and unfairly. These people are as angry at the manner in which they were treated as they are about what actually happened in their case. They are usually angry at a particular person who treated them poorly; do not let that person be you. Avoid the "I'm not going to explain to you—I don't have to" attitude. If you made mistakes, accept responsibility and apologize. Frequently, plaintiffs file civil suits based on principle to prove that you were wrong or made a mistake because you will not admit it.

There are worse things in life than being sued. If you are sued, you should consider the arguments being made by the plaintiff as dispassionately as possible. Perhaps you did jump to a conclusion too early, or you did not prioritize a particular interview properly. Everyone of us has "been there, done that," given that the child protection field is more an art than a science. Learn from the experience, and it likely will not recur. If you are defensive, rigid, or arrogant, you will accomplish one thing for sure: Your agency will pay the plaintiff a lot of money.

113

What Is the Role of the Caseworker in Juvenile Court?

■ Linda Spears

■ The Juvenile Court

Although the court is not involved in most cases that come to the attention of child protection services (CPS), it plays a fundamental role in addressing the safety and permanency needs of children who, in general, experience serious harm and are at the greatest risk of future abuse and neglect. Guided by federal and state statutes, the courts are responsible for authorizing and overseeing many of the critical decisions and responsibilities of the child protection agency and the caseworker. The court's responsibilities include ensuring the following:

- Reasonable efforts have been made to prevent the removal of the child from the home (or that there is adequate documentation of the need to waive reasonable efforts when such efforts are not warranted because they are not sufficient to protect the child).
- There is a sufficient legal basis for CPS intervention on behalf of the child.
- The child's best interests are adequately represented in court proceedings.
- The parents' due process rights have been protected in the court process.

- A case plan has been prepared for the child and parents.
- Reasonable efforts to reunite the family are made once a placement has occurred.
- The case is regularly reviewed to monitor progress toward the case plan goal.
- The child's need for a permanent family is addressed in a timely manner.
- Reasonable efforts have been made to secure a permanent family for the child when family reunification is not appropriate.

In its efforts to fulfill these responsibilities, the court relies on many individuals, including the child and parents, attorneys representing the parties to the case, guardians ad litem or court-appointed special advocates concerned with the best interests of the child or both, service providers, experts and other specialists, and the caseworker. The CPS caseworker's role is pivotal, beginning with the decision to involve the court in the protection of a child and extending throughout the court process. The caseworker's role includes the following:

- Documenting the allegations of abuse and neglect, the family's service history, and other factors that form the basis for court involvement
- Reporting on the purpose, nature, and outcome of service activities
- Reporting on key case activities and recommendations
- Preparing the child and family for court
- Preparing and submitting case plans and written reports to the court documenting case progress
- Giving testimony regarding case activities and agency recommendations

■ Working With the Juvenile Court

Sound casework skills and competent case practice are principal components of effective work with the court. This means caseworkers must have a range of skills, including those related to the following:

- Direct practice with children and families
- Effective interaction with service providers and other professionals
- Accurate case assessment and analysis
- Timely decision making that is grounded in both the facts and a well-reasoned assessment of the family situation
- Service planning that directly links family strengths and problems with the changes needed to achieve the case goal, the services to be provided, and the specific behavioral outcomes anticipated as a result of service participation
- Accurate, complete, and focused case documentation reflecting their work with the family

Next, caseworkers must understand how the court works. This not only means becoming familiar with the primary responsibilities of the court but also understanding the specific steps in the court process. The worker must also understand how particular casework activities relate to specific court oversight responsibilities and procedures. In so doing, the worker can more effectively link his or her work with the child and family to the court process. Appendix 10 provides a summary of the key phases of juvenile court activity and highlights some of the principal casework tasks associated with each phase.

Finally, the worker must be an effective participant during actual court hearings. Although most of the components of effective work with the court occur outside the courtroom, caseworkers must be prepared to respond to questions concerning the facts and handling of the case both in formal testimony and in judicial questioning during pretrial and review hearings. Competent case presentation means having a command of the facts and factors that support the agency's petition. It also requires an ability to articulate, in a clear and focused manner, the concerns for the child's safety, the need for intervention, and the rationale for proposed interventions.

To prepare for the court appearance, the caseworker should thoroughly review the case record not only to ensure that it is current but also to refamiliarize him- or herself with key events. The worker should also meet with the agency attorney before each hearing to review the overall handling of the case in court, including:

- Specific concerns regarding the child's safety
- Details of interventions offered and implemented and their outcomes
- The worker's plan for services to the family
- The attorney's plan for presenting the case to the court
- Any proposed agreements with the parties about the allegations in the petitions, the findings, or the services to the family
- Witnesses who may be called to testify
- The worker's testimony, including a review of questions that might be anticipated from attorneys representing the parents, the guardians ad litem, or the judge

■ Conclusion

Preparing for and appearing in court can be one of the most unnerving of the caseworker's responsibilities. Not only is the caseworker's work subject to review but also the caseworker must be able to defend his or her actions verbally and in writing. Although some caseworkers seem to bring courtroom skill with them to the job, many do not. Most work diligently to improve their practice, documentation, and courtroom skills. Through skilled supervision, legal consultation, and specific training in working with the court, caseworkers can become skilled in working with the court to protect children and strengthen families.

114

How Do I Feel Comfortable Testifying in Court?

■ *Paul Stern*

Once the investigation is complete, it is possible that the caseworker will be called to court to testify about the work he or she has done. Even if the work accomplished is of the highest professional quality, it may be severely compromised if the caseworker fails to adequately explain it in a courtroom. Decisions will be made based on the court's understanding of what was done and why; if the caseworker fails to clearly articulate his or her findings and opinions, disheartening decisions can be made.

Therefore, the caseworker must develop skills at testifying in court. The following are some basic rules that should guide all courtroom work:

- Understand the purpose of providing testimony.
- Appreciate the limitations of the courtroom.
- Recognize the limitations of the decision makers.
- Be professional.
- Be prepared.
- Know what you know, and know why you know it.
- Explain things in terms that everyone can understand.
- Be honest.
- Be a small target, and do not try to help.

■ *Understand the Purpose of Providing Testimony*

Judges and juries want to make the correct decision. The method used for their decision making, however, is to rely on the information provided to them by others: Neither judge nor jury has the ability or opportunity to independently investigate matters.

These decisions makers need information upon which to base their conclusions. They want this information, however, in a way that also allows them to maintain their sense of independence. In other words, they must be allowed to make logical decisions and not just be told what they should think. The effective witness supplies explanations, not just conclusions. The witness is their educator. He or she provides the information and background so that the decision makers can make the correct decision.

■ *Appreciate the Limitations of the Courtroom*

Courtroom testimony is generally brief and follows strict formalities. The decision makers—judges or juries—do not have an opportunity to get to know the witness. Decisions are frequently based on the swift impressions drawn from listening to and watching the person testify. The true credibility of the witness is sometimes difficult to ascertain in court. Decisions in court are often based on the witness's perceived credibility.

Perceived credibility is derived from appearances: The witness must look and sound believable. This means dressing appropriately for court. It is inexcusable for a witness to appear in court in informal or unclean clothing or to be poorly groomed. The courtroom should be treated as a place of respect. It is not a place to be casual and certainly not the place to make a novel fashion statement.

■ *Recognize the Limitations of the Decision Makers*

Often, those entrusted with making important decisions that impact the lives and safety of children do not have a good understanding of the dynamics of abuse or an appreciation for the issues involved. Jurors, for example, are usually disqualified from service if they have extensive training or experience in the area in controversy. In jury trials, in particular, the decision makers are purposefully ignorant of the subject matters involved.

The witness cannot assume the judge or jury understands important concepts about abuse or victimization. Again, the witness becomes the educator, providing understanding, knowledge, and perspective to allow for a rational and informed outcome.

■ *Be Professional*

This principle, of course, should govern all the work of the caseworker. The caseworker should appear unbiased, interested only in the truth. As both an investigator and as a witness, the caseworker must avoid appearing lax, incomplete, or lacking in objectivity. As a witness, he or she must be careful to neither overstate the evidence for one side nor understate the evidence for the opposing side.

Of course, a significant aspect of being professional involves knowing what one is talking about. This means being prepared.

■ *Be Prepared*

The witness must not only look professional but also sound professional. The caseworker is generally being called to court to provide information about the work that he or she has done. The caseworker, therefore, must be completely familiar with his or her own work.

Before going to court, the caseworker must review his or her case file, notes, and all relevant material several times. The witness can be assured that the attorneys will have done so and will be well versed about the material. If the caseworker appears confused, unsure of what work was accomplished or unfamiliar with his or her own work product, it reflects substantially on the worker's credibility.

The caseworker should also be acquainted with the leading research in the area that is the subject of the courtroom testimony. This does not mean the caseworker need know all the current articles and the details of research analysis. The caseworker, however, should have a grasp of the two or three leading articles in the field. The information that is provided within this book should provide sufficient information for the witness to discuss most issues competently and professionally.

■ *Explain Things in Terms That Everyone Can Understand*

In every profession, certain terms and phrases are shorthand for communication. For example, "I did a 379 investigation" might be an expression commonly used to explain that the work was undertaken pursuant to a particular statute number; "After the Roff hearing, we did an HSV" might explain that a home site visit was conducted after a certain legal hearing was held. This jargon must be avoided in court. Although these types of terms have meaning to the professionals involved, they will only lead to confusion or disinterest in laypersons.

Similarly, professional terms should be avoided and efforts made to explain them in understandable language. For example, medical terms or psychological syndromes should be explained in a manner to permit laypersons to understand what the witness is discussing. Showing people what a vast vocabulary one has may impress them, but it does not educate them.

■ *Know What You Know, and Know Why You Know It*

In court, the caseworker may be asked to share his or her opinion about the facts that have been presented. Recognize that the opinion itself is generally not as important as the reasoning for the opinion: Why do you believe what you believe? The witness should be prepared to explain this in a coherent, logical manner.

We all form opinions. Those that are put forward by seemingly thoughtful, careful people, however, are those most likely to be adopted by decision makers. Child psychiatrist Roland Summit observed, "What we choose to believe depends on whom we rely upon as our teachers." The witness' ultimate goal is to be someone decision makers will choose to rely on as their teacher.

■ *Be Honest*

Being a child advocate is fine: Who could find fault in those who seek to support and comfort children? In court, however, the witness should be an advocate for truth and not blindly for "the children."

The caseworker, through his or her investigation or involvement in the case, may have formed an opinion about the correctness of a certain outcome. As long as the opinion is reached after professional, careful, and objective consideration, there is nothing inappropriate about advocating for that opinion in court. The witness, however, must be certain to form opinions based only on careful and objective analysis. If the facts lead to a conclusion that the caseworker finds philosophically or personally distasteful, the caseworker must nevertheless base his or her decision on the facts. A witness will be rightfully criticized as a biased "advocate" when he or she supports conclusions that are not supported by the evidence.

■ Be a Small Target, and Do Not Try to Help

The job of the witness is to answer questions; the lawyer's job is to ask questions. One cannot, and should not, try to do the other person's job.

The witness should answer only the question asked and do so as succinctly as possible. If more information is desired, another question will be asked. The witness should not volunteer information beyond what is asked. Answers that wander beyond the specific question can cause at least three problems: They may violate prior court rulings or rules of evidence; they may run counter to the lawyer's carefully planned strategy; and the more the witness says, the larger the target he or she creates for cross-examination.

■ Dealing With Cross-Examination

The witness will first testify on behalf of the side that calls him or her as a witness. Then the opposing side has the opportunity to ask questions, which is called *cross-examination.*

Cross-examination allows the attorney greater abilities to try to control the testimony of the witness. The attorney will frequently ask only "leading" questions—questions designed to elicit brief responses from the witness, often no more than a mere one-word agreement or rejection.

The following are basic rules that might be helpful in dealing with cross-examination:

- Never answer a question you do not completely understand. Sometimes for tactics and sometimes through carelessness, questions are asked that are unclear or vague. Answer the question only if you understand it fully; otherwise, ask that it be rephrased or clarified.

- Do not give one-word agreement to a question unless you agree with it completely. If you agree with only part of the question, say so and explain. There is no rule that requires a witness to answer a question just "yes" or "no."

- Do not fight with the questioner. Be polite, be professional, be courteous, but be firm. Feel free to ask politely that a question be repeated, rephrased, or asked more slowly or in a less hostile tone.

- If you are asked to respond to reports of others, or about articles or other written information, and you are not completely familiar with the referenced material, ask to see it before you answer.

- The following is an overriding rule of dealing with cross-examination: Try to answer questions in court the same way you would in the real world. If you need more information, ask for it. If you need clarification, ask for it. Do so politely.

Cross-examination should be nothing more than a second opportunity to review your work and restate your conclusions and impressions.

■ *Further Reading*

Myers, J. E. B. (1998). *Evidence in child abuse and neglect* (3rd ed.). New York: John Wiley.

Stern, P. (1997). *Preparing and presenting expert testimony in child abuse litigation.* Thousand Oaks, CA: Sage.

115

How Do I Help Children Be Comfortable in the Legal System and Improve Their Competency as Witnesses?

■ *Julie A. Lipovsky*

Anyone who has testified in court knows that the experience is anxiety producing at best and frightening at worst. For a child who has been a victim of or witness to child abuse or neglect, the prospect of testifying in dependency or criminal proceedings is likely to be intimidating. Family members and professionals may be reluctant to include a child as a witness in court because of concern for the child's psychological safety. The child may have information for a judge or jury, however, that is essential to protect the child or punish an offender or both. Research suggests that testifying in court does not typically result in psychological damage to the child, although it may be stressful and uncomfortable. Children can be prepared for the experience of testifying, however, in a manner that reduces their distress and increases their ability to provide accurate testimony.

Court preparation for children typically focuses on educating the child about the rules and procedures of judicial proceedings and his or her role, assisting the child by teaching strategies to improve his or her ability to respond to questions truthfully, and

AUTHOR'S NOTE: This chapter was adapted from Lipovsky and Stern (1997).

providing emotional support. The primary goals of such preparation are to improve the child's ability to answer questions in court in the most complete and truthful manner and to minimize the likelihood that the child will suffer negative court-related consequences. Court preparation can be accomplished by a mental health professional or victim-witness advocate and the prosecutor. Child protective services workers can help this process by being available to the child and nonoffending parents for support and by answering questions the child or parent might have about courtroom appearances.

■ Components of Court Preparation

An anticipated court appearance is a significant, potentially stressful event that requires the child to understand his or her role as a witness and what will be expected of him or her in the courtroom. It may require the use of skills that a child has not developed (e.g., stress-reduction skills) or has not thought appropriate to this situation (e.g., familiar coping strategies). To maximize the child's ability to provide credible information and minimize accompanying distress, the child must be prepared, as for any other potentially stressful event. Court preparation can be conducted individually or in groups, and in some jurisdictions "court schools" have been developed to serve several children simultaneously.

Assessment

Prior to targeting skills for coping with the court process, the person preparing the child for court should assess factors that may affect the child's ability to provide accurate testimony or factors that might be stressful for the child. The first area to be assessed is the child's overall temperament and specific reactions to the abuse. Children who are experiencing significant emotional distress prior to court involvement may have a more difficult time coping with the stresses of testifying in court. Some of these children might be distressed to a degree that prevents them from being able to testify. In many cases, however, treatment by a mental health professional can help alleviate the precourt distress and teach the child skills for use in the courtroom. A decision about whether a particular child should testify may therefore be deferred until such time as the mental health professional has had a chance to work with the child on abuse- and court-related distress and can determine whether the child will be able to testify with a minimum of discomfort. The earlier the child starts treatment, the greater the likelihood that his or her precourt distress can be addressed well in advance of hearings or trials. Caseworkers can play an essential role by arranging assessment and treatment services for a highly distressed child soon after discovery of the abuse.

A second area to assess is the child's cognitive functioning and the extent to which cognitive limitations might affect the child's ability to provide accurate testimony. Third, the child's understanding of the court process and his or her anxiety related to testifying must be determined. In particular, the child's level of fear regarding facing the defendant and the meaning to which he or she attributes the court process must be assessed. Finally, the extent to which the child is able to receive emotional support from nonoffending parents or other family members or both is important because support is crucial to children's reactions to the legal process.

Caseworkers can assist with the assessment by providing the pertinent background information about the child and family. Observations regarding the level of parental support, the degree of child distress, and support systems available to the child and family can be valuable.

Education

Court preparation is an educational process. The child and family are provided basic information regarding the court process and specific court procedures (Table 115.1). The child should know the identity and function of each participant, from the bailiff to the judge. The child's role as a witness and courtroom procedures (e.g., oath, direct examination, and cross-examination) need to be explained. It is important that the family be informed as to when to expect proceedings to occur, with as much advance notice as possible. Expected courtroom behaviors are discussed with the child, including the importance of telling the truth while testifying and how to dress and behave. The child is

Table 115.1   Areas to Address in Educating Children About the Court Process

Who	Roles and responsibilities of all involved persons
What	Expectations for the child and the family during court process
When	Time frame and expected trial date
Where	Location of child and other persons involved in proceedings
How	Coping with specific problems

taught anxiety-reduction strategies and how to respond to confusing or misleading questions.

Courtroom Orientation

Bringing the child into the courtroom provides an opportunity to familiarize him or her with the physical layout and to practice answering questions from the witness stand. Several tools are available, including models of court, videotapes, and court notebooks, that can also help the child become comfortable with being a witness. There is no substitute for a trip to the courtroom prior to the court proceeding, however.

During the courtroom orientation, the professionals (prosecutor and mental health professional or victim advocate) can engage the child in many activities to increase his or her comfort in the setting and familiarity with the task of being a witness. The child is given an opportunity to take various perspectives in the courtroom, such as sitting at the prosecutor's table and on the judge's bench. As the child moves about the courtroom, he or she can be taught the identity and role of each participant. Once the child has gained some measure of comfort, he or she can sit on the witness stand. While the child is on the witness stand, the professionals who are preparing him or her can review courtroom procedures in sequence. For example, the child can be "sworn in" and then asked questions (by the prosecutor) about an experience he or she has had. These questions should not relate to the issues being decided by the court.

Strategies to Maximize Accurate Responses to Questions

Anxiety- and Stress-Reduction Techniques. High levels of anxiety interfere with a child witness's ability to attend and respond to questions accurately. Complete descriptions of stress-reduction techniques are beyond the scope of this chapter and are best left to mental health professionals with training in cognitive, behavioral, and affective approaches to psychosocial treatment. In brief, stress-reduction techniques provide the child with strategies to help manage feelings of anxiety. These strategies include deep-breathing exercises, deep muscle relaxation, imagery, development of positive self-statements, and role playing.

Communication Skills Training

Rules for how one converses in a courtroom are very different from those used in normal interactions. Words that have one meaning in normal conversation may have a different meaning in the courtroom. Children often do not understand these rules and meanings. Thus, they may misinterpret questions or respond with incomplete or inaccurate information. Therefore, it is helpful to practice how to answer the types of questions that may be posed in the courtroom using the language that is used in court. The child can learn the rules of courtroom interactions, how to respond to confusing questions, and what to do if he or she does not remember or know the answer to a question. Role playing, particularly in the courtroom, is an excellent method for teaching a child how to respond.

Emotional Support

Court preparation cannot be successful if the child does not receive emotional support from caregivers and concerned professionals. If the child is not believed or supported by immediate family members, it is essential to determine who is supportive of the child and facilitate contact between this person and the child. Professionals are supportive by clarifying the child's role in proceedings and by providing the child and family (if supportive) with information about the timing of events and expectations about the child's and the family's role in judicial proceedings.

■ The Caseworker's Role in Court Preparation

Interdisciplinary collaboration and coordination are essential for minimizing potential stress to a child witness. Therefore, the caseworker should communicate with other professionals involved in getting a child ready for court. The caseworker may share information that helps the prosecutor, mental health professional, or victim or witness advocate plan for the child's court appearances and focus on the child's safety in the justice system. Although a caseworker will not conduct actual court preparation sessions, he or she can assist in the process in many important ways. The caseworker can provide the person assessing and treating the child with important information about the child's level of functioning and sources of support to the child. In addition, the caseworker can be a resource to the child and family if they have questions about the court process. Finally, the most important role that the caseworker can fulfill is one of a supportive adult in the child's life by being available to talk with the child and family about concerns about testifying and providing emotional support.

■ *Summary*

Participation in the legal system can be daunting to anyone, but court preparation can facilitate the involvement of child witnesses by increasing the likelihood that they will provide accurate testimony and decreasing the likelihood that the experience will be overly stressful. For society to protect children from harm and to punish those who harm children, we must ensure that child victims and witnesses have a place in the justice system and that this system does not revictimize these children.

■ *Further Reading*

Lipovsky, J. A. (1994). The impact of court on children: Research findings and practical recommendations. *Journal of Interpersonal Violence, 9,* 238-257.

Lipovsky, J. A., & Stern, P. (1997). Preparing children for court: An interdisciplinary view. *Child Maltreatment, 2,* 150-163.

Saywitz, K. J., & Snyder, L. (1993). Improving children's testimony with preparation. In G. Goodman & B. Bottoms (Eds.), *Child victims, child witnesses* (pp. 117-146). New York: Guilford.

116

Why Is Communicating With Lawyers So Important and So Difficult?

■ *John E. B. Myers*

Oil and water do not mix. The same might be said of social workers and lawyers. Although social workers and lawyers are equally interested in solving problems and creating a just and fair society, they sometimes approach these goals from different, albeit overlapping, perspectives. Social work practice is founded on cooperation, affirmation, bridge building, and support. Litigation is rooted in adversarial confrontation. Lawyers believe the most effective way to arrive at the truth in court is for each side of a legal controversy to present the evidence that is most favorable to its position, to attack the evidence presented by the other side, and to let a neutral judge or jury sift through the conflicting evidence and decide where the truth lies. In the courtroom, the truth is thought to emerge through a clash of adversaries. Outside the courtroom, social workers and attorneys have more in common. Both employ similar processes of negotiation and compromise to solve problems. Thus, it is litigation in court that indicates most clearly the differences between social work and law.

Given the contrasting perspectives of social work and law, it is not surprising to see interdisciplinary sparks fly, with resultant communication snafus. Maintaining lines of communication, however, is vital. In the final analysis, social work and law are interdependent. Neither discipline can achieve its goals without the cooperation and assistance of the other.

■ *When Is It Permissible to Talk to a Lawyer About a Client?*

The principle governing this issue is confidentiality. Confidentiality is equally important to social workers and lawyers. The *Code of Ethics* of the National Association of Social Workers provides that "[s]ocial workers should protect confidentiality of all information obtained in the course of professional services" (1997, Standard 1.07(c)). Similarly, the *Rules of Professional Conduct* of the American Bar Association emphasize the lawyer's duty "to hold inviolate confidential information of the client" (1983, Rule 1.6, Comment).

Before communicating with a lawyer about a client, answer the following questions:

1. Who is my client? Sometimes the client is an individual and sometimes an entire family. In some cases, it is difficult to tell precisely who is the client.
2. What is my relationship with the lawyer? Is this my lawyer? The client's lawyer? The agency's lawyer? A third party's lawyer?
3. Is talking to the lawyer in my client's best interest?
4. Do I have the client's permission?
5. If I talk to the lawyer, what, if any, confidential information should I reveal?

If the client is an individual, then the social worker should obtain the client's consent before communicating with any lawyer, including a defense attorney, a prosecutor, or even the client's own lawyer. In discussing the matter with the client, the social worker should describe the pros and cons of communication between the social worker and the lawyer. The social worker should help the client understand that if confidential information is disclosed to the lawyer, the information may find its way into court or into the hands of other people.

Generally, a social worker has no legal obligation to talk to a lawyer over the phone, in person, or through correspondence. In many cases, however, communication with a lawyer—with the client's consent, of course—is in the client's best interest.

A lawyer may issue a subpoena that orders a social worker to provide testimony in legal proceedings or to produce documents (Myers, 1998). Although a subpoena is a court order that cannot be ignored, neither should subpoenas be blindly obeyed. Some subpoenas are invalid. In all cases, a social worker should (a) inform the client of the subpoena and (b) get advice from a lawyer on how to respond to the subpoena. For very useful advice on responding to subpoenas, see the report of the American Psychological Association's Committee on Legal Issues (1996).

■ *Further Reading*

Committee on Legal Issues of the American Psychological Association. (1996). Strategies for private practitioners coping with subpoenas or compelled testimony for client records or test data. *Professional Psychology: Research and Practice, 27,* 245-251.

Myers, J. E. B. (1998). *Legal issues in child abuse and neglect practice* (2nd ed.). Thousand Oaks, CA: Sage.

117

How Do I Work Effectively With Guardians Ad Litem, Court-Appointed Special Advocates, and Citizen or Professional Case Review Panels?

■ *Howard A. Davidson*

C hild protection personnel often work with others having related responsibilities. State legislatures and courts have provided the child protection system with "checks and balances" to help ensure child safety, permanency, and well-being and to independently review cases. A child's legal rights and interests can be advocated separately from—and not necessarily incompatibly with—the work of a child protective services (CPS) agency. One means of doing this is local juvenile or family court intervention.

The court—and those it appoints to help protect the best interests of the child—must

- make a fully independent assessment of the child's needs, and
- help ensure that judicial and CPS actions are more child sensitive and child focused.

There are various court-appointed, or otherwise involved, individuals and legal bodies with which you may interact. Laws require appointment of an independent representative for the child in court cases involving child abuse or neglect, and some laws establish state or community groups to separately review a case's status or agency handling or both.

You may have frequent contact with persons appointed as a child's legal counsel or attorney, and these persons are expected to follow their lawyers' ethical code. Note, however, that many laws label the child's appointed representative as a guardian ad litem (GAL). The GAL may or may not be an attorney. GAL roles differ from state to state based on applicable law and court practice, but GALs must always do the following:

- Conduct a comprehensive independent investigation of the child's situation
- Access and review all records and reports related to the case
- Take actions to protect the child's best interests
- Report to the court on their recommendations

In every state (but not every court), there are programs in which volunteer court-appointed special advocates (CASAs) serve to protect a child before the court.

States are also increasingly using volunteer citizen groups or professional interdisciplinary committees for case reviews of children known to CPS. These include children in the foster care system (e.g., foster care review boards), child death cases (e.g., child fatality review teams), and the more unusual child abuse citizen review panels that may examine CPS case handling. You may appear before such groups.

■ *How CPS Personnel Can Effectively Work With Independent Advocates and Groups*

First, consider court-appointed children's representatives (lawyers, GAL, or CASA) as potential allies to help you address the safety, permanency, and well-being of your abused, neglected, or abandoned child clients. If you have not been trained on how to interact with legal people, talk to the attorney who represents your agency in these cases. Ask about when and how information you have in your records can be shared with a child's attorney, GAL, or CASA. Their access to facts is critical to their work. Do not be surprised when they call to discuss the case or seek to meet for conferences or a discussion of case settlement possibilities.

Second, realize that you will likely interact with children's legal representatives throughout the case's progress if these advocates are doing their jobs correctly. You may find them helpful in obtaining services the child or parents or both need, and their advocacy—supplementing your advocacy—can be critical to get the child and family aid when resources are scarce. Legal counsel, GAL, or CASA for children should be actively involved in identifying safe alternatives to a child's removal from home and advocating for removal when necessary and, when appropriate, for family reunification, kinship placement, or termination of parental rights. They should be involved in precourt case settlement discussions and the rapidly growing process of child protection case mediation. They may also call witnesses on the child's behalf in court and may cross-examine witnesses, including yourself. Meet with the attorney representing your agency to prepare yourself for giving testimony and for being cross-examined by other attorneys. Before court, carefully review the entire case record. Again, you may expect to interact with children's legal representatives at case reviews, permanency hearings, and termination of parental rights hearings.

■ *Your Involvement With Citizen and Professional Case Review Groups*

You may expect, during the course of your child protection casework, to have cases in which

> a child has spent an inordinately long time in foster care;
> a child died or was severely reabused while in foster care or at home;
> there is critical attention by the media concerning your agency's handling of a case.

You may then appear before a citizen group, a gathering of professionals, or a "mixed" body to discuss such cases. Your agency's case practices and protocols may be critiqued. Before you attend any such meeting, review the entire case record and discuss your participation in the meeting with your supervisor and agency child protection attorney.

If the group is a foster care review board, it will likely want to examine

> why the child has not yet been placed in a permanent, legally secure, home;
>
> what steps you and your agency are taking to help make that happen; and
>
> why you may not have taken certain actions related to securing the child's permanency.

If the group is a child fatality review team, it may inquire as to

> what services were offered and aid provided to the family before the child's death;
>
> what help is now needed by the surviving siblings of the deceased child;
>
> how frequently you visited the family, and what you observed, prior to the death; and
>
> how similar deaths might be prevented in the future.

If the group is a child abuse citizen review panel, it may want to know

> whether laws or policies were complied with and how these might be improved;
>
> whether high caseloads, lack of sufficient training or supervision, or other factors inhibit successful outcomes for children and families involved with your agency; and
>
> what resources your agency might need to enable caseworkers to perform their responsibilities more effectively.

■ *Resources*

American Bar Association (ABA), Center on Children and the Law: Publications of the ABA include the monthly *ABA Child Law Practice* periodical, *A Judge's Guide to Improving Legal Representation of*

Children and an *Annotated Bibliography of Resource Materials for Child Fatality Review Teams* (1998), *A Guide to Federal Laws on Confidentiality and Disclosure of Information for Child Welfare Agencies* (1997), and *Standards of Practice for Lawyers Representing Children in Abuse and Neglect Cases* (1996). Website: *http://www. abanet.org/child*

National Court Appointed Special Advocate Association: Publications of this association include CASA training manuals and a quarterly periodical, *The Connection.* Website: *http://www.nationalcasa.org*

National Center for Child Fatality Review: This program is helping establish, support, and expand a national network of multiagency, multidisciplinary, local, regional, and state child fatality review teams. Website: *http://child.cornell.edu/ncfr/home.html*

Nusbaum Feller, J. (with Davidson, H. A., Hardin, M., & Horowitz, R. M. (1992). *Working with the courts in child protection.* Washington, DC: U.S. Department of Health and Human Services, Administration for Children and Families. (Bound with cover, 20-10016 [free]; unbound for photocopying, 00-10016 [free]; on disk, 02-10016 [$5.00])

Order from the National Clearinghouse on Child Abuse and Neglect Information at: *http://www.calib.com/nccanch* or send order and payment to:

National Clearinghouse on Child Abuse and Neglect Information, P.O. Box 1182, Washington, DC 20013-1182. Phone: (800) 394-3366 or (703) 385-7565; fax: (703) 385-3206.

Part X

CHILD PROTECTION PRACTICE

Special Issues for
the Practitioner

118

What Are the Core Competencies for Practitioners in Child Welfare Agencies?

■ *Joan Levy Zlotnik*

■ *What Are Competencies?*

To identify the "core competencies" that practitioners in child welfare agencies need, it is first necessary to understand what is meant by *core competencies*. This term is intended to mean the basic or minimal knowledge, skills, attitudes, and values that a worker needs to perform his or her job tasks effectively. In this chapter, I discuss the minimum knowledge that child welfare practitioners need and the skills that child welfare workers should have to do their jobs effectively.

There has been increasing focus on the need for "competent child welfare workers" because of concerns about poor child welfare service delivery; the increasing complexity of child welfare cases; the need for intersystem and intrasystem collaboration and coordination with mental health, juvenile justice, court, education, domestic violence, and substance abuse services; and the new legislative mandates of the Adoption and Safe Families Act of 1997 that require child welfare agencies to provide more timely and focused assessment and intervention services to the children and the families that are served within the child welfare system.

Multiple methods should be used to help child welfare workers acquire the necessary competencies. Acquisition of competencies should be a continual process. Child welfare practitioners should enter the field with a minimum background and knowledge (e.g., a bachelor's or master's degree in social work), which can then be built on through training, supervision, and on-the-job experience.

The National Association of Social Workers, the American Humane Association, and the Child Welfare League of America recommend that a bachelor's degree in social work should be the minimum entry requirement for most child welfare practice positions. For advanced child welfare practitioners and supervisors, a master's degree in social work is recommended. Social work is closely tied to preparation for practice in child welfare because much of the core knowledge and skills that are required for child welfare practice are integral to social work education.

In addition to the baseline that can be provided through social work education, child welfare agencies should mandate preservice and in-service training to ensure that staff have the necessary knowledge and skills to perform specific job tasks (e.g., foster care, adoption, family reunification, child protective services investigation, and resource development). Social work education grounds child welfare practitioners with a framework for practice. This should be enhanced through staff development opportunities offered by the agency so that workers are able to effectively perform their job tasks. Agency training should also include the policy framework under which the practitioners will operate.

Competencies can also be acquired through effective and ongoing supervision as well as peer support and consultative activities. Agencies should not expect that a worker enters the job with everything that he or she will need to know to perform that job. Training should be ongoing and based on an adult education model that draws on personal experience using a combination of didactic and experiential modalities and helps to build a sense of connectedness and community among the workers. To facilitate interdisciplinary work and interagency collaboration, child welfare workers should receive training together with staff from other agencies working with children and families so that they can understand each other's approach. This will assist them to work more effectively to meet families' needs.

■ *What Is the Philosophical Approach to Child Welfare Practice?*

The theoretical framework underpinning child-centered, family-focused child welfare practice includes the following:

- *Ecological perspective:* This perspective conceptualizes human behavior and social functioning within an environmental context.
- *Competence-centered perspective:* This perspective refers to practice methods and strategies that draw on the strengths of the children, families, and communities and promote the effective functioning of children, families, and their environments.
- *Developmental perspective:* This perspective refers to understanding individual human growth and development and family development from a life-span perspective and views individuals and families in transaction with the environment.
- *Permanency planning orientation:* This perspective embodies a mandate that all children have a right to permanent homes. Child welfare service delivery should be oriented toward safely maintaining children in their own homes or, if necessary, placing them permanently with other families.
- *Cultural competence perspective:* This perspective requires child welfare practitioners to understand the worldview or perspective of clients or peers who are culturally different and to adapt practice accordingly.

■ *Core Competencies*

To practice child welfare, workers need to have basic competencies on which more specific child welfare knowledge and skills will be built. The following general competencies that underpin social work provide a baseline of what a new worker should have before specialized child welfare knowledge and skills are added:

- Ability to develop and maintain relationships
- Ability to listen
- Ability to make individual and family assessments and develop an appropriate plan based on those assessments
- Understanding of child and adult development from a life-cycle perspective
- Understanding of the case management process and ability to provide case management services
- Understanding of crisis intervention and early intervention services and strategies
- Ability to broker and access services

Table 118.1 provides a detailed listing of the core values, attitudes, skills, and knowledge that child welfare practitioners need to be "fit" for child welfare practice. For further resources regarding child welfare competencies, see Appendix 11.

■ *Further Reading*

Pecora, P., Whittaker, J., & Maluccio, A. (1992). *The child welfare challenge: Practice, policy and research.* New York: Aldine.

Zlotnik, J. (1997). *Preparing the workforce for family-centered practice: Social work education and public human services partnerships.* Alexandria, VA: Council on Social Work Education.

Table 118.1   Core Child Welfare Competencies

Core Attitudes and Qualities	Core Values	Core Knowledge	Core Skills
Confident	Commitment to strengths-based, family-centered practice	Understands	Ability to
Self-aware		Family systems, the family in the environment, the family in a historical context, diverse family structures, and concepts of family empowerment	Identify strengths and needs and engage the family in a strengths-based, family-centered assessment process
Firm			
Belief in resiliency	Commitment to ensuring the safety of children in the context of their family		
Creative		Individual growth and development with particular attention to separation, loss, and identity development	Use self in relation to diverse children, families, and agency settings
Timely	Belief that each child has a right to a permanent family		
Caring			Write and communicate to meet a range of child welfare service needs
Committed	Respect for persons of diverse racial, ethnic, and cultural backgrounds and belief that there is strength in diversity	Working with involuntary clients and the use of authority in child welfare service delivery	Use family-centered case practice in a culturally sensitive framework
Honest			
Flexible			
Patient		Cultural diversity and the characteristics of special populations and the implications for assessment and intervention	Work with families in their homes and other out-of-the-office settings
Perceptive			
Respectful			Assess for abuse and neglect and the safety of the child and other family members in the family setting
Analytical	Belief that each child and family member should be empowered to work toward their own needs and goals	Special problems of poverty, oppression, and deprivation	
Understanding			
		Child welfare and child protection programs and models	Work with involuntary clients, including working with hostility and resistance
		Child abuse and neglect dynamics	Provide crisis intervention, parenting skills training, family counseling, conflict resolution, and individual and group work
		Substance abuse issues and their effect on children and families	
		Dynamics of community and family violence, including spouse abuse, and the impact of trauma on children and family members	Work together with the family to negotiate, implement, and evaluate the service agreement
			Work together with the family and other key supports to accomplish the service agreement goals

(continued)

Core Attitudes and Qualities	Core Values	Core Knowledge	Core Skills
		The role of out-of-home care and the principles of permanency planning for children, including the process for decision making and achieving permanency	Function as a case manager and a team member and collaborate with other service providers
		The continuum of placement services, including the foster care system, the residential care system, kinship care, placement prevention, maintaining familial ties, family reunification, and adoption	Assess for substance abuse and include treatment needs and referral in the service plan
			Assess for sexual abuse and provide or arrange for treatment of the child and his or her family
		Services available for children in the mental health, education, health care, and juvenile justice systems	Work with biological families to make and effect a permanent plan for a child in foster care, kinship care, or group care
		The legal system related to child welfare practice	Identify and use social supports to prevent burnout and stress while working in the child welfare system
		Process of political and funding advocacy as it relates to acquiring services for families and children	Work with the legal system, including documentation and court testimony
		Services available for families through the economic security, housing, education, substance abuse, mental health, health, and job training systems	Empower the child and family to enable them to sustain gains and use family and community supports
		Potentials for burnout, stress, and trauma that can occur in child welfare work	Work with children and adolescents at various developmental stages and with a wide range of needs, applying knowledge of human behavior and intervention skills

119

How Do I Protect My Personal Safety in the Community?

■ *Caroline L. Burry*

C hild protective services workers spend a great deal of time in the community assessing and treating families. Sadly, many workers have experienced threats and actual incidents of violence. Therefore, it is vitally important that workers be prepared to protect themselves as they carry out their responsibilities. Suggestions for protecting personal safety include considerations before making a home visit, while outside the home, while inside the home, in de-escalating verbal violence, and after the visit. In addition, ideas for safety while transporting clients and for agency policies are given.

■ *Before You Go*

In preparation for a home visit, read the file, searching particularly for previous threats or incidences of violence, substance abuse, or mental illness. Make sure someone in your office knows where you are going, whom you are visiting, and when you will return. If you are not returning to the office at the end of the day, make a plan to call the office and leave a message when you are done with your visit. Think through your plan for the visit, reflect on previous similar visits and what worked well and what did not work well, and ask your colleagues about the area you are visiting. It is also helpful to discuss your plan with your supervisor; talk about whether any safety concerns are based more on actual risks or on unfamiliarity with the family or area and about whether this is a situation in which you should have a colleague or police officer accompany you.

It may be possible to check with the local police to ascertain if and how often they have been called to the home you will be visiting and why. The best predictor of potential for violence is past violent behavior. This is an especially important step if you are making the first agency contact with this client because you have no agency history or record on which to draw.

Plan to arrive near midday and midweek when making home visits to anyone with a substance abuse problem. At these times, you will be somewhat less likely to visit a client who has a hangover or is actively using.

Leave valuables, jewelry, purses, and so on at home or locked in your office. Make certain you have clear directions, a full tank of gas, and a charged battery. A car phone is a necessity. Plan to dress sensibly. Women should consider wearing pants and definitely should wear flat shoes rather than heels.

Finally, a sensible precaution for all child welfare workers is to check with their local department of motor vehicles to make sure that their addresses are not given out to anyone who asks about a license plate. If this is the policy in your state, request a block on the dissemination of your address.

■ While You Are Outside

While you are outside the home, you should do the following:

- Look around and "size up" the environment and neighbors.
- Be certain you are parked in a way that will not allow your car to be blocked.
- Watch for hostile dogs, and do not get out of the car unless the dogs are chained up.
- Identify an escape route back to the car and out of the area.

- The most important qualities to have and project while you are outside are vigilance and alertness.
- Do not look vulnerable. If there is a large group of people in the client's home, consider leaving and rescheduling.
- If a dog approaches you in a hostile way, avoid eye contact with the dog while backing away toward your car. Your goal is to give the dog the message that you understand he or she is guarding his or her territory and that you are retreating.
- Do not get into an elevator with anyone who makes you uncomfortable; wait for the next car.

■ *While You Are in the Client's Home*

Sit close to an exit, and keep your keys in your pocket. It is a good idea to ask who else is home and if there is anyone there who has a problem with your visiting. Use a polite, calm, courteous, and impartial tone. Repeat yourself and explain your purpose. Keep a nonthreatening body posture; avoid putting your hands on your hips. If your client or another person in the home appears to be under the influence of alcohol or drugs, stop the interview calmly and leave. Also, if anyone shows you or indicates a weapon, stop the interview calmly; encourage the person to put down the weapon and then leave.

Be aware of signs that violence may be imminent, such as flushed faces, clenched fists, raised voice, pacing, or a threatening stance, and leave if they occur. Do not attempt to touch a client who seems to be escalating toward violence. Even a well-intended pat on the shoulder can trigger violence in someone "on the edge." Be prepared to trust your intuition.

■ *De-Escalating Verbal Violence*

Use a quiet, polite voice and slow conversational pace; keep a calm demeanor, and never argue. Do not use humor—it does not work in these situations. Allow the client to back away or leave. Sometimes, asking for a drink of water may de-escalate tension. Allow the client to ventilate and acknowledge his or her feelings.

If you do not know the answer to a question, say so. Do not make vague reassurances, such as "I'm sure everything will turn out OK."

Maintain physical distance, moving backward if necessary to do this. If you feel threatened, stop the interview calmly and leave. Remember that, although you are there to be helpful to the children and the family, they may be hostile because they perceive you to be there to "cause trouble" for the family. There are few things that enrage people more than feeling threatened about their children—it is a natural response.

■ After You Leave the Home

After you leave the home, do the following:

- Check under the car and in the back seat before getting in the car; someone may be hiding there.
- If you have had a home visit in which there were threats of violence, you need to document these carefully. Do not stay in front of the house or in the neighborhood to write your notes, however; return to the office.
- Seek consultation or supervision to debrief from your experience. If there has been violence, you should be prepared to get counseling. Posttraumatic stress disorder is common after work-related violence.

■ When Transporting Clients in a Car

Transporting clients is often overlooked as a risk; this can actually be a very dangerous situation. Try to have a second worker with you, especially if there has been previous violence. Also, as a practical matter, if you are transporting a child of the opposite gender, it would be helpful to have a worker who could accompany the child to the bathroom if necessary. When transporting a child, you should know whether the child has a history of running or has threatened to do so. Pull over immediately if you become concerned.

■ *Agency Issues*

Finally, you should advocate for personal safety in-service training in your agency, for the establishment of agency policies on worker teams, and for the practice of flagging records for potentially dangerous situations.

■ *Further Reading*

Newhill, C. E. (1995). Client violence toward social workers: A practice and policy concern for the 1990s. *Social Work, 40,* 631-636.

120

How Do I Prevent Burnout?

■ *Richard L. Norman*

■ *Prevention of Burnout*

Burnout is a process. It has a beginning with early warning signs and a middle in which isolation minimization and denial shield the destructive aspects from view and awareness of the victim. Finally, without interruption, the end stage literally burns out the victim's vital internal adaptive capacity. This understanding provides opportunities to prevent and interrupt the process as we identify it in others or ourselves. Prevention is the best approach to this insidious process. Once it begins, it can be extremely difficult to sort out from constructive attitudes and behaviors. The stress operates like a virus, coexisting with healthy functions until a critical mass is achieved, resulting in slow but accelerating breakdown of function.

Child protective services (CPS) work shares high stress factors with those of law enforcement, fire response teams, and emergency medicine. In each of these services, some of the critical decisions facing the worker are seen as having life or death implications. One never knows what a particular case will require in terms of time, degree of injury or risk involved, or level of authority required to intervene appropriately. Without understanding the stressful effects of this work, vulnerability is multiplied.

A general prescription to counter the likelihood of becoming burned out is a plan. The 3-year plan is based on the theory of a 3-year service life cycle of the typical CPS worker. The first year is devoted to learning the agency system and CPS service system as a subsystem of the agency. The second year is focused on achieving an acceptable level of competency with the knowledge and skills required to perform optimally on a consistent basis. The third year is devoted to putting it all together and establishing the ability to work at a consistently high level with the most difficult cases. The plan requires one to set knowledge and skill objectives for each of these years. When implemented, even your most difficult work time will also represent what you have gained personally as (value-adding) knowledge and skill.

In my experience, the observed effects of this prescription have been (a) improved supervision (you tend to get what you ask for), (b) a sense of accomplishment, (c) higher morale in the face of very difficult case assignments, and (d) increased involvement with others who share a similar approach. Each of these effects should be viewed broadly as protective and an enhancement of the worker's capacity to manage the stress of CPS. No matter how difficult or complex the case, it becomes a learning opportunity.

■ *Where There's Smoke, There's Fire!*

Again, burnout is a process and produces early warning signs. The following are some early warning signs and suggested action steps for the individual that may interrupt this process:

- There is a noticeable change in interest toward duties.

   Reexamine your goals and objectives. Have they changed?

- Your threshold for coping with anger begins to increase or decrease significantly.

   Discuss this with your supervisor. Determine if it is transient or part of a pattern.

- You begin to notice that you are taking risks that you previously avoided.

    Examine the basis for the change. Is it confidence based on experience, or is your internal risk monitor malfunctioning?

- You begin to minimize mistakes and judgment errors.

    Consider voicing this concern at a unit meeting for a supportive discussion of typical errors: Nobody knows everything.

- You notice a "Sunday night syndrome"—vague anxiety after sundown Sunday and staying up later than usual on Sunday night for no special reason.

    Talk with your supervisor or trusted experienced coworker or both about current work challenges.

- There is a pattern of taking "sick days"—you are not sick but you call in sick on a whim.

    This is hiding behavior. Talk with your spouse or a trusted friend, and commit to finding out why this behavior is occurring. Then take appropriate action.

This is only a sampling of possible early warning signs. Stay alert to the possibilities, and remember the importance of talking out your concerns. CPS work is stressful, but stress does not inevitably become burnout unless it is ignored.

■ *No (Wo)Man Is an Island*

Crisis is subjective and frequently not apparent to others in the early stages. Frequently, however, repeated crises, chronic stress, and burnout are quite apparent to everyone except the victim. It is ironic that the victim often thinks nobody knows and sinks increasingly deeper into the illusion of safety from awareness of what his or her behavior means. Isolation is not the answer. Sharing within the group or in other appropriate ways supports discovery of resources in individuals and the group that are enhanced every time they are used.

121

How Can Critical Thinking Contribute to Informed Decisions?

■ *Eileen Gambrill*

Critical thinking involves the critical appraisal of beliefs and actions to arrive at well-reasoned ones. Richard Paul (1993, pp. 20-23) suggests that critical thinking has the following characteristics:

- It is purposeful.
- It is responsive to and guided by intellectual standards (relevance, clarity, accuracy, precision, depth, and breadth).
- It is guided by intellectual humility, integrity, perseverance, empathy, and self-discipline.
- Critical thinkers routinely identify the elements of thought in thinking about a problem such that logical connections are made between the elements and the problem. They ask the following: What is my purpose? What precise question am I trying to answer? Within what point of view am I thinking? What concepts or ideas are central to my thinking? What am I taking for granted, and what assumptions am I making? What information am I using (data, facts, or observation)? How am I interpreting that information? What are my conclusions? If I accept the conclusions, what are the implications?

- It is self-assessing (self-critical) and self-improving (self-corrective) using appropriate standards.
- There is an integrity to the whole system. The thinker is able to critically examine his or her thought as a whole and to take it apart (consider its parts as well). The thinker is committed to be intellectually humble, persevering, courageous, fair, and just. The critical thinker is aware of the variety of ways in which thinking can become distorted, misleading, prejudiced, superficial, unfair, or otherwise defective.
- It yields a well-reasoned answer.
- It attends to opposing points of view and seeks and identifies weaknesses and limitations in one's own position. Critical thinkers are aware that there are many legitimate points of view, each of which (when thought through) may yield some level of insight.

Critical thinking involves clearly describing and taking responsibility for one's claims and arguments, critically appraising one's views no matter how cherished, and considering alternative views. It involves paying attention to the process of reasoning (how we think) and not just the product. It encourages us to identify and question our assumptions and to consider the possible consequences of different beliefs or actions. Critical thinking is independent thinking—thinking for oneself. Critical thinkers question what others view as self-evident. They ask the following: How do I know this claim to be true? Who presented it as accurate? Are vested interests involved? How reliable are these sources? Are the facts presented correct? Have any facts been omitted? Is there any reliable evidence that a claim is true? Have any rigorous tests of a claim been performed? Were they free of bias? Have the results been replicated? How representative were the samples used? Are there other promising points of view? If so, have these been tested?

Critical thinkers are skeptics rather than believers. They are neither gullible (believing anything people say, especially if it is in agreement with their own views) nor cynical (believing nothing and having a negative outlook on life). Critical thinking requires a keen interest in discovering biases and mistakes in our thinking. Truth (accuracy) is valued rather than "winning" or social approval. Values and attitudes related to critical thinking include open-mindedness, an interest in the views of others, a desire to be well informed, a tendency to think before acting, and curiosity. Critical thinking means being fair-minded—that is, accurately describing opposing views and critiquing both preferred and less preferred views using the same rigorous standards. Critical thinking encourages intellectual modesty by emphasizing the importance of being aware of what one does not know. It discourages arrogance, the assumption that we know better than others or that our beliefs should not be subject to critical evaluation. Popper (1992) stated, "In our infinite ignorance we are all equal" (p. 50). Critical thinking emphasizes self-criticism. It prompts questions such as the following: Could I be wrong? Have I considered alternative views? Do I have sound reasons to believe that this plan will help this client?

■ *Minimizing Biases That Affect Practice Decisions*

Guidelines for minimizing biases include the following. First, become familiar with common biases and their consequences. One example is the *fundamental attribution error*—the tendency to attribute a behavior to personal dispositions of individuals and to overlook environmental causes of behavior. A potential harmful consequence of this bias is selection of inappropriate service programs. Another example of bias is the *behavioral confirmation tendency*—the tendency to search only for data that support favored views and to ignore evidence that does not. Second, remember what is at stake. Clients benefit or suffer as a result of helpers' beliefs and actions. By focusing on service goals, you will also be focused on gathering information that reduces uncertainty about how to help clients. Third, view criticism as essential to learning and problem solving. Questioning the accuracy of your judgments will help you to pay attention to the uncertainty involved in making decisions and to shift from being a "believer" who does not question his or her beliefs to being an evidence-based "questioner." This involves paying attention to the gaps between knowledge needed, what is available, and what you do not know. Fourth, value mistakes as learning opportunities. Feedback is an essential part of learning. If you are not making mistakes, you are probably not learning. Fifth, use helpful questions, such as the following:

- What are my assumptions?
- How can I rigorously test my assumptions?
- Is there evidence against my point of view?
- How common is this behavior?
- Is it a question of fact? (Can data can be gathered to answer it?)
- Where did the sample come from? Is there a selection bias?
- Have I thought carefully about this decision?

Lastly, take advantage of helpful distinctions, such as between (a) widely accepted and rigorously tested, (b) good intentions and whether or not you help clients, and (c) a feeling that something is true and whether it actually is true.

■ *Further Reading*

Gambrill, E. (1997). *Social work practice: A critical thinker's guide.* New York: Oxford University Press.

Grey, J. A. M. (1997). *Evidence-based health care.* New York: Churchill Livingstone.

Paul, R. W. (1993). *Critical thinking: What every person needs to survive in a rapidly changing world* (3rd ed.). Santa Rosa, CA: Foundation for Critical Thinking.

Popper, K. R. (1992). *In search of a better world: Lectures and essays from thirty years.* London: Routledge Kegan Paul.

122

What Can I Do to Cope With the Death or Serious Injury of a Child From My Caseload?

■ *Norma Harris*

■ *Responding to Loss and Trauma*

Impact on Professional Involved

When children from caseloads sustain serious injury or death, it is not only traumatic for parents and siblings but also difficult for practitioners, who may experience a range of feelings, including shock, disbelief, guilt, anger, and grief. It is important that the professionals acknowledge their own loss by seeking out resources available to deal with these events. It is also important to understand that feelings of guilt and the desire to defend the practitioner's and agency's activities in the situation are normal reactions. It is important to seek guidance and counseling when these traumatic situations occur.

Impact on the Child Protective Services Unit

If the situation is highly visible to the community and the media coverage is extensive, the entire child protective services (CPS) unit may be involved. When press releases allege that CPS did not provide adequate protection, it can be demoralizing to the entire unit. In these situations, all workers should use agency support resources to put the matter in perspective.

■ 589

■ *Participating in the Agency*
Internal Support System

All CPS agencies should have internal support systems available to staff who encounter these kinds of situations. Within the agency, it should be considered standard practice for staff to seek support when a child in their caseload sustains serious injury or dies.

Counseling and Employee Assistance Programs

Counseling and other services may be offered by a qualified, trained person on staff, or they may be contracted. The purpose of the services is to assist staff in dealing with their feelings, to obtain clarity, and put the entire situation into perspective. Part of obtaining clarity involves putting the practitioner's role in the protection of children in proper perspective so that practitioners do not assume responsibility for children's injury or death. Although the counseling is ordinarily short term, arrangements should be made for staff who need longer term support.

■ *Participation in Agency Review*

Purpose

The agency must evaluate the circumstances in which a child sustained serious injury or died to determine if the agency did all it could to protect the child. In addition, the agency should conduct reviews to prevent future injuries or child deaths. Although the review process may be difficult, it is essential that the practitioner participate. Generally, there are specific policies and time frames related to informing management about the incidents. Practitioners involved with the child are usually responsible for providing background information, including dates of contact with the child or family or both, the nature of the activities (e.g., part of an initial assessment) and the ongoing relationship, collateral agency involvement, and other relevant information.

What to Do With the Review Findings

The review findings summarize the circumstances, identify possible deficiencies, and provide recommendations to prevent future incidents. Often, the incident occurred as a result of several factors. In addition to recognizing agency strengths, the results of the review can identify training needs, policies that need to be changed, problematic interagency relationships, and other needed changes. If the practitioner needs additional training, efforts should be made to provide this training.

■ *Participating in a Child Fatality Review*

Purpose

Child fatality review teams are multidisciplinary, with members representing several disciplines and agencies. One objective of these teams is to share information and clarify the circumstances contributing to the child's death. Another purpose of a local or state child fatality review is to reduce preventable child fatalities. Generally, child fatality review teams are responsible for reviewing all child deaths and not just those with CPS involvement. As such, state and local teams identify causes of preventable child deaths, work in partnership with each other to educate the public about the causes, and advocate for policies and programs to prevent further fatalities.

Procedure

When children from their caseloads have died, it is critical for CPS personnel to participate in assisting the teams' effort in collecting information promptly, routinely, accurately, and consistently. Although there are well-defined protocols for conducting reviews, often written records are not kept of the actual proceedings so that confidential and sensitive information does not become public.

Importance of Findings

Because these teams may review all child deaths, the findings can be very broad and comprehensive, affecting many agencies and the community. These teams generally have high visibility, and all agencies impacted by recommendations are expected to respond.

■ Dealing With the Media

Although the media, especially newspapers, tend not to be involved in serious injury situations, they almost always demand explanations for the deaths of children. In some communities, there is a tendency for the press to blame CPS for child deaths if the agency was involved with the children's families. Because there is a desire for practitioners to defend themselves, it is important not to overreact to statements in the media. Often, agencies have policies about who talks to the press and in what circumstances. Although there are ways in which agencies can effectively communicate with the media, confidentiality rules often influence how and what an agency releases to the public. If the practitioner has permission to communicate with the media and is inclined to do so, it is often helpful for him or her to use examples of how agencies conduct their business. Consultation with the agency's legal counsel is strongly recommended. For example, although the practitioner cannot talk about specific children, he or she can outline how the agency conducts safety assessments, indicating what factors are involved, how the agency makes decisions about out-of-home placement, and so on. Providing such examples often defuses allegations that the agency is trying to hide behind confidentiality laws.

It may also be helpful to acknowledge that the practitioner's ability to predict when a tragedy will occur is quite limited. Hindsight may make the course of events seem clear; the practitioner needs to be very cautious not to fall into this trap.

■ *Moving Forward*

Child welfare is a challenging field—one in which the turnover is high. Serious injury or death of a child presents significant challenges for practitioners, and these events can be difficult both personally and professionally for staff. This is a time when practitioners need to attend to their own well-being and use available agency supports. There are agency and community review mechanisms that will require the practitioner's involvement, but the final summary with recommendations is not the practitioner's responsibility. Although it may be difficult, the practitioner should examine the findings, learn from what has happened in terms of how to improve practice, and move forward to a productive career in this field.

123

How Do I Balance Common Sense, Personal Values, and Agency Constraints?

■ *Joan R. Rycraft*

C hild welfare practitioners are often required to make decisions regarding children and their families that abridge common sense and violate their personal values. Although agency constraints are often perceived as the primary cause of the dilemma, child welfare practitioners tend to select a system-oriented response rather than an individual client-oriented response in decision making. The key to surmounting this ongoing challenge is to find a balance among these factors and continue to provide needed services to children and families. Three major factors should be considered: (a) the realities of child welfare practice, (b) practitioner responses, and (c) finding a balance.

■ Realities of Child Welfare Practice

Child welfare is a highly regulated and complex social service system requiring knowledge and skills to navigate and to use the system for the benefit of children and families. Child welfare practice should be viewed as a continuum of problem solving and decision making based on collaboration among the practitioner, client, and key service providers within legal mandates and agency policy. Child welfare practitioners need to recognize the realities of the child welfare system:

- Legal mandates and policies are guidelines for practice.
- The child welfare system can be navigated.
- Advocacy is the role of the practitioner at both the case and system levels.
- Change is often difficult and slow but essential to effective practice.
- Making a positive impact may require personal and systemic change.
- Practitioners can become victims of the system.

■ *Practitioner Responses*

Faced with systemic obstacles such as changing policies, draconian rules and regulations, lack of resources, little agency support, and ethical conflicts, practitioners respond in a variety of ways:

- Falling into the rut of "practice as usual": The practitioner acquiesces to the constraints rather than working toward removing or decreasing obstacles. Constraints are unquestioned. Avenues of change are viewed as nonexistent or not worth the effort and hold the possibility of retribution.
- The "ain't it awful" griping game: Dealing with difficult decisions and insufficient resources, the practitioner places a mantle of blame on the system. Policies and procedures are quoted as reasons for obstacles to practice. A culture develops in which "nothing can be done" to make the system respond more positively.
- Attempting to be "all things to all people": Viewing the system as the barrier to effective practice and sound decision making, the practitioner takes total responsibility for client outcomes. This crusade is doomed. The practitioner will be unsuccessful and prone to disappointment.

- "Giving up" and "throwing in the towel": The practitioner fails to combat the problems of agency constraints. It is time to retreat and respond by doing only what is required. Clients receive minimal service with mediocre outcomes.
- "Meeting the challenge": The practitioner continues to work within agency constraints and takes action to rectify those found to be most challenging to common sense and personal values. A balance is established allowing the practitioner to function effectively in the agency.

■ *Means to Finding a Balance*

Child welfare practitioners are committed to children and families. Their valiant efforts to conquer insurmountable tasks require a balance of personal values, job functions, common sense, and agency policies and practices.

- *Identifying responsibilities:* All parties involved (agency, practitioner, client, and other service providers) hold a portion of responsibility for service outcomes. The determination of who is responsible for specific tasks is essential to balancing the demands of child welfare practice.
- *Self-awareness:* Self-knowledge provides a foundation for effective practice. Child welfare practitioners must be aware of personal values and their commitment to children and families and how they fit with agency policy, rules, and regulations. When in conflict, practitioners must determine how much, if any, of their personal values can be abrogated. The following question must be addressed: "Can I accept this and feel okay with myself?" If the answer is "no," then what changes need to occur to make it acceptable?
- *Strengths and limitations:* Building on strengths and improving on one's limitations are hallmarks of a professional. Finding a fit with specific tasks will enable the practitioner to balance demands and conflicts within the agency. With the assistance of a respected supervisor, a thorough assessment of how individual strengths and

limitations fit specific job assignments and tasks should be conducted. "Goodness of fit" with the job is instrumental in balancing expectations and conflicts.

- *Assessment, reframing, and letting go:* When imbalance occurs, an assessment of the perceived conflict must be conducted. To determine the magnitude of the conflict, the practitioner should explore the following: What is the underlying issue of conflict? Can it be resolved, and by whom? If not, what are the potential consequences? The approach to conflicts varies. Often, by examining the issue from a different perspective, the conflict can be reframed in a manner that supports resolution. A key element in finding balance is deciding when to let go of an issue. When all avenues of redress have been explored and no resolution has been reached, it may be prudent to move on and expend efforts on other issues.
- *Taking action:* Issues of imbalance may reach a point at which the practitioner calls for substantial changes in agency policy, rules, and regulations. This requires planning, thinking, and taking specific action. With a sound strategy, tenacity, and support, a practitioner can marshal change in the agency and maintain the balance between personal values, common sense, and agency constraints.

■ *Further Reading*

Pine, B. (1987). Strategies for more ethical decision making in child welfare practice. *Child Welfare, 66*(4), 315-326.

Walden, T., Wolock, I., & Demone, H. W., Jr. (1990). Ethical decision making in human services: A comparative study. *Families in Society, 71*(2), 67-75.

124

How Do I Use Case Record Keeping to Guide Intervention and Provide Accountability?

■ *Diane DePanfilis*

W
e are constantly being held more accountable for what we do. This chapter describes the primary purposes of record keeping and the principles of how we keep records, and it outlines content that we should record at each step of the process. In this way, we will not only be accountable to others but also can use the process of record keeping as a way of thinking and measuring the results of our work with families.

■ *Purposes of Client Record Keeping*

Keeping records is usually done because we have to do it and not because we like to do it. This is probably because we do not see how keeping records helps our work with our clients. Although some purposes of record keeping seem removed from our work, other purposes are directly related to our work. What are the purposes of keeping records?

1. Case records provide an ongoing "picture" of the nature of our involvement with families, the progress toward achieving outcomes, and the basis of decisions that eventually lead to case

closure. If we use this purpose as a method to analyze the progress we are making with our clients, not just to provide accountability for others, the process of record keeping helps to clarify and focus our work. The act of documenting one's work helps one reflect on the nature of one's efforts, on what is planned, and on how the case is progressing.

2. Case records also provide accountability for the agency and the worker. Records should describe who is served and not served, the kinds of services provided, the basis for all decisions, the degree to which policies are implemented, and other aspects of accountability and quality control. The record provides a statement about the quality of work that decreases personal liability should legal action be taken against the agency or the worker.

3. Case record keeping can also be a therapeutic tool for the worker and the family. This is particularly true if the worker and the family together define the purpose of their work, define outcomes and goals that will reduce the risk of maltreatment, and evaluate the progress toward the achievement of outcomes and goals. Many agencies use instruments and tools that seek input from clients during the process, and therefore the record provides an illustration of this collaborative process.

4. The case record is also a means to organize our thinking about our work. Structured presentation of factual information leads to more in-depth assessment and treatment planning. Sloppy recording and disorganized thinking often go hand in hand and will likely lead to poor service delivery to clients.

5. In addition to the previously described primary purposes (all of which can be useful in our work with our clients), the case record is also a means for supervisory review, statistical reporting and research, and interdisciplinary communication.

■ What Should Be Included in Case Records?

Case records should factually document both what we do (our assessment and intervention) and the results of our intervention and treatment (outcomes of child safety, permanence, and well-being) (see Chapter 77, this volume). Family records should include the following:

- Information about the nature and extent of the referral or report; identifying data on the child, family, and significant others; and the response of the agency to the referral (see Chapters 1 and 2, this volume)

- A record of all dates of contact and interviews (in person and phone) with all members of the family, collateral sources, and multidisciplinary team members and the locations and purposes of these contacts (see Chapters 13 through 19 and Chapter 21, this volume)

- Information about the initial assessment, including documentation of what may have already occurred (the alleged report of child maltreatment) and an assessment of risk and safety of the child (see Chapters 47 and 48, this volume)

- Information about diagnostic procedures that may have been part of the initial assessment (e.g., medical evaluations, X rays or other medical tests, psychological evaluations, and alcohol or drug assessments) (see Chapters 22, 23, 31, 32, 40, 41, and 43, this volume)

- Clear documentation of initial decisions with respect to substantiation of the alleged maltreatment, risk assessment and safety evaluation, the basis for placement in out-of-home care or court referral (if necessary), and reasons for continued agency involvement or for terminating services (see Chapters 20, 24-30, 33-39, 42, and 44-48, this volume)

- Documentation that the family members have been informed of the agency's policy on the release of information from the record (see Chapter 111, this volume)

- Inclusion of the safety plan if one was developed and documentation of referrals to other programs, agencies, or persons who will participate in the implementation of the safety plan (see Chapters 49 through 55, this volume)

- A record of the family assessment and a delineation of the treatment needs of the child, caregivers, and the family (see Chapters 56 through 75, this volume)

- Specification of the intervention outcomes that, if achieved, will reduce the risks of maltreatment and address the effects of maltreatment (see Chapters 76 and 77, this volume)
- Inclusion of the service plan, with specific measurable goals and a description of the process used to develop the plan (see Chapters 78 through 84, this volume)
- Documentation of the case activities and their outcomes, including information from all community practitioners who are providing intervention or treatment (written reports should be requested from all providers) and information about the family's response to intervention and treatment (see Chapters 85 through 105, this volume)
- Information about the progress toward the achievement of outcomes, the completion of service plans, the risk-reduction process, and reunification of children with their families or other permanency options (see Chapters 106 through 109, this volume)
- Information provided to the court if it was necessary (see Chapter 113, this volume)
- Inclusion of a case closing summary that describes the process of closure with the family (see Chapter 110, this volume) and an outline that summarizes the original reason for referral, the outcomes and goals that were established with the family, the nature of the services that were provided and the activities that various practitioners and the client undertook, a description of the level of progress that was accomplished with respect to outcomes and goals, a summary of any new reports of maltreatment that may have occurred during intervention, a brief assessment of the current risk and safety, an identification of problems or goals that remain unresolved or unaccomplished, and the reasons for closing the case

■ *Principles of Record Keeping*

The case record is a professional document and tool. Therefore, it should be completed in a professional manner, and confidentiality should be respected at all times. Principles of record keeping include the following:

1. All information maintained in case records should be relevant and necessary to the agency's purposes. We should record facts and distinguish them from opinions. When opinions are offered, the basis for them should be well established (e.g., "Mr. Smith appeared to be intoxicated, his eyes were red, he had difficulty standing without losing his balance, his breath smelled of alcohol").

2. We should record as much information as possible based on direct communication with our clients.

3. We should omit details of clients' intimate lives or their political, religious, or other personal views in case records if this information is not relevant to our purposes.

4. We should not include process recordings in case files. (The primary purpose of a process recording is to build the practitioner's skills. Therefore, they do not belong in an agency record.)

5. We should maintain and update records to ensure accuracy, relevancy, timeliness, and completeness. Errors should be marked as such but should not be erased or deleted.

6. We should use private dictation facilities to protect a client's right to confidentiality.

7. The client's permission must be secured before any session is audio- or videotaped.

8. Case records should be kept in locked files, and keys should be issued only to those who require frequent access to files. When a file is being used, there should be a clear record of the date that the file was removed and by whom.

9. Case records should leave the agency only in extraordinary circumstances with special authorization (e.g., if the record was subpoenaed for court).

10. Case records should not be left on desks or in other open spaces where janitorial personnel or others might have access to them.

11. Clients should be informed about the agency's authority to gather information, their rights to participate (or not) in the process, the principal purpose for the use of the information that they provide, the nature and extent of the confidenti-

ality of the information, and the circumstances in which information in records may be shared with others.

12. Clients should sign "release of information" forms prior to disclosure (verbal or written) of any information about them to other practitioners. An exception usually exists in state child abuse reporting laws to provide for sharing informa-

•   tion between members of a multidisciplinary team. Specific state laws and policies should guide these actions.

■ *Summary*

Quality record keeping is an integral part of professional practice. This chapter provided a brief overview of the purposes, content, and principles relevant to recording information about child protection practice. When the record is used as an opportunity to organize thinking and to integrate an approach to measuring the results of our work, it becomes part of the process rather than only documenting the process.

■ *Further Reading*

Child Welfare League of America. (1999). *CWLA standards of excellence for services for abused or neglected children and their families* (Rev. ed.). Washington, DC: Author.

Hepworth, D. H., Rooney, R. H., & Larsen, J. (1997). *Direct social work practice* (5th ed.). Pacific Grove, CA: Brooks/Cole.

Wilson, S. J. (1980). *Recording guidelines for social workers.* New York: Free Press.

Appendix 1
Advisory Group
on Chapter Topics

We thank the following individuals who helped identify topics for potential chapters or rated the importance of a draft list of chapter topics or both:

Veronica D. Abney, LCSW, Santa Monica, California

Nadine Bean, PhD, Bryn Mawr College, School of Social Work, Bryn Mawr, Pennsylvania

Steve Berry, Social Services Administration, Department of Human Resources, Baltimore, Maryland

Thomas Curran, JD, Defender Association of Philadelphia, Philadelphia, Pennsylvania

Pamela Day, MSW, Child Welfare League of America, Washington, DC

Kristina Debye, LCSW-C, Baltimore County Department of Social Services, Towson, Maryland

Joy Ernst, PhD, University of Maryland School of Social Work, Baltimore

Geoffrey Greif, PhD, University of Maryland School of Social Work, Baltimore

Esta Glazer-Semmel, LCSW-C, University of Maryland School of Social Work, Baltimore

Donna Harrington, PhD, University of Maryland School of Social Work, Baltimore

Clint Holder, MSW, ACTION for Child Protection, Denver, Colorado

Brenda Kess, LCSW-C, Baltimore City Department of Social Services, Baltimore, Maryland

Robert Lindecamp, Division of Child Protective Services, Wilmington, Delaware

John Curtis McMillen, PhD, Washington University, George Warren Brown School of Social Work, St. Louis, Missouri

Gisele Feretto Meek, LCSW-C, University of Maryland School of Social Work, Baltimore

Richard Norman, LCSW-C, University of Maryland School of Social Work, Baltimore

Margarete Parrish, PhD, University of Maryland School of Social Work, Baltimore

Peter Pecora, PhD, Casey Family Program, Seattle, Washington

Robert Pierce, PhD, Washington University, George Warren Brown School of Social Work, St. Louis, Missouri

Diane Pisano, LCSW-C, clinical social worker, Bowie, Maryland

Julia Rauch, PhD, University of Maryland School of Social Work, Baltimore

Marsha Salus, MSW, child welfare consultant, Boyd, Maryland

Stacey Saunders, MA, child welfare consultant, Columbus, Ohio

Maria Scannapieco, PhD, University of Texas at Arlington, School of Social Work, Arlington

Beverly Williams, LCSW-C, Child and Family Services Agency, Washington, DC

Charles Wilson, MSSW, National Children's Advocacy Center, Huntsville, Alabama

Dee Wilson, MSW, Department of Children and Family Services, Olympia, Washington

Joan Levy Zlotnik, PhD, MSW, Council on Social Work Education, Alexandria, Maryland

Ronald Zuskin, LCSW-C, University of Maryland School of Social Work, Baltimore

Appendix 2
The Michigan Alcoholism
Screening Test (MAST)

Circle the response "yes" or "no" depending on whether the statement says something true or not true about you. Please answer all questions. The test can be scored to let you know where you lie on a scale from social drinker to addictive drinker.

0. Do you enjoy a drink now and then?	Yes	No
1. Do you feel you are a normal drinker?	Yes	No
2. Have you ever awakened the morning after some drinking the night before and found that you could not remember part of the evening?	Yes	No
3. Does your wife, husband, a parent, or other near relative ever worry or complain about your drinking?	Yes	No
4. Can you stop drinking without a struggle after one or two drinks?	Yes	No
5. Do you ever feel guilty about your drinking?	Yes	No
6. Do friends or relatives think you are a normal drinker?	Yes	No
7. Are you able to stop drinking when you want to?	Yes	No
8. Have you ever attended a meeting of Alcoholics Anonymous?	Yes	No
9. Have you gotten into physical fights when drinking?	Yes	No
10. Has your drinking ever created problems between you and your wife or husband? A parent or other relative?	Yes	No
11. Has your wife, husband, or other family members ever gone for help about your drinking?	Yes	No
12. Have you ever lost friends because of your drinking?	Yes	No
13. Have you ever gotten into trouble at work or school because of your drinking?	Yes	No
14. Have you ever lost a job because of your drinking?	Yes	No
15. Have you ever neglected your obligations, your family, or your work for two or more days in a row because you were drinking?	Yes	No

16. Do you drink before noon fairly often?   Yes   No
17. Have you ever been told you have liver trouble? Cirrhosis?   Yes   No
18. After heavy drinking have you ever had delirium tremens (DTs)
    or severe shaking or heard voices or seen things that really
    were not there?   Yes   No
19. Have you ever gone to anyone for help about your drinking?   Yes   No
20. Have you ever been in a hospital because of your drinking?   Yes   No
21. Have you ever been a patient in a psychiatric hospital or on a
    psychiatric ward of a general hospital where drinking was part
    of the problem that resulted in hospitalization?   Yes   No
22. Have you ever been seen at a psychiatric or mental health
    clinic or gone to a doctor, social worker, or clergyman for help
    with any emotional problem in which drinking played a part?   Yes   No
23. Have you ever been arrested for drunk driving, driving while
    intoxicated, or driving under the influence of alcoholic
    beverages? (If so, how many times? _____)   Yes   No
24. Have you ever been arrested or taken into custody, even for a
    few hours, because of drunk behavior?
    (If yes, how many times? _____)   Yes   No

Your score is _____.   3 or less   Not alcoholic
                        4   Suggests alcoholism
                        5 or more   Alcoholism

Master Key

0.	<u>Yes</u>	<u>No</u>	0
1.	Yes	<u>No</u>	2
2.	<u>Yes</u>	No	2
3.	<u>Yes</u>	No	1
4.	Yes	<u>No</u>	2
5.	<u>Yes</u>	No	1
6.	Yes	<u>No</u>	2
7.	Yes	<u>No</u>	2
8.	<u>Yes</u>	No	5
9.	<u>Yes</u>	No	1
10.	<u>Yes</u>	No	2
11.	<u>Yes</u>	No	2
12.	<u>Yes</u>	No	2
13.	<u>Yes</u>	No	2
14.	<u>Yes</u>	No	2
15.	<u>Yes</u>	No	2
16.	<u>Yes</u>	No	1
17.	<u>Yes</u>	No	2
18.	<u>Yes</u>	No	2[a]
19.	<u>Yes</u>	No	5
20.	<u>Yes</u>	No	5
21.	<u>Yes</u>	No	2
22.	<u>Yes</u>	No	2
23.	<u>Yes</u>	No	2[b]
24.	<u>Yes</u>	No	2[b]

a. If DTs are reported, score is 5; for any other positive response, score 2.
b. Each arrest × 2 points.

Appendix 3
Likelihood of Sexual Transmission of and Basic Information on Sexually Transmitted Diseases

Robert A. Shapiro

Table A3.1   The Likelihood of Sexual Transmission of Specific Sexually
Transmitted Diseases (STDs)

STD	*Likelihood of Sexual Transmission*
Gonorrhea	Very high[a]
Chlamydia	Very high[a]
Syphilis	Very high[a]
Condyloma acuminata (venereal warts)	Possible
Trichomonas	Very high[a]
Herpes	Possible
HIV/AIDS	Very high[a]
Bacterial vaginosis	Low
Molluscum	Low
Pubic lice	Possible
Hepatitis B	Possible

a. The physician should consider other ways of transmission (e.g., birth process and blood transfusion).

Table A3.2   Sexually Transmitted Diseases (STDs): Basic Information

STD and Sites of Infection	Incubation Period and Symptoms	Transmission	Diagnostic Tests
Gonorrhea (*Neisseria gonorrhea*) Vagina Cervix Urethra Rectum Throat Pelvis (PID) Systemic	Vaginal infection in prepubertal girls usually causes discharge within 2 to 7 days. Rectal and throat infections in all ages, and cervical infections in adolescents, are often asymptomatic.	During delivery, an infant may be infected. Eye infections are most common and result in eye discharge within a few days of life. Vaginal and rectal infections are also possible. Vaginal infections beyond the newborn period should be presumed to be from sexual abuse. Little is known about the persistence of asymptomatic rectal and pharyngeal infections.	The only acceptable testing method is bacterial culture. A positive culture must be confirmed by two other identification tests before the diagnosis is made. Misidentification will occur if these methods are not followed.
Chlamydia (*Chlamydia trachomatis*) Vagina Cervix Urethra Rectum	Most chlamydia infections do not cause symptoms. Tissue culture tests should be positive 5 to 7 days after contact. Identification earlier than this is very unlikely.	Perinatal infection may be unrecognized for years. Asymptomatic vaginal and rectal perinatal infections have been documented for up to 3 years. A chlamydia infection should be presumed to be from sexual abuse if perinatal infection has been excluded.	The only acceptable method is positive bacterial tissue culture. Misidentification will occur if other methods are used.

(continued)

STD and Sites of Infection	Incubation Period and Symptoms	Transmission	Diagnostic Tests
Syphilis (*Treponema pallidum*) Primary infection causes a painless ulcer at the site of contact.	Primary infection usually occurs about 3 weeks after infection (range: 10 to 90 days). Secondary syphilis causes rash, fever, and other symptoms 1 or 2 months later. Condyloma latum, a wart-like rash, may be seen near the anus and vagina.	Perinatal infection often occurs. It is routine practice in newborn nurseries to screen for maternal syphilis at the time of delivery. Infection is almost always spread by direct sexual contact. Nonsexual transmission, other than perinatal infection, is extremely unusual. Infection should be presumed to be through sexual abuse unless acquired by perinatal (congenital) infection.	Although definitive diagnosis can be made by microscopic identification, adequate specimens are usually not available for this type of testing. Most cases of syphilis are diagnosed through serologic blood tests. A presumptive diagnosis of syphilis can be made if there is a positive nontreponemal test (rapid plasma reagin, VDRL, or automated reagin test) and a positive treponemal test (fluorescent treponemal antibody absorption or microhemagglutination test for *T. pallidum*).
Condyloma acuminata (venereal warts) Human papilloma virus Vagina Penis Anus	Infection may cause skin-colored growths that vary in size from a few millimeters to many centimeters. Infections may cause no visible warts. The incubation period may be 2 years or longer.	Infection may be transmitted during birth, through sexual contact, or by nonsexual contact. Sexual abuse should be considered in any child with anal or genital warts.	The diagnosis is usually made by their appearance on physical examination. The wart can be surgically removed and, in some centers, the virus type can be determined. More than 70 types of wart viruses have been identified. It is unclear if determination of the wart type is of value when evaluating alleged sexual abuse.

STD and Sites of Infection	Incubation Period and Symptoms	Transmission	Diagnostic Tests
Trichomonas (*Trichomonas vaginalis*) Vagina Urethra	Many infections are asymptomatic. Male urethral infection is often asymptomatic. Vaginal discharge may develop between 4 and 28 days after contact.	Perinatal vaginal infection may persist for many months following birth. Infection is usually by sexual contact. Nonsexual transmission is very unlikely, although it is possible.	It must be differentiated from other types of trichomonas if identified in analysis of urine or stool. The diagnosis is made by microscopic identification or bacterial culture of vaginal secretions.
Herpes (herpes simplex virus types I and II) Vagina Penis Anus Mouth	Painful ulcers occur within 2 weeks following contact. Reactivation of the infection often occurs and results in ulcers at or near the site of primary infection.	The most common infection in children is gingivostomatits, an infection of the mouth. It is not transmitted sexually. Infection of the genitalia or infection near the anus may be due to sexual contact. Nonsexual transmission is also possible.	The diagnosis can be made based on the appearance of the ulcers. The virus can be cultured if the diagnosis is in question. Type I and type II both cause genital and perianal ulcers. Identification of the virus type does not differentiate sexual from nonsexual transmission.
HIV/AIDS	Signs of illness are delayed for up to 6 years or longer. Symptoms include swollen lymph nodes, failure to thrive, and fungal and other infections.	Infection is spread by contact with infected semen, blood, cervical secretions, or human milk.	Approximately one in four infants born to mothers with HIV will be infected. Other methods of infection in children include contaminated blood or blood products during transfusion, intravenous drug abuse, and sexual abuse.

(continued)

STD and Sites of Infection	Incubation Period and Symptoms	Transmission	Diagnostic Tests
Bacterial vaginosis (*Gardnerella vaginalis* and other bacteria) Vagina	May cause vaginal discharge. Some infections are asymptomatic.	This organism is most often seen in sexually active women but has been found in girls and women who have had no sexual contact and have not been sexually abused.	Identification is made by microscopic analysis, bacterial culture, and other methods.
Molluscom contagiosum (*poxvirus*) This virus may occur anywhere on the body.	Small bumps appear with a central depression. The incubation period is 2 weeks to 6 months	This virus is spread by direct contact. It is most often transmitted by nonsexual contact	Diagnosis is made by the clinical appearance of the rash.
Pubic lice (crabs) (*Pediculus pthirus*) Eyelashes Eyebrows Genital hair Perianal hair Beard Arm pits Scalp (rarely)	The most common site of infection in young children is the eyelash. Nits (eggs) can be seen as can the movement of lice.	In adolescents, transmission is usually sexual. Nonsexual transmission through contaminated towels is possible. Sexual abuse should always be considered in children infected with pubic lice.	The diagnosis is made by the clinical appearance of the lice. Head lice do not infect eyelashes. Lice infestations of the eyelashes are pubic lice. Microscopic examination of the louse can be done if there is doubt about the type of louse causing the infestation.

STD and Sites of Infection	Incubation Period and Symptoms	Transmission	Diagnostic Tests
Hepatitis B (hepatitis B virus [HBV]) This virus causes systemic illness	Some children will have no symptoms. Others will have loss of appetite, stomach pain, and jaundice. Infection can cause death. The incubation period is 45 to 160 days after contact.	Perinatal transmission occurs if the mother is infectious. Both sexual and nonsexual transmission occur. Children who live with HBV carriers are at risk, as are children who live in institutions for the developmentally disabled. Infection is transmitted through infected blood, wound secretions, semen, cervical secretions, and saliva.	The diagnosis is made from serologic blood tests.

Appendix 4
Developmental Milestones[a]

Becky Frink Sherman and E. Wayne Holden

Skill	Months						
	0-3	3-6	6-9	9-12	12-18	18-24	24-36
Cognition	Follows movement of hands with eyes	Recognizes caregivers	Uncovers toy that has been partially hidden	Finds completely hidden object	Recognizes shapes in a puzzle board	Names five parts of the body	Engages in domestic make-believe play
Communication	Smiles at caregiver's voice	Turns head to locate sounds and voices	Uses vocalization for attention	Stops activities in response to "no"	Uses one word to express an idea	Uses familiar names of objects	Carries out two-step commands
Gross motor	Rolls from side to back	Rolls from stomach to back	Sits unsupported and reaches for toys	Walks with support	Walks alone	Picks up toy from floor when standing up	Walks up stairs with support, alternating feet
Fine motor	Grasps object when placed in hand	Bangs objects in play	Transfers objects from one hand to another	Grasps with finger and thumb	Holds crayon and scribbles on paper	Imitates stacking tower of four cubes	Builds tower of nine blocks
Self-help	Demonstrates sucking reflex	Reaches for and holds bottle	Manipulates finger foods	Drinks from cup with some liquid spilling from mouth	Removes simple garments on request	Ceases activity for nap time	Eats well with spoon; begins to use fork
Social	Quiets when picked up	Cries when left alone or put down	Plays peek-a-boo	Shows preference for one toy over another	Repeats a performance laughed at	Pays attention to other children	Initiates own play activities; plays in simple games

a. Approximate ages.

Appendix 5
Schedule of Preventive Health Care

While the age headings may suggest a preventive visit every two years from age 6 - 20 years, there may be a local recommendation for yearly preventive visits from age 2 - 20 years.

Screening Components / AGE	New Born	0-1 mos.	2-3 mos.	4-5 mos.	6-8 mos.	9-11 mos.	12 mos	15 mos.	18 mos.	2 yrs.	3 yrs	4 yrs.	5 yrs.	6 yrs.	8 yrs.	10 yrs.	12 yrs	14 yrs.	16 yrs.	18-20 yrs.
Health and Developmental History	X	X	X	X	X	X	X	X	X	X	X	X	X	X	X	X	X	X	X	X
Physical Examination (unclothed)	X	X	X	X	X	X	X	X	X	X	X	X	X	X	X	X	X	X	X	X
Health and Weight	X	X	X	X	X	X	X	X	X	X	X	X	X	X	X	X	X	X	X	X
Head Circum. **	X	X	X	X	X	X														
Blood Pressure								X				X	X	X	X	X	X	X	X	X
Develop./Mental Health Assessment	S	S	S	S	*	*	*	*	*	*	*	*	S	S	S	S	S	S	S	S
Vision	S	S	S	S	S	S	S	S	S	S	X	X	*	*	X	X	*	X	*	X
Hearing	S	S	S	S	S	S	S	S	S	S	X	X	*	*	X	X	*	X	*	X
Hereditary/Metabolic** Hemoglobinopathy	X	X	(X)										(X)							
Lead Assessment						X	X	X	X	X	X	X	X							
Lead-Blood Test **							X			X										
Anemia Hct/Hgb**							X	(X)	(X)	X	(X)	(X)			(X)					
Immunizations+	X	X	X	X	X	X	X	X	X	X	X	X	X	X	X	X	X	X	X	X
Health Education/ Anticipatory Guidance	X	X	X	X	X	X	X	X	X	X	X	X	X	X	X	X	X	X	X	X
Dental Assessment	X	X	X	X	X	X	X	X	X	X	X	X	X	X	X	X	X	X	X	X

KEY:

X   = Required
(X) = Required if not done previously
S   = Required, subjective assessment acceptable
*   = Required, subjective assessment acceptable, objective text recommended
** = Additional screening needed for individuals at risk
+   = Childhood immunizations for Hepatitis B, tetanus, pertussis, H Influenza Type B, polio, measles, mumps, rubella, varicella, and others as available should be given in accordance with the guidelines provided by the Advisory Committee on Immunization Practices (ACIF), the American Academy of Pediatrics (AAP), and the American Academy of Family Physicians (AAFP). The current recommended schedule of immunizations should be obtained from the child's health care provider.

Appendix 6
Limited Genogram of Mrs. R's Family

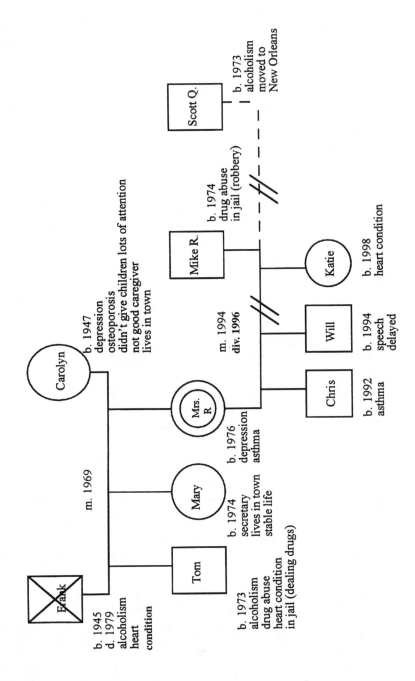

Appendix 7
Parenting Resources

Contributed by Sandra Azar

Table A7.1   How to Do Assessment in a Relationship-Building Way

Normalize
> "We do this with all parents as we enter our program."
> "I do this with each mom I work with—to help us get started."

Personalize
> "I have a set of questions I [we] find helps us to understand moms better . . . it is important we get to know what your life is like and what we can do to help."
> (If you are doing a selected assessment) "Last time we met, you talked a lot about being sad. I want to ask you more about this. I really get the sense you are suffering. I use these questions to make sure I understand how bad it is for you right now."
> (In an initial intake) "This set of questions might be especially important for the kinds of things you've already told me . . ."

Believe in what you are doing
> "This helps me to make sure I don't forget to ask about something important."
> "I find this really useful . . ."

Disarm
> "I hate forms myself, so I hope you'll be patient with all these questions . . ."
> "If any of the questions I ask are too personal, you let me know."
> "Some of these questions may seem silly [or may not apply to you]."

Practical tips
> Develop an introduction that feels right.
> Make sure you make lots of eye contact.
> Be familiar with the form.
> Go slow, but be efficient (set a time frame).
> If you hit a rough spot, say you will come back to this later, you want to hear more, stop briefly, spend a little extra time but move back to the instrument, and then stop.
> Teaching them how to use rating scales–Repeat instructions periodically–Use anchors and visual cues–Reward between forms—"Wow! We got through that one fast. . . . You're really getting the hang of this."
> Before ending, ask how it felt to be asked questions, ask for their reaction, and ask if there is anything you missed.

Table A7.2   Sampling of Skill Areas Required to Parent

Parenting skills
   Problem-solving abilities
   A repertoire of child management skills (balance of positive and negative strategies and discipline skills)
   Medical care and physical care skills (e.g., the ability to identify needs for medical assistance and the capacity to select nutritious foods)
   Safety and emergency response skills
   Capacities for warmth and nurturance (e.g., affective recognition and expression skills)
   Sensitive and discriminant interactional response capacities

Social cognitive skills
   Perspective taking
   Problem-solving capacities
   Appropriate expectations regarding children's capacities
   Cognitive reflectivity and complexity
   Balancing short- and long-term socialization goals
   Positive attributional style
   Perceptual and observational skills
   Self-efficacy

Self-control skills
   Impulse control
   Accurate and adaptive perceptions
   A positive interpretive bias
   Self-monitoring skills
   Assertiveness

Stress management
   Self-care skills
   Relaxation skills
   Recreational capacities
   The ability to marshal and maintain a social support network
   Positive appraisal style
   A breadth of coping capacities (problem-focused coping, emotion-focused coping, and avoidant coping)
   Financial planning skills

Social skills
   Interpersonal problem-solving skills
   Empathy
   Affective recognition and expression skills
   Assertiveness
   Social initiation skills
   Capacity to respond effectively to a breadth of individuals (e.g., family, friends, employers, social workers, and children's teachers)

■ *Sample Measures Referred to in Chapter 65*

Self-report inventories on parenting
- Child Abuse Potential Inventory (Milner, 1986)
- Adult/Adolescent Parenting Inventory (Bavolek, 1984)
- Parenting Scale (Arnold, O'Leary, Wolff, & Acker, 1993)

Measures of cognitive distortions
- Expectations (Parent Opinion Questionnaire; Azar, Robinson, Hekimian, & Twentyman, 1984)
- Role reversal (Bavolek, 1984)
- Problem solving (parenting, adult-adult relationships, and other areas) Hanson et al., 1995; Wasik, Bryant, & Fishbein, 1981)
- Negative intent attributions (child vignettes; Azar, 1990).

Observational protocols (Mash, 1991)
- For infants and toddlers
  ✓ Nursing Assessment Satellite Training Instruments (Barnard et al., 1989; Farell et al., 1991)
  ✓ Home Observation for the Measurement of the Environment (Caldwell & Bradley, 1984)
  ✓ Behavioral ratings for basic child care skills (Feldman et al., 1992)
- For preschoolers and school-aged children
  ✓ The Dyadic Parent-Child Interaction Coding System (Eyberg, Bessmer, Newcomb, Edward, & Robinson, 1994)
  ✓ Oregon Social Learning Theory Center protocol (Dishion et al., 1984; Reid, 1978)

Neglect issues
- Home cleanliness (Rosenfield-Schlichter, Sarber, Bueno, Greene, & Lutzker, 1983; Watson-Perczel, Lutzker, Greene, & McGimpsey, 1988)
- Home safety (Home Accident Prevention Inventory; Tertinger, Greene, & Lutzker, 1984)
- General family resources (Family Resource Scale; Dunst, 1986)

- Parent Outcome Interview (Magura & Moses, 1986)
- Emergency and medical care skills (Delgado & Lutzker, 1985; Tymchuk, 1990)

Symptom checklists
- Symptom Checklist-90 (Derogatis, 1983)
- Anger (Anger Scale; Novaco, 1975)
- Depression (CESD [Radloff et al., 1977] and Beck Depression Inventory [Beck et al., 1979])
- Alcoholism (Michigan Alcohol Screening Test; Selzer, Vinokur, & vanRooijen, 1975)
- Drug abuse (Skinner, 1982)

Child behavior problems
- Child Behavior Checklist (Achenbach & Edelbrock, 1983)
- Eyberg Child Behavioral Inventory (Eyberg & Ross, 1978)
- Issues Checklist (Robin, Kent, O'Leary, Foster, & Prinz, 1977)

Contextual measures
- Parenting Stress Index (Abidin, 1993; Lloyd & Abidin, 1985)
- Life Stress Scale (Egeland, Breitenbucher, & Rosenberg, 1980)
- Perceived Social Support from Family and Friends (Procidano & Heller, 1983)
- Social Support Inventory (Cyrnic, Greenberg, Ragozin, Robinson, & Basham, 1983)

■ *References for Measures*

Abidin, R. (1983). *Parenting Stress Index—Manual.* Charlottesville, VA: Pediatric Psychology Press.

Achenbach, T., & Edelbrock, C. S. (1983). *Manual for the Child Behavior Checklist and Revised Child Behavior Profile.* Burlington, VT: University Associates in Psychiatry.

Arnold, D. S., O'Leary, S. G., Wolff, L. S., & Acker, M. M. (1993). The Parenting Scale: A measure of dysfunctional parenting in discipline situations. *Psychological Assessment, 5,* 131-136.

Ayoub, G., Jacewitz, M. M., Gold, R. G., & Milner, J. (1982). Assessment of a program's effectiveness in selecting individuals at risk for problems in parenting. *Journal of Clinical Psychology, 39,* 334-339.

Azar, S. T. (1990). *Child vignettes.* Unpublished measure, Clark University, Frances L. Hiatt School of Psychology, Worcester, MA.

Azar, S. T., Robinson, D. R., Hekimian, E., & Twentyman, C. T. (1984). Unrealistic expectations and problem solving ability in maltreating and comparison mothers. *Journal of Consulting and Clinical Psychology, 52,* 687-691.

Barnard, K. E., Hammond, M. A., Booth, C. L., Bee, H. L., Mitchell, S. K., & Spieker, S. J. (1989). Measurement and meaning of parent-child interaction. In F. Morrison, C. Lord, & D. Keating (Eds.), *Applied developmental psychology* (Vol. 3, pp. 40-75). New York: Academic Press.

Bavolek, S. J. (1984). *Handbook of the Adolescent-Parenting Inventory.* Park City, UT: Family Development Resources.

Beck, A. T., Rush, A. J., Shaw, B. E., & Emery, G. (1979). *Cognitive therapy of depression.* New York: Guilford.

Bee, H. L., Disbrow, M. A., Johnson-Crowley, N., & Barnard, K. (1981, April). *Parent-child interactions during teaching in abusing and non-abusing families.* Paper presented at the biannual convention of the Society for Research in Child Development, Boston.

Caldwell, B. M., & Bradley, R. H. (1984). *Home observations for the measurement of the environment: Administration manual* (rev. ed.). Little Rock: University of Arkansas.

Cyrnic, K. A., Greenberg, M. T., Ragozin, S. A., Robinson, N. M., & Basham, C. (1983). Effects of stress and support on mothers and premature and full term infants. *Child Development, 54,* 209-217.

Delgado, A. E., & Lutzker, J. R. (1985, November). *Training parents to identify and report their children's illness.* Paper presented at the annual convention of the Association for Advancement of Behavior Therapy, Houston.

Derogatis, L. R. (1983). *SCL-90-R administration, scoring, and procedures manual-II.* Townson, MD: Clinical Psychometric Research.

Dishion, T., Gardner, K., Patterson, G., Reid, J., Spyrou, S., & Thibodeaux, S. (1984). *The family process code: A multidimensional system for observing family interactions.* Unpublished coding manual, Oregon Social Learning Center, Eugene.

Dunst, C. H. (1986). *Family resources, personal well-being, and early intervention.* Unpublished manuscript, Western Carolina Center, Family Infant and Preschool Program, Morganstown, NJ.

Egeland, B. R., Breitenbucher, M., & Rosenberg, D. (1980). Prospective study of the significance of life stress in the etiology of child abuse. *Journal of Consulting and Clinical Psychology, 48,* 195-205.

Eyberg, S., Bessmer, J., Newcomb, K., Edward, D., & Robinson, E. (1994). *Dyadic parent-child interaction coding system II: A manual.* Unpublished manuscript, University of Florida, Department of Clinical/Health Psychology, Gainesville.

Eyberg, S. M., & Ross, A. W. (1978). Assessment of child behavior problems: The validation of a new inventory. *Journal of Clinical Child Psychology, 7,* 113-116.

Farell, A. M., Freeman, V. A., Keenan, N. L., & Huber, C. J. (1991). Interaction between high-risk infants and their mothers: The NCAST as an assessment tool. *Research in Nursing and Health, 14,* 109-118.

Feldman, M. A., Case, L., Garrick, M., MacIntyre-Grande, W., Carnwell, J., & Sparks, B. (1992). Teaching child-care skills to mothers with developmental disabilities. *Journal of Applied Behavior Analysis, 25,* 205-215.

Hanson, D. J., Pallotta, G. M., Christopher, J. S., Conaway, R. L., & Lundquist, L. M. (1995). The parental problem-solving measure: Further evaluation with maltreating and non-maltreating parents. *Journal of Family Violence, 10,* 319-336.

Lloyd, B. H., & Abidin, R. R. (1985). Revision of the Parenting Stress Index. *Journal of Pediatric Psychology, 10,* 169-177.

Magura, S., & Moses, B. S. (1986). *The Parent Outcome Interview.* Washington, DC: Child Welfare League.

Mash, E. H. (1991). Measurement of parent-child interaction in studies of maltreatment. In R. Starr & D. A. Wolfe (Eds.), *The effects of child abuse and neglect* (pp. 203-255). New York: Guilford.

Milner, J. S. (1986). *The Child Abuse Potential Inventory: Manual* (2nd ed.). Webster, NC: Psytec.

Novaco, R. W. (1975). *Anger control: The development and evaluation of an experimental treatment.* Lexington, MA: Lexington Books.

Procidiano, M., & Heller, K. (1983). Measures of perceived social support from friends and family: Three validation studies. *American Journal of Community Psychology, 11,* 1-24.

Radloff, L. S. (1977). The CES-D Scale: A self-report depression scale for research in the general population. *Applied Psychological Measurement, 1,* 385-401.

Reid, J. B. (1978). *A social learning approach to family intervention: II. Observation in the home settings.* Eugene, OR: Castalia.

Robin, A. L., Kent, R., O'Leary, K. D., Foster, S., & Prinz, R. (1977). An approach to teaching parents and adolescents problem-solving communication skills. *Behavior Therapy, 8,* 639-643.

Rosenfield-Schlichter, M. D., Sarber, R. E., Bueno, G., Greene, B. F., & Lutzker, J. R. (1983). Maintaining accountability for an ecobehavioral treatment of one aspect of child neglect: Personal cleanliness. *Education and Treatment of Children, 6,* 153-164.

Selzer, M. L., Vinokur, A., & vanRooijen, L. (1975). A self-administered Short Michigan Screening Test. *Journal of Studies of Alcohol, 36,* 117-126.

Skinner, H. A. (1982). The Drug Abuse Screening Test. *Addictive Behavior, 7,* 363-371.

Tertinger, D. A., Greene, B. F., & Lutzker, J. R. (1984). Home safety: Development and validation of one component of an ecobehavioral treatment program for abused and neglected children. *Journal of Applied Behavior Analysis, 17,* 150-174.

Tymchuk, A. J. (1990). Assessing emergency responses of people with mental handicaps. *Mental Handicap, 18,* 136-142.

Wasik, B. H., Bryant, D. M., & Fishbein, J. (1981, November). *Assessment of parent problem solving skills.* Paper presented at the annual meeting of the Association for the Advancement of Behavior Therapy, Toronto.

Watson-Perczel, M., Lutzker, J. R., Greene, B. F., & McGimpsey, B. J. (1988). Assessment and modification of home cleanliness among families adjudicated for child neglect. *Behavior Modification, 12,* 57-87.

Table A7.3 Examples of Cognitive Problems

Problem	Example
Unrealistic expectations	Parents expecting children to comfort them when they are having a bad day; expecting a 4-year-old to pick out the correct clothing for the weather
Misattributions	Viewing an infant who cries all night as doing it "on purpose"; believing a 3-year-old's tantrum in the grocery store is intended to embarrass the parent
Negative biases	A mother perceiving herself as "bad" for not being able to get a child to behave; labeling a child "selfish" or "vicious" for behaving in developmentally appropriate ways
Failures to discriminate	A parent reacting to a child as if he or she were a negative figure in the parent's life (e.g., "He's just like his father!")

Table A7.4   Alternative Methods of Discipline

Prevention	If children fight before dinner, it is possible that they are hungry. Giving a snack might reduce the fighting.
Distraction	If children are fighting, rather than intervene directly when their voices get louder, the parent could ask one of the children to help him or her with something to distract them.
Time-out	Here, the child is removed from activities that he or she finds rewarding as punishment. He or she is placed in a neutral area of the house in which no rewards are available for a short period of time.
Logical consequences	Here, the punishment is a consequence of the misbehavior (e.g., cleaning up spilled milk).
Positive practice	Here, children are asked to repeat more appropriate responses (e.g., for slamming a door too loudly, they are asked to shut it quietly five times).

■ *Additional Parenting References*

Azar, S. T. (1989). Training parents of abused children. In C. E. Shaefer & J. M. Briesmeister (Eds.), *Handbook of parent training* (pp. 414-441). New York: John Wiley.

Azar, S. T. (1997). A cognitive behavioral approach to understanding and treating parents who physically abuse their children. In D. Wolf & R. McMahon (Eds.), *Child abuse: New directions in prevention and treatment across the life span* (pp. 78-100). Thousand Oaks, CA: Sage.

Becker, W. C. (1971). *Parents are teachers*. Champaign, IL: Research Press.

Egan, K. (1983). Stress management and child management with abusive parents. *Journal of Clinical Child Psychology, 12,* 292-299.

Fantuzzo, J. W., Wray, L., Hall, R., Goins, C., & Azar, S. T. (1986). Parent and social skills training for mentally retarded mothers identified as child maltreaters. *American Journal of Mental Deficiency, 91,* 135-140.

Feldman, A., Towns, F., Betel, J., Case, L., Rincover, A., & Rubino, C. (1986). Parent education project II: Increasing stimulating interactions of developmentally handicapped mothers. *Journal of Mental Deficiency, 90,* 253-258.

Patterson, G. R. (1971). *Families: Application of social learning theory to family life*. Champaign, IL: Research Press.

Sarber, R. E., Halasz, M. M., Messmer, M. C., Bickett, A. D., & Lutzker, J. R. (1983). Teaching menu planning and grocery shopping skills to a mentally retarded mother. *Mental Retardation, 21,* 101-106.

Tertinger, D. A., Greene, B. F., & Lutzker, J. R. (1984). Home safety: Development and validation of one component of an ecobehavioral treatment program for abused and neglected children. *Journal of Applied Behavior Analysis, 17,* 150-174.

Tymchuk, A. J. (1990). Assessing emergency responses of people with mental handicaps. *Mental Handicap, 18,* 136-142.

Tymchuk, A. J. (1992). Predicting adequacy of parenting by people with mental retardation. *Child Abuse & Neglect, 16,* 165-178.

Tymchuk, A. J., Yokota, A., & Rahbar, B. (1990). Decision-making abilities of mothers with mental retardation. *Research in Developmental Disabilities, 11,* 97-109.

Watson-Perczel, M., Lutzker, J. R., Greene, B. F., & McGimpsey, B. J. (1988). Assessment and modification of home cleanliness among families adjudicated for child neglect. *Behavior Modification, 12,* 57-87.

Wolfe, D. A., Sandler, J., & Kaufman, K. (1981). A competency-based parent training program for abusive parents. *Journal of Consulting and Clinical Psychology, 49,* 633-640.

Wolfe, D. A., St. Lawrence, J., Graves, K., Behony, K., Bradlyn, D., & Kelly, J. (1982). Intensive behavioral parent training for a child abusive mother. *Behavior Therapy, 13,* 438-451.

Wolfe, D. A., & Wekerle, C. (1993). Treatment strategies for child physical abuse and neglect: A critical progress report. *Clinical Psychology Review, 13,* 473-500.

Appendix 8
Assessing and
Maximizing Strengths

Family Functioning Style Scale[1]

Angela G. Deal, Carol M. Trivette, and Carl J. Dunst

Respondent _____ Date _____ Recorder _____

Directions
The scoring profile process is designed to facilitate accurate summation of responses on the Family Functioning Style Scale. The scoring sheet includes spaces for individual item scores, subscale scores, and category scores. The recorder should first enter the item scores on the scoring sheet and then sum them to obtain the subscale score. The subscale and category scores from the scoring sheets are transferred to the profile form by simply circling the number corresponding to the scores. The circled numbers are then corrected by pencil or pen to depict a family's profile of strengths.

1. SOURCE: Dunst, C. J., Trivette, C. M., and Deal, A. G. (1988). *Enabling and empowering families: Principles and guidelines for practice.* Cambridge, MA: Brookline Books. May be reproduced.

SCORING SHEET

Item	Commitment	Appreciation	Time	Sense of Purpose	Congruence	Communication	Role Expectations	Coping (I)	Coping (II)	Problem Solving	Positivism	Flexibility	Balance	C A T E G O R Y S C O R E
1	☐													
2							☐							
3											☐			
4		☐												
5						☐								
6				☐										
7													☐	
8					☐									
9												☐		
10								☐						
11											☐			
12			☐											
13							☐							
14									☐					
15										☐				
16			☐											
17								☐						
18						☐								
19					☐									
20									☐					
21										☐				
22				☐										
23	☐													
24												☐		
25		☐												
26													☐	
Subscale Score														

Family Identity   ☐ + ☐ + ☐ + ☐ + ☐ = ... ☐

Information Sharing   ☐ + ☐ = ... ☐

Coping/Resource Mobilization   ☐ + ☐ + ☐ + ☐ + ☐ + ☐ = ☐

FAMILY FUNCTIONING STYLE SCALE

PROFILE FORM

Family Identity	Commitment......	0	1	2	3	4	5	6	7	8
	Appreciation......	0	1	2	3	4	5	6	7	8
	Time.................	0	1	2	3	4	5	6	7	8
	Sense of Purpose..	0	1	2	3	4	5	6	7	8
	Congruence........	0	1	2	3	4	5	6	7	8
Information Sharing	Communications...	0	1	2	3	4	5	6	7	8
	Role Expectations.	0	1	2	3	4	5	6	7	8
Coping/Resource Mobilization	Coping I..............	0	1	2	3	4	5	6	7	8
	Coping II............	0	1	2	3	4	5	6	7	8
	Problem Solving....	0	1	2	3	4	5	6	7	8
	Positivism............	0	1	2	3	4	5	6	7	8
	Flexibility............	0	1	2	3	4	5	6	7	8
	Balance...............	0	1	2	3	4	5	6	7	8

Family Identity	0 .... 10 .... 20 .... 30 40
Information Sharing	0 .... 4 .... 8 .... 12 16
Coping/Resource Mobilization	0 .... 12 .... 24 .... 36 48

Table A8.1   Family Functioning Style Scale

Listed below are 26 statements about families. Please read each statement and indicate the extent to which it is true for your family. There are no right or wrong answers. Please give your honest opinion and feelings. Remember that no one family will be like all the statements given.

To What Extent Is Each of the Following Statements Like Your Family?	*Not at All Like My Family*	*A Little Like My Family*	*Sometimes Like My Family*	*Generally Like My Family*	*Almost Always Like My Family*
1. It is worth making personal sacrifices if it benefits our family	0	1	2	3	4
2. We generally agree about how family members are expected to behave	0	1	2	3	4
3. We believe that something good comes out of the worst situations	0	1	2	3	4
4. We take pride in even the smallest accomplishments of family members	0	1	2	3	4
5. We are able to share our concerns and feelings in productive ways	0	1	2	3	4
6. No matter how difficult things get, our family sticks together	0	1	2	3	4
7. We generally ask for help from persons outside our family if we cannot do things ourselves	0	1	2	3	4
8. We generally agree about the things that are important to our family	0	1	2	3	4
9. In our family we are always willing to "pitch in" and help one another	0	1	2	3	4
10. If something beyond our control is constantly upsetting to our family, we find things to do that keep our minds off our worries	0	1	2	3	4
11. No matter what happens in our family, we try to look "at the bright side of things"	0	1	2	3	4
12. Even in our busy schedules, we find time to be together	0	1	2	3	4
13. Everyone in our family understands the rules about acceptable ways to act	0	1	2	3	4
14. Friends and relatives are always willing to help whenever we have a problem or crisis	0	1	2	3	4
15. When we have a problem or concern, we are able to make decisions about what to do	0	1	2	3	4
16. We enjoy time together, even if it is just doing household chores	0	1	2	3	4
17. If we have a problem or concern that seems overwhelming, we try to forget it for awhile	0	1	2	3	4
18. Whenever we have disagreements, family members listen to "both sides of the story"	0	1	2	3	4
19. In our family, we make time to get things done that we all agree are important	0	1	2	3	4
20. In our family, we can depend on the support of one another whenever something goes wrong	0	1	2	3	4
21. We generally talk about the different ways in which we deal with problems or concerns	0	1	2	3	4
22. In our family, our relationships will outlast our material possessions	0	1	2	3	4

(continued)

To What Extent Is Each of the Following Statements Like Your Family?	Not at All Like My Family	A Little Like My Family	Sometimes Like My Family	Generally Like My Family	Almost Always Like My Family
23. Decisions such as whether to move or to change jobs are based on what is best for all family members	0	1	2	3	4
24. We can depend on one another to help out when something unexpected occurs	0	1	2	3	4
25. In our family, we try not to take one another for granted	0	1	2	3	4
26. We try to solve our problems first before asking others to help	0	1	2	3	4

Please write down all things that you consider being the major strengths of your family. Do not overlook the little things that occur every day, which we often take for granted (e.g., sharing the responsibility of getting your child fed and to school).

SOURCE: Dunst, C. J., Trivette, C. M., & Deal, A. G. (1988). *Enabling and empowering families: Principles and guidelines for practice.* Cambridge, MA: Brookline. May be reproduced.

■ *Further Reading* (Compiled by Diane DePanfilis, Vanessa Hodges, and Peter Pecora)

Beavers, W. R., & Hampson, R. B. (1990). *Successful families: Assessment and intervention.* New York: Norton.

Berg, I. K., & DeJong, P. (1996). Solution-building conversations: Co-constructing a sense of competence with clients. *Families in Society, 77,* 376-391.

Cowger, C. D. (1994). Assessing client strengths: Clinical assessment for client empowerment. *Social Work, 39,* 262-268.

Curran, D. (1983). *Traits of a healthy family.* Minneapolis: Winston.

De Jong, P., & Miller, S. D. (1995). How to interview for client strengths. *Social Work, 40,* 729-736.

De Panfilis, D., & Wilson, C. (1996). Applying the strengths perspective with maltreating families. *The APSAC Advisor, 9*(3), 15-20.

Dore, M. M., & Alexander, L. B. (1996). Preserving families at risk of child abuse and neglect: The role of the helping alliance. *Child Abuse and Neglect, 20,* 349-361.

Dunst, C. J., Trivette, C. M., & Deal, A. G. (Eds.). (1988). *Enabling and empowering families: Principles and guidelines for practice.* Cambridge, MA: Brookline.

Dunst, C. J., Trivette, C. M., & Deal, A. G. (Eds.). (1994). *Supporting and strengthening families.* Cambridge, MA: Brookline.

Friedman, S. (1992). Constructing solutions (stories) in brief family therapy. In S. Budman, M. Hoyt, & S. Friedman (Eds.), *The first session in brief therapy* (pp. 282-305). New York: Guilford.

Guildner, C. (1983). Growth promoting family therapy. In D. R. Mace (Ed.), *Prevention in family services.* Beverly Hills, CA: Sage.

Hill, R. B. (1971). *The strengths of black families.* New York: National Urban League.

Kaplan, L., & Girard, J. (1994). *Strengthening high-risk families: A handbook for practitioners.* New York: Lexington Books.

Kinney, J., Strand, K., Hagerup, M., & Bruner, C. (1994). *Beyond the buzzwords: Key principles in effective frontline practice* (Working paper). Falls Church, VA: National Center for Service Integration. (Individual copies may be obtained for prepaid postage and handling fee of $4.00 from the National Center for Service Integration Information Clearinghouse, 5111 Leesburg Pike, Suite 702, Falls Church, VA 22041)

Lewis, J. M., & Looney, J. G. (1983). *The long struggle: Well-functioning working class black families.* New York: Brunner/Mazel.

Lynch, E. W., & Hanson, M. J. (1992). *Developing cross-cultural competence: A guide for working with young children and their families.* Baltimore, MD: Brooks.

Maluccio, A. N. (Ed.). (1981). *Promoting competence in clients a new/old approach to social work practice.* New York: Free Press.

McCubbin, H., Thompson, A., & McCubbin, M. (1996). *Family assessment: Resiliency, coping and adaptation, inventories for research and practice.* Madison: University of Wisconsin Systems.

McCubbin, H. I., & Thompson, A. I. (1987). *Family assessment inventories for research and practice.* Madison: University of Wisconsin.

Mindel, C. H., Habenstein, R. W., & Wright, R. (1988). *Ethnic families in America: Patterns and variations.* New York: Elsevier.

Olson, D. H., Larsen, A., & McCubbin, H. (1983). Family Strengths Scale. In D. H. Olson, H. McCubbin, H. Barnes, A. Larsen, A. Muxem, & M. Wilson (Eds.), *Families: What makes them work.* Beverly Hills, CA: Sage.

Otto, H. A. (1963). Criteria for assessing family strengths. *Family Process, 2,* 329-337.

Rutter, M. (1985). Resilience in the face of adversity: Protective factors and resistance to psychiatric disorder. *British Journal of Psychiatry, 147,* 598-611.

Saleeby, D. (1992a). The strengths perspective in social work practice: Extensions and cautions. *Social Work, 41,* 296-305.

Saleebey, D. (Ed.). (1992b). *The strengths perspective in social work practice.* New York: Longman.

Saleebey, D. (Ed.). (1997). *The strengths perspective in social work practice* (2nd ed.). New York: Longman.

Schatz, M. S., & Bane, W. (1991). Empowering the parents of children in substitute care: A training model. *Child Welfare, 70*(6), 665-678.

Stinnett, N. (1983). Strong families. In D. R. Mace (Ed.), *Prevention in family services*. Beverly Hills, CA: Sage.

Stinnett, N., & DeFrain, J. (1985). *Secrets of strong families*. Boston: Little, Brown.

Trivette, C. M., Dunst, C. J., Deal, A. G., Hamer, A. W., & Prompst, S. (1990). Assessing family strengths and family functioning style. *Topics in Early Childhood Special Education, 10*, 16-35.

Walsh, F. (1998). *Strengthening family resilience*. New York: Guilford.

Weick, A., Rapp, D., Sullivan, W. P., & Kisthardt, W. (1989). A strengths perspective for social work practice. *Social Work, 34*, 350-354.

Werner, E. (1989). High-risk children in young adulthood: A longitudinal study from birth to 32 years. *American Journal of Orthopsychiatry, 59*, 72-81.

Wilson, M. (1984). Mothers' and grandmothers' perceptions of parental behavior in three-generational black families. *Child Development, 55*(4), 1333-1339.

Appendix 9
Assessing Family Needs, Resources, and Social Support

Table A9.1   Family Needs Scale

Respondent _____   Date _____

This scale asks you to indicate if you have a need for any type of help or assistance in 41 different areas. Please circle the response that best describes how you feel about needing help in those areas.

To What Extent Do You Feel the Need for Any of the Following Types of Help or Assistance?	Not Applicable (NA)	Almost Never	Seldom	Sometimes	Often	Almost Always
1. Having money to buy necessities and pay bills	NA	1	2	3	4	5
2. Budgeting money	NA	1	2	3	4	5
3. Paying for special needs of my child	NA	1	2	3	4	5
4. Saving money for the future	NA	1	2	3	4	5
5. Having clean water to drink	NA	1	2	3	4	5
6. Having food for two meals for my family	NA	1	2	3	4	5
7. Having time to cook healthy meals for my family	NA	1	2	3	4	5
8. Feeding my child	NA	1	2	3	4	5
9. Getting a place to live	NA	1	2	3	4	5
10. Having plumbing, lighting, and heat	NA	1	2	3	4	5
11. Getting furniture, clothes, and toys	NA	1	2	3	4	5
12. Completing chores, repairs, and home improvements	NA	1	2	3	4	5
13. Adapting my house for my child	NA	1	2	3	4	5
14. Getting a job	NA	1	2	3	4	5
15. Having a satisfying job	NA	1	2	3	4	5
16. Planning for future job of my child	NA	1	2	3	4	5
17. Getting where I need to go	NA	1	2	3	4	5
18. Getting in touch with people I need to talk to	NA	1	2	3	4	5
19. Transporting my child	NA	1	2	3	4	5
20. Having special travel equipment for my child	NA	1	2	3	4	5
21. Finding someone to talk to about my child	NA	1	2	3	4	5
22. Having someone to talk to	NA	1	2	3	4	5
23. Having medical and dental care for my family	NA	1	2	3	4	5
24. Having time to take care of myself	NA	1	2	3	4	5
25. Having emergency health care	NA	1	2	3	4	5
26. Finding special dental and medical care for my child	NA	1	2	3	4	5
27. Planning for future health needs	NA	1	2	3	4	5
28. Managing the daily needs of my child at home	NA	1	2	3	4	5
29. Caring for my child during work hours	NA	1	2	3	4	5

(continued)

To What Extent Do You Feel the Need for Any of the Following Types of Help or Assistance?	Not Applicable (NA)	Almost Never	Seldom	Sometimes	Often	Almost Always
30. Having emergency child care	NA	1	2	3	4	5
31. Getting respite care for my child	NA	1	2	3	4	5
32. Finding care for my child in the future	NA	1	2	3	4	5
33. Finding a school placement for my child	NA	1	2	3	4	5
34. Getting equipment/therapy for my child	NA	1	2	3	4	5
35. Having time to take my child to appointments	NA	1	2	3	4	5
36. Exploring future educational options for my child	NA	1	2	3	4	5
37. Expanding my education, skills, and interests	NA	1	2	3	4	5
38. Doing things that I enjoy	NA	1	2	3	4	5
39. Doing things with my family	NA	1	2	3	4	5
40. Participating in parent groups/clubs	NA	1	2	3	4	5
41. Traveling/vacationing with my child	NA	1	2	3	4	5

SOURCE: Dunst,, C. J., Trivette, C. M., & Deal, A. G. (1988). *Enabling and empowering families: Principles and guidelines for practice.* Cambridge, MA: Brookline. May be reproduced.

Table A9.2   Family Resource Scale

Respondent _____   Date _____

This scale is designed to assess whether or not you and your family have adequate resources (time, money, energy, and so on) to meet the needs of the family as a whole and the needs of individual family members.

For each item, please circle the response that best describes how well the need is met on a consistent basis in your family (that is, month in and month out).

To What Extent Are the Following Resources Adequate for Your Family?	*Does Not Apply (NA)*	*Not at All Adequate*	*Seldom Adequate*	*Sometimes Adequate*	*Often Adequate*	*Almost Always Adequate*
1. Food for two meals a day	NA	1	2	3	4	5
2. House or apartment	NA	1	2	3	4	5
3. Money to buy necessities	NA	1	2	3	4	5
4. Enough clothes for your family	NA	1	2	3	4	5
5. Heat for your house or apartment	NA	1	2	3	4	5
6. Indoor plumbing/water	NA	1	2	3	4	5
7. Money to pay monthly bills	NA	1	2	3	4	5
8. Good job for yourself or spouse/partner	NA	1	2	3	4	5
9. Medical care for your family	NA	1	2	3	4	5
10. Public assistance (SSI, TANF, Medicaid, etc.)	NA	1	2	3	4	5
11. Dependable transportation (own car or provided by others)	NA	1	2	3	4	5
12. Time to get enough sleep/rest	NA	1	2	3	4	5
13. Furniture for your home or apartment	NA	1	2	3	4	5
14. Time to be by yourself	NA	1	2	3	4	5
15. Time for family to be together	NA	1	2	3	4	5
16. Time to be with your child(ren)	NA	1	2	3	4	5
17. Time to be with your spouse or partner	NA	1	2	3	4	5
18. Time to be with close friends	NA	1	2	3	4	5
19. Telephone or access to a phone	NA	1	2	3	4	5
20. Baby-sitting for your child(ren)	NA	1	2	3	4	5
21. Child care/day care for your child(ren)	NA	1	2	3	4	5
22. Money to buy special equipment/supplies for your child(ren)	NA	1	2	3	4	5
23. Dental care for your family	NA	1	2	3	4	5
24. Someone to talk to	NA	1	2	3	4	5
25. Time to socialize	NA	1	2	3	4	5
26. Time to keep in shape and look nice	NA	1	2	3	4	5
27. Toys for your child(ren)	NA	1	2	3	4	5
28. Money to buy things for yourself	NA	1	2	3	4	5
29. Money for family entertainment	NA	1	2	3	4	5
30. Money to save	NA	1	2	3	4	5
31. Time and money for travel/vacation	NA	1	2	3	4	5

SOURCE: Dunst, C. J., Trivette, C. M., & Deal, A. G. (1988). *Enabling and empowering families: Principles and guidelines for practice.* Cambridge, MA: Brookline. May be reproduced.

Table A9.3   Family Support Scale

Respondent _____   Date _____

Listed below are people and groups that often are helpful to members of a family raising a young child. This questionnaire asks you to indicate how helpful each source is to your family.

Please circle the response that best describes how helpful the sources have been to your family during the past 3 to 6 months. If a source of help has not been available to your family during this period of time, circle the NA (not available) response.

How Helpful Has Each of the Following Been to You in Terms of Raising Your Children?	Not Available (NA)	Not at All Helpful	Sometimes Helpful	Generally Helpful	Very Helpful	Extremely Helpful
1. My parents	NA	1	2	3	4	5
2. My spouse's or partner's parents	NA	1	2	3	4	5
3. My relatives/kin	NA	1	2	3	4	5
4. My spouse or partner's relatives/kin	NA	1	2	3	4	5
5. Spouse or partner	NA	1	2	3	4	5
6. My friends	NA	1	2	3	4	5
7. My spouse's or partner's friends	NA	1	2	3	4	5
8. My own children	NA	1	2	3	4	5
9. Other parents	NA	1	2	3	4	5
10. Coworkers	NA	1	2	3	4	5
11. Parent groups	NA	1	2	3	4	5
12. Social groups/clubs	NA	1	2	3	4	5
13. Church members/minister	NA	1	2	3	4	5
14. My family's or child's physician	NA	1	2	3	4	5
15. Early childhood intervention program	NA	1	2	3	4	5
16. School/day care center	NA	1	2	3	4	5
17. Professional helpers (social workers, therapists, teachers, etc.)	NA	1	2	3	4	5
18. Professional agencies (public health, social services, mental health, etc.)	NA	1	2	3	4	5
19. (If there are others, write in here)	NA	1	2	3	4	5
20. (If there are others, write in here)	NA	1	2	3	4	5

SOURCE: Dunst, C. J., Trivette, C. M., & Deal, A. G. (1988). *Enabling and empowering families: Principles and guidelines for practice.* Cambridge, MA: Brookline. May be reproduced.

Table A9.4   Personal Network Matrix (Version 1)

Case Number _____   Date _____

This questionnaire asks about people and groups that may provide you help and assistance.
Listed below are different individuals and groups that people often have contact with face to face, in a group, or by telephone. Please indicate for each source listed how often you have been in contact with each person or group during the past month. Please indicate any person or group with whom you have had contact not included on our list.

How Frequently Have You Had Contact With Each of the Following During the Past Month?	*Not at All*	*1-3 Times*	*4-10 Times*	*11-20 Times*	*Almost Every Day (21 or more)*
1. Spouse or partner	1	2	3	4	5
2. My children	1	2	3	4	5
3. My parents	1	2	3	4	5
4. Spouse's or partner's parents	1	2	3	4	5
5. My sister/brother	1	2	3	4	5
6. My spouse's or partner's sister/brother	1	2	3	4	5
7. Other relatives	1	2	3	4	5
8. Friends	1	2	3	4	5
9. Neighbors	1	2	3	4	5
10. Church members	1	2	3	4	5
11. Minister, priest, or rabbi	1	2	3	4	5
12. Coworkers	1	2	3	4	5
13. Baby-sitter	1	2	3	4	5
14. Day care or school	1	2	3	4	5
15. Private therapist for child	1	2	3	4	5
16. Child/family doctors	1	2	3	4	5
17. Early childhood intervention program	1	2	3	4	5
18. Hospital/special clinics	1	2	3	4	5
19. Health department	1	2	3	4	5
20. Social service department	1	2	3	4	5
21. Other agencies	1	2	3	4	5
22. (other agency name)	1	2	3	4	5
23. (other agency name)	1	2	3	4	5

SOURCE: Dunst,, C. J., Trivette, C. M., & Deal, A. G. (1988). *Enabling and empowering families: Principles and guidelines for practice*. Cambridge, MA: Brookline. May be reproduced.

Table A9.5   Support Functions Scale

Respondent _____   Date _____

Listed below are 20 different types of assistance that people sometimes find helpful. This questionnaire asks you to indicate how much you need help in these areas. Please circle the response that best describes your needs. Please answer all questions.

To What Extent Do You Feel a Need for Any of the Following Types of Assistance?	Never	Once in a While	Sometimes	Often	Quite Often
1. Someone to talk to about things that worry you	1	2	3	4	5
2. Someone to provide money for food, clothes, and other things	1	2	3	4	5
3. Someone to care for your child on a regular basis	1	2	3	4	5
4. Someone to talk to about problems with raising your child	1	2	3	4	5
5. Someone to help you get services for your child	1	2	3	4	5
6. Someone to encourage you when you are down	1	2	3	4	5
7. Someone to fix things around the house	1	2	3	4	5
8. Someone to talk to who has had similar experiences	1	2	3	4	5
9. Someone to do things with your child	1	2	3	4	5
10. Someone whom you can depend on	1	2	3	4	5
11. Someone to hassle with agencies or businesses when you cannot	1	2	3	4	5
12. Someone to lend you money	1	2	3	4	5
13. Someone who accepts your child regardless of how he or she acts	1	2	3	4	5
14. Someone to relax or joke with	1	2	3	4	5
15. Someone to help with household chores	1	2	3	4	5
16. Someone who keeps you going when things seem difficult	1	2	3	4	5
17. Someone to care for your child in emergencies or when you must go out	1	2	3	4	5
18. Someone to talk to when you need advice	1	2	3	4	5
19. Someone to provide you or your child transportation	1	2	3	4	5
20. Someone who tells you about services for your child or family	1	2	3	4	5

The scales in this packet may be used as part of an assessment of family needs and strengths. Items that indicate problems or needs may then be the focus of intervention. Items that indicate strength may be emphasized to help a family cope with needs or problems.

SOURCE: Dunst, C. J., Trivette, C. M., & Deal, A. G. (1988). *Enabling and empowering families: Principles and guidelines for practice.* Cambridge, MA: Brookline. May be reproduced.

Appendix 10
Steps in the Court Process and Court-Related Caseworker Activities

Compiled by Linda Spears

Steps in the Court Process	Court-Related Caseworker Activities
Adjudicatory hearings	**Preparing for and appearing in court**
The adjudicatory hearing, or trial, is used to determine if the allegations of abuse or neglect are true and whether custody or supervisory authority should be removed from the child and placed with court or the CPS agency. Decisions about reasonable efforts, the child's placement, and services are also addressed.	Working with legal counsel to prepare • Service providers and others who may be called as witnesses to testify before the court • The child for the court appearance or testimony or both • Their own testimony in support of the petition
Dispositional hearings	**Case planning**
The dispositional hearing focuses on planning for the child's future after a finding of dependency. These hearings consider options for • Returning the child home • Continuing or making an out-of-home care placement • Making a kinship care placement • Court orders for services to the child and family	Preparing reports and a case plan detailing • The agency's recommended long-term plan for the child • A description of strengths and problems within the family • The changes needed to correct the concerns leading to CPS intervention • The specific services to assist the parents in making the identified changes • The specific tasks to be conducted by the parents to make the identified changes

(continued)

Steps in the Court Process	*Court-Related Caseworker Activities*
Review hearings	**Reporting on case progress**
Review hearings are usually held at 6-month intervals or less and provide the court with an opportunity to examine the status of the case, including • The parents' progress in making changes identified in the case plan • The continued need for placement or services or both to the child and family • The need for orders to further timely progress toward achieving the case plan goals • Reviewing and setting time lines for achieving the case plan goals	1. Updating the case plan to reflect changes in case plan goals, services, and parental activities 2. Reviewing progress with the family and seeking their input on case plan changes 3. Preparing a written report to the court documenting the progress in the case 4. Conferring with the supervisor and the agency attorney on proposed changes in the case plan or the status of the case 5. Conferring with the guardian ad litem or the court-appointed special advocate or both to review progress and changes in the case plan
Permanency hearings	**Permanency planning**
A permanency hearing must be held within 12 months of entry into care. This hearing is used to make a decision about how and when the child's need for a safe and permanent family will be met. Options include • Return home on specified date • Continuation in foster care with a plan for reunification • Adoption or guardianship • Permanent foster care	Conducting a thorough evaluation of the parents' progress toward the stated goal, including their potential to provide a safe and permanent home for the child. The evaluation includes • Meeting with the child and family • Collecting information from services providers • Consulting with the supervisor and legal counsel • Determining the viability of the current goal and making needed goal changes • Documenting the course of services, the rational for the recommended permanency goal, and a timetable to achieve the goal
Emergency removal	**Investigation and assessment**
When it is necessary to remove a child from the home on an emergency basis, the caseworker must typically rely on the courts or the police to provide authorization to conduct such removals.	1. Assessing the allegations of abuse and neglect, the child's current safety, the risk of future harm, and the interventions needed to achieve safety 2. Documenting the findings of the assessment and the rationale for removal of the child 3. Conferring with the supervisor to finalize the removal decision 4. Securing authorization for the removal from the courts or the police

Steps in the Court Process	*Court-Related Caseworker Activities*
Petition filing	**Legal guidance and petition preparation**
A sworn petition must be filed when court involvement is sought to protect the child. It should contain the facts about the alleged abuse and neglect and provide the basis for court involvement. A petition is needed when	1. Consulting with the agency's legal counsel to review the facts of the case and determine the legal basis for court involvement
• There has been an emergency removal • A nonvoluntary placement is recommended • Court supervision is sought to serve the family while the child remains at home	2. Working with legal counsel to prepare a complete and accurate written petition containing 3. Facts relating to the alleged maltreatment 4. Information describing agency efforts to protect the child and strengthen the family
Initial hearing and pretrial hearings	**Preparing for and appearing in court**
At the initial hearing, the court decides whether the allegations contained in the petition are sufficient to support court involvement pending a full hearing.	1. Preparing the child and family for court, including explaining the basis for the petition and the role of the court in making decisions about interventions and reviewing the purpose of the initial hearing
The court will also ensure that	
• The parents have been notified of the proceedings • The parents are aware of their rights, including the right to an attorney • A guardian ad litem or CASA has been appointed for the child	2. Working with the attorney to prepare for the hearing, including identifying potential witnesses, preparing for their own testimony in support of the petition, and updating the court regarding events subsequent to the filing of the petition
Pretrial hearings may also address	3. Working with law enforcement or prosecuting attorneys when the case involves criminal charges
• Reasonable efforts to prevent placement • The availability of kin to provide care • Court orders for evaluations or services • Arrangements for parent-child visitation • Coordination of criminal charges or court orders related to the allegations • Orders for child support	4. Implementing orders issued in the case, including ensuring that evaluations are conducted, services referrals are made, placement options are pursued, and visitation is arranged

Appendix 11
Resources on Child
Welfare Competencies

Compiled by Joan Levy Zlotnik

- Downs, S. W., Costin, L. B., & McFadden, E. J. (1996). *Child welfare and family services: Policies and practice* (5th ed.). White Plains, NY: Longman.
- Filip, J., McDaniel, N., & Schene, P. (Eds.). (1992). *Helping in child protective services: A casework handbook.* Englewood, CO: American Humane Association. (*http://www.americanhumane.org*)
- Zlotnik, J. L., Rome, S., & DePanfilis, D. (Eds.). (1998). *Educating for child welfare practice: A compendium of model syllabi.* Alexandria, VA: Council on Social Work Education. (*http://www.cswe.org*)
- California Social Work Education Center, University of California at Berkeley, School of Social Welfare has developed a comprehensive set of child welfare competencies focused on incorporating child welfare competencies into the master's in social work curricula.
- The Child Welfare League of America (440 First Street NW, Washington, D.C. 20001) develops detailed model standards for all aspects of child welfare service delivery. (*http://www.cwla.org*)
- National Center on Child Abuse and Neglect has developed a set of user manuals, which are available from the National Clearinghouse on Child Abuse and Neglect Information (phone: 1-800-394-3366; website: *http://www.calib.com/nccanch*).

University of Wisconsin-Green Bay, Department of Social Work has published a list of child welfare competencies to be acquired by bachelor's of social work students.

Appendix 12
National Organizations and Resources Concerned With Child Protection

ABA Center on Children and the Law, 740 15th Street NW, Washington, D.C. 20005; phone: 202-662-1720; fax: 202-662-1755; website: *http://www.abanet.org/child*

ACTION for Child Protection, National headquarters, 2101 Sardis Road North, Suite 204, Charlotte, NC 28227; phone: 704-845-2121 (NC), 303-369-8008 (CO); fax: 704-845-8577 (NC), 303-369-8009 (CO)

American Academy of Child and Adolescent Psychiatry, 3615 Wisconsin Avenue NW, Washington, D.C. 20016-3007; phone: 202-966-7300; fax: 202-966-2891; website: *http://www.aacap.org*

American Academy of Pediatrics, Department C-sexual abuse, P.O. Box 927, Elk Grove Village, IL 60009-0927; phone: 847-228-5005; fax: 847-228-5097; website: *http://www.aap.org*

American Association for Marriage and Family Therapy, 1133 15th Street NW, Suite 300, Washington, D.C. 20005-2710; phone: 202-452-0109; fax: 202-223-2329; website: *http://www.aamft.org*

American Association of Pastoral Counselors, 9504-A Lee Highway, Fairfax, VA 22031-2303; phone: 703-385-6967; website: *http://www.aapc.org*

American Humane Association, Childrens Division, 63 Inverness Dr. E., Englewood, CO 80112-5117; phone: 800-227-4645, 303-792-9900; fax: 303-792-5333; website: *http://www.americanhumane.org*

American Indian Institute, College of Continuing Education and Public Service, The University of Oklahoma, 555 Constitution Street, Suite 237, Norman, OK 73072-7820; phone: 405-325-4127; fax: 405-325-7757; website: *http://www.occe.ou.edu/aii*

American Professional Society on the Abuse of Children, 407 South Dearborn, Suite 1300, Chicago, IL 60605; phone: 312-554-0166; fax: 312-554-0919; website: *http://www.apsac.org*

American Psychological Association, 750 First Street NE, Washington, D.C. 20002; phone: 202-336-5500; website: *http://www.apa.org*

American Public Human Services Association, 810 First Street NE, Washington, D.C. 20002-4267; phone: 202-682-0100, 202-289-6555; website: *http://www.aphsa.org*

Annie E. Casey Foundation, 701 St. Paul Street, Baltimore, MD 21202; phone: 410-547-6624; fax: 410-547-6624; website: *http:///www.aecf.org*

Behavioral Sciences Institute, Homebuilders Program, 181 S. 333rd Street, Suite 200, Federal Way, WA 98003-6796; phone: 253-874-3630; fax: 253-838-1670

Center for Social Services Research, University of California School of Social Welfare, 16 Haviland Hall, Berkeley, CA 94720-7400; phone: 510-642-1899; fax: 510-642-1895

Chapin Hall Center for Children, 1313 E. 60th Street, Chicago, IL 60637; phone: 773-753-5900; fax: 773-753-5940; website: *http://www.chapin.uchicago.edu*

C. Henry Kempe National Center for the Prevention and Treatment of Child Abuse and Neglect, 1825 Marion Street, Denver, CO 80218; phone: 303-864-5320; website: *http://www.naccchildlaw.org*

Child Welfare Institute, 1349 W. Peachtree Street NE, Suite 900, Atlanta, GA 30309-2956; phone: 404-876-1934; fax: 404-876-7949

Child Welfare League of America, 440 First Street NW, Suite 310, Washington, D.C. 20001; phone: 202-638-2952; fax: 202-638-4004; website: *http://www.cwla.org*

Clearinghouse on Child Abuse and Neglect Information, 330 C Street SW, Washington, D.C. 20447; phone: 800-FYI-3366, 703-385-7665; fax: 703-385-3206; website: *http://www.calib.com/nccanch*

Cornell University, College of Human Ecology, Family Life Development Center, Van Rensselaer Hall, Ithaca, NY

14853-4401; phone: 607-255-7794; fax: 607-255-8562; website: *http://fldc.cornell.edu*

David and Lucile Packard Foundation, 300 Second Street, Suite 200, Los Altos, CA 94022; phone: 650-948-7658; website: *http://www.packfound.org*

Educational Resources Information Center, Clearinghouse on Disabilities and Gifted Education, 1920 Association Drive, Reston, VA 20191-1589; phone: 800-328-0272; website: *http://www.ericec.org*

Family Resource Coalition, 200 S. Michigan Avenue, 16th Floor, Chicago, IL 60604; phone: 312-341-0900; fax: 312-341-9361; website: *http://www.fcra.org*

International Society for Prevention of Child Abuse and Neglect, 401 N. Michigan Avenue, Suite 2200, Chicago, IL 60611; phone: 312-578-1401; fax: 312-321-6869; website: *http://ispcan.org*

National Adoption Information Clearinghouse, 330 C Street SW, Washington, D.C. 20447; phone: 703-246-9085; fax: 703-385-3206

National Association of Chiefs of Police, 1000 Connecticut Avenue NW, Suite 9, Washington, D.C. 20036; phone: 202-293-9088; website: *http://www.aphf.org/aphf.nsf/htmlmedia/safety.html*

National Association of Counsel for Children, 1825 Marion Street, Suite 340, Denver, CO 80218; phone: 303-864-5320; fax: 303-864-5351; website: *http://www.naccchildlaw.org*

National Association of Public Child Welfare Administrators, American Public Human Services Association, 810 First Street NE, Washington, D.C. 20002-4267; phone: 202-682-0100, 202-289-6555; website: *http://www.aphsa.org*

National Association of Social Workers, 750 1st Street NE, Washington, D.C. 20002-4241; phone: 800-638-8799; website: *http://www.socialworkers.org*

National Black Child Development Institute, 1023 15th Street NW, Suite 600, Washington, D.C. 20005; phone: 202-387-1281; fax: 202-234-1738; website: *http://www.nbcdi.org*

National Center for Missing & Exploited Children, 2101 Wilson Boulevard, Suite 550, Arlington, VA 22201-3077; phone: 703-235-3900; fax: 703-235-4067; 24-hour hotline: 1-800-THE-LOST (1-800-843-5678); website: *http://www.missingkids.org*

National Center for Prosecution of Child Abuse, American Prosecutors Research Institute, 99 Canal Center Plaza, Suite 510, Alexandria, VA 22314; phone: 703-739-0321

National Center for Youth Law, 114 Sansome Street, Suite 900, San Francisco, CA 94104; phone: 415-543-3307; website: *http://www.youthlaw.org*

National Center on Child Fatality Review, 4024 Durfee Avenue, El Monte, CA 91732; phone: 626-455-4585; fax: 626-444-4851

National Child Welfare Resource Center for Organizational Improvement, Edmund S. Muskie School of Public Service, One Post Office Square, P.O. Box 15010, Portland, ME 04112; phone: 800-435-7543, 207-780-5810; fax: 207-780-5817.

National Children's Advocacy Center, 200 Westside Square, Suite 700, Huntsville, AL 35801; phone: 256-533-0531; fax: 256-534-6883. website: *http://www. ncac-hsv*

National Children's Alliance, 1319 F Street NW, Suite 1001, Washington, D.C. 20004; phone: 800-239-9950, 202-639-0597; website: *http://www.nccan.org*

National Clearinghouse for Alcohol and Drug Information, P.O. Box 2345 Rockville, MD 20847-2345; phone: 800-729-6686, 301-468-2600; fax: 301-468-6433; website: *http://www.health.org*

National Clearinghouse on Families & Youth, P.O. Box 13505, Silver Spring, MD 20911-3505; phone: 301-608-8098; fax: 301-608-8721; website: *http://www. ncfy.com*

National Coalition Against Domestic Violence, 119 Constitution Avenue NE, Washington, D.C. 20002; phone: 202-544-7358; website: *http://www.ncadv.org*

National Conference of State Legislatures, Children Families Program, 1560 Broadway, Suite 700, Denver, CO

80202; phone: 303-830-2200; fax: 303-863-8003; website: *http://www.ncsl.org/public/cfh.htm*

National Council for Adoption, 1930 17th Street NW, Washington, D.C. 20009; phone: 202-328-1200; website: *http://www.ncfa-usa.org*

National Council of Juvenile and Family Court Judges, P.O. Box 8970, Reno, NV 89507; phone: 702-784-6012; website: *http://www.ncjfcj.unr.edu*

National Court Appointed Special Advocates Association, 100 West Harrison Street, North Tower Suite 500, Seattle, WA 98119-4123; phone: 800-628-3233, 206-270-0072; fax: 206-270-0078; website: *http://www. nationalcasa.org*

National Crime Victims Research and Treatment Center, Department of Psychiatry and Behavioral Sciences, Medical University of South Carolina, 165 Cannon Street, P.O. Box 250852, Charleston, SC 29425; phone: 843-792-2945; fax: 843-792-3388; website: *http://www.musc.edu/cvc*

National Criminal Justice Reference Service, P.O. Box 6000, Rockville, MD 20849-6000; phone: 800-851-3420, 301-519-5500; website: *http://www.ncjrs.org*

National Directory of Children, Youth & Families Services, P.O. Box 1837, Longmont, CO 80502-1837

National Family Preservation Network, P.O. Box 2570, Laurel, MD 20709; phone: 301-498-0103; fax: 301-498-2909

National Indian Child Welfare Association, 3611 SW Hood Street, Suite 201, Portland, OR; phone: 503-222-4044; fax: 503-222-4007; website: *http://www.nicwa. org*

National Information Center for Children and Youth With Disabilities, P.O. Box 1492, Washington, D.C. 20013; phone: 800-695-0285; website: *http://www.nichcy. org*

National Maternal and Child Health Clearinghouse, 2070 Chain Bridge Road, Suite 450, Vienna, VA 22182; phone: 703-821-8955; fax: 703-821-2098; website: *http://www.nmchc.org*

National Maternal and Child Health Clearinghouse, 2070 Chain Bridge Road, Suite 450, Vienna, VA 22182; phone: 703-821-8955; fax: 703-821-2098; website: *http://www.nmchc.org*

National Resource Center for Family Centered Practice, University of Iowa, School of Social Work, 100 Oakdale Campus No. W206 OH, Iowa City, IA 52242-5000; phone: 319-335-4965; fax: 319-335-4964. website: *http://www.uiowa.edu\nrfcp*

National Resource Center on Child Maltreatment, 1349 W. Peachtree Street, NE, Suite 900, Atlanta, GA 30309-2956; phone: 404-881-0707; fax: 404-876-5325

National Sudden Infant Death Syndrome Resource Center, 2070 Chain Bridge Road, Suite 450, Vienna, VA 22182; phone: 703-821-8955; fax: 703-821-2098; e-mail: *sids@circsol.com*

Parents Anonymous, 675 W. Foothill Boulevard, Suite 220, Claremont, CA 91711; phone: 909-621-6184; website: *http://www.parentsanonymous-natl.org*

Prevent Child Abuse America, P.O. Box 2866, Chicago, IL 60690; phone: 800-CHILDREN, 312-663-3520; fax: 312-939-8962; website: *http://www.childabuse.org*

Research and Training Center on Family Support and Children's Mental Health, Portland State University, P.O. Box 751, Portland, OR 97207-0751; phone: 503-725-4040; fax: 503-725-4180; website: *http://www.rtc.pdx.edu*

YouthInfo; website: *http://www.youth.os.dhhs.gov*

Index

About the Editors

Howard Dubowitz, MD, MS, is Professor of Pediatrics at the University of Maryland School of Medicine, and he also directs the Child Protection Program at the University of Maryland Medical System. He chairs the Maryland Academy of Pediatrics Committee on Child Maltreatment, and he is on the executive committee of the national board of directors of the American Professional Society on the Abuse of Children (APSAC). His clinical work has included all forms of child maltreatment, with an emphasis on neglect. His research has focused on child neglect, sexual and physical abuse, kinship care, and physician training in child abuse. He is currently principal investigator on a federally funded grant to study the antecedents and outcomes of child maltreatment. He is also actively involved in child advocacy at the state and national levels, and he chairs the APSAC legislative committee. He has presented at local, regional, national, and international conferences. He recently edited *Neglected Children: Research, Practice, and Policy* (Sage, 1999).

Diane DePanfilis, PhD, MSW, is Assistant Professor at the University of Maryland School of Social Work, where she teaches introductory social work practice and child welfare clinical practice and research courses in the MSW program. She has more than 25 years of experience in the child welfare field as a caseworker, supervisor, program manager, national trainer, consultant, and researcher, and she is a frequent consultant to child welfare agencies. She is currently principal investigator of a federally funded demonstration project that is providing early intervention to families at risk for neglect. Recent research and publications relate to the epidemiology of child maltreatment recurrences; child protective services risk assessment, safety evaluation, and decision making; the relationship between child maltreatment and adolescent parenting; the relationship between maltreatment and maternal alcohol or drug problems; the role of social support in preventing neglect; and outcome-based intervention to reduce the risk of neglect. She is particularly interested in ways to bridge the gap between research and practice. She is the past president of the national board of directors of the American Professional Society on the Abuse of Children, an interdisciplinary organization that works to ensure that everyone affected by child maltreatment receives the best possible professional response.

About the Contributors

Veronica D. Abney, Licensed Clinical Social Worker (LCSW) and Diplomat in Clinical Social Work, Santa Monica, CA.

Joyce A. Adams, MD, Associate Clinical Professor of Pediatrics, University of California, San Diego Medical Center, Division of Adolescent Medicine, San Diego, CA.

Sandra T. Azar, PhD, Associate Professor of Psychology, Clark University, Worcester, MA.

Insoo Kim Berg, MSSW, Director, Brief Family Therapy Center, Milwaukee, WI.

Lucy Berliner, MSW, Research Director, Harborview Center for Sexual Assault and Traumatic Stress; Clinical Associate Professor, University of Washington, School of Social Work and Department of Psychiatry and Behavioral Sciences, Seattle, WA.

Maureen M. Black, PhD, Professor of Pediatrics, University of Maryland School of Medicine, Baltimore.

Barbara W. Boat, PhD, University of Cincinnati, Department of Psychiatry, Cincinnati, OH.

Richard Bolan, MSW, Supervisor, Baltimore City Department of Social Services, Baltimore, MD.

Barbara L. Bonner, PhD, Associate Professor and Director, Center on Child Abuse and Neglect, Department of Pediatrics, University of Oklahoma Health Sciences Center, Oklahoma City.

Joaquin Borrego, Jr., MA, graduate student, PhD program in clinical psychology, University of Nevada, Reno.

Marla R. Brassard, PhD, Associate Professor of Psychology and Education, Teachers College, Columbia University, New York.

Sheryl Brissett-Chapman, EdD, ACSW, Executive Director, Baptist Home for Children and Families, Bethesda, MD.

Caroline L. Burry, PhD, MSW, Assistant Professor, University of Maryland School of Social Work, Baltimore.

Mark Chaffin, PhD, Associate Professor of Pediatrics, Director of Research, Center on Child Abuse and Neglect, University of Oklahoma Health Sciences Center, Oklahoma City.

David Corwin, MD, University of Cincinnati, Children's Trust, Department of Psychiatry, Cincinnati, OH.

Mark Courtney, PhD, Associate Professor, University of Wisconsin School of Social Work, Madison.

Lorine L. Cummings, MSW, Supervisor, Baltimore County Department of Social Services, Towson, MD.

Howard A. Davidson, JD, Executive Director, American Bar Association Center on Children and the Law, Washington, D.C.

Nancy Davis, PhD, clinical psychologist, Burke, VA.

Esther Deblinger, PhD, Associate Professor of Psychiatry, University of Medicine and Dentistry of New Jersey; Director, Center for Children's Support, Stratford, NJ.

Brett Drake, PhD, Associate Professor, Washington University, George Warren Brown School of Social Work, St. Louis, MO.

Mark D. Everson, PhD, Clinical Associate Professor of Psychology, University of North Carolina, Department of Psychiatry, Chapel Hill.

Monica H. Ferraro, MA, doctoral student, Clark University, School of Psychology, Worcester, MA.

Eileen Gambrill, PhD, Professor, University of California, Berkeley, School of Social Welfare, Berkeley.

Esta Glazer-Semmel, LCSW-C, Clinical Instructor, University of Maryland School of Social Work, Baltimore.

Geoffrey Greif, PhD, Professor and Associate Dean, University of Maryland School of Social Work, Baltimore.

Norma Harris, PhD, Colorado State University School of Social Work, Fort Collins.

Stuart Hart, PhD, Indiana University-Purdue University at Indianapolis, School of Education, Indianapolis.

Vanessa G. Hodges, PhD, Associate Professor, University of North Carolina-Chapel Hill, School of Social Work, Chapel Hill.

E. Wayne Holden, PhD, Research Director, MACRO International Inc., Atlanta.

Wayne Holder, MSW, Executive Director, ACTION for Child Protection, Aurora, CO.

Dennis Ichikawa, JD, Attorney-at-Law, Tukwila, WA.

Charles F. Johnson, MD, Professor of Pediatrics, Ohio State University College of Medicine, Columbus.

Brenda Jones Harden, PhD, Assistant Professor, University of Maryland Institute for Child Study, College Park.

David J. Kolko, PhD, Associate Professor of Child Psychiatry and Psychology, University of Pittsburgh Medical Center, Pittsburgh, PA.

John M. Leventhal, MD, Professor of Pediatrics, Yale University School of Medicine, New Haven, CT.

Julie A. Lipovsky, PhD, ABPP, Professor of Psychology and Director, Clinical Counseling Masters Program, The Citadel, Charleston, SC.

John R. Lutzker, PhD, Florence and Louis Ross Professor, University of Judaism, Department of Psychology, Agoura Hills, CA.

Kee MacFarlane, MSW, Social Work Consultant, Whispering Pines, NC.

Anthony Maluccio, DSW, Professor, Boston College Graduate School of Social Work, Chesnut Hill, MA.

Melissa N. McDermott, ACSW, CCSW, Coordinator, Child Protection Team, University of Maryland School of Medicine, Baltimore.

John Curtis McMillen, PhD, Associate Professor, George Warren Brown School of Social Work, Washington University, St. Louis, MO.

Chandler Scott McMillin, is Clinical Director of the Right Turn residential programs for adults and adolescents in Maryland and North Carolina.

Lisa Merkel-Holguin, MSW, Policy/Program Analyst, American Humane Association, Englewood, CO.

Thomas D. Morton, MSW, Executive Director, Child Welfare Institute, Atlanta.

John E. B. Myers, JD, Professor, McGeorge School of Law, Sacramento, CA.

Prasanna Nair, MD, Professor of Pediatrics, University of Maryland School of Medicine, Baltimore.

Kristine Nelson, DSW, Professor, Portland State University School of Social Work, Portland, OR.

Richard L. Norman, LCSW-C, Clinical Instructor, University of Maryland School of Social Work, Baltimore.

Margarete Parrish, PhD, Assistant Professor, University of Maryland School of Social Work, Baltimore.

Peter Pecora, PhD, Manager of Research, Casey Family Program, Seattle, WA.

Donna Pence, Special Agent, Tennessee Bureau of Investigation, Taft.

Barbara A. Pine, PhD, Professor, University of Connecticut School of Social Work, West Hartford.

Denise Pintello, MSW, doctoral candidate, University of Maryland School of Social Work, Baltimore.

Julia Rauch, PhD, Professor, University of Maryland School of Social Work, Baltimore.

Rebecca J. Roe, JD, Attorney-at-Law, Schroeter-Goldmark, Seattle, WA.

Ronald Rogers, MS, addictions consultant, Owings Mills, MD.

Ronald H. Rooney, PhD, Professor, University of Minnesota School of Social Work, Minneapolis.

Joan R. Rycraft, PhD, Assistant Professor, University of Texas at Arlington, School of Social Work.

Marsha K. Salus, MSW, child welfare consultant, Boyd, MD.

Maria Scannapieco, PhD, Associate Professor and Director, Center for Child Welfare, University of Texas at Arlington, School of Social Work.

Lorelei Schaffhausen, MSW, Project Coordinator, Prince Georges County Department of Social Service, Beltsville, MD.

Robert A. Shapiro, MD, Director of the Child Abuse Team and Attending Physician, Division of Emergency Medicine, Children's Hospital Medical Center, and Associate Professor of Clinical Pediatrics, University of Cincinnati, OH.

Becky Frink Sherman, former psychology intern, Department of Developmental and Behavioral Pediatrics, University of Maryland School of Medicine, Baltimore.

Charles I. Shubin, MD, Director, Children's Health Center, Mercy Family Care, Baltimore, MD.

Champika K. Soysa, MA, doctoral student, Clark University, School of Psychology, Worcester, MA.

Linda Spears, MSW, Director, Child Protection, Child Welfare League of America, Washington, DC.

Paul Stern, JD, Senior Deputy Prosecuting Attorney, Snohomish County Prosecutor's Office, Everett, WA.

Sherri Y. Terao, EdD, Psychologist, Child Protection Center, Department of Pediatrics, University of California Davis Medical Center, Sacramento.

Ross A. Thompson, PhD, Professor of Psychology, University of Nebraska, Lincoln.

Anthony J. Urquiza, PhD, Child Clinical Psychologist, Child Protection Center, Department of Pediatrics, University of California Davis Medical Center, Sacramento.

Robin Warsh, MSW, Lecturer, Boston College Graduate School of Social Work, Chestnut Hill, MA.

Susan Wells, PhD, Director, Children and Family Research Center, University of Illinois-Urbana Champaign, School of Social Work, Urbana.

Charles Wilson, MSSW, Executive Director, National Children's Advocacy Center, Huntsville, AL.

Dee Wilson, MSW, Regional Administrator, Department of Children and Family Services, Olympia, WA.

Joan Levy Zlotnik, PhD, MSW, Special Assistant to the Executive Director, Council on Social Work Education, Alexandria, VA.

Ronald Zuskin, LCSW-C, Director of Training, University of Maryland School of Social Work, Baltimore.